THE OPEN UNIVERSITY

MANCHESTER
1824
Manchester University Press

The Open
University

THE OPEN UNIVERSITY

A history

DANIEL WEINBREN

Manchester University Press
in association with
The Open University

Published by
Manchester University Press
Altrincham Street, Manchester M1 7JA, UK
www.manchesteruniversitypress.co.uk

in association with

The Open University
Walton Hall, Milton Keynes, MK7 6AA, UK
www.open.ac.uk

First published 2015

Typeset by
Servis Filmsetting Ltd, Stockport, Cheshire
Printed in Great Britain
by Bell & Bain Ltd, Glasgow

British Library Cataloguing-in-Publication Data
A catalogue record for this book is available from the British Library

Library of Congress Cataloging-in-Publication Data applied for

ISBN 978 0 7190 9626 6 hardback

ISBN 978 0 7190 9627 3 paperback

Contents

Illustrations

All images © The Open University unless otherwise stated.

Colour plates

Foreword by the Vice-Chancellor of The Open University

On 23 April 1969, the day The Open University came into being, our founding Chancellor Geoffrey Crowther set out his vision for the institution. It was a vision that went on to become our core ethos: to be open to people, places, methods and ideas.

Since then, we have continually strived to emulate Crowther's ideals. The OU has become the UK's largest university. The National Student Survey repeatedly ranks us at the forefront of British higher education. We dominate provision for part-time students. We offer access to higher education for people from economically or socially disadvantaged backgrounds. We're home to more students with disabilities than any other university. We have played a significant role in the development and expansion of prisoner education. We have pioneered the provision of free online courses. And our co-productions with the BBC are seen and heard by millions of people around the world every year.

Hundreds of thousands of people have studied with The Open University, with countless more people in their families, communities and places of work also feeling the benefits. Still more will have been educated elsewhere by teachers and lecturers who honed their academic skills here or began their studies with us. But the impact of The Open University has always gone beyond individuals. Since Harold Wilson first proposed a 'university of the air' in his 1963 'white heat' speech, The Open University has also had a central role to play in the continuous transformation of higher education.

When the university's first mailings were being dispatched in 1971, the Secretary of State for Education was Margaret Thatcher. In the decades that have followed, the world in which we live, work and study has changed beyond all recognition. There have been constant shifts in the cultural, technological and political context in which all universities operate and – as a practical laboratory of university education – The Open University has been both a subject and an agent of that change. Today it is at the heart of the debate about the future of higher education in the digital age, leading the UK's top universities into the world of Massive Open Online Courses.

At The Open University we have always looked to the future. But if we are going to continue the progress we have made since 1969, we must also take stock of where we are, remember where we have come from, and understand how we overcame the challenges and critics we encountered along the way. We have to grasp how, in just a few short years, The Open University made the transition from an 'electoral gimmick' (to quote one politician of the time) to its current status of 'national treasure' (in the words of the Vice-Chancellor at another university). The benefits of this historical perspective will also be felt further afield, as those who seek a greater understanding of the power of education will be able to learn from our experiences, our mistakes and our successes.

The Open University has been holding degree ceremonies for graduates since 1973, when the first was broadcast live on television from Alexandra Palace. In the years since then, ceremonies have been held across the UK and around the world, online and even in prisons.

While each degree ceremony is unique in its own way, all have a common theme. They're a very real representation of the values that Geoffrey Crowther laid out all those years ago, of our ongoing commitment to innovative, top-quality higher education that is open to all. And they're a reminder that central to the history of The Open University is the story of how an institution that many said could never succeed has done so much to help so many achieve what they once thought impossible.

Martin Bean
February, 2014

Preface

In 1976 a *Times Higher Education Supplement* journalist argued that 'the establishment and success of the OU will be remembered as one of the greatest achievements of this century'. He went on to suggest that 'it is a difficult task to evaluate its contribution to British Higher Education ... the book which can do this is still to be written'.[1] A generation later, the requirement for a considered, full-length history is still greater. The Open University has been called the 'greatest innovation' of the 1964–70 governments.[2] The Professor of Education and Vice-Chancellor of Keele University, Campbell Stewart, argued that the OU was innovative in nine different ways.[3] While the dramas of its earlier years have received attention, the long-run impact of what is much the largest and still the most distinctive British university requires a new study. New materials and analytical frameworks have permitted this account to explore other areas. A time of rapid change within the higher education sector makes this an appropriate moment for an assessment of the influence of the OU as it nears the end of its first half-century.

David Sewart, a former Director of Student Services and Professor in Distance Education, felt that the OU was 'like Athena springing fully grown and fully armed from the head of Zeus'; it 'appeared to have no mother and never to have had the opportunity to have been an adolescent, let alone a child'.[4] The passage of time has enabled us to view the OU within a longer context. The depth of its roots in correspondence courses, commercial television, adult education and the post-war social democratic settlement helps to explain its original ethos, distinctive culture and its continued growth and vibrancy. However novel the institution may have appeared, it had many parents. As Hilary Perraton has argued, an understanding of 'the British invention of The Open University is impoverished if we know nothing of ... 20th century British social history'.[5] Even this view may underplay the importance of distinct Scottish traditions and American influence.

This account is informed by scholarship in the social sciences, and in

educational and business studies. Christensen's model of 'disruptive innovation' is critically deployed as is Warner's notion of 'spaces of discourse'.[6]
Etienne Wenger's use of the concept of 'communities of practice' has also
been useful.[7] More generally, the perspectives of those social historians who
have placed education within a wide framework have informed the text.
Historian J. F. C. Harrison sought to examine the attitudes of those taking
part in adult education and concluded that the history of adult education
should be approached 'primarily in terms of social purpose rather than institutional form'.[8] There is also a debt to those who looked beyond official
institutions in the analysis of how students learned, and assessed the links
between informal learning and wider social formations.[9] In its use of interview material the book has also benefited from the considerable literature on
biography and personal testimony.

The materials for this study include official minutes of OU meetings and
the accounts of a range of staff members and students. Many people have
written about the OU over the years in the popular press, in scholarly journals and online. Uniquely for a history of a university, there has been access
to a complete set of teaching materials over the whole period of its existence,
including the broadcasts, books, posted experiment kits and the videos,
cassettes and digitised resources. From the outset the institution generated
survey data to assess the impact of its teaching, and this has been reviewed.
Attention has been paid to archives in the USA, notably the private papers
of the US Senator William Benton. Numerous previously unconsidered contemporary and sources which have only recently been made available at the
BBC and The National Archives have been considered. The archive staff
in The National Archives, Kew, the BBC Written Archive, Caversham, the
University of Chicago, Special Collections Research Center, Chicago, and, in
particular, The Open University Archive, Milton Keynes have been helpful
and supportive.

The text has benefited from access to thousands of recordings and photographs in the OU's own archive and to the recent recordings made for The
Open University Oral History Project. As its principal interviewer noted,
'oral history allows other stories of universities as places of pedagogy, culture,
social change and personal relationships to be told'.[10] The project would particularly like to thank (Lord) Asa Briggs, who was interviewed for this book
at the end of the most singular and comprehensive service to the university,
which began in its planning phase and culminated in his Chancellorship of
the institution. In addition, students have written accounts and posted them
on a specially created History of the Open University website. This open
source reflects the scope of popular narratives and understandings of the OU.

It is available for others to use. There are also personal accounts written by a number of those involved in the foundation and early years of the university.

Thanks are due to The Open University and its Vice-Chancellors Brenda Gourley and Martin Bean for funding the production of this book and to the members of the History of The Open University Project Committee for their thoughtful guidance and help. They are David Vincent (chair), Ruth Cammies, David Grugeon, Lorna Maguire, Rosemary O'Day (and Anne Lawrence when Professor O'Day was unavailable), Jean Seaton, Peter Syme, Mary Thorpe and Martin Watkinson. I would like to thank the staff of the Library and the Arts Faculty both of which housed this project. It was expertly managed by Rachel Garnham and Kirsten Dwight, both of whom offered support and advice. Thanks also to the staff of Learning and Teaching Solutions and the Communications Team, especially Christianne Bailey and Lucien Hudson, the Director of Communications, for helping with the publication. I am very grateful to the contributors of the two colloquia held by the project. Their ideas and enthusiasm made the events a pleasure to attend. Thanks for their reports on specific aspects of the OU's work are due to Anne Gaskell, Rachel Gibbons, Kim Hammond, Andy Northedge, Peter Syme and Martin Watkinson. Papers I presented about the history of the OU have been well received in London, Rhodes, Chicago and Milton Keynes, and I offer thanks to those who posed insightful questions and encouraged me to consider the OU in a different light. I have been delighted by the wide-ranging interest which has been shown in this project by the numerous members of the OU staff and former members of staff who have offered advice, artefacts and fascinating tales.

I have grown up with The Open University. I first heard of it in the 1970s when my mother began her journey towards an OU degree by studying the entry-level mathematics module. I took my first job at the university in 1986. Since then I have been an OU student, and I have worked full-time for the OU since 1999. My wife has a PhD from the OU, where she teaches, and our children attended the OU nursery. Writing about the OU has been a pleasure which has also had an impact on the lives of others. My personal thanks go to my immediate family, Rebecca, Jacob, Bethany and Miriam for so readily living with this book, and for distracting me from it. Thanks also to Jill Weinbren for introducing me to The Open University and, of course, a lot more.

Daniel Weinbren, Milton Keynes, 2014

SUCCESS BEGINS AT HOME

The University Correspondence College – backed by a 76 year record of success – offers expert, personalised tuition at home.
Highly qualified teachers
Moderate fees; instalments
GCE'O' to Degree Level Courses include :

English · French · Geography
German · History · Music · Chemistry
Maths · Physics · British Constitution
Economics · Economic History

Many other subjects available
Study to Degree Level with
University Correspondence College,
a non-profitmaking Trust.

Write for free prospectus to:
**UNIVERSITY CORRESPONDENCE
COLLEGE** (Dept. 56)
(Part of the National Extension College)
Shaftesbury Road, Cambridge

a

Is the OPEN UNIVERSITY your aim for 1972?

Start preparing now by similar methods of learning.
BBC broadcasts linked with three NEC "gateway" courses start again this month.
4,000 enrolled last year.

LITERATURE and HISTORY:

SOCIAL PSYCHOLOGY:

MATHEMATICS

Write or phone now for full details to:

**NATIONAL EXTENSION
COLLEGE, (ROOM Y4,)
8 SHAFTESBURY ROAD,
CAMBRIDGE CB2 2BP**
Telephone: 0223-63465

b

OPEN UNIVERSITY
—
GATEWAY COURSES

Courses in preparation for Open University in Maths, Sociology and Arts are offered by the

**Working Men's College,
CROWNDALE ROAD,
N.W.1.**

Details telephone 01-387 2037

c

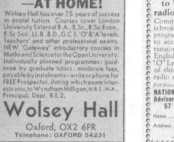

Read for a Degree —AT HOME!
Wolsey Hall has over 75 years of success in postal tuition. Courses cover London University External B.A., B.Sc., B.Sc.Econ., B Sc Soc .LL.B.,B.D.,G.C.E.'O'&'A'levels, Teachers' and other professional exams. NEW 'Gateway' introductory courses in Maths and Science for the Open University. Individually planned programmes; guidance by graduate tutors; moderate fees, payable by instalments—write or phone for FREE Prospectus, stating which exam interests you, to Wyndham Milligan, M.B.E.,M.A., Principal, Dept. B.E.2,

Wolsey Hall
Oxford, OX2 6PR
Telephone: OXFORD 54231

d

The modern way to 'O' Level English— radio and correspondence
Commencing Oct. 4th, the BBC is broadcasting a series of 24 weekly programmes in the Midland Region to accompany the National Extension College's GCE 'O' level English course. Do you want your 'O' Levels? Then take advantage of this opportunity for study by radio and correspondence
For free descriptive pamphlet cut out and post to
NATIONAL EXTENSION COLLEGE (EM)
Advisory Centre for Education Ltd.,
57 Russell Street, Cambridge
Name.................................
Address..............................

e

Five advertisements for courses for people returning to formal education: a) University Correspondence College; b) National Extension College; c) Working Men's College; d) Wolsey Hall; e) National Extension College.

Part I

Creating a university of the air

I

The challenge of
The Open University

The impact of The Open University (OU) has been enormous. It is available in many countries, has been reworked for many more and provides inspiration for a rich diversity of learners on their individual journeys. Through initiatives such as the National Open College Network some of its most successful ideas have been have spread across the UK.[1] It is widely admired. Prime Minister David Cameron called it 'a Great British innovation and invention'.[2] Others have noted its integration within the wider society. Bill Bryson rhetorically enquired 'What other nation in the world could have given us William Shakespeare, pork pies, Christopher Wren, Windsor Great Park, The Open University, *Gardeners' Question Time* and the chocolate digestive biscuit?'[3] However, the OU has become more than a much-emulated 'national treasure'.[4] Since its foundation in 1969 it has transformed the lives of the millions who have studied through it and challenged the very idea of a university. In the face of disdain and disbelief this unique institution has had impacts far beyond the higher education sector. It has drawn on the traditions of part-time education for adults, developed from the eighteenth century, on correspondence courses, associated with the rapid industrialisation of the nineteenth century and on university extension initiatives, which started in the 1870s. It has also developed ideas derived from sandwich courses, summer schools, radio and television broadcasts, for which there were precedents in the twentieth century. It owes much to its supporters, particularly its vast student body. Through its enthusiasm for learning and positive societal change the OU has affected the lives of people around the world, including those who, while not formally registered as students, acquired materials or watched broadcasts. This book examines its impacts by considering its structures, precedents, politics, pedagogies and personalities.

In defiance of the warning, attributed to Aristotle, that 'there are two human inventions which may be considered more difficult than any others – the art of government and the art of education', many of the key events in the creation of the OU occurred through swift government action between 1963 and 1969.[5] Having noted down his ideas for a 'University of the Air' on 14 April 1963, Harold Wilson, the Leader of Her Majesty's Opposition since 14 February 1963, proposed to a Labour Party rally on 8 September 1963 that which he later admitted was an 'inchoate idea' (Figure 1.1).[6] It was for 'the creation of a new educational trust'.[7] This 'University of the Air' would be provided with broadcasting time and government assistance.[8] Wilson swiftly and successfully embedded his uncosted and unproven proposal for a 'University of the Air' as soon as he came into the office of Prime Minister (PM) in October 1964. The new PM gave a trusted ally, Jennie Lee, the task of producing a White Paper on the subject before the next election, which was likely to be soon, as Labour's parliamentary majority was tiny. The White Paper was published and an election pledge was made to create

Figure 1.1 When Wilson proposed a university of the air in September 1963 the idea received a lot of coverage. The *Daily Mail*'s cartoon featured Wilson as the television host of an 'educational parlour game' called 'Double Your Diplomas'. A *Daily Mirror* cartoon portrayed the Conservatives as dismissive and envious, and the *Sunday Citizen* (a tabloid owned by the Co-Operative Press) also made a party-political point. When he opened the OU in 1969 Geoffrey Crowther acknowledged its role as an 'educational rescue mission', and in the *Citizen* Glan Williams showed Boyle's wooden vessel (Edward Boyle was Conservative Minister of Education 1962–64) as having sunk, leaving Wilson to rescue the poorly educated.

a 'University of the Air'. In 1966 Labour was returned with an increased majority, and work on the promised new university began. Drawing on the legal assistance of Lord Goodman, the support of some well-versed civil servants (including some within the Department of Education and Science – DES) and the use of some *ad hoc* arrangements (notably the creation of Advisory and Planning Committees outside the DES), Jennie Lee shaped Wilson's idea into a practical proposition. In 1969, shortly before the 1970 general election that Labour lost, The Open University was granted a Royal Charter, and by January 1971 the first OU students had received their mailings and watched the first television broadcasts.

Foundation

In Part I the focus is on the handful of innovators who 'were crucial' for the creation of the OU, which enjoyed a 'rapid gestation period'.[9] Phyllis Hall referred to the impact of 'a few powerful individuals'.[10] Harold Wilson, when recalling 1963, stressed the role of individuals (Figure 1.2):

> It certainly wasn't official Labour Party policy at this stage, except in the sense that I was running the party in a slightly dictatorial way; if I said something was going to happen, I intended it to happen.[11]

This was a feature of the OU that found echoes elsewhere. Dodd and Rumble noted that the 'personal commitment' of a minister was a feature common to the creation of a number of distance-teaching universities.[12]

While individuals were of importance, the OU was built on more than strong personalities. It is also in Part I that the wider social and political framework is considered. During 1963, the year of Wilson's announcement, ideas about rights, about the Cold War and about higher education gained wider salience. This was in part due to the coverage given to the publication of Betty Friedan's *The Feminine Mystique* (in February), to Kennedy's 'Ich bin ein Berliner' speech in West Germany (in June), to Martin Luther King's 'I have a dream' speech in Washington (in August) and to the opening of another new university, the University of East Anglia (in September). While there were countervailing tendencies, the notion gained traction that a university could be committed to teamwork and discussion, widening access to power, promoting cross-class engagement in civil society and enabling the systematic facilitation of social and economic mobility. The OU's values were reflected in its Charter, which was based on that of the University of Warwick, opened in 1965. In its emphasis on openness, the OU echoed the

Figure 1.2 Harold Wilson addresses The Open University.

motto of another new university, Lancaster (opened 1964): *Patet omnibus veritas* (Truth lies open to all). However, unlike other universities, it had a commitment to the 'educational well-being of the community'.[13]

Wilson was also able to build on existing ideas within and around his party. In 1945 Ellen Wilkinson, the Minister of Education 1945–47, proposed the broadcast of lectures.[14] In 1960 Professor George Catlin, a member of the National Broadcasting Development Committee, called for a television university based not on the BBC, which had rejected his ideas, but on a new third channel. Woodrow Wyatt introduced a bill to the Commons in 1961 to facilitate the expansion of adult educational broadcasts, and the Pilkington Committee on the future of broadcasting, which reported in June 1962, assessed educational broadcasting.[15] In March 1962 Hugh Gaitskell, the Labour Party leader, established a Labour Party study group, chaired by Lord Taylor, to consider higher education. Its report, with a foreword by Harold Wilson, called for a 'University of the Air'.[16] The interest of the left was noted. In 1966 the *Times Educational Supplement* described the OU as a 'cosy scheme that shows the Socialists at their most endearing but impractical worst'.[17] Sociology professor Norman Birnbaum, who taught in both the US and UK, recalled that 'when I visited Milton Keynes in 1972, I was struck by the utter familiarity of the rhetoric of the Open University'. He went on to argue that it was not simply a 'secularised version of socialism' but also an 'appeal to prescient technocrats unburdened by socialist aspirations' and 'an answer ... to the problem of rising educational costs'.[18]

The values which framed the institution, the recognition of the benefits of pluralism, dissent, equity and the belief that humans can and should shape the world have often been associated with social democracy. When Michael Young (who worked for Labour and later became a Social Democratic Party peer) argued that 'the tap-root of socialism was in working-class communities [where] the poor were helping the poor' he provided an image of altruism expressed in the form of reciprocity which informed the thinking behind many of the schemes to which he contributed, including the OU.[19] A number of those who had some responsibility for the foundation and design of the OU had similar political perspectives. Walter Perry (the first Vice-Chancellor) was twice Social Democratic Party deputy leader in the Lords, and, as OU Professor Stuart Hall noted, the OU was 'filled with good social democrats. Everybody there believes in the redistribution of educational opportunities and seeks to remedy the exclusiveness of British education.'[20] He later pointed out 'it would have been funny to come to the OU and not to be committed to redistributing educational opportunities'.[21] The university certainly attracted some staff with left-wing views. Arnold Kettle was a member of the Executive Committee of the Communist Party of Great Britain, David Potter had been fired from his previous university because of his association with the left and Aaron Scharf, the first Professor of Art History at the OU, only came to England after he was victimised by Senator McCarthy and accepted an invitation from a fellow art historian, the spy

Anthony Blunt. Others at the OU noted that there was wide support among staff for the bolstering of social democracy through the utilisation of modern centralised systems of production and distribution.[22] Many at the OU sought not to reproduce the privileges and dominance of the ruling class or to justify inequitable access on grounds of merit. The OU had its left-wing critics, who saw it as a 'pale reflection of the conventional class-ridden establishments'. It had been 'perhaps overeager to win the acceptance of the rest of academic society'. Nevertheless, it remained a 'great liberal experiment'.[23] It was, to quote its Planning Committee, firmly located within the British tradition of 'being liberal expansionist in tone, empirical and specific as to numbers and money'.[24]

Wilson presented his idea about a 'University of the Air' to the 1963 Labour Party conference within the context of a speech about 'Labour's plan for science'.[25] In this, he argued that social progress and peaceful developments could be achieved by investment in research, particularly in science and technology. It was, Tony Benn recalled, an 'industrial speech' which broke away from the 'romantic attitude' of the Tories.[26] Wilson proclaimed:

> The Britain that is going to be forged in the white heat of this revolution will be no place for restrictive practices or for outdated methods on either side of industry. We shall need a totally new attitude.

The University of the Air was going to contribute to the cultural life of the nation and also provide more scientists and technologists. This was a period in which scientific intellectuals with technocratic expertise and an enthusiasm for rational planning were gaining higher status.[27] Norman MacKenzie, founder of the Centre for Educational Technology at the University of Sussex, sat on the Advisory Committee (which wrote the 1966 White Paper on the 'University of the Air') while representatives from the Ministry of Technology attended committee meetings. The expansion of higher education, the restructuring of the science policy machinery and the 1968 report on the civil service by Lord Fulton led to a technocratic zenith during the 1960s.[28] The 1964–70 Labour government substantially increased spending on higher education and scientific research, much of it carried out in universities. The graduation rate for scientists and engineers rose higher than that of many other countries.[29] During a surge in economic activity in North America and Western Europe that 'seemed powered by technological revolution', the OU appeared to be an intellectually and economically feasible, rational and efficient means to maintain that drive.[30] However, although in 1971, the year that the first OU students began their studies, the computer scientist Alan Kay told a meeting that 'the best way to predict the future is to invent it', the OU thrived not because of technology, but as a consequence of the ways in which the familiar was deployed to aid learning.[31]

The OU was able to rely on popular support for state expenditure on higher education. A report from a committee chaired by Sir Samuel Gurney-Dixon in 1954 suggested that poor educational structures resulted in many people, adults and children, failing to realise their potential.[32] Geoffrey Crowther chaired a committee which concluded the proportion of pupils studying to the age of eighteen should rise to 50 per cent and there should be an expansion of higher education in the interests of reducing wastage and contributing to justice.[33] The 1962 report of the Standing Advisory Council on the Training and Supply of Teachers led to the expansion of places in colleges of education. In 1963 a report by the former Chief Education Officer for Hertfordshire, Sir John Newsom, rejected the notion of a limited pool of ability and demanded 'Education for all'.[34] A new type of university might help to resolve the problems. Harold Macmillan's Conservative government had commissioned a review of universities in 1961 and when Lionel Robbins reported in 1963, his proposals for the expansion of the sector were swiftly adopted by the Conservative leader of five days' standing, Sir Alec Douglas-Home. The 1960s was a period when funding was provided and universities enjoyed governmental approval. There was a rapid expansion of the higher education sector, which grew faster than any major national enterprise.[35] It was, said Annan, 'the golden age of the don', while in 1969 Harold Perkin claimed that 'university teaching is the key profession of the twentieth century'.[36]

The OU was also deployed to indicate how the modern media could be employed by the state. This was in contrast to Conservative-favoured pirate radio entrepreneurs, who flouted the internationally agreed allocation of radio frequencies.[37] The OU demonstrated the worthiness of state broadcasts. Asa Briggs noted that the 'appeal of the pirates depended on the triumphs of a new ... technology that in a quite different context figured prominently in Wilson's campaign speeches of 1963'.[38] He also noted that within a few months of a newspaper interview with Edward Short, the Postmaster-General, which was headlined 'Why I'm sinking the pirates', he became, in 'what was doubtless a coincidence', Secretary of State for Education. Briggs linked this development to the introduction of a Granada quiz programme, *University Challenge*, and a *Daily Mail* headline about television and universities, 'Top of the Profs'. There was a parallel to be drawn with pop's defiance of radio's formal conventions and its enthusiasm for spontaneity and greater engagement with personal emotions and the everyday. Briggs concluded that

Questions of 'education' and of 'pop music' should not be treated, therefore as separate historical topics. Nor at the time were they kept in entirely separate files ... The agenda and the chronologies of education and pop music criss-cross.[39]

Educational television was, argued Peter Smith in 1972, 'a symbol of a new type of government'. Certainly, as OU students noted, there was 'very little' commercial educational broadcasting.[40] The political assumptions of the 1950s and 1960s rested on the notion of economic growth. The OU was seen as an opportunity to build upon the level of prosperity and technological development which had only recently been attained. For example, the introduction of transmissions on very high frequencies meant that 99 per cent of the UK population could receive BBC1 television in 1960 and 60 per cent could receive BBC2.[41] If society had become one in which, as Harold Macmillan claimed in 1957, 'most of our people have never had it so good', the OU showcased how the state could support consumers.[42]

Part of the context in which, in 1964, Jennie Lee established an Advisory Committee 'To consider the educational functions and content of a University of the Air as outlined in a speech made by Mr Harold Wilson in Glasgow on 8th September 1963' was that the roles of women were changing. In 1952 Edith Summerskill MP introduced a bill to help women whose husbands failed to pay them maintenance. Her activities led to the 1963 Married Women's Savings Act. From 1961 female public servants received the same pay as their male counterparts and in 1964 the Labour government expressed its commitment to universal equal pay. Part-time work for women quadrupled in the 1960s and 1970s, and the official figures for part-time women workers who paid tax and national insurance were 779,000 in 1951, 1.85 million in 1961 and 2.75 million by 1971. Increasingly women with children were being employed in paid work.[43] While there were new opportunities for educated women as teachers and social workers, others articulated their discontents. Following an article in the *Guardian* and a letter to the newspaper, the Housebound Housewives Register was begun in 1960. In 1966 a study by Hannah Gavron indicated the disillusion felt by many housewives.[44] Barbara Castle introduced the Equal Pay Bill in 1970, and Margaret Thatcher also spoke in Parliament defending the rights of mothers to work.[45] Legislation, notably the Abortion Act, 1967, the NHS (Family Planning) Act, 1967, the Divorce Reform Act, 1969, the Matrimonial Property Act, 1970, and the Equal Pay Act, 1970, indicated the development of new frameworks for women. Part-time education became more attainable and desirable as affluence rose, opportunities in the workplace improved and legislation altered the possibilities for women's lived experiences.

The enthusiasts for the OU were able to draw on a variety of resources. The university was built on the widespread interest in opening access to higher education and in using the apparatus of the state to redistribute power. It offered to resolve the contemporary problem of how to increase swiftly and efficiently the numbers of technologists and those trained in science. The key figures produced a blended approach to distribution which recognised the capacities of existing delivery methods, notably night schools, correspondence, radio, television, summer schools and tutorials. The interest in creating a post-war world which was efficient, democratic and technologically advanced occurred at a time when notions of student-centred active learning were being popularised. Moreover, increasing numbers had access to radio and television, more time to study and sufficient incentive and confidence to approach the new university.

The 1970s and 1980s

Part II of the book is about the first two decades of the OU. There is a chapter on the social and political framework and another one on the OU's teaching processes and its support for learners. Being 'one of the most revolutionary new policies' of the 1964–70 Labour governments, the OU faced considerable party-political opposition.[46] It was designed to fit within an administrative and economic framework which was shortly to lose its popularity within government. In 1970 Jennie Lee lost her seat, Harold Wilson became Leader of the Opposition, and the Conservatives gained power and retained it for much of the OU's first forty years. There were detractors and sceptics in the BBC, Whitehall, Westminster, the higher education sector and the press. Within days of Wilson's initial speech *The Economist* concluded that such a university would 'not nearly be as replete a sign as a degree from say, Oxford'. Nevertheless, it was supportive, saying that Wilson's idea was 'one of the best things he has done'.[47] Others argued that the OU was of little value as demand was not proven, many students would leave early and degree-level work could not be taught in such a way. *The Times* felt that a university education 'demands direct personal contacts between teachers and learners and even more, among the students themselves. It is doubtful that the network of summer schools and study centres will be able to support it.'[48] 'Many academics', noted Professor Arthur Marwick in 1969 in regard to television, 'remain convinced that programmes, highly successful as mass entertainment, could never be used for serious purposes.'[49]

The OU could have become politically isolated. However, it adapted to changes and indeed contributed to the creation of new roles allocated to universities. As Education Secretary in the early 1970s Margaret Thatcher ignored the patrician voices in her own party which derided the newly opened OU and opted to retain Labour's project. She then sought to broaden the remit of the OU and allow it to accept eighteen-year-olds (to whom the franchise was extended in 1969) not just adults aged over twenty-one. The notion of education as a product to be paid for by consumers (students) with the corporation (university) accountable to shareholders (taxpayers and voters) was popularised by those associated with Margaret Thatcher and has greatly influenced the OU. As one of the OU's founders, Norman MacKenzie, told her 'This is exactly what you should be supporting. You think all the universities are against you, you think that nobody pays any attention to hard working independent people, this should be Thatcher University.'[50] From the first, when the OU addressed learners it sought to realise them as citizens who paid taxes (as workers) and also fees (as students) and who sought to gain skills for work and pleasure by building ideas together.

While the OU was shaped by a number of commercial businesses, notably companies running television and correspondence courses, part of the OU's distinctiveness was its use of a corporate, industrial model. In 1969, as the OU was opening, the government presided over the opening of Longbridge, the biggest car plant in Europe. Other universities of the 1960s saw themselves in the tradition of communities of investigative scholars. Sussex, for example, was called Balliol-by-the-Sea. However, the OU has been described by one of its first deans as 'an industrial revolution in higher education'.[51] It was built on industrial precedents, and this is reflected in the language developed by its early staff, with 'lines of study' and the 'production' of 'units' of teaching materials. Greville Rumble, who joined the OU in 1970 and was head of the OU's corporate planning office in the mid-1970s and also in the late 1980s, suggested that 'during the 1970s industrialisation came to be seen by many as a defining feature of distance education'.[52] Others adopted a similar view.[53] Two of the OU's first deans stressed both the egalitarian ethos and the use of a systems approach at the OU.[54] The concept of a 'system', a term which, along with the phrase 'evidence-based policy' was part of the *lingua franca* of the period, indicated the ambition to combine academic enquiry with assembly-line manufacturing techniques to create educational materials for mass consumption.

Although educational broadcasting had commenced in the early twentieth century and teaching by correspondence had a longer history, it was often the case that completion rates were low. There was little research on the impact of these delivery methods.[55] By contrast, in order to ensure its suitability for the support of learners in a variety of circumstances, the OU evaluated the impact of its teaching from the outset. Its use of a system included a feedback loop. In common with much associated with what has been termed Fordism, the OU appeared to thrive in the protected national market, able through the efficiency of a complex organisation to mass-produce products at low cost by fragmenting work tasks.[56] During the 1980s Desmond Keegan argued that an essential element of any comprehensive definition of distance education should be that it was 'the most industrialized form of education'.[57] Similar ideas were being expressed elsewhere.[58]

Born in an era of economic expansion, the OU has also thrived during periods of restraint. It appointed a marketing director in 1970, and many of its fee-paying students sought to enhance their employability. Nonetheless, it still needed to demonstrate that it was a wise investment of public money. As the certainty and level of its central government income fell so the university's reliance on its students' fees rose. After a £3 million grant was lost, students faced fee rises from £55 to £67 in 1979 and then up to £120 in 1982. The OU started to sell packs designed for a wide range of learners. At the same time it developed an international mission. Education and culture had significant roles in the Cold War. Governments felt that building trust and giving access to educational opportunities were likely to increase their global influence, and the OU collaborated with the British Council in promoting opportunities for study around the world. By the 1980s there was greater interest in charging 'full cost' fees (initially for overseas students) across the higher education sector. There was advocacy of the corporatisation of university governance in the 1985 Report of Sir Alex Jarratt, which encouraged a move from decisions being made by academics towards greater control by university administrators. A Green Paper emphasised the need for universities to serve the economy, the first research exercises took place, new funding arrangements were made and, at the end of the decade, Kenneth Baker, the Secretary of State, called for greater engagement with private resources. In 1991 the Committee of Vice-Chancellors and Principals Academic Audit Unit set out guidelines for a new system of quality-assurance mechanisms for the design and teaching of degrees, which the OU, already familiar with such notions, swiftly adopted. The intention was to increase the efficiency and maximise the benefits of the higher education system by developing mechanisms for running universities that were closer to what were assumed to be the practices of the commercial sector. As a university with fee-paying, and mostly tax-paying, students, the OU could appear as a harbinger of a Conservative as well as a Labour future.

In the second chapter in Part II the focus is on another distinctive aspect of the OU, its teaching methods. While the technologies and structures have changed over time, the OU has consistently used a multi-media blend of materials and approaches in its pedagogy. The concept of teaching through a variety of media had been used by the National Extension College. This paved the way for the OU's use of books, cassettes, broadcasts, models, experiment kits, online materials, tutorials and residential schools.[59] It also promoted

> the idea that no course is really educational unless it has a 'cultural' as well as exam-passing aspect; that we were writing not for captive adolescents, but for free adults, with whose other interests we were, in a sense, competing ... above all that the student should be not only instructed, but also stimulated, entertained, enlivened and encouraged.[60]

The OU built on this approach, promoting the notion that learning was not simply the acquisition of knowledge by individuals but a process of ubiquitous social participation in knowledge construction.

The precedents on which the OU was built included notions honed at existing universities. It was associated with the European ideal, developed since the early nineteenth century, of universities as communities of scholars and students who together sought advancement of knowledge by investigation.[61] It performed the functions expected of modern universities by contributing to policy-making and curriculum development, to the provision of high-quality, accredited, teaching and to serious research. Jennie Lee was adamant that the OU should be comparable to other universities in terms of its academic standards, rather than merely representing an educational second chance for the marginalised. By enabling its students to gain new skills it has had an economic impact, while by making its teaching materials available to the population at large it has had an effect on the cultural and intellectual life of the nation.[62]

However, the OU also had other educational precedents. In the 1920s there was a well-established sense that adults could be taught through broadcasts which could 'lead on to more formal or more intensive study'.[63] In 1929 the inventor Dr Edmund Edward Fournier d'Albe proposed a 'wireless university'.[64] While the radio group-listening schemes of the 1930s fell away after the Second World War, lessons were learned from their demise. The importance of central organisation, reliable transmissions and robust agreements between the BBC and bodies associated with education became clear.[65] Moreover, television group viewing, as used in half a dozen countries by the 1950s, became so popular that wide viewing screens were built especially for these adult educational viewers.[66] It was also in the 1950s that it was concluded that 'children can be taught by television just as effectively as when they have a teacher in front of them'.[67] The idea that it is wiser not to select students for adult education, rather than appealing to an educational elite, was part of the 'Great Tradition in University Adult Education' according to one of the OU's planners, Harold Wiltshire, in 1956.[68] In Canada there was substantial interest in using television for adult and university education.[69] There was evidence from the USSR, and the conclusion that 'much might be learned from developments in the USA' was heeded by the developers of the OU.[70] In 1963, when Wilson wrote his first notes on the 'University of the Air', there were eighty educational television stations in the USA, some broadcasting university-level programmes; the idea of building television into a teaching system was outlined in the *Times Higher Education Supplement* and the Oxford University Department of Education held an Anglo-American conference on education by correspondence and television. In 1964 Marshall McLuhan claimed that since the spread of television, 'nobody is happy with mere book knowledge of French or English poetry. The unanimous cry now is "Let's talk French" and "Let the bard be heard".'[71] Television programmes, it was declared in 1966, 'have helped to create the self-questioning Britain and to make sure the questions asked are the right ones'.[72] The contribution of the OU was to adopt, to adapt and to recognise that new tools did not need to do the tasks of old ones: that, for example, video did not need to duplicate theatrical performances but could be used to move beyond existing information structures and assist the understandings of individuals in new ways.

In addition to broadcasting, the OU also consistently sought to adapt other technologies to enhance learning. The 1967 edition of the American *Yearbook of the National Society for the Study of Education* was devoted to programmed learning, a new field of interest in the 1960s. This was the idea that technology could be used to deliver small amounts of information at the pace desired by the learner and with an inbuilt prospect of a response to the learners' input. A 1970 Report to Congress about Instructional Technology argued that 'Technology can make education more productive, individual and powerful, making learning more immediate; give instruction a more scientific base; and make access to education more equal.'[73] It was also argued that algorithms, logical trees and decision charts were the best way to present instructions and that programmed learning was a technique which, because it 'can help to reduce "teaching" to "telling" has definite advantages'.[74] The university's pedagogy was informed by 'programmed learning' and there had to be a 'rational curriculum planning approach'. It was also argued that teaching at the OU needed to be student-centred as 'irrelevant scholastic displays must be eliminated', declared Brian Lewis of the OU's Institute of Educational Technology.[75] After a few years one analysis concluded that 'at the OU it was clear that "telling" was often to be the central operation' and that 'the OU teaching system is in reality as conventional as its logic, as dehumanised, as elitist as ever, albeit in a modernised and rationalised way'.[76]

Programmed learning was not the only influence on the development of ideas at the OU. By 1971 the benefits of group discussion within higher education had already been established.[77] The OU modified such ideas in order to support its often isolated individual learners. Their part-time status meant that they almost all had competing interests and many also had little experience of formal education. The OU promoted study groups. It assessed their impact and recognised that peer learning aided the development of a sense of community.[78] In 1975 a senior counsellor emphasised that an OU tutor was not 'the course team made flesh to the student; instead he [sic] becomes a facilitator of learning both to the individual student and the group'.[79] One study pointed out that the staff-to-student ratio of 1:8 found in 1976 in face-to-face universities in a residential setting

> does not foster peer relations in academic life ... The Open University could capitalize on its disadvantages [by] encouraging peer relationships in academic ... situations and through this fostering more autonomous learning.[80]

The OU critically assessed the competing pedagogic approaches of the period and forged its own frameworks and delivery methods.

The mix of the division of labour associated with the production line and the democracy associated with liberal thinking was found within the teaching structures of the OU. Unlike other universities, OU materials were produced by teams on a module-by-module basis.[81] These teams were infused with elements of the institution's ethos. The chair of the second level module which was devised by staff from the Faculties of Technology and Science, *An introduction to materials*, TS251, 1973–81, described the allocation of work. The staff tutor linked the team to regional tutorials and counselling staff, and there was also an editor, a BBC producer and a technician with defined roles. The educational technologist 'advises the academics on the structuring of the teaching materials they produce and on continuous assessment and examinations'. He noted the mix of a 'corporate drive' with teamwork, with one member helping another or responsibilities for content being reallocated. In addition, an interest in equity was maintained. The 'provision of some wine at course team meetings' aided conviviality, and decisions were made 'fairly democratically'.[82]

The OU's headquarters was physically situated in the new town of Milton Keynes. Its students studied at home, where they faced the constant threat of intellectual isolation. In response, the university supplemented its use of the media with a physical network of local, regional and national offices in thirteen locations and hundreds of study centres.[83] Having these local contacts became an important means by which the OU was developed. Ken Boyd, who worked for the OU in Ireland from 1970 to 2001, recalled 'I would find it not too difficult to get a meeting with a Permanent Secretary, or even with a Minister in Northern Ireland'.[84] Other regional staff made similar points about the value of local contacts. In addition to offering tuition by correspondence and broadcasting, the OU employed part-time, locally based tutors and counsellors around the country. They offered face-to-face group tutorials and counselling and, together with centrally based academic staff, taught in residential summer schools which were held on hired university campuses. The emphasis was on discussion and collaboration. Students were expected to locate, evaluate and apply knowledge while tutorial staff members were expected to promote critical engagement with the materials and to offer appropriate encouragement and correction. The OU was a very early user of computers for teaching, initially via regionally based mainframes, later through home dialup. In these ways, geographically distributed learners could share knowledge, exchange links, provide support for one another and develop a sense of belonging and community.

The 1970s and 1980s saw the OU, centralised in its production and in much of its assessment, offer the same teaching materials to all students, no matter where they lived within the UK (and further afield in some cases). At the same time, it promoted the production of knowledge at numerous sites. While this model involved some tensions (for example, between the national and the local) it also enabled a sophisticated model of teaching and learning to be developed, critically evaluated and improved.

The 1990s and beyond

Part III is about the period since the 1990s. It has two chapters. The first is about the political framework, positioning the OU within the patterns of convergence and divergence in the expanding higher education system of the late twentieth and early twenty-first centuries. The other chapter in Part III is an assessment of the ways in which, since the 1990s, the OU has sought to enable learners to work together to create knowledge.

One way to understand the development of the OU is in terms of a business model. Clayton Christensen saw a pattern whereby new services which took root at the lower end of the market could displace competitors higher up the market, if the goods and services of the latter were complicated, expensive and inaccessible. The university sector of the 1960s might be described as being for the upper end of the market and ripe for such 'disruptive innovation'.[85] The OU provided products which were simple, affordable and convenient to many.[86] The applicability of Christensen's ideas has been acknowledged at the OU and other universities.[87] The OU was able to challenge established traditions of delivery and access, and the scale of participation, and to deploy technology in new ways to help customers (whether government or adult learners) to 'do more easily and effectively what they were already trying to do'.[88] The OU also reached out to markets which would not otherwise be served. For example, it offered mature students the flexibility of not having to leave home or work (Figure 1.3). Insofar as watching television and reading books were familiar activities, its correspondence and broadcast materials were 'simple' products. This aided the rise to prominence of the part-time adult learners' sector. However, there are some caveats. Christensen's focus was on the USA, where there was a different attitude to universities. By contrast, as the Vice-Chancellor of the University of Warwick, Nigel Thrift, noted, British universities 'have never been able to build the kind of solidarity with the British mentalité that exists in the US'.[89]

Christensen also marginalised the role of the state, conceptualising it as a freestanding, sealed system, as if its internal workings were opaque and unchanging. However, the OU has been significantly affected by the

Figure 1.3 Studying almost always involved negotiations with other occupants of the home.

British state structures. Between 1980 and 1997 the OU shared the overall 45 per cent reduction in the higher education sector's state provision.[90] During the 1990s, the OU ceased to be funded in a different way from most universities and polytechnics. Its planning, funding and auditing became more aligned with the practices of other universities. Most universities were funded through the University Grants Committee. Polytechnics, run by local government, offered low-cost courses, often tailored to the local jobs market. When, in the 1990s, the funding of these higher education bodies was merged the OU was also netted with rest of the sector. Higher education, while still maintaining the idea of a collegium of scholars, came to have more in common with work-oriented, commercial, government-regulated bodies. The OU, which had built on ideas from both sides of the polytechnic–university divide, and was familiar with working to short-term financial considerations accompanied by ministerial interventions, fitted into the new arrangements and became less distinctive.

While the distinctiveness of the OU needs to be recognised, understandings based on Clayton Christensen's model of 'disruptive innovation' continued to inform decision-makers. In 2011 David Willetts, the Minister for Universities and Science, said of the university sector that 'the biggest lesson I have learned is that the most powerful driver of reform is to let new providers into the system'.[91] He sought 'new models' to create 'a genuinely open system that encourages real student choice'.[92] The OU, in this instance, was seen as one of the older providers. Conceptualising the OU in business terms highlights that it has recognised the importance of engagement with issues of employability and relevance and that it built pedagogical content through purposeful attention to, respect for and reciprocity with the communities, not just individual students, that sustain it. Its partners have included the Royal College of Nursing, with which the OU sought 'to encourage greater participation in learning and development'.[93] There has also been a partner-ship with Unionlearn (which helps trade unions provide opportunities for their members to learn) and with the government strategy for widening participation in higher education (Aimhigher).[94] Since 1984 the OU has pro-duced, with support from the global body for professional accountants, the Association of Chartered Certified Accountants, and with Barclays Bank, a quarterly survey of small business in Britain.[95]

The development of the OU was also framed by the wider expansion of the higher education sector. In the academic year 1970/71, there were 621,000 stu-dents in higher education. In 1984 there were forty-eight universities in the UK and 15 per cent of young people went to university.[96] Student numbers almost doubled between 1990 and 1996. Over 41 per cent of 17- to 30-year-olds participated in higher education in 2002/03, and the government set a target of 50 per cent.[97] By 2007/08 there were 2.5 million students in higher education in the UK, and 106 universities.[98] One of the effects of this growth has been that the cost of providing higher education has risen. UK governments began to decrease the state contribution per student: public funding per student for higher education declined from a value of 100 in 1976 to 60 in 1994 and while between 1979 and 2011 student numbers increased by 320 per cent, public expenditure on higher education rose by only 165 per cent.[99]

The abolition of maintenance grants (which had a limited impact on OU students), the introduction of limits on student numbers and the requirement that students pay fees shifted the focus within the financing of higher education towards the reduction in the use of public resources. The abolition of the block grant made to universities to support the costs of teaching the arts, humanities and social sciences and the reduction of the grant paid to teach medicine and the natural sciences led many universities, including private institutions with appropriately designated courses, to become more reliant on loan-backed fees rather than direct government funding. The overall impact was that market and commercial relations were widely promoted and competition between institutions for funding and to achieve the best benchmarks and performance indicators increased. There was an interest across the higher education sector in strategic partnerships which would reshape teaching and research, promote knowledge transfer to private firms and blur the boundaries between public and private provision.[100] A sign of the greater integration of the OU into the reconfigured sector is that in 2012 the universities admissions website UCAS carried messages highlighting financial support for part-time study and featured a new search tool which listed The Open University's part-time courses.

The OU found itself more often in the same market for customers. As governments encouraged the higher education sector to look beyond degrees, to make interventions into the market to support part-time, mature students and to charge fees, so the OU drew on its experiences of providing vocational, non-degree materials, levying fees and offering places to those otherwise marginalised from universities. The interactions between the OU and its rivals became increasingly complex. On the one hand the OU started to offer degrees with titles similar to those of other universities. On the other hand, more universities adopted the modularisation and credit system familiar to OU students and started to compete for part-time students. Universities began to evaluate and be evaluated and the results were publicly tabulated, a notion long familiar at the OU. Where the OU had been virtually alone in its use of computers, now the whole of higher education in modernised countries communicated with their students through the internet. By the early twenty-first century almost 96 per cent of 'conventional' universities in the USA offer some kind of online coursework.[101] In the UK the shifting of political power away from London and towards Belfast, Edinburgh and Cardiff, and Brussels, had significant implications for the economics and structures of the OU. Material had to be designed not simply for the UK but in conformity with several legal frameworks and educational structures. In these ways the distinctiveness of the OU was reduced. Yet the university retained its cost-effective scale, its fully open access, and its deep experience of the application of communication technologies to high-quality learning. Its difference was at once more qualified and more vital to its mission.

In Part III there is also consideration of the OU's overseas roles. When the OU was being designed it was, in part, in response to the apparent success of the USSR in training many of its engineers at a distance and in promoting the values of what became known as *Homo Sovieticus*. On being given responsibility for the creation of a 'University of the Air', Jennie Lee appointed an advisory committee. This was 'essentially a political committee'.[102] After it fulfilled its brief a further committee was appointed to plan the OU in more detail. This was dissolved when the OU's first council was created in 1969. Norman MacKenzie sat on all of these three bodies. He had worked in radio propaganda during the war and later for MI6 in Eastern Europe, and he was influential on the committees.[103] The OU became part of the effort to spread Western values. It was funded to support similar 'open universities' in Iran, Pakistan, Venezuela and a number of other countries. By the twenty-first century the OU's overseas activities and the structures it developed were focused in different ways. It expanded in Europe, found partners in Asia and opened institutions in the USA and the Middle East. It developed a concept of stakeholdership in Africa.

During the 1990s fresh ideas about how best to support learning among its students were developed at the OU. It sought to provide the tools for the social construction of new perspectives. From the launch of the first OU modules, students who took history modules at the OU were encouraged to study their own histories while the teaching materials provided by geographers included both imaginative historical material and literary prose and poetry. Materials for tutors emphasised the importance of building learners' confidence and acknowledging the individual's perspective. This commitment to supporting the social learning of adults was reinforced when computers began to be widely used within teaching at the OU. As networked computing became available, an online-focused pedagogy and online communities were developed. Dialogue and discussion retained their importance.[104] A tutor-counsellor, noting the popularity of courses which enabled 'some freedom of choice', argued that students should be free to develop their own study programme and be involved more in 'what to study how and when'.[105] The aim was to provide opportunities for people to separate themselves from their familiar social practices and power relations and begin to learn, and eventually to master, concepts. The space they created to do this was one where they could construct new ideas about the world and forge links to other students. Structures were put in place which helped learners to become members of the OU's student body, which was itself in dialogue with the OU. Similar ideas about both methods and content were spread through much of the higher education sector and these informed, and were informed by, the OU.

Using interactive materials, new communication methods and a renewed emphasis on the importance of communities, the OU continued to build on its assets, its conventions and the life experiences of those who studied with it. Students were encouraged to work together throughout and beyond their programmes of study. Some continued to take courses; others adapted the teaching materials they had used and studied together in the informal sector. The OU deployed digital technology to reduce the sense of alienation among learners and disrupt expectations about adult distance learning. Students could more easily communicate directly with one another. They might themselves become researchers and could contribute to the creation of new knowledge. The role of the university's tutorial staff developed over this period with an increasing emphasis on supporting the construction of knowledge by students. There was an increased flexibility in the practical side of learning. New solutions were found to the questions of where and when people could study and how they could receive advice and support from tutors, other staff and fellow students.

Learners

Having considered the political and pedagogic influences upon the OU, and framed it within developments in those areas in Part II and Part III, the emphasis in Part IV is on the experiences of people who remade themselves through their learning at the OU. As Malcolm Chase has suggested, it is important when considering the history of adult education to avoid an 'uncritical teleology' which emphasises institutional provision rather than the reception by students.[106] In 1974 Michael Macdonald-Ross and Robert Waller, two OU educational technologists, also argued that the focus should not be exclusively on the institution:

In our opinion the University works not so much because we are expert at distance teaching, but because, in the main, students are keen, intelligent and hardworking.[107]

Many students' accounts of their journey with the OU refer to the growth in their confidence, the pleasure to be gained from studying and the ways in which their careers and lives have been transformed. Mass mailings of texts aimed at generic learners, rather than focused on the individual, have made for mass consumption. However, the OUs structures have enabled learners to participate, to engage – to become part of the OU. To emphasise the constitutional and organisational arrangements should not marginalise the vitality, the pleasures of studying and the struggling with deadlines, unfamiliar concepts and different perspectives which have been central to many students' experiences.

Taking an overview can, of course, miss critical detail. John Kirkaldy, a tutor and counsellor for many years, remembered how, in 1979, he prepared to meet his new students: 'Tommy, I decided, was thirty-something; drank bitter and was keen on football.' She turned out to be an elderly woman. He went on:

I had received my first lesson about typical OU students – they do not exist … No generalisation about a quarter of a million graduates and current students [this was written in 1994] is possible.[108]

Although rarely physically present on the Walton Hall campus in Milton Keynes, the student body has been at the centre of the OU. By taking 'lectures' into living rooms, and holding examinations in a Polaris submarine, the OU expanded the notion of open learning. It has also helped to shift the concept of 'open', deploying it as a way both to be competitive and also to support collaboration. For the OU an important challenge has been how best to appropriate emerging technologies of learning in order to realise the vision of an early honorary graduate, Paulo Freire, that 'through learning [people] can make and remake themselves'.[109] Its ethos has helped to pave the way towards more open intellectual property and data standards, and sharing and remixing for non-commercial purposes. As critical, active readers engaged with texts (which could include broadcasts and web-based material) and as participants in dialogue, students have created both spaces for learning and a sense of identity and reciprocity with fellow learners. They helped themselves and each other through collective and individual self-help. The students have made the OU, just as it has been part of a virtuous circle which has made them. Yet while students have come to many different conclusions about the impact of their studies, common threads about the effects of the OU can be discerned.

Surveys carried out since the 1990s indicate that according to the students the most common reasons for participating in higher education are interest in the subject, expectations for personal growth, and aspirations for career progression or development. More than any other university, personal development has been the most salient gain for those who studied with the OU.[110] OU students tend to be distinctive from students who study part-time elsewhere. The latter are more likely to take a vocational and less flexible course at an institution near their home.[111] Moreover, those who study part-time tend to mention financial or domestic concerns such as being unable to afford to stop being in paid employment or being unable to move home in order to study. A survey of 2008 found that 88 per cent of part-time graduates said that their studies helped them to develop as a person, 78 per cent claimed an increase in self-confidence and 55 per cent in their overall happiness, and employers also valued the improved productivity and efficiency of part-time students.[112] Taken as a piece, learners' narratives indicate that, through the OU, people were able to change their understandings, to alter their own lives and the lives of those around them, and to contribute to the society in which they lived.

As a result of the political and pedagogic developments outlined in the first three parts of this book the OU came to be unconventional institution. It has offered convenient and accessible learning and teaching materials to those unable or unwilling to undertake residential higher education, many from groups otherwise marginalised within UK higher education. These include adults without A-levels, serving military personnel, prisoners, people with disabilities and those living abroad. It challenged long-held assumptions that learners should have only one chance to study for formal qualifications and that they needed to be full-time and in the same place at the same time to learn. The OU has significantly increased access opportunities and come to dominate part-time adult university provision. It made 'the bold move of ignoring entry standards and concentrating entirely on exit standards. This task we perform with excellence.'[113] The OU introduced novel design, analytics, monitoring and assessment, and developed learning journeys with the BBC.[114] It was the first higher education institution comprehensively to embrace modular academic structures, credit accumulation and transfer, the accreditation of prior learning, the use of multi-media learning technologies, the provision of extensive student guidance and support systems, and the issuing of transcripts as records of achievement.[115]

The OU was also conventional, in that it aspired to be a community of scholars who engaged with teaching and research. Moreover, many OU students were, in some respects, conventional in comparison to popular notions of students. When Michael Young described the socialisation and selection processes in place in the 1950s, he referred to an iconic artefact of the period. He argued that the educational system was

> rather like that strange water chute at the Festival of Britain [of 1951, although the chute remained open until the 1970s]. Most people flood straight through the ordinary schools and out to a job at 15 [whereas for the wealthy there were] channels leading straight from Nanny to New College.[116]

By the time the OU opened the dominant image of students had shifted from any association there might have been with Nanny or the 'varsity japes' epitomised by Bertie Wooster's trouble-making younger cousins Claude and Eustace, and towards greater alarm and hostility.[117] After a wave of strikes and sit-ins by students, universities were viewed with less enthusiasm.[118] In 1969 Donald Hutchings answered the question 'Has the student image reached a new low?' in the affirmative. He claimed that students were perceived as 'a pampered lot ... wasting time (paid for by tax-payers) on sit-ins and marches'.[119] This was the context in which *The Times* reported the OU's opening: 'the fact that it has started in the present economic and political climate is a minor triumph'.[120] 'Youth', lamented E. P. Thompson when writing in 1970 of the students he admired at the University of Warwick, where he taught, 'if left to its own devices, tends to become very hairy, to lie in bed til lunch-time, to miss seminars.'[121] That most of the members of the Angry Brigade who faced trial for a bombing campaign in Britain between 1970 and 1972 had been students was not lost on the press: 'Dropouts with brains tried to launch bloody revolution' claimed one headline.[122]

The OU demonstrated that universities need no longer be focused on wealthy, often male, youths or even only on those with prior qualifications.[123] In 1974 the Department of Education and Science funded a pilot scheme for the OU to admit 500 students aged between eighteen and twenty-one. Half of them had sufficient A-levels to ensure them a place at a conventional university and the rest had no A-levels.[124] In 1975 John Ferguson suggested that one reason why there were concerns about the admission of younger students to the OU was the fear that they were not as hard-working as its other students.[125] When *The Times* referred to the 'remarkable dedication of ordinary men and women which the OU has harnessed and channelled with such distinction and success', it promoted the OU as a state body which could yoke together ordinary people and – by helping them to override the social exclusivity, lawlessness and laziness associated with other universities – take the country not back to the 1950s but forwards to stability.[126] The first Dean of Arts connected the conventional and the novel when he noted that

> our revolutionary achievement, which is real and startling, has been carried out within the framework of traditional Western higher education.[127]

The OU was a space for the production and circulation of expertise where tutors could critique and elaborate upon teaching materials and students could learn from them. It could enable dialogic forms of engagement and facilitate the ethos of a pedagogy which emphasised non-hierarchical processes of learning and the fostering of resistance to conventional perspectives. Those whose voices had previously rarely been heard could challenge the conventional view of themselves as audiences and present themselves as participants. While there were hierarchies and asymmetries of power there was an aspiration to plurality. In 1971 the *Times Higher Education Supplement* squared the circle of the different elements of the OU:

> Although the Open University is a quiet, well-behaved institution with few radical ambitions the very principles on which it is based are an implicit challenge to many of the assumptions about the nature of all higher education – including polytechnics – that are generally accepted. It is bound to be a more democratic institution than the rest of higher education: it is more available to women, to the middle-aged and to people who were denied proper opportunities for education when they were young.[128]

The OU offered relatively conventional opportunities for people whose pathways to study had previously been blocked by financial, personal or social obstacles to learn, at many stages of their lives, from material developed in advance in a variety of locations from fellow learners and from tutors. More unconventionally it has stood at right angles to conventional higher education within and beyond the borders of the United Kingdom because it sought not to reproduce the privileges and dominance of the ruling class or to justify inequitable access on grounds of merit. Rather, it has tried to place wider participation and fairer access at the heart of mass higher education. Although the centre of gravity of the UK higher education sector has shifted towards The Open University's initial vision, the university's methods, its scale and its ambitious exploitation of the latest information technology have ensured that it remained a radical outlier in the much-expanded university system.

The OU's impact can also be gauged through increased prosperity. A study of the incomes of part-time students who had graduated from six different institutions, one being the OU, found that their pay rose following their studies, while a study of OU graduates, 1990–95, came to a similar conclusion about earnings.[129] Further evidence of the effects of the OU can be found in the descriptions of those students who have taken their knowledge and confidence into their communities and the wider world. Gordon Lewis used his *Third world studies* knowledge to bring water to a village in Nairobi; Sue Wilson designed a microwave iron after studying *Design and innovation*. For others, the impact of the OU has been at a familial level. The principles of sleep management were disseminated through the community education pack *Living with babies and toddlers*, while the fastest London marathon runner over the age of 60, Gordon Booth, felt that his change in lifestyle (a decade earlier he had been living on fast food and did no exercise) was due to the OU study pack *Health choices*.[130]

Students often find it hard not to engage with the OU. While working as a regional director in London, Peter Syme noted that

> The OU seems to have a particularly large and loyal constituency among London cab drivers, making many a journey an informal course choice and educational counselling session.[131]

Engagement with the OU has been expressed in other ways. Ben Palmer, Director of Assessment, Credit and Qualifications, recalled that at a degree ceremony in Belfast, 'the first person to come across the stage did a somersault, stood up and shook [the Vice-Chancellor's] hand. The look on the face of the person who was second in line was something to wonder at.'[132] Wakes have been held by students who have felt so attached to their studies that they had to mark the passing of specific courses. The formation of societies based on OU studies is also evidence of the effects of the OU. Personal narratives indicate the enthusiasm for critical thinking and the acceptance of ambiguity rather than black-and-white solutions. Through the letterbox, the airwaves or the ether the OU has entered people's homes and people's lives. Once there, this disruptive stranger has often treated as a friend and supporter of learning rather than an intruder.

Conclusion

The confident suggestion made by the historian E. P. Thompson, when receiving his honorary doctorate in 1982, that the OU appeared to be 'an inevitable invention of a nation with this kind of history' requires qualification.[133] The rise from being an institution of which *The Times* asked, in June 1968, 'is there a demand for the service?' to being one that Conservative Minister of Higher and Further Education Nigel Forman called 'a jewel in the crown of UK higher education' in October 1992 was not predestined.[134] Several of the attempts to replicate the OU which have had only a small impact indicate that the OU could have had a different fate. The Open College, which sought to copy the OU at the further education level and started to broadcast in 1987 on Channel 4, did not flourish. However, it spawned the National Open College Network, which provides quality assurance and accreditation, and the Open College of the Arts, which teaches the creative arts. The Open Polytechnic failed to take off when the distinction between polytechnics and universities was blurred, and the UKe-University only lasted three years before being closed. The OU did not invent education through broadcasting or correspondence; neither was it the first to hold summer schools or to use production lines or to explore the best ways to support collaborative learning. Rather, it made use of existing delivery methods and it continued to seek out and develop the formats which were best able to buttress learner-centred supported open learning.

Amid the jokes which rely for their humour on the juxtaposition of working people and intellectual endeavour or on footage of hirsute men pontificating on late-night television, two images of the OU from popular culture illustrate key characteristics which contributed to this national status. In the 1980 play (and 1983 film) *Educating Rita* the OU was portrayed as a force not only for education, but for profound personal transformation of the eponymous student, who in turn changes the lives of those around her, including that of her tutor. About a quarter of a century later in the TV series *Life on Mars* (first broadcast 2006–07), the time-travelling central character's understanding of his situation was significantly improved through a late-night OU-style television programme which offered highly relevant knowledge. The OU also served as a quintessentially 1970s cultural marker. Both images of the OU present it as distinctive, pervasive and informative. Within a few years of its opening it had rendered novelty as revered normality. It was by intention and outcome a disruptive innovation.

At its opening, the OU's first Chancellor Lord Crowther claimed that 'the University will be disembodied' (Figure 1.4). In the face of the dominant model of the bricks-and-mortar university he foresaw a form of higher education in which all that was solid could melt into the airwaves. The subsequent development of digital technology made possible still more ambitious and imaginative ways of transmitting knowledge and building communities of

Figure 1.4 Geoffrey Crowther, the OU's Foundation Chancellor, giving his speech, which defined the OU as being disembodied and also open to people, places, methods and ideas.

scholars. Crowther also compared the human mind 'to a fire which has to set alight', which reminded listeners of the importance of air for combustion, and hinted at how the circulation of air can ensure that thinking is not congested and how the airwaves could be used to deliver the materials and support the interactions necessary for learning. Yet, while OU broadcasts travelled through the ether, the university did not emerge out of thin air, nor were its subsequent achievements confined to the realm of the abstract. It was a product of high politics and deep planning, and its expansion stemmed from a specific combination of excellence and pragmatism.

The OU has had to develop in the face of changes in societal values, economic prosperity and university funding. Since it was founded there has been a growth of the sector (in terms of student numbers and the number of institutions) and in the recognition of a continuing need for well-educated, highly skilled professional entrepreneurs. There has also been greater interest in those able to adapt to portfolio careers and an increase in the importance attributed to student choice, to enhancing the experience of learners and to the role of the market within the sector. It has weathered the development of a global higher education economy and of new relationships between the state, the student and higher education. The significance that was attached to higher education institutions having a research role has increased, as has the international outreach of many universities. Central to the OU has been the idea that education is not simply about transmission from experts to learners, but is a relationship which provides learners with opportunities to construct themselves as producers of knowledge as well as consumers of education. It has presented students with the opportunities to gain sets of skills and accumulate learning outcomes, to become absorbed by a topic, wonder at the universe, develop self-confidence and be excited by intellectual challenges and dialogue and the value of a lifelong quest for knowledge. It has inspired, informed and illuminated customary practices in new ways; supported learning as part of the everyday experiences of people of all ages and backgrounds in all manner of places; and involved learners, teachers, researchers and many more in the development of universities, communities, wider societies and the lives of millions.

2

Opening a castle of the air

The Open University has its roots in more than a century of engagement with those excluded from conventional higher education. It drew upon long-established practices of open access and correspondence courses. In the shorter term its commitment to supported and accessible learning was built on post–1945 values, assumptions and educational structures. Yet the institution far exceeded the sum of its context and influences. This chapter will address the crucible in which the OU was formed in terms of politics, socio-economic developments and innovations in teaching.

Unlike other universities founded at about the same time, the OU was not part of a national plan developed by the University Grants Committee (UGC) in collaboration with the Committee of Vice-Chancellors and Principals (CVCP), local authorities and academics.[1] Neither was it the subject of significant consultation or lobbying by educational or local authorities. Rather, Harold Wilson, Labour Party Leader from 1963 and Prime Minister from 1964, was key to the foundation of the OU. The first of the three sections in this chapter concentrates upon the activities of Wilson and a small group around him who were responsible for the creation and early running of the university.

Despite its roots in the Labour Party, the OU faced opposition from the political left, where there was concern that the OU would result in less funding for and attention to the polytechnics and existing part-time provision. The historian E. P. Thompson, who began his career teaching for the Workers' Educational Association (WEA), argued that the money earmarked for the new university should be spent on the WEA as the OU was crowding out liberal adult education.[2] The second section focuses on how Wilson won support for the OU not only by building on the ideas and skills of others but also by drawing on the emerging wider interest in universities for their potential to support economic and social development. Since the Second World War there had been numerous official reports which promoted the benefits of wider participation within an enlarged education system; there was also considerable post-war expansion of the higher education sector in the UK and across Europe. The OU was developed by a government that conceived an active role for the state in the diffusion of knowledge. It recognised there would be high demand from both students and employers and embraced the potential of technology and science to revitalise the economies of democratic societies.

Richard Hooper, a former Senior Producer for the BBC and OU who has been credited as one of founding forces of the university, argued that the OU 'has, in a real sense, two ancestries. One is technological. The other is ideological.'[3] This pair of formative influences resulted not only in the OU's foundation but also in the specific form of its pedagogy. The third section is about the educational roots of 'the first distance teaching university that was truly multi-media in nature'.[4] It examines the ways in which the OU adapted and transformed established models. The university was built on the premise that television, radio, correspondence and external assessment systems could be combined successfully for educational purposes. A blended system of open, supported learning could be created partly because of existing antecedents. Several features which have become almost synonymous with the OU – sandwich courses, summer schools, radio and television broadcasts, correspondence courses and programmed learning – had previously been trialled, some over many decades. The university also built on traditions of part-time education for adults, which had developed from the eighteenth century; the rise of correspondence courses, associated with rapid industrialisation; and university extension initiatives, which started in the 1870s. Six of the universities opened in the 1960s used continuous assessment and several of those institutions experimented with projects, long essays and 'unorthodox examination techniques'.[5] The OU was able to have a significant impact because it was fashioned initially by a small number of people, it employed familiar methods and it was created within a broader consensus about the value of education.

The political components

In 1963 Clark Kerr, economist and the first Chancellor of the University of California, Berkeley, analysed the role of the modern university. He argued that following specialisation and fragmentation in academic fields, the notion of a university as a single community of scholars was replaced by a multiversity of many, sometimes competing, communities including undergraduates and postgraduates, administrative staff and academics, social sciences and scientists.[6] He suggested that this challenge to the university as a monolithic entity had aided the democratisation of access and promotion, resulted in advances in research and provided better services to the nation.

There were similar moves in the United Kingdom to reassess the role of universities. Lord Robbins chaired a Committee on Higher Education between 1961 and 1963, the conclusions of which were accepted by government. His assumptions – that there would be a narrowing of income inequality and an upgrading of jobs – were proved correct by developments in much of the following two decades, in part due to the legacy of the post-war settlement. A number of factors coincided to drive the increase in student numbers from 50,000, before the war, to 68,400 by 1947 and 107,700 by 1961. These included the removal of some educational costs in 1944, demobilised service personnel entering higher education, full employment and the increase in the number of sixth-formers. The number of institutions granted charters to be universities rose.[7] This was a period, argued Geoffrey Price, when 'British universities were on a path of increasing involvement with, and service to, the goals of the nation, as defined by central government'.[8] While the political goals of university expansion were national, the impetus to establish individual institutions was often decidedly local: a number of universities of the 1960s were 'created entirely through local initiative by proud, entrepreneurial and dynamic local government executives'.[9] In 1958, when Brighton Corporation's scheme for a university was approved, it had been discussed in the town for almost half a century.[10] There were plans for the University of East Anglia (UEA) dating back to 1918, and the seeds of the University of Warwick were sown in the 1940s.[11]

By contrast, the foundation of a national, widely accessible university, designed to support part-time learners principally through correspondence and broadcasting, was closely associated with only a few individuals at the centre of government. As John Pratt put it, 'The Open University was devised and set up quite explicitly by a handful of civil servants'.[12] This unusual path to foundation had an impact on the way in which it developed. According to Pratt, it was a 'very eccentric institution [because it was] funded directly by the state, and run by a direct grant from the state'.[13] Moreover, the British parliamentary system enabled a relatively small number of people to work, not via the conventional body which administered universities, but through ministerial fiat.

In September 1963 Harold Wilson, the Leader of HM Loyal Opposition, produced, in a speech in Glasgow, an idea for 'a new educational trust ... a University of the Air ... to cater for a wide variety of potential students [including] technologists who perhaps left school at sixteen'.[14] This was done without circulating his speech to the Shadow Cabinet or the Labour Party Executive prior to delivery. He reiterated his scheme at the Labour Party

conference in October 1963, stressing that he sought 'to provide an opportunity for those, who, for one reason or another, have not been able to take
advantage of higher education'.[15] By placing his intention to create a university of the air within his speech about the white heat of technology Harold
Wilson associated the OU not with the dreaming spires of the university
where he was educated (he was an undergraduate at Oxford) but with scientific modernity and economic activity.[16] He restated 'socialism in terms of
the scientific revolution' and linked automation to the case of socialism. As
it became clear that service industries, such as universities, were of economic
importance so the perception spread that the production of knowledge could
be seen as similar to the production of raw materials.[17]

   Wilson's text contains echoes of a speech made a year earlier by President
Kennedy, committing the USA to putting a man on the moon during the
1960s.[18] Kennedy placed the space race in the context of the Cold War. He
credited research conducted in universities with driving progress and voiced
his support for those who sought to answer as yet unformulated questions.
Wilson followed Kennedy in arguing that social progress could be achieved
by investment in research, particularly in science and technology. Both
leaders linked these forms of progress to the cause of peace. Kennedy stressed
the universal aspects of space exploration, which he claimed represented an
'opportunity for peaceful co-operation', while Wilson called for the kinds of
resources previously devoted to research into military defence to be dedicated
to research supporting peaceful industrial development. The OU became,
according to one commentator, 'a tacit hymn of praise to the generosity of
space and its exploration'.[19] Within days of the first moon landings in 1969
the OU was opened by Lord Crowther, who made an explicit link between
the aspirations embodied by both endeavours:

   we start on this task, in this very week when the Universe has opened.
   The limits not only of explorable space, but of human understanding,
   are infinitely wider than we have believed.

While the OU reflected the enthusiasms of its age as an industrial, technological business, the terms in which it was described also echo the era's idealism.[20]
   Harold Wilson's proposals for cost-effective, modern and flexible standardised training for adults furthered Labour's ambition to be seen as the
party for socially aspirational voters. He linked Labour to higher education,
economic regeneration, increasing productivity, the elimination of social
inequalities and the promotion of social justice. The government's general
commitment to opening up opportunities for citizens in order to demonstrate

the benefits of British social democracy and stability was employed to justify the OU.

However idealistic the rhetoric, a practical plan was needed to bring the university into being. Wilson's original idea was to connect existing extra-mural departments, the WEA, broadcasters, correspondence courses and night classes together to create a scheme for degrees to be awarded by an established university. He did not initially envisage an institution with a charter and autonomy but a consortium of existing universities using television and the post. There needed to be 'facilities for home study to university and higher technical standards', nationally organised correspondence teaching and a structure open to 'a variety of people'.

Wilson sought not only to increase the supply of 'technicians and technologists', but also to enrich British cultural life and living standards. To achieve this aim learning materials would be made available not only to enrolled students but to the public at large, principally through television broadcasts. Interest in using the medium for educational purposes had been developing since the beginning of the decade. In 1961 former Labour MP David Hardman proposed an Institute of Educational Television. A year later there were ITV conferences on educational television, and in 1963 an inter-university television link was created when Oxford University hosted an Anglo-American conference on education by correspondence and television.[21]

The modernity of television would enable traditional adult education to be brought within the orbit of the technological revolution. Wilson's enthusiasm for the medium echoed an early American proponent of educational broadcasting, William Benton.[22] In 1960 Benton sponsored him to address the University of Chicago, a liberal arts college at Carleton and the Federal Reserve Board in Washington. Wilson met twenty senators and went on to make similar trips in 1961, 1962 and 1963.[23]

William Benton

Benton was an American millionaire who made his money in radio advertising and then turned to using radio and film for educational purposes. He became a vice-president of the University of Chicago in 1937 and a trustee of many other educational institutions. He ran a scheme to support learning among early high school leavers.[24] Benton's politics, 'pro-business and pro-state, dedicated to private profit and to regulatory reform', were informed by early twentieth-century American corporate liberalism.[25] From 1943 he owned *Encyclopaedia Britannica*; shortly afterwards he purchased what soon became Encyclopaedia Britannica Films; in 1952 he started publishing the *Great Books of the Western World* series, which presented the Western canon in 54 volumes. He sought to enlighten citizens against communism by connecting higher education, commerce and high culture. As a US senator, 1949–52, Benton promoted a 'Marshall Plan for Peace' and called for the expulsion of Senator Joseph McCarthy.[26] After he lost his seat he worked closely with leading Democrats, toured many countries promoting his books and films and supported the creation of non-commercial education television stations in the US.

Benton wanted television to be used for educational purposes, arguing that it 'could be the greatest force ever known to deepen our understanding and broaden our knowledge'.[27] A 'key figure in elite media circles whose work focused on the task of manufacturing consent', he wanted to marginalise Soviet involvement and spread liberal ideals.[28] Benton argued that 'the cold war between the open and closed societies is likely to be won in the world's classrooms, libraries, and college and university laboratories' and that to bar entry to higher education on grounds of poverty 'stands athwart the American Dream'.[29] The first Vice-Chancellor of the OU, Walter Perry, claimed that Benton was one of the men whose vision of education for all, through correspondence teaching and the use of the mass media, contributed to the decision to found the university.[30] He died aged 73 in 1973.

Benton was lavish in his praise of Wilson and arranged for his first honorary degree at the University of Chicago. He sent gifts and invited him to meet influential people aboard his ocean-going yacht.[31] The seeds were sown for a critical future relationship when he held a dinner in London for Wilson and Geoffrey Crowther, then Vice-Chair of the Editorial Board of the *Encyclopaedia Britannica* and a governor of the London School of Economics. Asa Briggs, who would later become the OU's Chancellor, went on to edit a ready reference version of the *Encyclopaedia Britannica*, and Perry considered purchasing 280 sets of the 27 volumes in order to equip study centres.[32]

Geoffrey Crowther

Geoffrey Crowther was born in 1907 in Leeds. He studied at the University of Cambridge and was awarded a Commonwealth fellowship to Yale. After working on Wall Street and then in a London merchant bank he became an economic adviser to the Irish government on the recommendation of John Maynard Keynes. In 1932 he joined *The Economist* and was its editor from 1938 until 1956. He became a director of Economist

Newspaper Ltd in 1947 and managing director after he ceased to edit the magazine. In 1963 he became the company chair, and the magazine 'warmly welcomed' the OU.[33] His wartime service included stints at the Ministries of Supply, of Information and of Production. As chair of the Central Advisory Council for Education (1956–60) he was responsible for *The Crowther Report: Fifteen to Eighteen* (1959). This indicated that a large number of those who left school at the first opportunity were highly intelligent, and it galvanised many progressives. As David Grugeon recalled, 'we were losing talent all over the place. And so there was a huge flurry and interest in new ways of approaching things.'[34] Crowther went on to become the OU's Foundation Chancellor, until his death in 1972.[35]

Despite its association with technical progress, Wilson was not wholly comfortable with television.[36] He had 'intense suspicions of the BBC' with which his relationship was 'awkward'.[37] Instead, he preferred commercial television and wrote enthusiastically to Benton about 'the possibilities of television as a medium of popular education'.[38] On his return from his first sponsored trip to the USA, Wilson wrote to thank Benton and added that he was willing to help him with his 'problem' concerning the British quota on the number of foreign films shown.[39] He later suggested that: 'On Ency. Brit. matters ... my discussion with the television authorities suggest that it would not be difficult to propose a small change in the regulations which would be of benefit in regard to educational films.'[40]

In February 1963, as new Leader of the Opposition, Wilson gave a party political broadcast in which he stressed that 'We can't afford a higher educational system where only a small proportion of students who have the necessary qualifications get into a university, or a college.' This passage is marked in Benton's copy of the speech.[41] Benton sent Wilson notes on how best to promote a 'television university' and how television was used in the USA.[42] After Wilson gave his speech announcing his plans for a university of the air, Benton told two aides to provide 'every single argument that he can use politically here in his advocacy of this idea. Manifestly this is a terribly important goal for us in line with our interest in EBF [Encyclopaedia Britannica Films] and EB [*Encyclopaedia Britannica*].'[43] Wilson discussed the proposals with the Labour-Party-supporting owners of Granada TV.[44] He provided information for Benton and offered to broker a deal.[45] In February 1965 Wilson proposed three ideas; that the ITA (Independent Television Authority) could broadcast OU programmes, that the BBC could (and advertise during its late-night programmes), or that both could broadcast, together with two universities.[46] Wilson was able to forge these aspirations and practical concerns into a personal commitment to the new university because, like Benton, he saw how business and politics could be used to widen access to knowledge.

Wilson's importance to the OU has been widely recognised.[47] Professor Ralph Smith felt that 'political willpower, to Prime Ministerial level, played a large part in ensuring the successful launch of the British OU'.[48] The Chancellor of the Exchequer, James Callaghan, wrote, 'I am conceding the "Open University" and the necessary expenditure in exchange for a substantial cut in public expenditure' and he later recalled Wilson's emphatic enthusiasm for the OU.[49] Just two months before the general election of June 1970 Callaghan's successor, Roy Jenkins, also bowed to Wilson's wishes, though he 'regretted the need to make a concession on The Open University because to do so was not in accordance with his own assessment of priorities'.[50] According to Conservative MP Sir Paul Bryan there were 'no supporters for this University ... The most truthful reason for it came to me from a Socialist, who said, "Well, Harold insists on having it".'[51] The sense of personal ownership of the project was apparent in Wilson's recollections of 14 April 1963: 'That Easter Sunday I spent in the Isles of Scilly. Between church and lunch I wrote the whole outline of a proposal for a University of the Air.'[52] This positioning of the OU's origins as lying between Christian worship and home cooking presents it as a personal decision rather than the outcome of consensual deliberation within the government. It was, he later claimed, 'a brain child of mine, worked out by me privately in the early sixties'.[53]

It has been argued that 'higher education policy has rarely been a major concern of the Labour Party in the second half of the twentieth century' and that 'higher education in general, and in particular part-time higher education, adult education and lifelong learning have rarely had a high profile with Labour'. Nonetheless, through a mixture of long-term vision and short-term tactics Wilson was able to place access to universities on the Party agenda and eventually in the 1966 election manifesto.[54] He wrote an introduction to Lord Taylor's *The Years of Crisis: The Report of the Labour Party's Study Group on Higher Education* (1963), which called for higher education to be seen as a right. However, his envisaged vehicle for access was not immediately accepted. Wilson noted that the Labour Party's National Executive Committee was 'not committed to every detail proposed'.[55] Although *The Times* reported the 'university of the air' as a conference decision, items for the manifesto required that a resolution had to be passed by a two-thirds majority.[56] Labour returned to office in 1964 'on the ticket of technical competence, purposive planning ... faster growth and higher social spending', but its specific promise was only to 'carry out a programme of massive expansion in higher, further and university education'.[57] The National Executive Committee, which saw the manifesto as an important instrument for achieving accountability, did not recognise the OU as policy because it was not specifically mentioned. As one minister put it, 'we have been sent to Parliament to carry the mandate out. ... Now, what could be more immoral than entering Parliament and failing in our faith to the party outside?'[58] In response Wilson strategically convened meetings of the necessary Clause 5 Committee at the end of the Parliament, when members were impatient to leave and therefore more likely to accept a *fait accompli*.

Wilson grasped how the strengths and limitations of correspondence courses could complement the potential of television. His employment of the slogan 'a university of the air' captured imaginations and connected his party to a broader enthusiasm for greater educational opportunities. His success owed much to his ability to connect a variety of approaches to education to the post-war consensus and the values and aspirations of his party. Brian Jackson, referring to Wilson's claim to have written his proposal for the OU 'after church on Easter Sunday morning', noted 'that this may give the impression of an inspiration from the blue. Of course it wasn't like that and the old strands still interweave.'[59]

Harold Wilson announces the OU

Today I want to outline new proposals on which we are working, a dynamic programme providing facilities for home study to university and higher technical standards, on the basis of a University of the Air and of nationally organised correspondence college courses. These will be intended to cater for a wide variety of potential students. There are technicians and technologists who perhaps left school at sixteen or seventeen and who, after two or three years in industry, feel that they could qualify as graduate scientists or technologists. There are many others, perhaps in clerical occupations, who would like to acquire new skills and new qualifications. There are many in all levels of industry who would desire to become qualified in their own or other fields, including those who had no facilities for taking GCE at O or A level, or other required qualifications; or housewives who might like to secure qualifications in English Literature, Geography or History ... . What we envisage is the creation of a new educational trust, representative of the universities and other educational organisations, associations of teachers, the broadcasting authorities.

Glasgow, 8 September 1963[60]

Wilson built on the work and ideas of Michael Young, who had already begun to explore the possibility of connecting existing institutions with more adventurous configurations. Young had, as a Labour Party employee, worked with the BBC on the 1945 election broadcasts and retained an interest in broadcasting.[61] Appointed to the University of Cambridge in 1960 he found this 'orthodox university' to be 'uncongenial'.[62] He felt that 'the spirit of 1945 was still in the air, and some of the enthusiasm that had once gone into socialism had emigrated into education of the new sort'.[63] David Grugeon explained:

> he felt that Cambridge was an almost impossible place to get any decent change going, and that he could do in London in a week what it would take ten years to get done in Cambridge.[64]

Young himself recalled that 'one crucial moment was in 1960' when Brian Jackson 'urged me not to get absorbed by the comfortable haven of Cambridge and do something like starting a new university. He said he would help.'[65] In 1961 Geoffrey Crowther suggested using existing facilities to take more students.[66] Young took up the idea in March 1963 and piloted his 'dual Cambridge' plan to establish a 'Battersea University in King's Parade'.[67] He used part of Churchill College for fifty students to attend a one-week residential course, which was extended by the use of radio, television and correspondence courses.[68] This prefigured Harold Wilson's Glasgow speech of September 1963 in which the Labour leader 'outlined a similar proposal'.[69] Although Young's precise model was not adopted, his passion for social justice would inform the ethos and structures of the OU. He helped to ensure that the plight of the 'unlucky generation of 1947', marginalised by the education system, was not ignored. He also insisted that a variety of media were employed at the new university, that it was not simply a university of the air.[70] This role was acknowledged by Peter Laslett, who referred to Young's persuasiveness; by John Griffith, the National Extension College's first Executive Director, who called Young and Jackson 'the true founding fathers of the OU'; and by Asa Briggs, who felt Young 'created' the OU.[71]

The National Extension College

In 1963 Michael Young left Cambridge and founded, with Brian Jackson, the 'Invisible College of Cambridge', the National Extension College.[72] Jackson's role was significant. The intention was that it would offer courses, largely through correspondence, but with some use of television.

This, the open multi-media college was 'set up precisely for the purpose of piloting a university of the air'. The National Extension College drew on the private sector for support,[73] but the public sector was also represented.[74] Initially, Young wanted to make use of correspondence, telephones, live tutorials and television to run the National Extension College first of all as a pilot and then as a nucleus for an open university. The Chair was Michael Young, and its Director (Brian Jackson) and Treasurer (Howard Dickinson) were shared with the Advisory Centre for Education (ACE). The one staff member of its own, David Grugeon, was a teacher who was seconded for a year as Administrator. Some courses were run in conjunction with Anglia Television. These were linked to correspondence and a residential element.[75] It merged with the private University Correspondence College and by 1967 had 7,000 students taking O- and A-levels. Shirley Williams, Secretary of State for Education and Science, 1976–79, felt that the National Extension College was 'a very important milestone' on the route to the OU.[76] The *Guardian* was enthusiastic:

> the Advisory Centre for Education's plans for a National Extension College are now rapidly taking shape ... we should all be grateful to the college for this important pioneering work, leading towards ACE's vision of the 'Open University' – certainly a better name than Mr Harold Wilson's original 'University of the Air' since much of the work must necessarily be done on the ground.[77]

However, the National Extension College's interest in wide adult education rather than degrees marginalised it once the decision had been made to establish a university rather than a college.

In its formative phase, the OU received little support from the other major parties. The Liberal leader Jo Grimond stated:

> of adult education I am sceptical. The intense desire for knowledge which existed fifty years ago seems to have evaporated or is now satisfied by TV and the papers. By all means let universities run extra-mural courses but modern adult education of people over twenty-five is largely a matter of providing 'third programmes' in various ways outside the educational system itself.[78]

Labour included adult education in its 1966 manifesto, while the Liberals focused on other issues.

There was little discernible enthusiasm on the Conservative benches. Christopher Chataway, who had been a junior minister for education before the 1964 election, suggested that the OU might be dropped.[79] He cited the view of *Education* that the topic about which most nonsense was talked was educational television. He went on to call the notion of a university of the air 'a bright red herring [with] qualities of superficial smartness and underlying irrelevance which made it irresistible as an election gimmick'.[80] In the same vein, Iain Macleod, the future Conservative Chancellor of the Exchequer, dismissed the project as 'blithering nonsense'.[81] Charles Wedemeyer, who was consulted by the Conservatives, felt that 'the Tory position regarding the University of the Air-cum-Open University was not one of either outright opposition or support, but was characterized by restrained criticism'.[82] Perry recorded that 'during the life of the Planning Committee the Conservative Party never went on record with any public statement about their attitude to the Open University'. The Tory spokesman on education, Sir Edward Boyle, was unsupportive, though he offered only 'the mildest attack on the Open University'.[83] Shortly before the 1970 election the Conservative leader, Edward Heath, was asked for the stance of a future Conservative government in regard to the newly launched OU, which had yet to receive its first student, but would not commit himself.[84]

There was only cautious engagement from the BBC, which had had its own plans for a 'College of the Air' and was concerned about control over content and airtime.[85] David Puttnam recalled that 'the creation of the OU was initially opposed root and branch by the BBC as being an imposition on its editorial independence'.[86] The *Times Higher Education Supplement* mentioned the 'many rumours that the death warrant was only waiting to be signed by Iain Mcleod when he died' and the 'constant sniping' by the *Daily Telegraph*.[87] This included the claim that the OU was deemed 'grossly expensive' and there was parliamentary pressure (from the Conservative majority) for it to be closed.[88] William van Straubenzee, the Conservative junior minister for higher education in the 1970–74 government, was reported as saying of the OU 'I would have slit its throat if I could'. He blamed the outgoing Labour education minister Ted Short for some 'nifty, last-moment work with the charter that made the OU unkillable'.[89] In the face of indifference and hostility, the OU needed a champion.

Jennie Lee

A coal miner's daughter, born in 1904, she could not afford university fees and became an undergraduate with the support of the Carnegie Trust and the Fife Education Authority. She developed an interest in education. In 1925 she read a founders' account of the WEA, a choice which her biographer pointed out was 'an unusual book for an Edinburgh undergraduate'.[90] In 1926, having read WEA lecturer Richard Tawney's *Education*, she persuaded her Labour Club to run him for rector.[91] Reflecting on her youth, she said that Hardy's *Jude the Obscure* was 'one of the formative books for me when I was a young student – the struggle for self-education, the struggle in circumstances [of poverty]'.[92] In 1929 she won a by-election and became the youngest MP and one of the first women in the Commons. Having lost her seat in 1931 she returned to the Commons in 1945. In 1934 she married Labour MP Aneurin ('Nye') Bevan. He had become a miner on leaving elementary school. He helped to pay for his sisters to attend college and he wrote of how 'tenaciously we clung to the hope of superior educational opportunities for those of our family who could benefit from them'.[93] She recalled that the origins of the OU went

> back to all the years when Nye Bevan and myself were together [he died in 1960]. We knew, we both of us, from our backgrounds, that there were people in the mining villages who left school at 14 or 15 who had first-class intellects. The problem was how could you devise a scheme that would get through to them without excluding other people?[94]

Norman MacKenzie said that 'Jennie always had a mental picture of her father in a break in the day's mining with his headlight on, sitting reading Karl Marx in a mine'.[95] Others made the same connection. Brian Jackson claimed that whereas some had emphasised the importance of equality to the OU,

> Wilson fashioned it differently. His was then the politics of the 'white heat of technology' ... To re-read the scheme for a University of the Air today is to find simply a listing of the virtues and services of the Mechanics' Institutes of the nineteenth century and the Technical Colleges of this, speckled all over by the marks of the new technology.[96]

Stuart Hood called the concept of an open university an

> historical fossil from the days of the Workers' Educational Association and the National Council of Labour College ... [its supporters were]

obsessed with the days when bright boys like Aneurin Bevan could not obtain an education commensurate with their gifts.[97]

Michael Young wrote of Jennie Lee that 'The OU was built by one person, though she had many able lieutenants and one ace card ... the direct support of the Prime Minister ... It was a stunning performance' (Figure 2.1).[98] Clive Ponting inverted the relationship, claiming that the OU was created because Wilson was both 'determined' and 'deferential towards Jennie Lee'.[99] The OU benefited from it being the only plan singled out for the attention of a minister who was known to be close to the PM and from Jennie Lee being a powerful figure in her own right. Her role was recognised by the OU, which has named two buildings on its Walton Hall campus in her honour. MSP Claire Baker called Wilson the father of the OU and Lee the midwife.[100] Geoff Mulgan felt that Lee attained the status of a 'sanctified figure' for her support of the OU.[101] Briggs suggested that, if this was the case, such status was deserved:

Figure 2.1 Jennie Lee, Walter Perry and Louis Mountbatten. Earl Mountbatten of Burma laid the OU's foundation stone at Walton Hall on 18 May 1970. He was educated at home before he attended a school and then the Royal Naval College. After serving in the First World War he became a mature university student. He later returned to the Royal Naval College as an adult learner. His membership of the Institute of Electrical Engineers and presidency of the United World Colleges were reminders of the OU's international and economic roles and its appeal to prescient technocrats.

> She was the real heroine of the story, resolute, determined and able to confront Labour party leaders who were not committed as she was to creating a real university of quality ... no one but Jennie, backed by Goodman – and, just behind the scenes by Harold Wilson, – could have done it.[102]

After losing her seat in 1970 she was elevated to the Upper Chamber. She died in 1988.

Once he became Prime Minister, Wilson could not give as much of his attention to the creation of a new university. In March 1965, to ensure delivery of the University of the Air, Jennie Lee was moved from the Ministry of Public Buildings and Works (where she was Minister of Arts) to become a Parliamentary Under-Secretary of State at the DES.[103] She chaired the Parliamentary Committee convened to investigate the practicability of Wilson's 'University of the Air' project (Figure 2.2). Her personal role was made possible only by challenging the structures of influence and control in higher education. Wilson recognised at the outset that an unconventional institution could not be entrusted to the conventional mechanisms for managing the university system. Left to the existing authorities, the OU would be smothered in its cradle. The UGC, which channelled funds to most of higher education, was known to be unenthusiastic about the proposed new project. As early as 1946, when R. H. Tawney, a Labour appointment to the UGC, called for the expansion of higher education, the idea was not adopted and both the UGC and the CVCP were opposed to change.[104] Wilson also felt that officials in the Department of Education and Science were unsympathetic, and sought to isolate the proposed OU from other plans for expanding the face-to-face sector.[105] He had expressly stated in Scarborough that the University of the Air 'was not a substitute for our plans for higher education ... for new universities ... or for extending technological education'.[106] Jennie Lee, although only a junior minister, was able to by-pass the higher-education power brokers and deal directly with the Treasury and with the Prime Minister.

But she faced an uphill task. Wilson recalled:

> After the election I had every kind of obstruction. No ministers were really keen on the University of the Air. The Treasury and the Department of Education were determined to kill it – The DES on the grounds that they would only get so much money and they had to give some of it to this idea they would have less for other things.[107]

Figure 2.2 Membership of the Parliamentary Advisory Committee (AC), the Planning Committee (PC) and the first Council (C) of the OU.

	AC	PC	C
Professor K. J. Alexander	x		
Sir William Alexander		x	x
Lord Annan	x		
Sir Eric Ashby		x	
Dr E. W. H. Briault	x	x	
Professor Asa Briggs		x	
Professor John Currie Gunn			x
Lord Fulton		x	
Lord Goodman		x	x
Brian Groombridge		x	
Professor Hilde Himmelweit		x	x
Dr Sidney Holgate			x
D. J. G. Holroyde	x		
Mr I. Hughes		x	
Sir Byrnmor Jones	x	x	
Dr Kathleen Kenyon			x
Professor K. W. Keobane			x
Peter Laslett	x		
Jennie Lee	x		
Dr F. J. Llewellyn		x	
Professor F. Llewellyn-Jones	x		
Norman MacKenzie	x	x	x
R. MacLean		x	
A. D. C Peterson	x		
Dr O. G. Pickard	x		
Dr A. J. Richmond		x	
Professor Lord Richie-Calder		x	
John Scupham	x	x	x
Professor Roy Shaw		x	x
Frank Thistlewaite			x
Dr Bryan Thwaites			x
Sir Peter Venables		x	x
Professor Harold Wiltshire	x	x	x
The Lord Wynne-Jones			x
The Vice-Chancellor (ex officio)			x

Among the ministers there was interest from Anthony Crosland (Education Secretary 1965–68), though his main focus within the higher education sector was on the polytechnics, the subject of his 1966 White Paper. His successor, Ted Short, was more supportive.[108] However, both had competing priorities, and in the first Labour administration money was tight from the outset. After the 1964 election there was a run on the pound. In 1965 the government 'deferred' the building costs of 20 per cent of the proposed construction on university sites and in 1966 the pound was devalued.

The proposal benefited by being kept away from senior ministers who might have sought to save money by pruning the plans. Jennie Lee was able maintain the momentum of the project and in the House of Commons in April 1965 commit the government to 'implementing the University of the Air', which would be autonomous and independent, and would support open access and award degrees.[109] The isolation of the new university was so complete that when in 1966 two White Papers were published on higher education, one on polytechnics, the other on the OU, neither referred to the other.[110] In accordance with the National Plan, 1965, 60,000 full-time students by 1969–70 were envisaged. They were to study in possibly thirty or more newly designated polytechnics.[111] However, there was some rivalry. Eric Robinson argued strongly for the development of the local authority colleges such as the colleges of advanced technology and the polytechnics.[112] Magnus Turnstile (a nom de plume) in the left-leaning *New Statesman* suggested of the OU that 'the press was lukewarm, educators were doubtful about ends, broadcasters were dubious about means and the public was apparently unstirred'.[113]

Jennie Lee put the idea of a new university to the Ministerial Committee on Broadcasting, a standing Cabinet Committee. As a result an Advisory Committee to explore 'educational functions and content' of a University of the Air was created. Organisation and finance were referred to the Official Committee on Broadcasting, composed of civil servants and headed by members of the Ministerial Committee. Jennie Lee chaired the Advisory Committee and gave it a specific remit: 'To consider the educational functions and content of a University of the Air as outlined in a speech made by Mr Harold Wilson in Glasgow on 8th September 1963'. The Committee contained five vice-chancellors, the leaders of two education authorities, John Sculpham (Controller of Educational Broadcasting at the BBC), Harold Wiltshire from Nottingham University extra-mural department, Peter Laslett from the National Extension College and Norman MacKenzie from Sussex. Notable by their absence were representatives from the principal university providers of adult education, Birkbeck, London Extra Mural and Ruskin College.

It was clear that there was now a policy that the new university would award degrees. Labour had a tiny majority and the Committee was asked to swiftly produce a White Paper before the 1966 general election. The Committee was, Asa Briggs felt, 'of fundamental importance to the whole concept and the subsequent development'.[114] In attendance at the Advisory Committee stage were representatives from the DES, the University Grants Committee, and officials and officers of the Ministry of Technology and the Scottish Education Department. There was also John Scupham, who had previously collaborated with Brian Jackson of the National Extension College.[115] Scupham was still was working on his own plans.[116] Donald Grattan recalled that there were 'discussions going on at the highest level' of the BBC:

> a number of us would meet in the evenings in Broadcasting House ... we'd sit down with people like Ralph Toomey ... and others from the DES, to talk about what we might do if we got more airtime ... we came out with some outline plans of what a set of courses might do, and we knew that you had to have some form of accreditation, but not necessarily degree-giving accreditation.[117]

These ideas were now swept up into Jennie Lee's larger project.

The Advisory Committee established the principle of open access: 'Enrolment as a student of the University should be open to everyone ... irrespective of educational qualifications, and no formal entrance requirement should be imposed.' This part of its report in August 1965 was produced unchanged as paragraph 8 of the White Paper published in February 1966. Jennie Lee rejected the case for offering qualifications other than degrees.[118] A full university could have been a deterrent to some potential applicants and there already existed a part-time route to degree-level qualifications through technical colleges, which were attended by many working-class students. But Jennie Lee was adamant. She chaired the original Advisory Committee and when the topic arose, made her preference for a university clear.[119] She later argued that the OU 'has to be a university with no concessions ... I didn't believe we could get it through if we lowered our standards.'[120] She insisted that the new institution should be autonomous and independent, a 'full university' with degree-granting powers, as only this structure would provide 'genuine equality of opportunity to millions of people for the first time'. Furthermore, they would be offered 'the best', just as her late spouse Nye Bevan had promised when he launched the National Health Service in 1947.[121]

The intention was to avoid reproducing the inadequately funded, poorly supported adult education institutions that already existed. Jennie Lee

characterised the Conservatives as old-fashioned and in favour of unneces-
sarily harsh conditions for learners:

> We have a great tradition of adult education in this country but we have
> to be careful that it does not become a little dowdy and mouldy. The
> days when people would go out to the old-fashioned night schools and
> sit on hard benches are receding. They are now looking for a different
> kind of environment. There was a kind of passion for hair shirts from
> hon. Members opposite today, a passion I do not share.[122]

She was clear that pre-university education for adults 'had no glamour' and
she chose 'largely to ignore the world of adult education'.[123] She insisted
that the institution must be able to award recognised academic degrees with
no compromise on academic standards. Her February 1966 White Paper, *A
University of the Air*, made it clear that

> There can be no question of offering to students a makeshift project
> inferior in quality to other universities. That would defeat its whole
> purpose. Its status will be determined by the quality of its teaching.[124]

Her desire for an autonomous, independent university equal to any other
was related to her enthusiasm to beat the established order at its own game,
to 'outsnob the snobs', as she put it. She referred to previous, marginalised
educational broadcasting attempts:

> I am not enamoured of the idea of dawn patrols and midnight parades.[125]
> It is astonishing how we can talk of learning in uncomfortable circum-
> stances for other people, especially those of us who have had extremely
> comfortable university careers.[126]

The Cabinet and Labour Party's National Executive Committee met at
Chequers prior to the 1966 election. Richard Crossman claimed that in
1966 'the manifesto was drafted under the complete personal direction of
the PM'.[127] Jennie Lee was instrumental in the promise to create the OU, and
Wilson recalled her contribution:

> At the end of the afternoon anybody was free to speak on anything.
> Jennie got up and made a passionate speech about the University of
> the Air. She said the greatest creation of the previous Labour govern-
> ment was Nye [Bevan]'s National Health Service but that now we were

engaged on an operation which would make just as much difference to the country. We were all impressed. She was a tigress.[128]

She then needed to persuade the Party of the financial viability of the proposal. Although there was Treasury control of public expenditure in the 1940s it was not as tight as it had been during the 1930s. From 1961 the planning and control of public expenditure were mediated by the Public Expenditure Survey Committee. This was never consistently effective at either the planning or control of expenditure and, as Christopher Pollitt noted, there was considerable departmental bi- and trilateral horse-trading with the Chancellor and the Prime Minister.[129] In the face of deflationary policies Jennie Lee campaigned for the fourth television channel to be devoted to the OU, despite the estimated cost of £17 million (Lee) or £40 million (the Treasury's Chief Secretary).[130] The idea was defeated in Cabinet and she had to amend her 1966 White Paper.[131] In these manoeuvres Wilson's personal solicitor, who was also the chair of the Arts Council, Lord Goodman, 'assisted Jennie Lee' to create the OU.[132] Indeed, she had 'no more ardent, more able and active supporter' than him.[133] His financial estimates were low and he spread confidence and optimism about financial support.[134] In 1966, when costs were estimated 'at something under £4 million', he suggested that £2 million might be 'obtained from the Ford and Benton Foundations'.[135] The next day Benton wrote to Wilson about the same meeting and put the emphasis on a different matter: 'I told Lord Goodman that the Britannica would be prepared to explore the question of cooperation in the development of courses.'[136]

The White Paper outlined plans for 'the general improvement of educational, cultural and professional standards' and indicated that:

> There can be no question of offering to students a makeshift project inferior in quality to other universities ... Its aim will be to provide, in addition to radio and television lectures, correspondence courses of a quality unsurpassed anywhere in the world. These will be reinforced by residential courses and tutorials.

The 1966 Election Manifesto had a section entitled 'Higher Education', which promised that there would be the expansion of 'higher education provision in the universities, the colleges of education, and the leading technical colleges' and a section entitled 'The OU' which promised to 'establish the University of the Air'.[137]

Some individual officials assisted the project. In 1963 the UGC established the Brynmor Jones Committee to consider audio-visual aids in higher scientific education. Norman MacKenzie claimed that the OU owed much to the DES officials who drafted the Brynmor Jones report of 1965.[138] He added, 'there would not have been an Open University without Ralph Toomey, you can say that quite positively. He believed in it, he fought for it, he acted quite outside the bounds of his Civil Service brief.'[139] Asa Briggs wrote of DES official Ralph Toomey that his 'backstairs role was in its own way as important as that of Wilson'.[140] There was, however, little concerted support for the OU. Jennie Lee stressed that 'The civil servants hated it – all very irregular. But it was the only way you could get a new job done.' She felt that 'the press was against us, the Cabinet was indifferent or hostile, the opposition totally hostile ... [and the civil servants were] snobs'. [141] Others echoed this, describing how she drove through the project in the face of what Brian McArthur called departmental 'scepticism' and Patricia Hollis referred to as 'carping, criticism, disbelief and downright obstruction'.[142] Asa Briggs said of the DES, 'the civil servants there were awful ... almost intolerable and patronising'. He recalled that the CVCP was sceptical and that once the university had come into existence, the new Vice-Chancellor was only permitted to join it after a 'very hard' battle.[143]

Labour's majority increased at the 1966 election and Jennie Lee was reappointed to oversee the new university. She commissioned new work on the cost of the venture. Following consultation with Hugh Greene, Director General of the BBC, Arnold Goodman put this at £3.5 million annually. In 1967 Lee and Goodman attempted to raise investment in the US, and William Benton was approached. On the recommendation of the Advisory Committee, a Planning Committee, chaired by Sir Peter Venables, began to 'work out a comprehensive plan for an Open University, as outlined in the White Paper [A university of the Air]'. The committee sought to provide opportunities for 'all those who ... have been or are being precluded from achieving their aims through an existing institution of higher education'.[144] Asa Briggs, who served on the Planning Committee, recalled that it brought together a variety of expertise:

> I was very keen that there should be some kind of gateway element, an introductory element into the courses ... there should be some inter-disciplinary element and that there should be no great gap in the university between one set of courses and another. That there should be very considerable freedom to move from one course to another... that people should take as long as they liked to get their degrees. And I found all this extremely exciting ... not a great deal of resistance on the Committee, but an immense amount of scepticism outside.[145]

In line with the original Advisory Committee's notion of independence, it rejected partnerships with the College of Preceptors (regarding teachers), with correspondence colleges and with the National Extension College (which offered to act as the correspondence arm of the OU comparable in status to the BBC). To ensure greater autonomy, it was decided to create a new publishing department rather than use the BBC's. Planning, production, presentation and the regional structure were to be controlled by the university.[146] Charles Weymeyer attributed the creation of the OU to

> The vision of Harold Wilson, the steely determination and leadership of Jennie Lee, the extraordinary work of Sir Peter Venables and his committee, the commitment of the Labour Party and the support of the Government, and the absence of strong and sustained political opposition during the critical period of formation.[147]

Ian Donnachie recalled concerns about the OU's association with Labour:

> there was just this air of uncertainty about it all. There was an enormous ideological commitment on the part of the people that had come on board ... This seemed to be something really new and innovative and interesting, and, I think everyone was affected by that. Also affected by the uncertainty of it all ... people had a realisation that maybe the Tories would shut it down.[148]

There was concern that decisions about funding the venture were made on party political grounds.[149] However, support was broadened by the prevailing enthusiasm for technology as both a subject of and a mechanism for learning, and a general feeling that higher education could drive social and economic improvement. This wider rationale was sufficiently flexible to enable the Conservatives to adapt themselves to the project once it had been launched in 1969. Following their victory in the 1970 election the new Secretary of State for Education and Science, Margaret Thatcher, required the OU to examine 'the contribution it can make to the development of higher education provision in the future'. She recognised that the OU was likely to aid the occupationally mobile and to be relatively inexpensive. It was showing signs of being able to work at unprecedented scale, and was, and would remain for more than a quarter of a century, the only public university in the UK to charge fees. She cut the OU's budget and sought to place it in direct competition with other UK universities by encouraging younger students to study with it.[150] The OU was born at the moment when the post-war consensus on the state as a moral agent, taking responsibility for the welfare of its citizens, was beginning to be challenged by the emergence of neo-liberalism and a new popular compact between the individual and the market. Driven into existence by the most passionate Labour politician of her generation, the university began its working life under the direction of the most determined of the new breed of Tory iconoclasts.

The economic and social components

When educationalist Brian Simon referred to a post-war 'change of consciousness among the British people' in regard to education, he was one of several who noted the strength of the political consensus about the need to improve educational opportunities and to increase spending on higher education.[151] In 1946 the Barlow Report on 'Scientific Manpower' noted that many intelligent people did not attend universities and that if the number of universities was doubled the number of science graduates could be doubled. This was a theme adopted in a further report on scientific manpower made to the Minister for Science by a committee chaired by Solly Zuckerman in 1959.[152]

In 1963 the Robbins Report concluded that higher education should be available to all those who were qualified by ability and attainment to pursue it and who wished so to do. There should be more university places and more instruction by television.[153] It was a popular message. The only official reports to have sold more copies than Robbins are Beveridge on social insurance and Denning on Christine Keeler.[154] The benefits of universities were said to include 'improvements in health through the diminution of crime rates to better parenting skills, enhanced awareness of citizenship and increased social cohesion ... education could be seen as transformative of the individual self'.[155]

Between the end of the war and the oil crisis of the 1970s expenditure on education soared.[156] Moreover, as the OU's founding Professor of History noted, during the 1960s 'the arena of most conspicuous boom was that of education, higher education in particular'.[157] The first new post-war university, the University College of North Staffordshire, later Keele University, was founded in 1949 and had a long and careful gestation. It grew slowly, overseen by Oxford, Birmingham and Manchester universities for the first twelve years of its life. By contrast the seven new campus universities ushered in by Robbins received the right to grant their own degrees immediately.[158] Established universities expanded at the same time, with Durham opening a new college in 1959 and Southampton making nearly 200 new appointments between 1963 and 1965.[159] Information about universities became more available not only to those involved in higher education, but to the general public, as press and television coverage of them grew. Social surveys of British and American parents and students revealed 'a keen awareness of the vocational opportunities opened up by additional education'.[160] Higher education became the topic of the moment. In 1963 the *Daily Express* and the *Daily Mail* appointed university correspondents, leaving education correspondents to deal with schools, and Granada made a film about Lancaster University, which also commissioned its own film.[161] Asa Briggs, who was involved in the creation of both Sussex and the OU, saw the 1960s as one of those 'rare decades when education was a "focalizing issue" that captured the headlines'.[162] A door for innovation had been opened and if the moment was seized, an idea as radical as the OU could be smuggled through. Gerry Fowler observed that, 'if the Open University had not been founded in 1969, it is likely that it would never have been founded at all'.[163]

The enlargement of the sector was driven in part by the expansion in the number of eighteen-year-olds from 642,000 in 1955 to 963,000 in 1965. This increased the volume of those qualified by conventional routes to enter higher education. At the same time there was growing concern about those denied opportunity by the school system created by the 1944 Butler Education Act, or who had grown up in earlier decades when secondary education to the age of eighteen was still more restricted to the middle and upper classes. Harold Wilson cited academic research which indicated that many of the children of manual workers were 'just as intelligent as those of professional workers' and proposed to offer opportunities to 'those who for one reason or another, have not been able to take advantage of higher education' (Figure 2.3).[164] In 1964 there were more people with A-levels but there were also many schoolchildren who were not selected for grammar schools but who attended elementary schools. It appeared that 'social inequality was being reinforced rather than reduced'.[165] Some of the new universities began to respond to this agenda by modifying their entrance practices. In 1964 admission to York was not 'wholly dependent on GCE results' while Lancaster University accepted its first students 'many of whose A level results did not qualify them for a university on accepted standards'.[166] These precedents bolstered the notion that opportunities to study for degrees should be offered to adults who had not gained formal qualifications.[167] There were parallel developments in technical higher education. Following reports from the 1944 Hankey Committee and the 1945 Percy Committee, Colleges of Technology were created to meet an anticipated need for more scientific training.[168] These colleges helped to spread the idea of vocationally orientated higher education through their sandwich courses (courses containing a work placement element) and close links to industry. They received university status in the 1960s and their continuing acceptance of students with Ordinary National Certificates, who had left school at 15

"Since grandad became a student we've had nothing but demonstrations!"

Figure 2.3 As Stanley Franklin's cartoon – *Daily Mirror*, 29 January 1969 (captioned 'Since grandad became a student we've had nothing but demonstrations') – appeared before the OU was opened he felt it necessary to remind readers (top left corner) that there were to be 'TV university courses for everyone'. The scenario captures the unease about the new university's challenges to conventions. An older working-class man, possibly swayed by the donnish theorising of the mortar-boarded figure on the TV screen, has been moved to make demands of a working housewife. He has become one of the stereotypes of the period, the revolting student.

and subsequently received part-time education, further challenged the dominance of the A-level entry route.[169]

Developments elsewhere in the world informed the debate about the future of British higher education. Wilson argued that 'we cannot as a nation afford to cut off three quarters or more of our children from virtually any chance of higher education. The Russians do not, the Germans do not, the Americans do not and the Japanese do not and we cannot afford to either.'[170] William Benton's work in the USA was a formative influence on Wilson's thinking. American correspondence education had grown symbiotically alongside conventional educational facilities.[171] In other countries, what became known as 'distance universities' were developing from the correspondence education structures established in the large, sparsely populated parts of the USA, Canada and Australia in the nineteenth century. A number of universities offered distance education courses. Armed services used this delivery method during the First

World War and Canada used it for citizen education.[172] It enjoyed popularity among veterans after the Second World War. The emphasis was on individual success rather than learning communities.[173] In addition, Peter Scott's view of universities in general can be applied to distance universities: that is, that they 'are national institutions that retain the early modern mission of service to the state'.[174] In South Africa from 1946 UNISA, the University of South Africa, Division of External Studies, promoted the Afrikaner identity through inequitable racial quotas, Afrikaner-domination of the teaching staff, segregated graduation ceremonies and residential schools, and a racist curriculum.[175] An open university was started in Finland in 1970, and in 1972 a national distance university was established in Franco's Spain. It promoted a Castilian curriculum and provided no concessions to the Basque and Catalan languages or regional autonomy.[176] In 1973 and 1974 distance universities were created in Germany, Israel, Pakistan and Canada. An American study concluded that East Germany's distance teaching materials were 'overtly political, notably *The Management of Socialist Economy* series'.[177] In 1976, after the conclusion of the Cultural Revolution in China, when the campuses were in ruins, television was used to broadcast to students.[178] Governments have long used higher education 'to attempt a rapid change in the social structure of society, to increase the growth of industrial technological proficiency and to control scholarship for propagandistic purposes'.[179] Moreover, the OU was a partner of the BBC, which promoted national unity, 'played a crucial role in conceiving and cementing notions of "Britishness"' and 'presumed a "national community" whose general interests the BBC had a duty to serve'.[180]

In the UK particular interest was shown in Russian distance education, which had begun in the 1870s. By the 1950s the USSR had 'the first well-structured and organised model of nationwide distance learning'.[181] Correspondence study in the USSR may have widened educational opportunities and enabled people to combine study with productive work.[182] Lectures were broadcast on the central TV station from Moscow, and by 1965 half of all students in higher education were part-time and at a distance. In 1957, when the USSR demonstrated its technological superiority by launching Sputnik 1, a UNESCO report indicated that the UK had far less university provision per head than most European countries.[183] Both Michael Young and Harold Wilson were impressed by the apparent success of the Soviet model of correspondence courses and radio broadcasts followed by a year on a campus. Wilson was particularly struck by the discovery that that 60 per cent of Soviet engineers obtained their degrees in part from distance teaching.[184] When Robert Williams, Chair of the Electronics and Communications Section of the Institution of Electrical Engineers, called for a 'televarsity, a university using television to provide educational opportunities for everyone', he mentioned the USSR.[185] The Russian system also impressed William Benton, who wrote 'I am greatly interested in the Soviet plans for the use of television in the field of higher education'.[186]

The difficulty for Western observers was separating the mechanism from the function. A study in 1963 concluded that 'the Soviet ideology of higher education aims at maintaining a doctrinal uniformity within the educated class [and the] propagation of the Marxist-Leninist ideology'.[187] In 1964 *Soviet Education* announced that in regard to correspondence education, 'the really important thing is not economic considerations' but the fact that 'this policy is in complete accord with the tasks of the present phase of the comprehensive building of communism'.[188] Writing about 'television for instructional purposes' as employed in the USSR, Stuart Hood suggested in 1967 that it was didactic and that 'in Russia there is little alternative to the heavy-handed instructive documentaries that occupy much of the screen time there'.[189] Reflecting many years later, Alan Tait noted that this system of distance teaching supported the creation of a cadre of communist functionaries.[190]

While its name suggests that the OU was heir to a long tradition of universities, it was not only a reinterpretation, in terms of a notion of social justice and overtly industrial and business needs, of the metaphysical themes associated with universities in the past. It was also a product of other influences. These included party political and more generic ambition. The OU was both evidence of Labour's plans and also a project of the British state, upholding and promoting a notion of a national culture at home and internationally. Numerous post-war reports, commissioned to address a range of concerns, had concluded that widening access to higher education would be socially and economically advantageous, beneficial at both private and public levels. Such conclusions were popular with baby boomers and many of their parents. Moreover, other countries had modelled successful delivery methods for distance education and demonstrated its potential for facilitating change. Jennie Lee and Harold Wilson stressed the need to break away from night school and 'learning in uncomfortable circumstances', and the OU conformed to some of the conventions of the university.[191] Nevertheless, it had roots and connections in a wide number of institutions and ideas.

The pedagogic components

The OU's pedagogy was built on shaky foundations. The poor reputation of many of the teaching methods associated with adult and distance learning posed an obstacle to winning over early critics of the proposed university. As Michael Young argued, by the early 1960s education by correspondence 'had got itself a bad name. The profit motive had often worked against good standards.'[192] In 1960 Børje Holmberg claimed that many distance-education courses were little more than school books with self-checking exercises and recurring tasks for submission.[193] The poor image of distance education encouraged proponents of the OU to stress that it was a university of the air. Critics, however, pounced on the name. *The Times* noted that

> The very term is an illusion in the sense that it holds out hopes that it cannot possibly fulfil ... to encourage hopes that the television viewer will be offered the range and depth of courses open to the university student. This would be misleading nonsense.[194]

This view did not take into account the full range of materials that the OU would in fact provide: the posted texts, home experimentation kits, face-to-face learning at residential school and tutorials, and counselling in local study centres. Despite the popularity and glamour associated with television, the name was changed from the 'University of the Air' to 'The Open University'.[195] This name change might better reflect the full range of materials and teaching methods provided as well as the key dimension of open access, but television remained an important part of the OU's offering. By the end of the 1960s almost 95 per cent of the population had access to television. It was seen as a better bridge between the academy and popular audiences than correspondence study. Through the visual medium students and a mass public could gain a sense that they had met and engaged with academic staff.

Out of the air

The term 'University of the Air' was used by Harold Wilson on 8 September 1963 when he announced 'a dynamic programme providing facilities for home study to university and higher technical standards, on the basis of a University of the Air'. He used the term again in an address to the Labour Party Conference on 1 October 1963. On 25 February 1966 the Labour government published a White Paper, *A University of the Air*.

These were not the first times the phrase or similar ones had been employed. George Catlin used the term in 1960 and Michael Young and also Brian Jackson in 1962.[196] Anglia TV broadcast a series called *College of the Air* in 1963. There were also precedents overseas. Asa Briggs noted that 'I found out that the phrase "University of the Air" was used in the University of Southern California before anybody thought of using it in any British university'.[197] There was a TV College, which was opened in

Chicago in 1956.[198] Through this students could attain degrees using television, study guides and correspondence elements. Commencing in 1954, Stanford University aired broadcasts to Latin America under the banner of The International University of the Air. A few years later the Canadian Broadcasting Corporation (CBC) broadcast a radio series called *University of the Air*, which consisted of recorded lectures. The CBC used the name *University of the Air* for a television series aired between 1966 and 1983.[199] In Australia a School of the Air opened in Alice Springs in 1951. In 1946 in the UK the Air Service Training was reopened as the University of the Air.[200] In 1939 thousands listened to America's *Town Meeting of the Air*.[201] In 1938 Disney sponsored the *Mickey Mouse Theater of the Air* radio series and the Mercury Theatre on the Air started to broadcast live radio dramas. An *Inter-American University of the Air* was broadcast by the National Broadcasting Company between 1935 and 1956, and this was linked to the University of Chicago's home study courses, a project of which William Benton was proud (Figure 2.4).[202]

The *Wisconsin College of the Air* broadcast from 1933, the *Wisconsin School of the Air* from 1931 and the *Ohio School of the Air* from 1929.[203] The annual Institute for Education by Radio yearbook, first produced in 1931, was entitled *Education on the Air*. The *Radio Times* referred to programmes for the WEA as 'University of the Air' in 1927.[204] In 1924 'A broadcasting university' was the front-page headline of the *Radio Times*.[205] Perhaps the earliest use of the term occurred in May 1922, when an American radio magazine concluded that a 'people's university of the Air will have a greater student body than all our universities put together'.[206]

Figure 2.4 Wilson adapted the idea of a 'University of the Air' having visited Chicago. William Benton was vice-president of the University of Chicago, 1937 to 1945.

The promise of television contrasted with another form of part-time adult study which, in the UK, was also associated with industrialisation: night school. The first of these opened for adult mechanics in Salford in 1772 and similar institutions soon followed. Technical education for adults developed as did sandwich courses at universities.[207] From the 1870s some universities offered courses to non-enrolled students, and a London Society for the Extension of University teaching was established.[208] The extension system also introduced credit transfer.[209] The WEA, founded in 1903, was connected to the extension movement. It won state aid for tutorials, which the extension movement had not, and demonstrated that adults were capable of learning part-time and often alone. The WEA promoted state provision in the name of social justice and became informally linked to the Labour Party.[210]

The University of London had a well-established system of assessment for students not resident in London. The syllabus was widely available and students could sit its exams in many countries.[211] While Jennie Lee recognised the value of this model she decided not to adopt it.[212] The university did not provide tuition for its distance learners, many of whom gained support from private colleges or by attending colleges which taught its materials and subsequently became the universities of Reading, Nottingham, Exeter, Southampton, Leicester and Hull.[213]

Forms of electronic communication had been applied to education from almost the moment of their invention, particularly in countries whose populations were thinly distributed over large distances. There were examples of radio being used for universities and school in Australia in the early twentieth century.[214] In the USA radio telegraph and radio telephone experimentation took place in at least a dozen colleges and universities before the First World War. The University of Iowa used television in 1932, and there were thirty-five educational stations on the air in the USA in 1941.[215] By 1948 at least five universities were using television for educational purposes.[216] Henry Ford was educated through home studies, and in 1956 the Ford Foundation financed Chicago's college of the air, which integrated TV lectures and written work, telephone tutorials and face-to-face teaching. It focused on students with fewer resources. The Foundation also financed other programming including the Midwest Airborne experiment, which broadcast from an aeroplane to schools in six Midwest states. Others offered college credits for work done via television, and by 1961 there were over 50 channels reserved for education and perhaps 80 educational television stations. High school physics teachers could learn about recent developments in their field through dedicated television broadcasts.[217] The stations were licensed, were not permitted to carry advertising and typically featured low-budget programming presented by educational bodies. Peter Laslett visited the USA and concluded that 'television with other visual aids, is helping to transform American education' and that it 'may yet out-date the printed word as a teaching instrument for many purposes'.[218]

In Alberta, Canada, radio programmes commenced in 1923. The University of Alberta started broadcasts of lectures in 1925 and soon, supported by a government grant, a radio station was built on campus.[219] The National Farm Radio Forums (slogan 'Read–Listen–Discuss–Act') started in 1938. Farmers met to listen to broadcasts and assess problems together. Printed study material was available, and their discussion conclusions could be noted and submitted to a provincial office. The idea spread to other countries.[220] In France 'teleclubs' were created in 1951, and these too spread.[221] Elihu Katz and Paul Felix Lazarsfeld developed a theory which supported this teaching. They proposed that mass-media information was channelled by opinion leaders who were similar to those they influenced and were able to explain and diffuse the content.[222] These media were also used for educational purposes in East and West Germany and in Mexico.[223]

James Donald argues that it makes 'sense to examine education and broadcasting as overlapping cultural apparatus or technologies' because both structure people's everyday lives, particularly in the case of the OU.[224] The BBC commenced educational radio broadcasts, with associated printed materials, in 1924.[225] By 1930 there were over five million listeners to mid-evening talks and 1,000 BBC listener groups in existence.[226] The number of groups grew to about 50,000 during the war, when educational programmes were seen as beneficial to morale and national unity. Listener groups were also established in the USA, Germany and the USSR. Training films and courses prepared people for the armed forces and industry, and closed-circuit television was used for educational purposes in civil defence and military training and in hospitals as well as in the education of mechanical engineers.[227] A Forces Education Unit was run between 1945 and 1952.[228] The Beveridge Committee on Broadcasting, 1949–51, charged with considering all aspects of broadcasting in Britain, concluded that 'further research and experiment will be needed to work out the most effective methods' of supporting adult education and that 'the use of broadcasting for adult educational purposes should be developed to the fullest practicable extent'.[229] In 1951, following the suggestion of a farmer, the BBC took its educational strategy in a different direction and started to broadcast an educational radio soap, *The Archers*.[230] The BBC World Service and the World Service Trust – its charitable arm, which specialised in development projects – employed the format elsewhere, and other countries also used soap operas for such purposes.

There were many radio discussion programmes, including *The Fifty-One Society*, broadcast between 1951 and 1962. These programmes helped to forge links between academics and the BBC and to harness the power of broadcasting to the values of liberal education. Many of the contributors were adult education tutors, and the style and content of the programmes had about them 'something of the early university class tutorial movement'. Discussions were designed to educate and speakers included a number of people who later came to be associated with the OU, including Harold Wilson, Raymond Williams and Asa Briggs.[231] The Midlands Region of the BBC broadcast six weeks of programmes based on the GCE O-level syllabus and a year later a national course, *After School English*.[232] Brian Groombridge suggested that

> broadcasting has been a major force, probably the major adult educational force in contemporary British society, both through much of the general output and through the range and quality of its specialised provision in radio and television.[233]

Commercial television companies provided further examples of the use of television for education. The BBC lost its monopoly as a television broadcaster in 1955, and two years later Associated-Rediffusion transmitted its first television programmes for schools. In 1962 the Pilkington Committee on Broadcasting criticised the existing commercial television licensees for purchasing American westerns and crime series, and concluded that the output of ITV fell 'well short' of good public broadcasting.[234] Wilson told Benton that one outcome of the Pilkington Report would 'be tremendous opportunities for Encyclopaedia Britannia'.[235] Perhaps in order to sway decision-makers regarding the allocation of the third channel, shortly afterwards ATV started to broadcast weekly lessons in English, French and public administration. The 1963 Television Act allowed the BBC to run the third channel and BBC2, which broadcast from 1964, became the first home of the OU. In 1963 ITV was broadcasting more adult education than the BBC, providing some associated written material and residential courses.[236] Associated Television and the University of Nottingham produced a thirteen-week course, which 1,250 people completed. It included programmes, written notes, two tutorials and a residential weekend attended by 200 people.[237] Harold Wiltshire of the University of Nottingham's Department of Adult Education wanted to develop the scheme. He proposed a National Teleteaching Institute with its own permanent staff of authors, tutors, producers and administrators, and with broadcasts by both the ITA and the BBC. The courses he proposed included some which were ancillary to the WEA and others which would lead to degrees. A Universities Council for Adult Education pamphlet published in 1965 also suggested a permanent institution. This would offer a range of qualifications up to degree level but not make its own awards.[238] Its organiser, Peter Laslett, concluded that 'the introduction of university television on a large scale might transform the teaching potential and the teaching practice of all our institutions'.[239] Michael Young suggested that 'if TV and radio courses were arranged to tie in with their written work and reading correspondence college students would be a great deal better off than they are now'.[240]

The experience of collaboration between teaching staff and broadcasters aided the educational use of television. The existence of career paths within educational television paved the way for collaboration between the education and broadcasting sectors. One of the members of the Ministerial Planning Committee of the OU who sat on its Council from 1969 until 1978 was the first Controller of Educational Broadcasting at the BBC, John Scupham. He started with the Schools' Broadcasting Council in 1946. Richmond Postgate and Donald Grattan from the BBC played considerable roles within the OU; the CCTV systems at Leeds and Glasgow universities were created by former BBC producers.[241] The first head of the BBC OU Production Centre, and an advocate for an open university from 1963, Peter Montagnon,

> used what amounted to a small course team in *Parliamo Italiano* in 1963 and anticipating the Open University he had associated television programmes with other teaching and learning materials.[242]

Sussex deployed closed-circuit television for classroom observation in teacher training, to record and play back lectures and to display teaching materials. The university also had audio-visual units, language laboratories and some programmed learning. By 1965, twenty-four universities, thirty-four colleges of advanced technology and technical colleges, nineteen colleges of education, thirteen training colleges and nine secondary schools had closed-circuit television.[243] Hull University built its own television studio. The first session started with a conflict as the studio staff interpreted the purpose as teaching television techniques and set up the equipment accordingly, while the academics felt that the intention was to enable students to see how they taught. There were further debates about the form that the pedagogy took once television was used.[244] The Gulbenkian Foundation funded a working party, chaired by Peter Laslett, to draw up plans for an inter-university network. The Advisory Centre for Education (ACE) ran a TV week in June 1965, and the University of East Anglia appointed a Director of Television and a former head of outside broadcasts at Harlech TV to direct its Audio Visual Centre. The University Grants Committee funded the equipment at UEA but declined to finance links to other institutions.[245] The outcome of these trials was growing confidence that integrated university courses could be offered which employed a variety of media and that, in Brian Jackson's words, 'the unwalled University of the Air lies within sight'.[246]

During the early 1960s there was a growth of expertise within Whitehall. In 1962 a new Research and Intelligence Section was created at the Ministry of Education. One of its tasks was to co-ordinate policy on educational broadcasting, including television. In January 1964 an interdepartmental committee was established to report on the technical, financial and organisational implications of educational broadcasting. Although it was dissolved by Parliament, interest in this subject continued and in 1965 a Ministerial Committee on Broadcasting was created.[247] The variety and number of precursors to the use of television for education meant that Harold Wilson could be assured that plans for a University of the Air were realistic: educationalists, the BBC and commercial television companies had all considered the issues, experimented, examined examples from around the world and concluded that using television as part of a multi-media teaching package was feasible.

A May 1963 report by *Which?*, the magazine of another Michael Young initiative of the time, the Consumer's Association, found correspondence courses standards to be 'deplorably low' and 'uninspiring'. It also found that 'material was often drearily presented, sometimes cramped and badly duplicated' and that 'people in ordinary education are on the whole contemptuous of the correspondence method'.[248] While it is possible to trace this mode of learning back to the Chinese imperial examinations of the Sui Dynasty (519–618 CE) and while there are examples of correspondence courses being offered in 1728 in Boston, USA and in 1733 in Lund, Sweden, in Britain the technique was associated with nineteenth-century industrialisation.[249] The need for a better-educated workforce was combined with the spread of literacy, the mass production of books and pens, and the creation of a cheap, reliable postal service and an efficient transportation system. For the post-1945 generations, initially it seemed neither a cost-effective nor a modern method of instruction.

However, the OU sought to revive correspondence, initially by a new method of instruction called programmed learning. For many years it had been recognised that animals could be taught through a system of rewards for tasks completed. During the 1950s machines were developed which enabled human learners to proceed at their own pace and, through rational responses to questions, to acquire new material only once they had mastered the previous steps.

They too could be guided to a reward. Psychologist Burrhus Frederic Skinner wrote about 'teaching machines' in 1954 and subsequently, and said that he was consulted about the OU before it was opened and that he was enthusiastic about its methods (Figure 2.5).[250] Skinner became associated with the view of knowledge as a permanent and cumulative commodity which could be mass

Figure 2.5 During the 1980s B. F. Skinner visited the OU (seen here with Professor of Biological Psychology, Frederick Toates, left). Skinner said that he had been consulted during the early stages of the OU and approved of the mission and outcomes of the OU. In 2009 Professor Toates' book *Burrhus F. Skinner* was published.

produced and was best placed within individual minds by a limited number of teachers. This gained popularity in the 1960s and attracted attention in Britain. In 1963 Michael Young envisaged 'teaching machines and programmed text-books' at the National Extension College.[251] Aided by the support of a government committee on university teaching methods, the notions reached teacher training and many universities.[252] In 1964 a Central Training Council was created to promote programmed instruction in industrial training, and the West Riding Education Authority set up its own Programmed Learning Unit. In 1965 Hooe Primary School trained its teachers in the methods.[253] In 1966 an Association of Programmed Learning was formed, and a survey suggested that the idea of programmed learning was accepted within industry.[254] That year the Labour Party manifesto argued that:

> We must also make the most effective use of teachers, by encouraging the use of audio-visual aids and programmed learning; and by providing the teacher with the ancillary help which he [sic] increasingly needs.[255]

The Department of Education and Science also expressed interest in 'teaching machines' and programmed learning.[256] Universities engaged with the idea.[257] By 1968 programmed learning was being used in at least twenty-nine universities in the UK. Electronic systems were developed such as the Edison Responsive Environment, known as the 'talking typewriter', and audio-visual material was also used. One training journal reported that 'it is already technically possible to plug little Johnny into a computer which will teach, mentor and prescribe remedial work, possibly with the help of a satellite'.[258]

When, in 1969, the Planning Committee of the OU was faced with the problem of creating a structure which would enable multi-disciplinary, multi-media courses to be produced and distributed, it looked to democratic, industrial processes which could be mimicked.[259] The interest in programmed learning informed educational technologists at the OU.[260] Many of them were 'people coming out of programmed learning and people who'd been in the armed forces doing education'.[261] Walter Perry also suggested a mechanistic argument for television programmes when he noted that they 'function as a pacing mechanism. In science they are vital for demonstrations.'[262]

The development of structures for teaching which echoed the production systems around it was noted in a report on the OU's teaching of systems:

> The OUs teaching materials were more structured, logical, and comprehensible than any others before them as they were designed for students to use at home with little tutorial support.[263]

In 1974 only three British universities offered systems-based courses and degrees, and these were focused on postgraduate education and research and, in two cases, on hard systems. At the OU under John Beishon, the Founding Professor of the OU Systems Group, the emphasis was on the undergraduate teaching of systems and on combining both hard and softer approaches to create clear, accessible methodologies and approaches. Bob Bell from the OU's School of Education suggested that some course team members acknowledged that what they were providing was 'perhaps not programmed learning in the full Skinnerian sense but certainly a learning progression highly organised from the centre', while Tony Bates recalled that 'the first UK Open University courses were based on instructional systems design'.[264] A programmed approach also operated at the level at which the teaching was understood. Barry Smith – who left school aged 15 and a decade later, in 1971, was a shift worker and studying with the OU – was an enthusiast:

> What I really like about the Open University is that it really is programmed learning. If I am going to try and pick my own way through, it's better to have someone say 'Here is what you learn and this is the way to learn it'. You can absorb more by them telling you what to learn than by simply trying to work it out for yourself in a vacuum.[265]

At the same time that programmed learning was spreading, criticisms of it and of computer-marked tests also spread. It was felt that this approach was mechanistic and rigid and gave the student no chance to question the 'teacher' or to ask for elucidation. Studies of the Royal Navy and others carried out in schools indicated that 'programmed learning is more effective when combined with teacher instruction'.[266] In 1971 Michael Young argued that:

> students themselves should be in the dialogue, helping build their own courses – pressing on the university and never switching the TV knobs in passive isolation. No university, anywhere, anytime, has had such fertile and varied experience latent in its student body as the Open University.[267]

Others expressed similar concerns. During a period when more flexible regulatory regimes were becoming familiar within industry, cognitive approaches (rather than the behaviourist analysis associated with programmed learning) were becoming more popular within psychology. Many within the OU took the view that students were not passive recipients of centrally produced knowledge. They were encouraged to gather data, assess theories and engage in collaborative research. In order for them to perform experiments and

Figure 2.6 Television, sometimes presented as a passive medium, was used to encourage students to engage with debates.

assess primary sources, the OU provided home experiment kits and broadcast versions of canonical dramas. David Grugeon's *Handbook on course tutoring*, 1973, emphasised the importance of two-way communication and dialogue between tutors and students.

The OU's pedagogy was adapting and merging ideas derived from the experience of correspondence courses, the BBC and other broadcasters, from technologies developed in association with theories of learning and human behaviour and by learning from those who worked and studied within adult education. The delivery methods were outlined in the 1966 White Paper, which listed television, radio, correspondence, programmed instruction, tutorials, practicals, the residential element and the use of study centres (Figure 2.6).[268] Once it was opened, the OU quickly cultivated its own ways of supporting learners. However, in order to reach that point, it relied upon the enthusiasm and confidence of experienced practitioners from a number of fields in order to convince the sceptics that a university of the air was a viable concept and not merely a castle in the air.

Opening the OU

Albert Mansbridge, the WEA's founder, argued that 'the real University is mystical and invisible; it is to be found wherever scholars cooperate for the extension of the bounds of knowledge. It is not in one place, or in selected places. It is intangible, undiscernible, but none the less real.'[269] On 23 July 1969, two days after a human walked on the moon, the OU Charter was awarded and the Congregation of The Open University held its first meeting. Geoffrey Crowther, the Foundation Chancellor, opened the OU with words which echoed those of Mansbridge, but reflected other sources as well:

This University has no cloisters – a word meaning closed. Hardly even shall we have a campus. By a very happy chance, our only local habitation will be in the new city that is to bear two of the widest ranging names in the history of English thought, Milton Keynes. But this is only where the tip of our toe touches ground; the rest of the University will be disembodied and airborne. From the start it will flow all over the United Kingdom.

But it is already clear that the University will rapidly become one of the most potent and persuasive, and profitable, of our invisible exports. Wherever the English language is spoken or understood, or used as a medium of study, and wherever there are men and women seeking to develop their individual potentialities beyond the limits of the local provision (and I have defined a large part of the world), there we can offer our help. This may well prove to be the most potent form of external aid that this country can offer in the years to come. The interest of those all over the world who are wrestling with the problem of making educational bricks without straw has already been aroused, and before long The Open University and its courses, electronically recorded and reproduced, will be for many millions of people their introduction to the riches of the English language and of Britain's heritage of culture.

There are no boundaries of space.[270]

Conclusion

The Open University was the most original innovation in twentieth-century British higher education. Yet it can be argued that it invented almost nothing, as precedents existed for its component elements nationally and internationally, reaching back into the nineteenth century and beyond. Peter Venables' 1969 report on behalf of the OU Planning Committee referred to correspondence schools in Japan, radio in Australia and television in Chicago.[271] In the UK, there were powerful precedents in the development of correspondence, extension and sandwich courses. Other factors which contributed to its foundation included the growing conviction that widespread social and economic benefits would follow from widening participation in higher education. Universities were associated with economic regeneration, increasing productivity and with the promotion of soft power on the cultural and technological fronts of the Cold War. The enlargement of higher education was closely linked to science and technology, which were perceived as a means of increasing productivity and competitiveness.

The ferment of growth in higher and further education in the 1960s created a sense of unbounded possibilities. Established universities expanded, new ones were founded, thirty-two polytechnics were created and funded to enable as many students to be admitted as local authorities wished, and colleges were upgraded. In terms of sheer volume, more people had more opportunities to gain accredited skills than ever before. The availability of funding and the spread of knowledge about universities as more places became available drew attention to those who had missed out. For eighteen-year-olds, the later 1960s were a time of unprecedented opportunity. However, their society included tens of millions of older men and women whose opportunities had been restricted by earlier shortcomings in secondary and tertiary education. If education was to be capable of eliminating social inequalities, aiding social justice and helping to make citizens, then those now excluded by age and the daily responsibilities of earning a living and raising families deserved to be heard.[272] The perception that formal qualifications, professionalism and vocational training were of value raised questions about the skills of those now in work.

All of these developments pointed towards The Open University, but none of them guaranteed its creation. In a sense the sheer vitality of the debates surrounding higher education in the 1960s was the greatest obstacle to the new institution. Wilson's big project faced opposition not just from the upholders of the old elitism but more critically from informed enthusiasts who shared its values and aspirations. Obstruction might be expected from Oxbridge-educated civil servants and from Vice-Chancellors anxious to enhance their own influence and budgets. More damaging was the fire aimed at the evolving concept of the University of the Air by influential and creative figures committed to rival solutions to the challenge Wilson had identified. Proponents of adult-education networks, extra-mural departments, educational broadcasting, polytechnics and colleges of advanced technology fought for their own ventures and resisted an alternative which appeared to cut across the pathways to which they were committed and the funding which they needed. In 1967, with nothing yet settled, Jennie Lee protested to her senior civil servant, Ralph Toomey, 'that little bastard that I have hugged to my bosom and cherished, that all the others have tried to kill off, will thrive'.[273] Not merely to conceive, but actually to make happen a university which sought to match the standards of the best in the sector but had no admission requirements, which attempted to employ print, correspondence and television in a way which transcended the potential of each, which made a reality of reaching every kind of learner in every corner of the United Kingdom, required a vast act of faith and a bloody-minded determination. How it thrived will be the subject of the following chapters.

Part II

The first two decades

3

Growth and acceptance, 1969–89

The Open University embraced a dual commitment. Two founding Deans argued in 1971 that 'higher education is the democratic right of anyone who can profit by it and it is in the nation's interests to make maximum use of human resources'.[1] The rationale of individual rights on the one hand and benefits to wider society on the other informed the development of the institution during its first two decades. The university took shape during a period when higher education across the UK and around the world was characterised by a new focus on efficiency and on access for a wider range of people.

The first section of this chapter outlines the development of the OU's structures. As a university created by central government and directly accountable to the Department of Education and Science during its formative period, it drew upon models of authority familiar to Whitehall. But as an institution founded on an idealistic vision it also aspired to become a community of collaborative scholars. The tension between hierarchy and collegiality can be understood within the broader social and political aspirations that accompanied the OU's early history. The OU was a product of the 'great reappraisal' of the 1960s when governments – first the Conservatives, then Labour – sought to create a 'developmental state' as a means of revitalising the economy.[2] Modernisation, the central issue in the 1964 general election, was promoted as a response to Britain's perceived decline, the 'staple assumption of every subsequent election over the next three decades'.[3] This era was characterised by concerns about the effect of economic decline on the nation. At the same time there was a renewed interest in extending the welfare state following the publication of an influential work on poverty.[4]

The second section examines how the OU became part of the UK's educational landscape and influenced developments overseas. From the outset the footprint of the university reached far beyond its new base in Milton Keynes. Successive governments supported the dissemination of its teaching materials through the expanding medium of television and more conventional print

" DO YOU MIND? WE'RE STUDYING INTER·PERSONAL RELATIONSHIPS ON OPEN UNIVERSITY "

Figure 3.1 Dean of Arts John Ferguson complained that 'It is a common delusion about the Open University that we "give lectures on TV." We do not "give lectures" at all.' Nevertheless, cartoonists continued to present another image. Keith Waite's 'Do you mind? We're studying inter-personal relationships on Open University' (*Daily Mirror*, 3 November 1975) connected the OU to sex, television and, through the screen image of the bearded lecturer with a pointer and a blackboard with a picture of an apple on it, conventional teaching methods.

technologies. The ambition was to stimulate an appetite for learning among the wider public and at the same time challenge conventional teaching methods in the established university sector (Figure 3.1). In this process, the university's curriculum became exposed to public and political scrutiny on a scale unknown in the private worlds of the face-to-face institutions. The consequence was by far the most overt conflict between the state and the content of university teaching that has been seen in modern Britain. Alongside the domestic dramas, the OU almost at once became a major cultural export. It was encouraged by the government and its agencies to play a significant role in the reform and extension of higher education in developing countries around the world.

The third section assesses the OU's exposure to the growing crisis in public finances. The institution's rapid expansion meant that not only its curriculum but also its costs attracted increasing political concern. Despite its broader national and international role the OU's programme remained heavily dependent on government funding, and thus it was vulnerable to the currents of change from the early 1980s when, to reduce public expenditure, university funding was cut and efforts were made to increase the contribution of higher education to the national economy. There was a merger of liberal and vocational forms of education and a separation for many within the expanding HE sector of research from teaching.[5] In this context, the OU's close engagement with the dynamics of political, social and economic change was both its weakness and its strength. It was able to mobilise a broad public constituency to ward off the more serious threats to its budget. And within higher education these sector-wide shifts in some ways served to reduce the distance between the OU and other higher education institutions. The university had long been attuned to short-term financial considerations, to teaching staff who were not paid to research and to the provision of vocational subjects. Moreover, it was accustomed to working with national political priorities, and had developed an ability to engage with governments to transform education systems around the world. These characteristics ensured that it was able to contribute as well as adapt to the new rules of the game.

Learning and teaching the OU way

The OU has always enrolled students with no prior qualification on to undergraduate programmes of study. They have been located all over the country and indeed the world. Most have been in full-time employment. Their learning has long benefited from the use of a mainly asynchronous teaching model. Learning alone, without the benefit of mixing with, and learning from, peers, they have required well-designed teaching materials. These have always had to be effective and easy to access for those unfamiliar with academic work or formal learning. Students have had to be fairly assessed across time and space. A student located in Kent studying a module in 2005 should have had access to as much support and have had their work marked in a similar way to another student studying the same module in Dublin in 2010. Nowadays the OU is organised around familiar academic disciplines and faculties. These have changed in number and title over the years. The faculties currently consist of Social Sciences, Arts, Science, Mathematics, Computing and Technology, Health and Social Care, Education and Languages, and Business and Law. Modules (formerly courses) have almost always been designed centrally by module teams (formerly course teams). The members of these have typically been academic staff, media designers, editors and administrative staff. In general, modules have been designed for undergraduate students at any one of three different levels. Students often selected to study courses in an appropriate order, starting with the Foundation or first level. The teaching materials consisted largely of books written by the course teams. There have also been course-specific radio and television programmes, cassettes, CDs and DVDs, and often additional materials collated by the course teams but not written by them. Typically, students receive a pack of materials and instructions through the post, and these materials can also be accessed and downloaded from the web, via desktop, laptop and mobile devices. Some modules are available only online. Students are assigned to a group of other students studying the same course, and this group is tutored by an associate lecturer of The Open University.

As well as studying at home, students on many courses were invited to attend face-to-face tutorials in the area in which they lived or worked. Some had to travel long distances to attend these tutorials. Typically, there were six of these for each 32-week ('full credit') course, each one lasting two hours. Each tutorial was staffed by a tutor. This person was employed on a part-time basis to teach the course materials. Many tutors had full-time lecturing posts at other educational establishments. They also marked the written assignments which students submitted to them by post or electronically. They were instructed that the analysis offered to the students as part of the marking should be detailed and that they should both comment on the material submitted and also teach the student generic skills. Often the six or so written assignments constituted 50 per cent of the overall assessment of the course. There were also examinations which were sat in centres where students gathered to be invigilated. Some courses had a variety of forms of assessment. Allowances were made for the fact that some students did not have access to tutorials or television (Figure 3.2).

Many courses had a residential element. The OU hired parts of a university campus during the summer. Students would be in residence for typically one week. Once there, they would attend lectures and seminars, work in the laboratories or go on field trips. The residential schools were staffed by regional and central staff and often tutors and guest lecturers. In addition, staff were employed in the OU's regional centres to counsel students in regard to their studies.

Figure 3.2a Tutorials sometimes involved students attending study centres to listen to or watch broadcasts which had been recorded for them.

Figure 3.2b

Moreover, many OU materials – first via the television, later online – were available for free and it has provided tools and support to facilitate the use of these openly available items. In 2008 the OU was one of the first UK universities to join iTunesU, which enables users to obtain high-quality content for free. The OU has also developed its own free podcasting site and YouTube channel.

The formal approach to learning and teaching has four key elements: high-quality learning materials; individual academic support to each student; effective administration, logistics and increasingly learning analytics; and teaching rooted in research. This model owes much to the cybernetic models of Pask's work in the 1970s but is also underpinned by a socio-constructivist approach to pedagogy and the conversational model later developed by Laurillard.[6] Although the print and broadcast media were conceptualised as methods of transmitting information, the OU sought to promote active, independent learning. Many printed texts included in-text exercises for self-assessment, and students were advised to watch television broadcasts while sitting forward with a notepad, rather than sitting back watching passively.

In addition to its own checks on quality and consistency, since the 1990s the OU's teaching and research have been subject to the same processes and procedures to ensure quality as every other higher education institution in the UK. It has been in the top three in the national rankings for student satisfaction for teaching since ranking began in 2005.

Structures

The OU's distinctive engagement with the ideals of social democracy and the methods of scientific management can be seen in the structures that framed its managerial and teaching provision. Initiated in Whitehall, the OU was to run as a centralised body with regional offices. However, confidence, in Douglas Jay's dictum, that 'in the case of education, the gentleman in Whitehall really does know better what is good for people than the people know themselves' had faded.[7] Although directly accountable to the Department of Education and Science (DES), the OU did not adopt wholesale the civil service's convention of vertical structures designed to provide clear lines of management and accountability. Rather, it adapted hierarchical structures to the needs of an institution with a mission to promote egalitarianism. An example of the way the OU sought both conformity and difference can be found in its Charter. The first stated objective was to advance and disseminate learning and knowledge. This was similar to statements in the charters of other universities of the 1960s: York's focus was on enabling 'students to obtain the advantages of University education'; Lancaster wanted to use the 'influence of its corporate life'; and the University of Warwick has almost identical wording to these two. However, the OU's Charter contained an additional object, 'to promote the educational well-being of the community generally'.[8] The university was unique in its mission to reach out beyond the conventional campus and its own formally registered learners. The Charter modelled how the OU would unite strangers and support co-operation between learners, and committed the institution to being inclusive, innovative and responsive.

'If your social status is insecure you need a good address' said Jennie Lee.[9] Initially, the OU was based in offices in the 'opulent and palatial' Belgrave Square, London, but before long it had to select a site for its permanent head-quarters. Building in the capital would be costly but the consensus was that proximity to the BBC studios in Alexandra Palace was important. After a search conducted by early OU staff, it was decided that Milton Keynes, a new town not far north of London, provided a compromise between expense and access. The new university was welcomed by the Milton Keynes Development Corporation, and Walton Hall, a site to the south of the town, was selected.[10] The OU was unusual among universities in that it was never intended to be run from only a single location. At the hub were to be the administrators, other support staff and a small number of academics, who would have access to only a limited infrastructure for research beyond that focused on educational methods. The spokes of the university that would deliver the teaching were to be based around the UK, in the form of regional centres (Plate 1). The Planning Committee concluded that 'it will be upon the success of the Regional Directors that the corporate spirit of the University will largely depend'. It appointed a Director of Regional and Tutorial Services, Robert Beevers, in February 1969.

While many of the issues faced by new universities were shared, the OU faced a particular challenge. The University of Warwick, which opened in 1965, was close to Coventry, and the universities of Kent, Essex and East Anglia could draw on Canterbury, Colchester and Norwich for support. One of the OU's differences, maintained Planning Committee member Harold Wiltshire, was its unusual location.[11] Milton Keynes, a town founded in 1967 following the New Town Act of 1965, had been 'pitched like a new baby born into a fast-changing world, into the era of de-industrialisation'.[12] One result was that, as many recalled, there was little local accommodation for staff.[13] There were also few amenities, so the OU opened its facilities to local people.[14] At first the buildings that the OU used were not designed for a university. They included several former RAF huts and a former stud farm. Some OU activities were based in nearby villages and it was only in 1971 that a warehouse was acquired, at Wellingborough (Figure 3.3).

On the Walton Hall site was a large former family home which had been used by Milton Keynes Development Corporation. The university used this building for offices and, following a grant from the Aneurin Bevan Memorial Trust, its cellars were converted into rooms for social and recreational pur-poses, in order to 'establish friendly contacts with members of the general public and other institutions in the area'.[15] The building itself was situated, said Joan Christodoulou, within 'a sea of mud, and mud predominated in the first month and everyone was allocated slippers' (Figure 3.4).[16] She also called

Figure 3.3 Students relied on the mass mailing of teaching materials.

Figure 3.4 Building work churned up the ground and Walton Hall, Milton Keynes, was often surrounded by mud. Staff wore wellington boots outside. Slippers were allocated for indoor use.

it a 'wilderness'.[17] Harold Lowndes remembered that as they were putting in some foundations for the lab buildings 'I dashed over and said, "Can I show you where I'd like an electrical point to come out for lathes and things?"'[18] Christopher Harvie recalled that:

> the campus was so covered in mud that people had to trample around in welly boots. People were issued with slippers when they went into the teaching rooms. Walter Perry greeted us like Trevor Howard in a Second World War movie. He said, 'Some of you chaps might be wondering why you have been brought here.'[19]

Because of its location the OU became associated with the hopes for socially mixed, sustainable, aspirant communities, and a New Towns Study Unit was established at the university.[20] The egalitarian ethos of new towns was echoed in the sense of community between academic and support staff, who were all faced with the same mud and pressing deadlines. In the face of limited facilities and bulldozers there developed a sense of camaraderie and of 'urban pioneering as well as educational pioneering'.[21]

During the construction of its headquarters, many of the OU's administrative functions were geographically dispersed. Initially, the OU used the computing facilities at nearby Cranfield as 'we didn't have a computer at Walton Hall until early in 1971', while the payroll was run from Southampton.[22] However, it was soon felt that the OU needed to adopt its own computer systems to aid the management of assessment and staff–student allocation (Plate 2).[23] In 1971 the examination budget was £130,000 and this had risen to £220,000 by 1973. As an example of the administrative challenge posed by the early volume of students, it took only 10 per cent of a Foundation course cohort to be on an examination borderline for the results of 600 individuals to be reconsidered. Performing such a task manually would be expensive and time-consuming, and computer use at the OU soon increased. In 1973 the Student Computing Service consisted of thirty staff and three Hewlett Packard 2000B time-sharing systems located at Walton Hall, Newcastle and Alexandra Palace, with a further 180 terminals around the UK. This service also offered practical computing activities for the Mathematics Faculty, as from 1971 about 10,000 students were taking courses that involved a computing component (Figure 3.5).

The Planning Committee envisaged a small number of central academic staff and an extensive number of consultants on short-term contracts to create the course materials.[24] At the start of 1969 four staff members were in post. These were the Vice-Chancellor, the Secretary of the University, one administrative assistant and one personal secretary. Other staff members

Figure 3.5 Students received a variety of items through the post. The MSc programme in *Industrial applications of computers* involved substantial home kit components, including the HEKTOR III microcomputer system.

were seconded from the DES. For example, Ralph Toomey acted as the Assessor of the Department on the Planning Committee, while D. V. Stafford was the Committee's secretary. The plan was for four deans (all professors) to head 'lines of study' with three or four specialists (one senior lecturer, two lecturers and maybe an additional professor) working to each dean. In addition, there would be full-time educational technologists and media specialists. Most other academic staff would be contracted for part-time work. There were also plans for developmental testing of all course materials, including home experiment kits and written materials. The production of materials for teaching was 'a process more akin to an industrial process than the normal unstructural, unchecked work of an academic in a conventional university'.[25]

It was soon realised that laboratory and field work required more time than the original scheme had allowed. The OU's relationship with the BBC also needed clarification as it too had its own systems. While at other universities decisions about the curriculum were taken on academic grounds, at the OU such issues had to be weighed with other factors. The Head of the BBC/ Open University Productions at Alexandra Palace argued that resources and structures were a central consideration:

A powerful academic pedigree for a subject should not, by itself, be adequate justification for its presentation as an Open University course, if it does not translate into our system.[26]

The system needed some adjustment when it became clear that briefing academic consultants was more time-consuming than had been anticipated. While it was felt that to produce teaching materials for Foundation courses 'Nobel prize winners are not necessary', the need to hire more central academic staff was conceded.[27]

For a university founded by the Labour Party, the change of government in 1970 posed a threat to its existence before the first student had been recruited. Despite the association with the outgoing administration and the scepticism of some of her colleagues, the new Education Minister, Margaret Thatcher, did not, perhaps surprisingly, seek to close the OU. Rather, it has been argued that 'she did save the Open University'.[28] Although she felt that 'the ethics of the DES was self-righteously socialist' and she had 'no love of universities', her concern was to produce 'low unit costs' – something the OU could promise with its efficient production methods. She sought to amend the OU's entry rules to encourage greater competition, arguing that this 'specialised form of adult education' which was 'given comparatively generous support' should consider, 'as a matter of urgency', admitting qualified school leavers.[29] She requested a full report by May 1971 and told *The Times* that the OU ought to admit students under the age of 21.[30]

While allowing the OU to proceed with a few amendments, Margaret Thatcher also gave her support to a very different venture. During the late 1960s money was raised for Britain's first private university, and by 1973 (the year that saw the first OU graduates) a company was formed. In 1976 Mrs Thatcher unveiled the foundation stone of the University College of Buckingham. In common with the OU it accepted students who had not passed any A-levels and it was given powers to grant degrees. Moreover, the DES allowed local authorities to pay student awards. Unlike the OU there were few students at first (47 enrolled in 1975 and there were still fewer than 250 by 1978), and although it had a computer link to a bookshop in Oxford it focused on a 'system of personal tuition' rather than teaching at a distance.[31] Despite its location a mere fifteen miles from Walton Hall, it had little to do with the OU. One of the earliest decisions of the OU Planning Committee was to reject the idea that OU students could transfer at the end of their foundation year to an accelerated degree at Buckingham.[32]

As the activities undertaken by the OU began to grow and more staff were taken on, governance structures had to be developed. While the University

Grants Committee took an overview of activities and expenditure at most universities, its remit did not cover the OU. Instead, in October 1969 an Academic Advisory Committee with a membership from outside the OU was established to maintain standards.[33] Subsequently, a Working Group on the Review of Academic Staff, chaired by Professor Malcolm R. Gavin, was appointed to report to the DES and the OU Council. Gavin recommended that additional staff be recruited so that the OU could more fully engage in research.[34] Rather than employing consultants to be supervised in the production of teaching materials, a large, permanent, academic base was created. To manage these people and properties a number of formal bodies were created. These included executive and policy bodies, notably Senate, which took responsibility for academic standards and regulation, and Council, 'the executive governing body of the university'. These were decreed within the Charter. There were also the Finance Committee and Congregation, a meeting of Senate and Council and general and advisory bodies, such as a non-executive general assembly, 'the organ through which the feeling of a corporate institution would be generated'.[35]

Initially, all academics were members of Senate. Soon senior BBC staff and some library and educational technology staff were admitted.[36] Colin Robinson recalled speaking at Senate and how those who, like himself, were not academics were 'keen ... to be seen to be part of the university'. He added 'we'd certainly take part in faculty boards and of course in course teams ... it was very good that we felt part of those teams'.[37] The membership of Senate grew from 8 to 163 members between June 1969 and May 1971, and then to 284 by January 1972; soon it reached 335 and met every month. During the same period the number of full-time regional staff rose ten-fold from 35 to 333. Walter Perry complained that 'at one Senate meeting in 1971 each member received 487 pages of typescript weighing 2lbs 15 oz'.[38] John Horlock said that 'in theory 700 people could attend Senate' when he was Vice-Chancellor, but in practice only 'a couple of hundred' attended.[39] The volume of policy formulation that was required was vast and an infrastructure was developed to reflect this need.

Project working groups were established and the Vice-Chancellor's Committee formed. This was a small group empowered to co-ordinate short-term planning and executive action, to make swift decisions and initiate project working. It met weekly, while the larger Senate met monthly. That it soon became the executive body of the OU can be demonstrated by the fate of the 186 items sent from the Vice-Chancellor's Committee to Senate. Only 16 were referred back, amended or not accepted.[40] It was able to take on this role for two reasons: firstly, because attendance at committee meetings fell over time, meaning they became less representative; and, secondly, because of the volume and complexity of Senate business. Moreover, policy matters sometimes did not reach Senate. David Murray, who chaired the Senate Agenda Committee from 1971–73, recalled his concerns about how an interest in overseas projects might tilt the OU away from its core concerns. He said that Walter Perry almost arranged for Open University courses and course material to be distributed in the USA, even though the commercial publishers required that teaching materials could be amended. However, after Murray pointed out that academic content was a matter for Senate, and there was 'a good set to on that issue', the matter was dropped.[41]

To manage the university, academic bodies were given a high level of responsibility. In April 1970 six faculty boards, in effect standing committees rather than *ad hoc* working groups, were formed.[42] Foundation course teams assumed the functions of faculty boards but then membership was widened to include members of other faculties and BBC staff.[43] Many of the staff members who worked in the Applied Education Sciences Unit (later called the Institute of Educational Technology) were accorded academic status.[44] Initially limited to an investigation into the NEC/BBC preparatory courses, this unit's tasks soon included developing courses, supporting members of course teams through the process of preparing material for distance learning, and carrying out surveys of students to gain evidence about the students attracted to the OU and the impact of the OU's teaching. In 1986 responsibility for staffing and the financing of teaching (including course production and presentation) was devolved to heads of units.[45] One member of staff felt that 'the organisation was brilliant [it] worked from the foundation committee all the way down, via the faculties, to the course teams and the working groups'.[46]

The production of teaching materials formed what David Murray called 'the industrial end of the university' which he said 'had to be mechanistic ... routinised ... highly organised' (Figure 3.6). New posts were created to run these operations.[47] Walter Perry appointed a Pro-Vice-Chancellor (Resources). John Horlock, who succeeded Walter Perry as Vice-Chancellor, recognised that 'the range of duties is greater than in a conventional university and the size of the administrative staff is much larger' and created the post of Deputy Vice-Chancellor and appointed a new Secretary.[48] Posts were created at the OU for which there were no parallels at other universities. Although the structures created had the appearance of hierarchies, in practice there was considerable debate and flexibility. When the management of the OU was reviewed there was considerable input. A University Infrastructure Review Group established in December 1981 received 155 pages of comments regarding the future of the General Assembly, a third statutory body, besides Senate and

Figure 3.6 Industrial-scale processes were central to the OU. It was built on the assumptions of mass production. There was a warehouse to deal with the need to supply thousands of students with books and equipment. Bletchley Post Office was overwhelmed by the correspondence so Post Office staff worked on the Walton Hall site and dispatched items directly to the railway station.

Council. While the Vice-Chancellor wanted more Pro-Vice-Chancellors there was 'a sustained attempt to develop and extend existing practice' in order to delegate and decentralise power.[49] There was also recognition that it was beneficial if staff co-operated rather than simply obeyed. Ruth Young, the senior packing supervisor, encouraged the academics to see the process of packaging and posting of teaching materials for themselves. Charles Cleverdon saw these interactions as another example of OU egalitarianism:

> such strong ties and relationships were formed between these packing ladies, who were paid the lowest wage on earth, and these senior academics and they adored each other ... They would get invited to go over to lunch with the Dean or a professor who applauded them as part of the team.[50]

There was less flexibility with regard to Whitehall's interventions. Despite its Royal Charter the university's finances were subject to close government scrutiny. Its grant was reviewed annually and it was forbidden to carry over income from one year to another unless the expenditure was for the development of teaching materials.[51] In addition, the OU could not accumulate reserves, nor own property against which it could borrow money. Formally, there was little scope for errors in budget management. However, costing such an innovative venture was difficult and in practice there was some flexibility, perhaps because the OU was not treated as other universities were in that it was not within the remit of the University Grants Committee. Walter Perry noted that 'our financial health has been maintained not so much because of lucky budgetary guesses in those early years but because of the extremely understanding and sympathetic way in which the DES has viewed our problems'.[52] It was crucial that the fledgling university was not directly competing for funds with powerful and unsympathetic conventional universities. Asa Briggs noted that

> the University benefited immensely from the fact that it was not part of the system to begin with [i.e. was not funded via the University Grants Committee] ... in the Planning Committee, we did spend a bit of time talking about our relationship to the University Grants Committee ... we benefited from being outside.[53]

As the university became more established, the demerits of this mode of funding began to outweigh the benefits. It was difficult to plan over the medium term because of the numerous challenges which required immediate resolution. Short-term resource allocation, in response to specific events or initiatives, was favoured, as 'it mattered to our masters at the DES when £500,000 was overspent one year (from a budget of well over £100 million)'.[54] There was also concern that funding decisions were made on party-political grounds.[55] John Horlock complained that 'the civil servants liked to have their fingers in the OU pie, whereas I hardly saw a civil servant in all my time at Salford' (where he had previously worked). He also noted that while the government determined student numbers, discouraged research and denied proposals for postgraduate funding, 'ventures close to its own policies' received support.[56]

Although strategic planning was not widely employed within universities and there were few qualifications in higher-education management available, the role of administrator was gradually becoming professionalised. In 1961 the Conference of University Administrators (following a merger this became the Association of University Administrators) was founded. Within the OU Joe Clinch promoted a high level of performance. A later Vice-Chancellor, John Daniel, said that as Deputy Secretary he built a sophisticated and effective system for student administration and ... as Secretary he ... put in place personnel policies and procedures that empower OU staff to serve students well.[57]

The importance of planning was increasingly recognised, with a strategic planning body reporting to Senate and Council and responsible for the triennial submission to the DES. Annual plans during the 1980s could be criticised – 'uninspiring, inward-looking and focused on the short-term', according to Martin Watkinson – but they illustrate that attempts were made to prepare for the future.[58]

In addition to responding to financial constraints in the 1970s, the OU along with other universities had to answer criticisms of the higher education sector during the 1980s. Although some scholars, notably Rothblatt and also Sanderson, argued that universities had modernised, Keith Joseph, Secretary of State for Education 1981–86, adopted Martin Weiner's view that the impact of the university-educated elite of the UK had been economically detrimental as it was wary of commercial and industrial activity.[59] Keith Joseph's 1985 White Paper, *The Development of Higher Education into the 1990s*, envisaged a smaller higher education sector. The sector, meanwhile, responded to the prevailing climate by consciously adopting industry-based models of management, which were endorsed in the Committee of Vice-Chancellors and Principals' Jarratt Committee report of 1985.[60] The Committee, which was chaired by an industrialist, emphasised an enterprise culture and specific managerial styles and structures. It also called for improvements to strategic planning and resource allocation within all universities and proposed performance reviews.[61] This framework was already relatively familiar to the OU, as its public outputs and position within the DES had led to frequent scrutiny of its activities, budgets and teaching materials. The OU argued that it had already created structures which were in line with the recommendations of the Jarratt Report, notably a Vice-Chancellor's Management Team and a Senate and Council connected to the Strategic Planning Resources Committee.[62] Other universities took steps to implement its main recommendations.

A further aspect of the OU's relationship to the DES was that a Visiting Committee was appointed in order to advise the minister on financial and other plans. Between 1982 and 1990 it was chaired by Sir Austin Bide.[63] This was a period when the amount of government grant per undergraduate fell by over a quarter in real terms.[64] Its eleven members visited a summer school and Walton Hall in 1982 and proposed improvements to the assessment system, which were implemented. Although the Visiting Committee caused 'some difficult staffing adjustments', it accepted that the OU should undertake research and it helped to persuade the DES to offer 'more flexible funding arrangements'.[65] When the OU sought to expand postgraduate teaching and to fund some undergraduate-level courses in the continuing education programme through the core funding, it had to make its case through the Visiting Committee.[66] Sir Austin Bide was also a member of the Croham Committee which, as part of a wider brief, reviewed the relationship between the OU and the University Grants Committee. It received evidence from the OU's Vice-Chancellor and others at the OU and did not recommend the integration of the OU.[67] It did, however, propose the replacement of the University Grants Committee by a group half drawn from outside the world of education.

In the development of its management systems the OU was in some respects further down a path which all universities would have to follow. However, its spatial identity remained wholly distinctive. In common with many other post-war projects the OU developed out of the centralised wartime state as a unitary institution to serve the whole nation. This reflected attitudes in the 1960s when there was little interest in nationalism in Scotland and Wales. The assumptions of centralism were illustrated by the editor of the *Times Educational Supplement*, who in 1971 called it 'England's Open University'.[68] Although the OU's administrative structures and its Charter and Statutes had much in common with other contemporary universities, its regional organisation was unique, as was the influence that regions had on its policy. It was intended that a General Assembly, representative of both students and staff, would elect representatives to the Council and Senate through regional assemblies. The Planning Committee set out the aims as

> first to ensure as far as possible the smooth operation of the new institu-tion, and second to provide for the growth, among the staff and students of some sense of belonging to a real, definable and vital organisation ... this sense of belonging can be fostered only by an administrative struc-ture related to the needs and problems of the regions. Thus the two objectives are closely interwoven.

The Planning Committee went on to indicate the significance of the regions and nations, noting that 'regional directors will play a vital role in developing close co-operation with many interests of various kinds'.[69]

Regardless of the debates about the status of the regions within the uni-versity, staff had to create a system which would enable the OU to be local to many of its students and staff. To cover England, nine regions, based on the geographical boundaries of the Regional Advisory Councils for Further Education, were created. Scotland and Wales were also designated as regions, and later nations (Plate 3). London was split from its south-east hinterland, and as there were 'few students in Northern Ireland', that part of the UK was initially run from Manchester.[70] Each region was headed by a Director able 'to respond to an immense interest in and ignorance of what The Open University was going to be'.[71] The regions looked after teaching and counselling staff. Overall management was placed in the hands of Robert Beevers. Described as a 'quiet figure' who didn't really bring the regional end into the fore of discussions, he enabled the regions to develop some degree of autonomy.[72] Beevers recalled that at first 'we had no idea whether we could provide tutors on a regional basis, let alone a local basis'.[73] However, with over 12,000 applicants, 5,000 part-time tutors were found and started work in the summer of 1970.[74]

The regional structure enabled the OU to adapt to differences within the United Kingdom. For example, it was only in 1971 that legislation was amended so that, for teacher trainer accreditation purposes, OU degrees were given the same status as degrees awarded by the Council for National Academic Awards and the Scottish universities.[75] As the political salience of nationalist sentiment grew, so within the OU, despite the constrictions of the centralised production model, there was adaptation to cultural, legal and economic developments within the nations of Ireland, Scotland and Wales and within the different regions of England.[76] The integration of the OU as part of the educational systems of Wales, Northern Ireland and Scotland was aided by the ways in which OU staff nurtured networks within those locations. This was done in many ways, including by sitting on committees and contributing to the communities within which the OU was situated.

The OU had been particularly influenced by Scotland from its inception. Harold Wilson first announced his plans for a 'University of the Air' in Glasgow Concert Hall, and Jennie Lee and Walter Perry brought their experiences of Scottish universities to the OU.[77] Professor F. Llewellyn-Jones, Principal of the University College of Swansea, was on the Advisory Committee, and a member of the Scottish Education Department was in attendance. Members of the Planning Committee included Lord Ritchie-Calder, Professor of International Relations at the University of Edinburgh; Roderick Maclean, Director, University of Glasgow Television Services; and Ienan Williams Hughes, Warden of Coleg Harlech. Winnie Ewing, Scottish National Party President 1987–2005, suggested that the honorary doctorate she received from the OU in 1993 was 'in recognition of my role in establishing it'.[78] The Scottish local authorities were given the right to nominate a member of the OU's Council. They brought with them the confidence that working-class students could attend a university, a notion with a longer pedigree in Scotland than in England. Since the nineteenth century there had been a large number of bursaries for university places in Scotland. In the 1860s 1 in 1,000 people went to university in Scotland compared with 1 in 5,800 in England, and 20 per cent of students at universities in Scotland were of working-class origin.[79] It has also been argued that 'in Scotland traditions of independent working-class education have been particularly strong'.[80] In addition, Scottish personnel brought experience of specific features of higher education that were particularly relevant to the OU: the four-year degree was widely accepted in Scotland; the Scottish Universities Council for Studies in Education had already explored credit transfer systems;[81] The University of Stirling offered modular degrees from its inception in 1967. These precedents encouraged the OU's planners to believe that a modular system, necessary as students often took breaks within their studies or did not seek to complete an entire degree, could successfully be developed.

Walter Perry initially demonstrated little interest in the regions and nations, claiming that he used an amended version of the further educational administrative boundaries because 'we had no coherent plan for the regions when we started; they were simply allowed to evolve'. Nevertheless, the model of central planning was soon amended to encompass the specific needs and aspirations of nations. For example, following anger when the first advertisement for a Regional Director for Wales made no reference to the need to speak Welsh, a new Welsh Advisory Committee, chaired by Walter Perry, was established. The Committee included figures from the Welsh Joint Education Committee and the University of Wales. A new advertisement was written. The unique geographical and political situation of Northern Ireland provided an opportunity for the OU to register its first students outside the UK with the Belfast Centre delivering OU courses to students in both Northern Ireland and the Republic of Ireland. This was a complicated task, as it had to operate within two separate sovereign jurisdictions with separate political, educational and public service systems – and even differing currencies. It was also the first part of the UK to negotiate a collaborative teaching agreement with a non-UK institute, the Plassey Management and Technology Centre at the University of Limerick.

Neil McCormick (an arts staff tutor in Scotland) noted that the Scots working in Edinburgh felt obliged not only to appoint and supervise staff in Scotland, but also to adapt OU teaching to local conditions. He reminded 'pleasant English colleagues [that] Scotland had a different legal system, different educational traditions, an Established Church of its own and a richly distinctive cultural history'.[82] The students were not always like those from England. Among the first ten cohorts of OU graduates, 44 per cent were teachers, but this was only 37 per cent in Scotland, where there had long been many graduate teachers; the percentage of teachers without previous degrees was 41 per cent across the UK but only 29 per cent in Scotland.[83] In addition, 20 per cent of Scottish students were geographically remote. The distance between the university's central administration and its furthest flung students put a lot of mileage on its Scottish staff, as Neil McCormick noted: 'Stornaway Tuesday, Milton Keynes Thursday'.[84] Soon after the tuition fees doubled in the course of four years he pointed out the inequalities of access in Scotland. 'The better-off can travel from Arran to Aberdeen, just for a day school, if they want to. The others may not be able to, even once a year.'[85]

The teaching methods had to be adapted as the reception of broadcasts was unreliable in some parts of Scotland and the distances people were required to travel if they sought to attend tutorials were vast. However, there were compensations: staff who went to Kirkwall and Lerwick returned with sides of lamb from appreciative local organisers.[86] For part-time staff with more generic roles, location counsellors, location centres (rather than study centres) and telephone and later video conferencing were employed. Telephone tutorials were developed for those who lived in remote locations, some disabled students and those on some low-population courses. Research was conducted and materials were developed to support this form of teaching.[87] Heddwyn Richards, a senior counsellor in Wales, was one of the pioneers of the use of telephone tutorials.[88] Judith George, another prominent developer, worked in Scotland.[89] The experience regions had gained in responding to distance proved valuable in adapting to other kinds of needs. Students who were unable to travel to tutorials because of their remote location and lack of access to public transport were offered additional support by part-time counsellors. It was Cardiff which merged the roles of tutors and counsellors and appointed the first assistant student counsellors.[90] Communication between Milton Keynes and the national offices was not always straightforward. Gordon Macintyre, the Regional Director, Northern Ireland, 1972–92, felt that he was sometimes marginalised, while Roger Carus, the first Scottish Director of The Open University, ignored '"instructions" from Milton Keynes when he believed they did not meet Scottish needs'.[91] Those in the regions communicated with one another, as one of the first Regional Directors, Norman Woods, recalled: 'we met regularly about once a month and [there were] constant circulars'.[92] This may have helped them to act in concert. In 1972 there was a 'virtual walk-out of Senate representatives from the OU's Regional Services [after] the VC handled Senate rather badly'.[93]

The offices in Edinburgh, Cardiff and later in Manchester promoted the OU through liaison with national figures and bodies in Scotland, Wales and Northern Ireland. As Walter Perry acknowledged:

A regional director, on appointment in 1969, found himself carrying a large share of the burden of attempting to enlighten public opinion about the Open University and of fending off some of the most ill-informed criticisms of our objectives.[94]

The role of those who shaped these offices, and the status of the OU, was confirmed when some of them were awarded honours.[95] The Scottish Director of The Open University from 1988, John Cowan, an educator of international reputation, was involved in many local issues and networks and active in securing access to university education for the Highlands and Islands.[96] Harford Williams, the Director in Wales from October 1969, was born in Carmarthenshire but when appointed was working as a Principal Scientific Officer at the Marine Laboratory in Aberdeen with responsibilities in the university's Department of Zoology.[97] Nevertheless he recorded eight television interviews for Wales, gave twenty lectures within a few weeks of his first press conference in 1970, and was responsible for a rise of over 10 per cent in applications within the country.[98]

In Northern Ireland the provision for adult education was transformed over a brief period of time. Students started at the New University of Ulster in October 1968, at The Open University in January 1971, and at the polytechnic formed by the amalgamation of existing institutions in April 1971. Gordon Macintyre represented the OU on the Council for Continuing Education, as a member from 1974 until 1982 and then as chair until 1986. He was a member of the Advisory Committee on the Supply and Training of Teachers from 1976 and chaired this Department of Education for Northern Ireland body from 1979 to 1982. In addition, he worked within a number of government bodies relating to schools' policies and to teacher training.

The regions and nations took on tasks such as providing counselling for all students. This proved to be more complex and important than the planners had realised. It was at the regional and national level that contacts with adult educational bodies and local union branches were secured and maintained. Connections were made by many others within the three nations. Robert Walker recalled that he was influenced to join the OU because a technology staff tutor, David Channing, addressed him and young engineering lecturers at University College, Cardiff in 1971.[99] For many years Rees Pryce, a staff tutor, lectured in University College, Cardiff on the sociology of Wales. Another staff tutor, Terry Thomas, collaborated with Paul Ghuman to produce research on the people of Wales.[100] In addition, a collaborative system was developed which enabled OU students to gain credits for University College, Cardiff courses and vice versa. The OU also created community education courses and packs. These were rolled out across Wales, where 30,000 people joined 1,800 groups. In addition the OU has been represented at the National Eisteddfod, the annual Welsh cultural festival. These examples of integration into the national life demonstrate how the OU became part of the lived culture. It was in recognition of the importance of all the nations that the Vice-Chancellor, John Daniel, paid tribute to his Welsh roots and chose to be installed in Cardiff in 1990.

Gordon Lammie was aged 26 in 1970 when he joined the OU in the East Midlands. His main task was to select staff. He recalled that 'the number of people appointed was around about three hundred ... without interview, references, or anything of the sort, they were just selected on the basis of their applications ... it was absolutely frenetic'.[101] The offices of the regions had to change as the functions developed (Plate 4). David Grugeon, the first Regional Director for East Anglia, initially had a desk and a secretary in a little room and utilised nearby space, including the local pub.[102] The extra-mural department of Nottingham University loaned the OU two rooms until the staff were able to secure a larger space, and in Belfast, when there was an office move, Ken Boyd recalled 'I got the female staff to carry the furniture, I drove the van and we moved about half a mile down the road'.[103] In 1989 it was noted that regional centres 'too often resemble insurance offices'.[104] Joan Christodoulou charted improvements from 'a horrible brick college' in Aylesbury through the superior Parsifal College, London to the 'really superb tuition rooms' in Camden.[105] Naomi Stinson recalled that 'it was all very relaxed ... at the end of the day nobody wanted to go home ... everybody just sort of sat around talking'.[106] Although most of the teaching materials were delivered to students by post, when the first mailings coincided with a national postal strike regional staff stepped in. They collected materials from Walton Hall and delivered them to regional centres, study centres and even students' homes. In some areas they also collected student assignments.[107]

Tutors, who were employed part-time in the regions, taught using the centrally provided materials. An early distinction between correspondence tutors, who assessed the written work, and class tutors, who conducted face-to-face tuition, was later dissolved. These staff members became course tutors, later known as associate lecturers. Counsellors advised students about the nature of their courses, the OU's regulations, and how to study, obtain library books and work at home. They had a wide brief to offer guidance, training and advice about admission and the pattern of studies. Senior counsellors worked full time and were based in the regional offices. They were responsible for helping to train staff, run residential schools, liaise with local adult-learning institutions and arrange courses for students and staff. A link between these categories of staff was provided by full-time staff tutors who were based in a specific region and reported both to their faculty in Walton Hall and to the Regional Director. They connected the region to the Walton Hall campus, arranged tutorials and advised course teams. These practical tasks were combined with a broad understanding of academic outcome. By September 1970 almost all of the fifty-six staff tutors had been appointed. Twenty-six senior counsellors were appointed to guide, co-ordinate and supervise the part-time counsellors in their novel roles. The tutor-counsellor system became the human face of a university operating on an industrial scale. David Sewart argued that 'the OU accepted industrialisation of production' but added that

> the broad theme of industrialisation in the OU embraces the creation of a product but also the relationship with the students, how it was organised initially … The notion of individual customer care on an industrialised scale only properly emerged in the tutor counsellor [TC] system in 1976 in which the TC really became 'the face of the OU' for each student. … The TC system lasted almost without change for some 20 years.[108]

While there were hierarchies and changes, the elements of teamwork, discussion and stability were in place at regional level.

Conversations continued about the role of the OU regions. Those who advocated the importance of regions could point to variations between students in different locations.[109] In 1987 and 1988 three inter-regional symposia were held on their role and future. All the staff involved felt that the regions played an important role in widening access and that they were both integral to and marginalised within the OU. They argued that they were better able to offer personal contact than Walton Hall, acting as an intermediary or buffer 'between the student and the bureaucracy and between the individual student's needs and highly standardised materials'.[110]

The distinctive organisation of the OU reflected its roots both in democracy and in mass production. There needed to be parity and equity across the UK, provided by nationally consistent teaching materials, rigorous assessment strategies and the supply of detailed teaching guidance to tutors. There also had to be opportunities for students to gain personal support. The distributed structure of engaging with students was an attempt to ensure that these aspects of the OU's educational system were delivered in a consistent manner. The industrial processes of centralised course production were given a human face by the regional and national centres. The balance between the regions and the centre was a matter of constant internal debate, with the parameters shifting as the United Kingdom began to engage with constitutional devolution. At the same time the challenges posed by this unique model of higher education generated a stream of organisational and technical innovations. In particular the problem of bridging centrally produced materials to dispersed groups of students led to new teaching models and the use of computers in higher education.

Study centres

Since the 1966 White Paper it had been envisaged that, possibly through liaison with the WEA and local authorities, a network of regional study centres, where tutors could meet students, would be created (Figure 3.7).[111] Walter Perry noted that in order to function, the OU had to be 'parasitic' upon other institutions in regard to the provision of study centres.[112] Locating and equipping these was the responsibility of Regional Directors and it was sometimes difficult to find suitable, inexpensive rooms preferably with storage facilities. Unlike other universities, the places where tutors and students met one another, be they study centres or residential schools, had to be equipped to enable users to access a variety of electronic and electrical items given that, from 1971, some mathematics courses required students to be able to access a computer terminal.[113] Harold Wiltshire (who was both a member of the Planning Committee and Head of Nottingham University's extramural department) helped Norman Woods to find rooms in the East Midlands. In Belfast one of the first centres was in a school. Ken Boyd recalled 'adults getting their knees under grammar school pupils' desks.'[114] Tutorials were often devoted to offering students opportunities they could not otherwise obtain, notably group discussions or engagement with scientific experiments and demonstrations. Study centres began to be seen as potential media resource centres (Figure 3.8). Some were stocked with collections of videos and video players. In 1976 the OU set up the CICERO project with three courses with online requirements.[115] In 1981 students could attend centres in order to use Europe's first 'interactive videodisc' and there were more than 250 study centres in the dial-up network; most had Teletype or VT100 terminals. In 1982 about 95 per cent of students lived within five miles of a study centre computer terminal.[116] The 'connect hours' increased by 50 per cent due to the introduction of the courses *Computing and computers*, M252 and PM252, studied by nearly 3,000 students. It was in 1982 that a telewriting system or an 'electronic blackboard' known as Cyclops was introduced (Plate 5). A telephone line connected to a TV monitor enabled drawings made on screens to be

Figure 3.7 The distribution of study centres by type of host institution in 1971.

Technical Colleges and Art Colleges	120
Colleges of Further Education	55
Schools	30
Adult Education Centres	20
Colleges of Education	14
Polytechnics	12
Universities	11
Teachers' Centres	6
Others	6
Total	274

Source: David A. Hoult, 'The Open University: Its structure and operation' (Dip. Ed. thesis, University of Hull, 1971), p. 99.

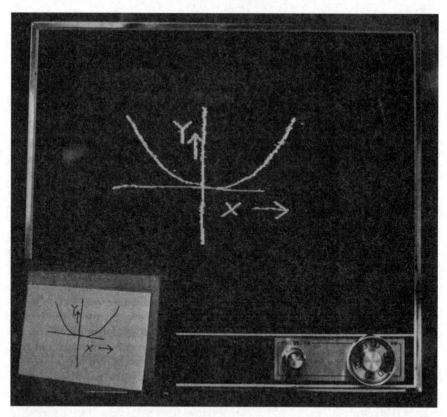

Figure 3.8 The remote blackboard was first used at the OU in 1975. Developed by John Monk and Chris Pinches, a tutor could write using an electronic pen and television screen and the results could be seen immediately by students in distant locations.

seen in other locations. Eight study centres were connected in a trial run in the East Midlands. This lasted for two years and was funded by British Telecom.[117] Norman Woods recalled that it was used on courses where the visual element was particularly valuable and which, by comparison to the Foundation courses, had relatively few students: 'the tutor could be in a central position in one of the study centres with a group of students there, talking to little groups in another three or four centres as well'.[118] John Daniel noted of the 1980s both that governments sought to reduce their expenditure and that there was an increased interest in 'home electronic entertainment (e.g. video players and micro computers) as opposed to network TV'.[119] These were trends which had an impact on the roles of the study centre.

Spreading the word

To Walter Perry it appeared obvious that, with its insistence on high standards coupled with its many innovations, the OU could challenge the norms of higher education.[120] He argued that

> the standard of teaching in conventional universities was pretty deplorable. It suddenly struck me that if you could use the media and devise course materials that would work for students all by themselves, then inevitably you were bound to affect – for good – the standard of teaching in conventional universities. I believed that to be so important that it overrode almost everything else.[121]

The government encouraged the OU to reach out to the wider population. Its programmes could be watched by anybody with access to television. Some of the mystique of traditional universities was eroded when the OU positioned students as interactive learners and presented learning as a problematising and experiential activity. There was, however, no certainty that the university's experiment would register either with public opinion or with those trained in the existing universities and for so long accustomed to conventional higher education. The scale of what it would take for the OU to become known and its methods accepted was alluded to by one senior counsellor who argued that 'the load of advertising the Open University must be shared between students and graduates as well as central administrators, faculty and regional academics'.[122] The need for this 'advertising' is underlined by a study which found that in 1971 only a third of the population had heard of the OU and that women and working-class people tended to be less knowledgeable, possibly

Figure 3.9 Peter Maddocks' work for *Sesame* presented a council cleaner who studied while working (a book held in place on his broom so that he can read and sweep at the same time). While gently mocking aspirations, this rendered the university experience as attainable and appropriate for the streets and homes of people who might never have been to a university or met a student. The press releases and publications of the OU reinforced the message that universities need not only be for Sebastian Flyte (the aristocratic drunkard Oxford undergraduate in Evelyn Waugh's novel *Brideshead Revisited*). They could also be for Harry.

because press coverage was largely within the 'quality' press (Figure 3.9).[123] One of the most important ways that understanding of the OU spread was through the use of its teaching materials by others.[124] Rex Watson, an OU tutor from 1973, noted:

> The standard of OU written and other material is rightly in my view regarded highly, as a general rule. I have myself learnt quite a bit of new mathematics, and have often pinched ideas to use in my other work![125]

The impact of this new approach was reflected in the comments of those outside the OU. Two academics from Brighton College of Education noted:

> Lecturers, who for years had been saying they needed time to prepare more meaningful courses, found them ready-made by the Open University production system. [The teaching material] was the envy and despair of those in more traditional institutions of higher education.[126]

All but one of the UK's universities and polytechnics purchased off-air recording licences, which permitted them to record OU broadcasts. A review carried out by the DES and the OU in 1991 acknowledged the impact the OU had on the higher education sector through its published materials, as 1,500 course units were sold to seventy higher education institutions and a further 2,000 units to bookshops near campuses:

> It is generally recognised that the University's materials have been widely disseminated within the educational world and that they have had a widespread effect on teaching in conventional universities.[127]

The OU's Scottish Director 1987–97, John Cowan, explained the popularity of OU materials in other institutions:

> The OU had produced materials which were so splendid that they were pillaged on a widespread basis. The OU had trained and employed members of staff in established institutions who were so pleased to work for the OU and so inspired by some of the things that the OU stood for.[128]

Many OU teaching ideas were spread by the early students who had been teachers. They took the OU's methods and concepts and translated them for use in classrooms and lecture theatres.[129] The dissemination by enthusiastic users was rapid. By 2009 the OU was being placed at the top of the list of 'the most influential educational innovations of the twentieth century'.[130] At the same time, the forces of inertia within the higher education system remained an obstacle.[131] Jocelyn Bell Burnell, a tutor, consultant, examiner and professor of physics at the OU, recounted that her 'one regret' about working in the university was that

> the rest of UK higher education hasn't learnt more from the way the OU has taught, and pinched more of its ideas and things because it is really excellent stuff … There'll be some individuals who work in normal higher education physics departments, and there will be physics tutors for the OU who will be shipping material between the two, and that's great, but I'm just sorry that it hasn't happened more.[132]

The dissemination of its teaching materials meant that the OU, unlike other institutions, had placed its curriculum effectively on the public stage. A crisis arose when a national debate over alleged political bias in the OU's course materials took place. This coincided with proposals to reduce the OU's funding. Beginning in the 1970s there was a long-running debate about the national curriculum which, in 1988, was introduced into all state schools in England, Wales and Northern Ireland. There were also allegations of political bias in the content of courses at a number of institutions.[133] While the lectures of staff at other universities were largely hidden from view, OU teaching materials were readily available for scrutiny. In at least six of the years during the period 1976–85 there were allegations that OU course materials were politically biased. The OU expended much time and energy addressing these concerns. It provided opportunities for views to be exchanged through articles and letters in the OU's newspaper, Sesame, and students were surveyed as to their opinions.[134] After Caroline Cox, the Head of Sociology at the Polytechnic of North London 1974–78, contributed an article to Sesame entitled 'D302: a platform for blatantly political views', the course chair, Andy Blowers, wrote a response: 'Students have freedom to decide for themselves.'[135] The following issue carried letters on this debate.[136] The Times asked 'Is there a Marxist bias at the Open University?' It concluded, on the basis of an analysis of 10 of the 2,000 units that the OU produced that year, that there was bias. It was also claimed that

> The students saw it as their job to learn and reproduce what was in the course book … Working mostly on their own the students do not ask critical questions.[137]

In 1977 accusations of Marxist bias were met within the OU with debate and the airing of a variety of views, including those of students and the Chancellor.[138] Other elements of the national press joined The Times in covering the debate.[139] David Harris, an OU researcher, countered claims of Marxist bias, arguing that students typically found Marxism 'strange, counter-intuitive [and] unrealistic' and did not engage with it, and that, moreover, the OU 'reproduces the features of advanced capitalism [and] sterilises the content of courses'.[140] Fresh evidence fuelled the debate in 1981 and 1982, leading to internal inquiries as to bias in materials.[141]

Having listened to radio broadcasts, the philosopher Roger Scruton felt that one OU sociology course was 'certainly biased' and concluded that a student 'who learns to write a perfect examination answer in Marxism' would be rewarded. He also claimed that OU students' minds 'are neither impressionable nor truly open'.[142]

In 1984 George Walden (the Parliamentary Private Secretary to the Secretary of State for Education and Science) was critical of the OU and promised 'an efficiency study' of it. [143] The following year, Sir Keith Joseph, the Secretary of State for Education and Science, assessed the contentious material and visited Walton Hall.[144] Considerable preparations for the visit were made as there was a concern that the inquiry might adversely affect The Open University's funding.[145]

Keith Joseph's Permanent Under-Secretary, David Hancock, commissioned a report by economists which found two OU course units which presented an 'essentially Marxist' view. John Horlock was invited to review the material.[146] After the minister referred the issue to the Visiting Committee, John Horlock reported that 'the visit appeared to have been very successful'.[147] The resulting review concluded that the existing standards were 'impressive', but that procedures for maintaining academic standards could be improved. Some modifications were made to Block 2 of D102 for the presentation of the course in 1986.[148] Horlock recalled being 'summoned to what proved to be a very difficult interview' with Keith Joseph. Anastasios Christodoulou (the University Secretary, 1968–80) said that the minister 'didn't like the OU at all' and thought that the OU 'was politically motivated, ideologically unsound and its standards suspect and I'm almost quoting'.[149] Asa Briggs (the OU Chancellor, 1978–94), felt that while 'some courses in the Open University were pretty Marxist in structure and in content' they were qualified by other views. He spoke with Keith Joseph and concluded that 'he was not really a serious threat, but he produced a lot of alarm in the Open University'.[150]

The principles of the OU spread through its work as a model for similar institutions in other countries. As early as 1971 there were 146 visitors from overseas to the OU.[151] A report was prepared for the Commission on Post-Secondary Education in Ontario which compared the OU to the Telekolleg and Funkkollege, while another report on the OU for Canadian universities proposed that they make more use of television.[152] In addition, the government invited the OU to support various overseas ventures as part of its diplomatic efforts. The terms of reference within which planning committees worked in India specifically mentioned the need to 'study the details of the Open University'.[153] By 1972 three US universities were using OU television programmes, and by 1975 there were twenty US institutions using OU course materials. A New-York-based British Open University Foundation was created which enjoyed some success supporting whole-course-user universities in North America. Gordon Lammie recalled it as being 'a three person operation … it started in Washington and moved to New York'. He was part of this project, which involved over '1,000 people in different universities at any one time studying OU courses'. However, this was relatively limited growth. In 1978 Rosemary O'Day was an associate professor at the University of Maryland at College Park. She found that on her appointment 'nobody knew anything about the OU or its materials and it took two months to obtain programme videos'.[154] Gordon Lammie felt that there was an element of 'Not Invented Here syndrome ... a British product in the US in the field like higher education is a challenging task'.[155] The OU forged links with the National University Consortium, which arranged for students to enrol via participating local colleges and public television stations and, subject to that college's academic control, receive broadcast and print material from the OU. The colleges paid the consortium and the OU received royalties for each student enrolled on each course. By contrast to this modest success, a consortium which sought to create an American Open University had to abandon its plans.

The OU's Consultancy Service negotiated a contract for assistance to the Free University of Iran. Between 1973 and 1975 several members of the OU's staff worked on the project and eventually a two-year deal was signed in 1975.[156] The OU played an important role in the creation of the Israeli Open University, established in 1974.[157] Three senior staff, including Pro-Vice-Chancellor Ralph Smith, were seconded to the People's Open University in Pakistan (now the Allama Iqbal Open University (AIOU)). This trip was funded by the UK government, which also financed the provision of books and equipment for the AIOU library, its Institute of Educational Technology and the Mailing Section. The British Council was among those bodies which assisted in the provision of consultancies, training courses, fellowships, books, materials and equipment. Open University staff helped with the planning and development of the university's academic programmes, and the administrative and regional structures and procedures. Several of the new university's academic, administrative and regional personnel were trained at the OU. Joe Clinch was seconded to spend ten months in Pakistan, where he helped to create distance education systems.

The OU also had a contract with the Universidad Nacional Abierta in Venezuela and worked in the Netherlands and Surinam. The emphasis was not on reproducing the OU model, but on adapting OU approaches to local needs. Reporting from Venezuela in 1977 for *Open Forum 16*, Professor Mike Pentz stressed:

> We are not trying to say this is what we've done and you blokes ought to do the same. Nothing of the sort. On the contrary we are trying to help them get an insight as to why we have done things the way we have so that they, in their quite different contexts, can work out for themselves how they should transfer the experiences to their situation.[158]

In 1977 the Consultancy Service was replaced by the Centre for International Cooperation and Services (OUCICS), which developed contacts with external agencies, institutions and individuals concerned with distance education, and provided policy and technical assistance to new institutions in Costa Rica, Israel, Thailand and Nigeria. It instigated collaboration with China and the marketing of materials in Canada, India, Venezuela and China. However, it was never self-financing and was closed within a few years. The OU ceased actively to market its resources and expertise and became 'essentially re-active, not pro-active'.[159] Although the university continued to collaborate with the British Council in response to requests for advice and assistance, other universities began to be commissioned by the British Council, UNESCO and other aid agencies to undertake distance education consultancy assign-ments. Moves by many universities towards extending their global reach and opening overseas campuses echo the ways in which the OU spread its concepts of education across the world in the 1970s and 1980s. Supported by the Bernard Van Leer foundation, in 1978 the OU hosted the executive heads of sixteen open universities from fourteen countries. This led to the develop-ment of the International Institute for Distance Learning.

The commitment to enhancing access to high-quality, affordable and rel-evant education ensured that the OU not only had an impact within the UK but that it was influential around the world. While it had many contacts with ministers and officials, the way in which the students engaged in promoting the OU reflects the enthusiasm with which it was treated and the ways in which it became integrated into people's lives.

Costs, cuts and efficiency

During the 1960s higher education had been a 'focalising issue' that 'captured the headlines' and gained airtime.[160] Ideas of social democracy, the welfare state and educational opportunity were in the ascendency.[161] Expenditure on education increased and 'the arena of most conspicuous boom was that of education, higher education in particular'.[162] However, during the 1970s and 1980s economic and labour policies came to have a higher status, and educa-tion had to fit within the framework dictated by concerns about economic difficulties. In 1975 the *Wall Street Journal* ran the headline 'Goodbye, Great Britain', advising investors to get out of sterling; by 1976 confidence in sterling was so low that the government sought help from the International Monetary Fund. The price for the $3.9 billion loan (the largest ever made by that institu-tion) included an agreement to make deep cuts in public expenditure. In the years 1974, 1976, 1977 and 1981 there was a fall in real living standards in the UK. In 1979 economic troubles were exacerbated by a second oil crisis, and widespread protests were generated by an unpopular decision to deploy mobile American middle-range nuclear missiles in the UK. The titles of books of the period reflect a sense of dislocation: *Is Britain Dying?*, *Britain Against Itself*, *Britain's Economic Problem*, *The Breakup of Britain* and *Policing the Crisis*.[163] In the light of these concerns, the economics of the OU were subject to considerable scrutiny during the 1970s and 1980s. Its income from the government fluctuated and it sought to supplement this by charging higher fees and by broadening its appeal by offering vocational, often non-degree courses.

The OU was assessed on its cost-effectiveness after being open for only three years. It was concluded that it cost less than a third of other universities to teach an equivalent undergraduate course. The unit cost per graduate was about half and it appeared the OU 'would seem to have a substantial cost advantage over conventional universities, particularly when capital costs are taken into account'.[164] Critics noted that the OU only allocated 1 per cent of its expenditure to the library, compared to 3–4 per cent by other universities.[165] Although the initial costs were high and difficult to predict, as the pace of innovation slowed there was consolidation through evolutionary and incremental changes designed to improve performance and services. Routines became established, and the likely expenditure of the OU could be more easily determined.[166] Further reports on the OU economy assessed how much was spent to produce a graduate, the cost to individuals and to the public sector and the economic efficiency and adaptability of the OU.[167] Comparisons were difficult. Many students did not complete degrees but studied courses. The OU did not have to provide accommodation for its students. Its students were part-time (the Robbins formula was that each one should be measured as equivalent to only two full-time students). Most of them were older (which had an impact on the number of years they might earn prior to retirement) and in contrast to others studying for degrees within the UK they did not receive mandatory grants. Indeed, many paid taxes as they studied. The categorisation of fixed costs (such as the creation of television programmes, correspondence materials and radio broadcasts) and variable costs (such as the cost of printing and postage and the hire of study centres and summer school locations and the salaries of academics), and the decision as to which costs ought to be allocated to teaching and which to research, were open to dispute.

Nevertheless, by 1974 it was being argued that the OU had already demonstrated its cost-effectiveness.[168] Subsequent studies bolstered this view.[169] Indeed, by 1978 the idea of the financial value of the OU had gained the status of 'a dangerous myth'.[170] Hülsmann sought to calculate the cost of producing 'one student learning hour' using various educational technologies and concluded that face-to-face teaching was less expensive.[171] However, his concept of the 'student learning hour' was not universally accepted, and other approaches were taken.[172] Although if the number of students who did not complete degrees is taken into account the OU looked less financially appealing, it continued to be perceived as efficient. In 1991 a government review concluded that the costs of the OU were between 3 and 47 per cent lower for ordinary degrees than those of other universities, and between 55 and 80 per cent lower for honours degrees.[173] Perraton found the OU to be relatively cost-efficient in terms of costs per graduate.[174]

Research develops[175]

In 1963 the Robbins Report on higher education accepted the notion of academic tenure and that academics could 'pursue what personal studies and researches are congenial'.[176] The OU's 1969 Charter committed the university to 'the advancement of learning and knowledge by teaching and research' and obliged the university 'to make provision for research and for the advancement and dissemination of knowledge'.[177] However, the Department of Education initially funded teaching but not research at the OU. This contrasted with the new universities of the mid-1960s, which supported both activities. The Vice-Chancellor and his senior colleagues at East Anglia 'were determined that [UEA] should become an outstanding teaching university'; the Essex Vice-Chancellor said, 'one thing above all else: we want to establish that good teaching really matters'. Despite this emphasis on teaching, both institutions were also funded for research.[178] The founding staff of the OU recognised the connection that was made between good university teaching and research practice. Its aspiration to become a research university was derided by Rhodes Boyson, a head teacher who was to become a Conservative MP in 1974. He speculated in 1970 that the OU's suggestion that it provide facilities for postgraduate studies was 'because it expects that no one will accept its degrees as worthy of postgraduate extension'. He opposed this 'empire-building'.[179]

Despite difficulties and scepticism, research played an important role at the OU from the beginning. Steven Rose, the OU's first professor of biology, established the Brain Research Group (now the British Neuroscience Association), which was important in the development of the new field of neuroscience. He recalled the situation when he first arrived: 'I made it very clear at the start that I wouldn't go unless there were research facilities ... this was going to be a university like any other university'. He received funding from the Medical Research Council, 'so from the very beginning ... we'd actually got research going'. He paid tribute to two Vice-Chancellors, saying that it would have been impossible without Perry and that Horlock 'was passionately committed to research'. He added that 'people would say "I didn't know they did research at the Open University". And that's a real bloody nuisance for at least getting on half a century.'[180] The author of some three hundred research papers on memory and the brain, he has received several medals and awards, including a Medical Innovation Award for a potential therapy for Alzheimer's disease developed at the OU with his colleague, Dr Radmilla Milusnic. The OU awarded its first PhD in 1972 and counted several significant researchers among its staff.[181] These included Clive Emsley and Doreen Massey. Emsley's work on the history of crime and policing has attracted numerous research grants and top-class researchers to the university and to the International Centre for Comparative Criminological Research that he co-founded. Massey's work on space and place, global urbanisation and labour resulted in her being awarded the Victoria Medal of the Royal Geographical Society in 1994 and the prestigious Prix Vautrin Lud (the 'Nobel of Geography') in 1998. While central academic staff members at the OU were at first expected to focus on the production of teaching materials, some were enthusiastic researchers, despite the initial lack of research equipment, such as laboratories and a well-stocked library. By 1990 there twenty-one research assistants funded by the OU and four research groups operating in the highest rating level. The value of new grants to the OU in that year was £2.5 million.[182]

By the 1980s the post-war consensus on macro-economic management was being countered by the spread of monetarist ideas, which advocated the reduction of public expenditure on higher education. The state relinquished ownership of numerous enterprises and there was an increased focus on fiscal scrutiny. An Audit Commission was created to improve efficiency within the public sector. In 1981 the UK's universities were given one month to make an 18 per cent cut in their budgets, and 3,000 academic posts were eliminated. This cut was not evenly spread. Salford (where the OU Vice-Chancellor John Horlock had previously been Vice-Chancellor) had a cut of 40 per cent over three years. The OU had its grant cut by £3.5 million in 1980, a 9 per cent cut from its 1979 grant. A further £1.5 million was cut in 1981. The capital grant was halved in real terms in 1982. In 1983 the OU was required to reduce expenditure by £3 million and then by a further £10.5 million over the following two years. *The Times* argued that the OU was held in high esteem by Conservatives.[183] However, John Horlock concluded that, although the 'major crisis' over bias was 'not overtly linked' to funding, he still felt that 'the whole affair had clearly done us no good in the eyes of the Tory government ... I am sure that he [Joseph] would willingly have closed the OU down if it had been politically possible to do so, particularly after the affair of academic bias.'[184]

The OU also encouraged students 'to alert people in positions of influence to the University' as to the situation. An External Relations Committee was established which ran 'a well-organised public relations exercise' involving articles in the press and radio and television appearances, which was awarded a prize by the professional association of PR consultants.[185] The OU strove to be non-party-political, and David Grugeon (a member of the organising committee) recalled that

> one of our sharpest supporters was Nicholas Winterton [a Conservative MP] who put down PQs [Parliamentary Questions] for every Government Department, asking how many OU students and graduates they had. We eventually had to assist the Department to prepare answers to the growing range of PQs.

John Horlock said: 'we got out amongst the students and so that the students knew we were in trouble. We didn't in fact encourage students directly to write to the Department of Education and Science, but many, many did.'[186] A series of *Briefing Notes* and a *Pocket Guide to OU Figures* were produced, as was a booklet, 'An Open And Shut Case'. Bob Masterton (later Director of Open University Worldwide and Vice-Chancellor at United States Open University) provided data which suggested that in many parliamentary constituencies the number of OU students was greater than the majority that the MP had. By August 1984 over 1,000 representations had been made to the DES and over 100 parliamentary questions had been asked about the OU. This was more than any other single education issue. There was considerable press coverage, and the DES had to produce a rebuttal.[187] Senate noted that it 'regretted the damage being caused by excessive cuts' and the OU complained to the government, but ministers remained adamant.[188] Keith Joseph referred to the government's 'determination to contain public expenditure' and noted that while 'support is not lacking ... nevertheless, continued restraint in public expenditure is necessary and the OU as a substantial consumer of such expenditure, must play its part in the process'.[189] Its funding was reduced. Nevertheless, the OU's position, in terms of finance and the reputation of its teaching materials, appeared to improve.[190] An additional grant of £5 million was made in 1989, measures were taken to contain costs and increase income, and by 1990, 'for the first time for a number of years', the Vice-Chancellor declared the financial situation to be 'tranquil and stable'.[191]

One way of dealing with the reduction in its income from the government was to charge students more. Some OU students received local authority funding for summer schools, but it was largely the case that OU students were expected to pay their own fees or secure contributions from their employers.[192] In 1971 a full-credit undergraduate course (that is, a 60-point module) cost an individual learner £20. It cost £25 in 1976 for a full-credit course (excluding summer school fees) and £55 in 1979. There were substantial rises in the 1980s when fees rose by about 70 per cent in real terms, and at one point increased by 80 per cent over two years (i.e. from £67 to £120 per 60 credits). A full-credit course cost £120 in 1982, £202 by 1990 and £279 by 1995 (Figure 3.10).

In 1973 an Associate Student Programme began, offering modules intended to serve as refreshers, enabling learners to update or retrain. These were self-funding and some of the earliest were aimed at professional development, such as *Reading development*, PE261 (for teachers). In 1975 *The handicapped person in the community*, P853, became the first health and social welfare course. The fees charged to associate students were set at £360 in 1990.[193] By this time the fee income covered about 16.5 per cent of the costs of the undergraduate programme, or 22.5 per cent including summer school fees and other income (Figure 3.11). In 1980 the comparable figures were

Figure 3.10 Division of OU expenditure 1982–85 in £s.

	1982		1983		1984		1985	
	Staff	Non-staff	Staff	Non-staff	Staff	Non-staff	Staff	Non-staff
Research Committee	240	240	281	169	333	138	292	117
Academic units	703	293	714	298	803	280	400	280
Higher Degrees Committee	/	197	/	203	/	206	/	192
Institutional Research	/	58	/	50	/	5	/	/
Academic Computing	/	25	/	25	/	21	/	22
Sub-total	943	813	995	745	1136	650	692	611
Grand total	1756		1740		1786		1303	

Figure 3.11 Fees in the 1980s.

Fees in £s.	1980	1983	1984	1985
Undergraduate 60-point course (actual)	67	127	133	141
Undergraduate summer school (actual)	62	82	88	94
At constant 1983 price levels	85	127	126	128

Source: *Into the 1990s: The role of the Open University in the national provision of part-time higher education* (Milton Keynes: The Open University, 1986), p. 54 .

9 per cent and 13.5 per cent.[194] From 1982 the DES paid the OU to cover the cost of the fees of unemployed students. Assistance from these funds rose by 34 per cent between 1985 and 1990. As tuition fees rose, student demand fell and assistance for students from local authorities withered away. There was a continuing effort to make study accessible to people from all walks of life, which was reflected in the ambition (not always realised) to keep the fee rises in line with the Retail Price Index.

A further way of gaining additional income was to broaden the scope of the OU. In 1975 the university set up the Committee for Continuing Education, chaired by Peter Venables. The Planning Committee Report had referred to 'professional, refresher, updating and post-experience courses' and his report supported expansion into the wider field of adult and continuing education in co-operation with other relevant bodies.[195] The OU began to produce courses and study packs that were not part of a degree programme. In 1977 the first packs were produced by the Community Education programme: *The first years of life*, P911, and *The pre-school child*, P912, were aimed at parents with young children. These were early examples of collaboration, as P911 was funded by the Health Education Council and P912 by the Pre-School Playgroups Association. In 1977 the first diploma programme – the Diploma in Reading – was launched. Continuing education at the OU was financed through fees and grants by other bodies, not through the DES. The number of post-experience courses, and those taking them, continued to grow, and in 1978 the Interim Delegacy of the Centre for Continuing Education was created. By 1985 more than 27 per cent of the OU's income came from sources other than the DES.[196] This included grants for its continuing education programme.[197] Although there were concerns expressed that this expansion would result in the notion of social justice 'being thrust into the background', in practice this development paved the way for growth into the subject of business and social health.[198]

The OU was able to respond to this greater emphasis on a wider range of modes of provision for work-based learning because of its existing relationship with workplaces. Robin Wilson recalled one student who told him:

'I work for china clay in St Austell in Cornwall, and we've just been doing linear programming as part of the course'. He said 'I learnt this from the OU course, and I thought that our china clay works could work more efficiently so I worked out a way of doing this, using what I had just learnt in the Open University unit, and I went to my boss, and my boss fortunately was very open to the idea, and tried it, and the result was, it did work more efficiently, and I got a promotion.' That was directly out of what he had just studied in that course.[199]

The OU became the first university to be granted awarding body status by the National Council for Vocational Qualifications.[200] The Council for Industry and Higher Education, a body comprising thirty-two heads of large corporations and twelve heads of higher education institutions, called for access to and more variety in higher education along with a shift towards science and technology provision.[201] In the mid-1980s the OU introduced the BSc degree, the MMath and the MEng, and the PGCE.[202] The OU began to offer courses in English law (in association with the College of Law). Social relevance was exemplified by the emphasis within the OU on business education and the teaching of foreign languages. The Open Business School opened in September 1983, initially for those with a degree and aged over 27. At first 974 people studied *The effective manager*. Courses on *Accounting and finance for managers* and *Personnel selection and interviewing* were also launched. Within a decade it was producing 20 per cent of all the UK's MBAs. Initially, the teaching of languages at degree level was felt to undermine the principle of open access to the unqualified, and was seen as becoming a possible competitor to languages courses offered by the Further Education Advisory Council of the BBC. A course, *Understanding German*, was proposed and then cancelled in 1985. It was only in 1991 that a foreign language, French, was offered. German and Spanish soon followed.

In 1985 the idea that higher education as whole needed to be more responsive to the needs of the economy was promoted in a DES report which noted that

There is continuing concern that higher education does not always respond sufficiently to changing economic needs. This may be due in part to disincentives to change within higher education, including over-dependence on public funding, and to failures in communication between employers and institutions.[203]

A closer relationship between education and work was promoted by the Employment Department, which in 1987 launched Enterprise in Higher Education in sixty universities in co-operation with the DES, Scottish Office, Welsh Office and the Department of Trade and Industry. This sought to encourage change in the universities so that they would better prepare students for workplaces. The Confederation of British Industry also became involved.[204] The DES encouraged vocationally relevant higher education and a wider range of modes of provision, including part-time, distance and work-based learning. At the same time it introduced changes to its relationship with universities, taking greater central control over some of the activities of universities while devolving other responsibilities to them.[205]

Research developments

Funding was used to employ research assistants and for the use of laboratory space at other universities. A Research Unit was set up in Oxford, in a rented house, to provide some research facilities for physicists and technologists. The programme for conventional internal postgraduate research students began in 1969 with a handful of students and grew as fast as accommodation would allow, reaching 79 by 1975. For distance postgraduates, a more innovative system had to be developed based on 'research credits' for the BPhil, MPhil and PhD awards. A prospectus published in July 1972 attracted 450 applicants, 60 per cent of whom were teachers in schools, colleges or universities. Eighty students were registered in 1972, rising to 209 in 1975. Research was not confined, as some had imagined, to the analysis of teaching and learning. For example, Monica Grady, who started at the OU in 1983, worked within the Centre for Earth, Planetary, Space and Astronomical Research on meteorites and the development of instruments for international missions to Mars (Plate 6).[206]

Despite the efforts of many staff members, supported by the Vice-Chancellors, the OU was not widely seen as a university with a research focus. When the first national audit of university research took place in 1986 the OU was not considered as part of this state-supervised peer-review process designed to support the selective funding of research. This was because only the outputs of those institutions funded by the University Grants Committee were assessed, and this excluded the OU, which was funded by the DES. The 1988 Education Act abolished tenure and provided academics, under Section 202, with the 'freedom within the law to question and test received wisdom, and to put forward received ideas ... without placing themselves in jeopardy of losing their jobs or privileges'.[207]

There were further audits of research, in 1989 and 1992. Research excellence became a critical restructuring agent and helped to determine the direction that the OU took once it was classified with the other universities. The research income of the OU rose. In two fields the OU was awarded the highest possible grade. 'A very respectable outcome', commented the Vice-Chancellor.[208] New structures to allocate research funds were created.[209] There was further improvement when the next audit occurred in 1996.[210] In addition, the number of postgraduates increased and the amount of its research grew as more staff became research active.[211] The response to the government's decision to concentrate research funding so that a few select institutions took most of it led the OU to retain its interest in research, not to abandon it.[212] Pelagios, which was a system of linked projects about classical antiquity, connected open data about places in the historic past, while the OU-based Reading Experience Database created a dataset of over 30,000 searchable records of reading in Britain between the mid-fifteenth and mid-twentieth centuries.[213] These projects pooled data and encouraged additional contributions from students and others.

Governments sought to promote research deemed appropriate to the needs of the economy. Labour's policies for higher education, notably the 1998 White Paper *Our Competitive Future: Building the Knowledge-Driven Economy* and the 2002 White Paper *Investing in Innovation: A Strategy for Science, Engineering and Technology*, echoed some Conservative strategies, notably the 1993 science and technology White Paper *Realising our Potential: A Strategy for Science, Engineering and Technology*.[214] The Education Minister, Charles Clarke, argued that the focus should be on 'harnessing knowledge to wealth creation'.[215] In 2003 the Lambert Review of Business–University Collaboration sought to improve collaboration.[216] 'Public funding for basic research', it argued, 'is intended to benefit the economy.' It noted that while the OU did not rate among those universities which received large sums from the Higher Education Funding Council for England or research councils, it had a large number of industrial grants and contracts. It also proposed that the impact of research be measured, an idea that was widely adopted. The Director General of the Confederation of British Industry, Richard Lambert, later reiterated that 'skills and employability should be seen as part of the return on the substantial public investment that is already made in the sector. That's why we all pay taxes.' University education and research should aim to support 'the needs of business'.[217] In 2011 the Wilson Review of Business–University Collaboration noted that 'universities form the supply chain for business'.[218] The OU was well placed to address such concerns as it was already engaged with the notions of developing skills and employability.

Conclusion

By 1989, The Open University had become an accepted part of the national and international higher education landscape. Its survival owed much to its capacity to appeal to contrasting agendas. Alan Woodley observed that

> The Open University has been well looked after because Labour think it's about educating the working class and the Conservatives think it's about people standing on their own two feet and paying for their own courses.[219]

In 1990 the OU celebrated its twenty-first birthday and awarded its 108,000th degree. Lord Wilson and eight MPs, including three Secretaries of State, visited the Walton Hall campus that year, and nine MPs and one MEP attended graduation ceremonies. Several ministers launched continuing education packs. By this point over a million people had studied with the OU; 63,000 applied to study in that year alone.

There were more students with disabilities at the OU than at all the other universities put together; there was a higher proportion of women students, about 50 per cent, than most other universities; and over 700 students had registered in 1989 in Belgium, the Netherlands (where there was a study centre which was also used by the Dutch OU) and Luxembourg (Figure 3.12). Approximately half the OU's students had fathers with 'blue-collar' jobs compared to about 20 per cent in most universities. Three-quarters of the OU's students had full-time work, and 60 per cent of those classified as 'housewives' (who constituted about 12 per cent of the total OU student population) when they started their degree courses joined the workforce during or after their studies. In the period since the Business School had opened in 1985, 5,500 companies had sponsored its 40,000 students. The OU's graduates (about 9 per cent of all the graduates in the country) were a minority among the OU's students. Many studied individual modules or self-contained packs, or were focused on specific offerings such as the in-service training of teachers or courses leading to certificates and diplomas.

Figure 3.12 This advertisement appears to have been designed to attract men to the OU. Note the address was Bletchley, as Milton Keynes was still a tiny village. Even after Milton Keynes Development Corporation's offer of a long lease of a seventy-acre site for the OU was accepted there were problems related to the lack of infrastructure. Students might have been able to 'work at home for an Open University degree', but Milton Keynes-based staff found it difficult to find accommodation.

The Good Study Guide, written by Andrew Northedge, almost achieved 'best-seller' status.[220] The OU had its own purpose-built television studio complex at Walton Hall, which enabled it to produce, for example, a video which generated three-dimensional images of the brain for the *Biology: Brain and behaviour* course. It was also where radio programmes were made for broadcast to students and non-students via the new day-time, easy-listening Radio 5. Samuel Beckett's *Endgame* was given its television premiere on an OU transmission of 90 minutes' duration.

After nearly ten years, Vice-Chancellor John Horlock was able to claim that millions had, through the OU broadcasts, 'obtained further education "by osmosis"' and that the OU was

> no longer a strange new immature organisation, but a massive national resource, with a high international reputation [and] the most successful development in the development of higher education in the latter part of the 20th Century ... the best arguments for the Open University are its students, who study with such dedication, enthusiasm and perseverance.[221]

The status of the OU was reinforced when the Prince of Wales accepted an honorary degree (Figure 3.13).

Figure 3.13 The Chancellor and Vice-Chancellor were in attendance when, to mark the first decade of the OU, the Prince of Wales was awarded an honorary degree.

If Harold Wilson was 'the man whose idea gave birth to the University', as Vice-Chancellor John Daniel said, and Jennie Lee was the 'midwife' of the OU, as Robin Wilson claimed, then its stepmother was Margaret Thatcher.[222] Both she and Jennie Lee had an impatience with the traditional university sector. Both were willing to back an educational experiment which could use modern communications technology and rigorous production processes to challenge the restrictive conventions of face-to-face education. In a post-colonial world, both saw in the OU a means by which the UK could render a vital service to developing countries.

Within the institution its founding leaders and the early cohorts of staff wrestled with the conflicting demands of centralised management, collegial decision-making and devolved delivery of services. All the systems and pro-cesses had to be invented; this required endless debate and improvisation. The end of the first two decades of innovation marked merely a way-station in a long and uncompleted journey. By the late 1980s there was in place a working structure and system unlike anything that had been seen in higher education. Visitors poured into Walton Hall from all over the world because here was a menu of practices that could be adapted to many different politi-cal, social and economic contexts. Very few countries attempted to replicate the OU in its entirety. But all could learn from the solutions to the task of delivering scalable, high-quality higher education.

Although the OU's educational ambitions were too radical and the tensions between its democratic ambitions and its operational requirements too deep to find a resolution in this period, its innovations anticipated many changes which later became widely accepted within higher education. It was a popular university where the students paid the fees; it anticipated the shift towards a higher percentage of part-time, mature students; it pioneered the blend of teaching technologies and adapted early to the growing interest in vocational teaching and research. Monitoring of students' and tutors' activities, survey-ing the learning process in order to gauge the impact of modules, checking assessment and teaching materials by external parties were familiar practices at the OU which eventually became more widespread. It had widened the brief of higher education far beyond the traditional offer of degrees. All the same, in 1989 the OU was still an outlier in the system whose basic teaching methods had been enriched rather than transformed by the experiment taking place in Milton Keynes and across the institution's regions. Its impact on educational innovation in the developing world was in many respects much swifter and more profound, but the many partnerships and consultancies had only a marginal impact on the OU's business model. The university remained a UK institution with an extremely interesting set of global interactions.

The major threats to the university's future in this era came from the politi-cal class which had done so much to bring it into existence. The increase in the number of students led to greater government expenditure. This was at a time when the public sector optimism of the 1960s was evolving into an era of uncertainty and retrenchment. The OU was almost from the outset challenged to demonstrate that its idealism and technological innovation were not being pursued at the expense of good management and operational efficiency. Eventually the very content of the OU product was attacked for its alleged hostility to capitalism and the market economy. What saved the university, and prepared it for a further phase of growth in the 1990s, was precisely the combination of democratic values and practical competence which it had striven so hard to keep in balance. By the late 1980s its delivery of access and quality had built up a body of affection in the country among tens of thousands of current and former students and among millions of late-night television viewers whom it could draw upon in times of political confrontation. When pressed, employers in both the public and private sector came out in support of the university's contribution to the economy, and when enquiries were made into value for money and quality-assurance pro-cesses the rigour of the OU systems generally proved robust. The university was in some respects a machine, but it also promoted individual opportunity and social progress.

4

Sensemaking and sociability: the first two decades of learning

'The first and most urgent task before us', said Lord Crowther in his foundation speech, 'is to cater for the many thousands of people, fully capable of a
higher education, who, for one reason or another, do not get it.'[1] The Open
University's first Chancellor made it clear that teaching and learning were
to be at the core of the new institution. His ambitious target was to support part-time and mature students without prior qualifications to complete
modules which need not necessarily lead to a degree.

The teaching methods of other universities – the lecture, the seminar and the
tutorial which had been developed for young, full-time students with A-levels –
required adaptation. The thousands of new students led one commentator to
remark that 'the distinctiveness of the teaching situation stems from the sheer
complexity and size of the OU teaching system'.[2] By 1977 the total OU student
body consisted of 57,820 students (of whom only 390 were postgraduate
students and only 50 were full-time). There were 288 central and 196 regional
academics who developed course materials and supervised part-time tutors,
respectively. There were 5,262 part-time tutor-counsellors and course tutors.[3]
The first two sections of this chapter examine the innovative methods of creating and delivering the curriculum. In the third section these developments are
discussed in the context of the shifting nature of the student body.

The first section considers the OU's distinctive approach to the organisation of teaching and learning. Although a state-funded university, the OU
drew on methods more familiar in the private sector. In the words of one
commentator, 'like most organisations of our age the Open University has a
production-line system like that of the Model T Ford'.[4] The aim was to ensure
that students received high-quality teaching which was sufficiently similar,
whatever their circumstances, to enable them to study assessed modules over
many years in order to gain a degree. This required teams of academics and
other specialists who would centrally control the production and distribution
of a blend of media, notably print, television and radio.

In the second section the focus is on the debate surrounding what one OU academic characterised as 'a systems-based industrial model of academia'.[5] Teaching at the OU was never simply the creature of administrative or political pressures or economic models of efficient production and nor was it ever entirely free of those constraints. According to David Harris, the 'teaching system was shaped as much by administrative and political pressures as by any particular educational goals'.[6] There was an inherent tension between the scalable methods and the anti-elitist approach to education. The OU was the most pedagogically conscious university in the UK. It maintained a critical stance towards conventional higher education and at the same time subjected its own methods to continual assessment and review. Broadcasting was seen as 'everyman's classroom' in 1972 and became the most outwardly distinctive aspect of the university's delivery mechanism. At the same time it did not enable the OU to challenge 'the idea of what a classroom was [in] a flash', as has been claimed.[7] The broadcast material was perceived as lightweight by some, overweight by others and (particularly in the case of radio) sometimes unpopular with students.[8] Over the course of twenty years, elements of the initial pedagogic framework were perceived by internal critics to be passive, hierarchical and resistant to supporting dialogue. The conception and design of programmed learning were deemed 'largely male areas' (while the materials were delivered to a large number of female students), and the innovative course teams which produced the teaching materials came to be seen as unwieldy, long-winded and argumentative.[9]

In the third section the impact of the OU's teaching strategies during its first two decades are presented in terms of the development of an active student body. Kitchens, ships and the airwaves became new locations for university learning where the social order could be re-imagined. The OU developed strategies for teaching adults, many of whom were long out of school, who often had unpleasant memories of their own formal education and who were physically separated from one another. Participation, dialogue and self-help were encouraged. Technological developments such as cassettes, videos and computers were deployed to personalise the learning process. The student body was not constrained by the boundaries of a campus but was a transitory cultural formation in several places at once, sustained by shared engagement in texts and programmes and supported by tutors. The OU's efforts to enable learning to become lifelong and ubiquitous were dramatised by a play, later a film, *Educating Rita*.

The production of learning

Unlike many other universities the OU was able to start afresh, with few of the constraints associated with funders' desires, academic traditions or location. The course team, one of the OU's distinctive contributions to teaching and learning, embodied many of the attributes which helped the OU in its first two decades. During the 1970s and 1980s, ideas derived from industrial production informed this new concept which became 'the power house of the university'.[10] The notion of flexible project groups was proposed by the Planning Committee.[11] At its first meeting Senate agreed to make the course team the basic academic unit responsible for the development of a multi-media course. Academics, project managers and BBC staff formed teams within what Walter Perry called a practical system 'designed as a whole from scratch'.[12] They were joined by educational technologists who, it was argued by one of their number, 'made a crucial difference to the work of course teams'.[13] While they were often involved in activities 'akin to an industrial process', they were also structured in such a way as to enable opportunities for intellectual challenge and stimulating debates.[14] Two OU academics reflected on the role of teams. Kate Bradshaw felt they were

> a very methodical, and innovative process where material was proposed, approved, written, read, commented on, rewritten, modified, re-commented upon and then edited by people in house and edited by the Course Team Chair. It was extremely thorough.[15]

Robin Wilson, who 'was quite excited by being in this melting pot of all these different people with different skills', noted that 'those with industrial experience could bring it to their teaching which no one in Oxford could' (Figure 4.1).[16]

The concept of the course team was lauded by the BBC's Chairman, George Howard, while the Corporation's Director General, Charles Curran, saw it as effective. It was seen by the Vice-Chancellor as way of enhancing the relationship between the OU and the BBC.[17] Teams were said to provide moral support for staff and aid their professional development. They led to 'an improved regard for teaching'.[18] Raymond Williams considered that the idea of a package of materials which were to be used for each specific week of study, the course units, was an outcome of this 'uniquely valuable experiment'.[19]

From the start a systems approach informed plans on how to create courses.[20] The idea was that all the components of the process of deciding on the right subjects to teach, preparing the materials and delivering the teaching needed to be seen in relation to one another. Once courses had been delivered, through broadcasts, books and tutors, there would be a cyclical link back to

Figure 4.1 Robin Wilson's innovative and supportive teaching of mathematics has been fondly remembered by many students who arrived at the OU with memories of the frightening and incomprehensible method used when they were at school. A report on the OU's use of television made in 1974, when this image was first broadcast, noted that a 'significant number' of programmes were 'a film of a classroom lecture albeit with elaborate or rather clever devices to replace the blackboard'. This style of delivery was parodied by graduates of other universities such as those who made the 'Open University blooper reel', for the BBC series *A Bit of Fry and Laurie*. In this Hugh Laurie played a mathematics don called Robin.

the creation of new courses or the improvement of existing ones. However much thought was put into course design, plans needed to be amended in the light of real-world experience. For example, it was realised that laboratory and fieldwork required more time than the scheme had initially allowed and that the role of the BBC needed clarification.[21] The process of course production was lengthy and paperwork-intensive. Teams completed a proposal form for a course up to seven years before the course was to be presented to students, and then completed at least ten other forms in subsequent years. This process was still largely in place in the 1990s.[22] The detailed nature of the course-production process was not an exercise in bureaucracy for its own sake, but was aimed at creating a continuous cycle of improvement. Brian

Lewis's twelve-page flow chart included structured liaison and feedback loops which, once courses were produced and delivered, enabled analysis of their impact in order for them to be improved.[23] It was these evaluation exercises that the Director of the OU's Institute of Educational Technology (IET) argued made the university 'the only higher educational system that is self-improving through the use of objective data'.[24] Researchers at the IET emphasised the importance of feedback: 'educational technology prides itself on its devotion to evaluation and improvement'.[25] There remained room for debate about the operation of the process. Alan Woodley, an IET researcher, sounded a note of caution, recalling that 'They'd got this very mechanistic view of a course having errors that would be corrected. Now I went to course team meetings and it was very obvious that life isn't like that, the course isn't like that.'[26] Nonetheless, a mechanism had been put in place for keeping the outcomes of the course teams under systematic review.

Just as the OU borrowed some of its production processes from industry it was also optimistic about the role of technology to deliver teaching. Television, as part of a blend of media, was seen as an ideal medium for the OU which would enable the best teachers to reach a large number of learners (Figure 4.2). In 1965 C. P. Snow (who had spoken of 'two cultures' dominating the educational system in the Rede Lecture of 1959) was Parliamentary Secretary to the Ministry of Technology. He argued that 'the educational use of television could be of real value to the nation'.[27] A government report declared in 1969 that it was 'no longer necessary to argue that the broadcasting media, when imaginatively used, are efficient means of instruction' as part of a broader educational system, 'since that has now been established by an adequate body of research'.[28]

Through television the OU promoted learning to millions unfamiliar with higher education. It widened access and bolstered the confidence of those on the brink of imagining themselves capable of advanced study. It was through television that the OU entered the popular consciousness (Figure 4.3). Perry noted that at first 'the University was widely regarded as a creature of the BBC. As a result many of the enquiries both from within Britain and from abroad were directed to the BBC and not to the University itself.'[29] In 1973 Martin Trow, an American commentator on British higher education, saw the OU as evidence that 'higher education at the high standard of British universities can be offered to men and women in their own homes through the imaginative use of new technologies' (Figure 4.4).[30]

When using television, the OU built on the communication styles familiar to producers and academics. Often this was the lecture. In 1964 the Hale Committee Report on university teaching methods started 'from the

Figure 4.2 Making recordings with the BBC was an important part of the process of teaching. The relationship between the BBC and the OU operated at many levels. Jennie Lee proposed that BBC2, launched in 1964, be focused on educational programming, and it was proposed that the BBC should be given a permanent seat on the University Council. It was decided that the remit of BBC2 would be broader and that there would be a series of agreements between the OU and the BBC. There were disputes: for example, in 1970 the Corporation's Controller, Finance, complained that 'Perry appears to be obsessed about controlling the BBC'.

Figure 4.3 'I hope that Kenneth Clark is going to present the Arts course for us' wrote Jennie Lee, and indeed Clark's 1969 television series *Civilisation: A Personal View* was used as a benchmark. Nevertheless, there was also a wide range of presentation styles. This is TS282, being presented in 1972.

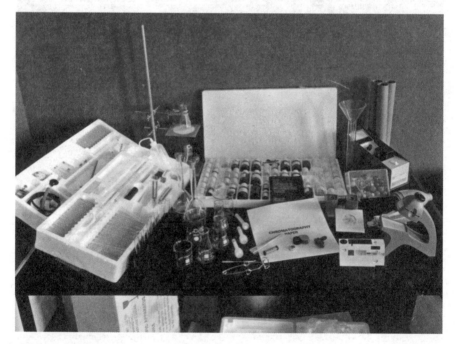

Figure 4.4 Home experiment kits, such as this one, were mailed to students' homes enabling them to take part in practical experiments.

standpoint that the main object of a university course should be the development of a student's capacity to think for himself and to work on his own'. It concluded that

> one important justification advanced for the central position given to the lecture is the immaturity of students who are thought to learn more rapidly by listening than reading ... [N]o one doubts that university students are not sufficiently mature to dispense with oral teaching.[31]

This interest in lectures was adopted by the OU Advisory Committee, which intended to broadcast talks by distinguished lecturers. In 1971 Richard Hooper, a consultant to the US Commission on Instructional Technology, argued that 'the lecture as the medium of college communication could now be set fair, thanks to television, for another 100 years'.[32]

Through the Arts Foundation course *Humanities: An introduction*, A100 (1971–77), several thousand students were introduced to university-level study across a range of subject areas, including art, civilisation, culture, drama, history, literature, music, philosophy and poetry. The Dean of Arts called it

> frankly a compromise, one worked out through many months of patient negotiation, between a variety of sometimes conflicting opinions and interests. Sometimes it achieves an integrated approach; sometimes it is interdisciplinary; sometimes it is merely multidisciplinary.[33]

One of its broadcasts, *Music 1*, on the topic of 'sound', took the form of a studio-based lecture. In another, on reading poetry, three academics discussed a seventeenth-century poem. The poem was read out while the text scrolled across a black screen and viewers were invited to offer their own analysis. A third programme, *Primary sources: A case study of Stratford upon Avon*, involved an informal, multi-voiced, conversational style with a lively dialogue between historians. Material related to D. H. Lawrence's *The Rainbow* included a recording of Bertrand Russell's memories of Lawrence.[34]

The need to reiterate ideas and to address a wide audience had an impact on delivery. 'Uses and abuses of television', a broadcast made for the Arts Foundation course A101 (1978–86), started with a lecturer explaining the aim and included two men reading the same script in different styles and differently edited versions of the same event. Words appeared behind the speaker (as if on a blackboard) and later across images. Viewers were asked to assess and categorise images and to make notes. In subsequent programmes there was reiteration and repetition, examples from course materials, discussions and references to exercises in the broadcast notes.

For *Haemoglobin*, Programme 1 of *Biochemistry and molecular biology*, S322 (1977–85), Max Perutz used a static model, moving graphs, equations, diagrams, a clip of an experiment and a view down a microscope as well as lecturing to camera. Robert Bell, an OU lecturer, recalled 'seeing an early Maths programme shot on a rubbish dump, and certainly many of them involved ingenious working models that would have been unavailable then in a conventional university'.[35] John Brown, a student on the first presentation of the Technology Foundation course, felt that 'TV is useful because the models come across very well' and that television programmes were easier to follow: 'a child could because they don't attempt to show you the more difficult ideas which are contained in the [written course] units'.[36] The materials for *Drama*, A307 (1977–81), included the transmission of sixteen fifty-minute plays. BBC producers were course team members, whose intellectual and creative input was appreciated.[37] BBC producer Nick Levinson recalled that he was given greater freedom with drama for the OU than for documentaries. Once the script was finalised, he was allowed to take on a role akin to the director in the theatre.[38] The A307 teaching materials included a written section on 'Using television in a drama course', a studio plan, a camera script and a radio programme discussion about the adaptation of stage plays to television.[39] Although drama had been taught at the University of Bristol since the late 1940s, the idea that the meaning of a play had been fixed by the playwright remained a popular one.[40] By contrast, Brian Stone, Reader in English Literature at the OU, argued that students should be able to see plays for themselves. His A307 teaching materials explicitly instructed students: 'Do not regard each programme as definitive … you should bring your free and concentrated response and your informed critical judgment.'[41] Students were also encouraged to perform dramas for themselves while at residential summer schools.[42] The classicist Professor John Ferguson, Dean of the Arts Faculty, introduced the scenes but there were also efforts to develop students' critical awareness of how each performance of a play was an interpretation of the text. This was done through multi-camera work in the studio. For A100 (Arts Foundation) students were offered written material about the sources for information about Socrates and televised scenes from Aristophanes' *Clouds*, in which Socrates appears as a character.[43] In the broadcast's introduction John Ferguson is shown with cameras around him and there is a moment when both a Greek character – Strepsiades, played by Juan Moreno – and the Dean are in shot. Similarly, Shakespeare's *Hamlet* was not presented as an uninterrupted performance. Instead academics discussed different ways of interpreting individual scenes. These interpretations were illustrated through performances by actors. Cicely Havely, then a lecturer in literature, recalled that the intention was to counter the notion of a single definitive performance.[44] She noted that there were different opinions about how to perform the nunnery scene from *Hamlet*, telling students:

> you may suspect that such differences are very artificial and have nothing to do with the play on the stage but a proper critical attitude is as necessary to the producers and actors as it is to the student reading the play. ... There are no stage directions for Hamlet's tone of voice, no gestures marked in. The producer and the actors have to add these things themselves by responding to the text creatively and critically.[45]

For most courses the aim was that students should spend about ten hours a week viewing and listening to broadcasts and another hour reading the related commentaries. The Survey Research Department reported that first-year students spent between eleven and thirteen hours per week in this way.[46] In 1972 Maureen O'Connor felt that when rigorous broadcast material was linked to written material, the OU 'is in the process of proving itself in some ways superior to the traditional universities'.[47] The challenge was to ensure that such connections were consistently made. A 1974 study concluded that 'examples of truly integrated television, radio and study units are rare, most often the integration is at a superficial level'.[48] But even where the programmes fell short of their ideal form, the content was policed by its public exposure. The standard of material remained high because, as Professor John Beishon noted,

> You are being watched by the general public, students and other colleagues. Institutions stand or fall by their teaching, scholarship and the material they produce, so ours has to be damn good.[49]

The Times pointed out that

> The OU was always more than television broadcasts. Indeed the title University of the Air was grossly misleading. Since about 90 per cent of the work took the form of correspondence, the University of the Post Office would have been a more apt title.[50]

The Planning Committee made it clear that it was 'neither practically possible nor pedagogically sound to rely on broadcasting as the principal or exclusive means of instruction in an operation designed to provide disciplined courses of university level'.[51] In 1971 Raymond Williams noted:

> We can't be too often reminded that the Open University isn't just a series of television and radio programmes. People looking in on it from outside are of course very likely to gain that impression.[52]

In the same year one of the OU's lecturers felt it necessary to stress that 'the television and radio components form only 10 per cent of the students' work-load'.[53] A report in 1974 did not focus on television. Rather it noted that the courses 'rely heavily on written material with relatively little face-to-face tuition'.[54] Nevertheless, in 1975, John Ferguson complained that

> people used to speak loosely of 'the BBC university' and I have heard a senior Conservative politician explain the initial hostility of his party to the Open University as arising from 'suspicion of those left-wingers in the BBC' ... The written word remains paramount.[55]

In an era before it was possible for most people to record television broadcasts, some students could not watch the OU programmes, for example those at work, in prison or out of broadcast range. Material that was broadcast was therefore not central to assessment. Nevertheless, the perception was maintained that the OU 'made extensive use of television to support its teaching programmes. These programmes were also available to the general public on a free-to-view basis and they did a lot to publicise the new institution.'[56]

The model of industrialised delivery also influenced expectations about the interaction between students and teachers. At first the importance of these staff members to all students was not recognised. The first Vice-Chancellor, Walter Perry, argued that the centrally produced material would be of such strength that there would be 'no need for face-to-face tuition – except remedially'.[57] In *Teaching by correspondence in the Open University*, 1973, tutors were told that 'the main function of the course tutor is his [sic] correspondence work'. However, many with experience of face-to-face lecturing tended to offer 'minimal interaction with the students', rather than developing an effective discussion.[58] Tutors, in an analysis based on tutorials recorded in 1980, felt that 'there is an irresistible pressure for them to "talk and chalk"' and that they were hired 'to transmit information'.[59] A survey of 602 tutors and 457 students found that there were differences between disciplines and that tutors' conceptions of tutoring were often more elaborate than those of students. One tutor felt herself to be a cog within an alienating system. Referring to 'the loneliness of the long distance tutor', she noted that 'if I grade out of line the computer will pick up my aberration, or if I write too few comments my staff tutor will phone me ... I am infinitely replaceable.'[60] Analysis of two OU foundation courses concluded that the effect was 'to constitute the students as a mass and the tutorial staff as a powerless subordinate priesthood'.[61] A course chair said of his own course that there was 'a good deal of truth' in the view that it was 'packaged and administered knowledge, [and] constructed its students as passive learners'.[62] Nick Farnes of IET noted that an OU student had few responsibilities: 'in our teaching system all decisions are made for him: what is be learnt, the sequence in which it is be learnt, the material he is to study, when in relation to other materials he should read page 38, when to watch television and listen to radio'.[63] In 1976 Harris and Holmes also described the OU system of pre-selection and pre-pacing as one of centralised control.[64]

However, expectations about the duties of tutors and the role of students began to change. For *Mass communications and society*, DE353 (first presented in 1977), there were formal examinations and group-based projects, which carried a collective grade. In 1984 *Education for adults*, E355, included a core of readings with a 'wrap-around by the course team who suggested frameworks, rather than defining the field of study'. Students were encouraged to add readings to the collection. Although the examination date and the continuous assessment deadlines were fixed, there was some flexibility in regard to the order in which texts were studied and there was a project on a topic which individual students selected for themselves. All but one of the assignments 'was deliberately designed to be concerned with the individual life experiences of the students either as teachers or learners'.[65]

Two of those involved in creating the course emphasised the active nature of learning:

> This not only facilitates a 'pick and choose' approach by students but also directly involves them in the challenge of developing their own interpretations of the very diverse nature of the literature and research in the field.[66]

A year later a staff tutor argued for 'the notion of teaching becoming less central to education than the notion of "self-direction" and "participation"'. He went on to propose that knowledge 'is not something that can be easily fixed or pre-packaged but is something more uncertain, tolerant of contradiction and individually and socially dependent'.[67] In 1985 Woolfe suggested the OU had had a major impact in challenging the view of tutors as employed to fill 'empty vessels or disembodied brains ... full of facts or to impart a body of knowledge'.[68]

In order to encourage tutors to support students' learning, training was developed from 'a cottage industry into a well-developed and comprehensive system'.[69] When technologies were introduced, tutors were provided with ideas about their effective use. In 1973 Heddwyn Richards established a system in Wales whereby students used free-standing loudspeaker telephones. After press reports of this, the GPO complained but later a concession was granted. It was important to ensure that students were offered comparable experiences, no matter where they lived or who their tutors were. It was recognised that students needed to have opportunities to scaffold each other's learning and to communicate what they understood. In the first edition of the OU-based journal *Teaching at a Distance* Hilary Perraton pointed to the importance of dialogue:

> There's that old Oxbridge theory that education is something that you get off the walls along with the ivy that grows on them, and that story about the talks into the small hours over cups of coffee as the central part of the university experience. There is an appalling amount of inherent snobbery in the idea, but there is also a germ of truth in it. The germ of truth is that we look for some kind of supporting network within which we learn things.[70]

At first OU tutors were offered little advice as to how to use the broadcast programmes. In 1973 material for tutors suggested that they train students 'to make the best use of broadcast materials' but that they should 'work out their own ways of doing this'.[71] Bates recognised that 'we have surprisingly little knowledge about how students can make best use of broadcasts and what problems they encounter in learning from broadcasts'. As a consequence he aimed to 'provide a framework within which you, as counsellor or tutor, can provide advice for the students [as] there is obviously a job to be done by tutors and counsellors in *training* students to make the best use of broadcast materials'.[72] He wanted students to avoid passive listening and employ a questioning and active approach. In 1982 it was noted that 'there is still a great deal to be understood about successful learning from television' and that students needed to develop 'a critical approach and a good visual memory'.[73] Generic advice to tutors was replaced with more detailed broadcast notes and course-specific guidance for both students and tutors. For example, the cassette handbook for *Culture and belief in Europe 1450–1600*, A205 (1990–99), provided instructions about what students should do to prepare for the programme and the questions they would need to consider. More generally tutors were encouraged by Richard Lewis to develop an 'enabling role', and to support self-help study groups. They were urged to 'take an interest in self-help groups' by Gibbs and Durbridge, who listed the qualities of a good tutor, which included 'an informal egalitarian style'.[74]

Standardised testing, homogenised curricula and batch processing of cohorts of students may have been important features in the initial teaching model, but it soon became apparent that learning was more effective when staff and materials encouraged each student to participate fully, to play to their individual strengths, to be respected and to gain a sense of belonging. The process of reflection and review that was built into the university's pedagogic systems, together with the very public nature of its televised output, caused a series of modifications to the use of technology and the roles of staff and students. As we shall see in more detail in the next section, within a framework of a saleable product and a consistent user experience, tutors were encouraged to take a more creative role and students were expected to become more active learners.

Beyond production lines

An industrial model implies a linear process along a production line. At the OU, however, staff and students invented, disseminated and shared ideas about teaching and learning. Collaboration was multi-directional and technology was not simply adopted, but adapted. The commonly held perception of the OU as transmitting knowledge through the air or via tutors puts an emphasis on methods of delivery which fails adequately to capture its anti-elitist ideals.[75] During the 1970s the work of the educator Paulo Freire became more influential within the university. He proposed that much education reinforced existing social relations by separating teachers and learners and by encouraging the teacher to 'fill students with the content of his narration'. He was concerned that, in dominant educational models, students were being treated as 'receiving objects', presented with packaged sets of pre-prepared materials, marketed as desirable learning outcomes and delivered by part-time academic labour. Freire described such teaching as 'educational banking' because a teacher narrated – that is, made a 'deposit' – which filled the listener's head, irrespective of the relevance of this activity.[76] 'Banking' impeded the development of a student's critical consciousness, as it required students to be passive and did not encourage dialogue.

Before the OU opened, the model of the lecturer as didactic expert who would transmit to students had begun to be displaced by a model which valued experiential and interactive learning. In the 1950s Professor G. P. Meredith initiated the use of 'mutual tuition' groups in the Psychology Department at the University of Leeds, in which students were encouraged to work with one another. The experiment led to the institutionalisation of the idea at Leeds by 1962. Other universities developed student-directed learning groups. There was analysis of collaborative approaches.[77] In 1970 Norman MacKenzie was among those who argued that a student's colleagues often represented the least recognised, least used and possibly most important of all the resources available to him.[78]

A study of medical students suggested that 'the optimum length of a lecture may be 30 instead of 60 minutes'.[79] Learners forgot and had attention lapses, while their processing and retrieval procedures interfered with the efficiency of the lecture. Others acknowledged the ineffectiveness of monologues. The OU staff had a strong sense of leading change in the higher education system. One Dean, echoing the university's founding Vice-Chancellor, claimed that 'much that goes by the name at teaching in the conventional universities is utterly unworthy of the name'.[80] Another recalled that, prior to being appointed to the OU, he taught at a campus university where 'the way we were teaching people left a lot to be desired'.[81] At the same time the very public nature of the OU experiment generated a critical commentary. Even the use of new technology was not in itself enough to overcome the problems of traditional academic lectures. In 1979 a TV critic called OU programmes

> heavy-going material ... showing an intense teacher, lacking style and bad at conveying enthusiasm. Lecturing straight to camera in a mono-tone from notes on a blackboard. [82]

It was also difficult for the lecturer. OU academic Dave Elliott commented that 'after about ten minutes reading an autocue you tended to glaze over'.[83] One researcher claimed that the OU 'represents the logic of "banking" at its clearest: the remoteness of academic staff, the impossibility of detailed discussion between students and staff, the underlying belief in education as telling, the anonymous abstractness of courses, the pervasive assessment scheme'.[84]

Efforts were made to resolve the problems. There was an increased use of self-assessment questions and 'pause for thought' text boxes, which were designed to encourage learners to suspend their reading of a text in order to engage in specified reflective tasks. A formal recognition of the need to employ the most appropriate pedagogy was made in 1973, when the OU awarded Freire an honorary doctorate at the first OU degree ceremony (Figure 4.5).

Educating Rita

Any association made between the OU and the notion of educational 'banking' was weakened by the popularity of playwright Willy Russell's two-hander about the relationship between a 26-year-old female OU student and her tutor. Educating Rita, first performed in 1980, with a film version released in 1983, shifted attention from the centralised production of materials to the personal experiences of individual students

(Figure 4.6).[86] Following a student from the time she overcomes the difficulty of entry to higher education – she is literally impeded, as she cannot open the door at the start of the play – to her final entrance and scene when she is calm and confident about her ability to succeed within the conventional academy, the emphasis was on personal liberation through learning.[87] It positioned the OU as part of a long tradition of motivating forces in tales of women who through their own transformations transform others. Russell's conventionally structured play echoes the tale (recounted by Ovid in the eighth century CE) of the sculptor Pygmalion, who fell in love with a statue he had carved. Ovid's tale was the basis for G.B. Shaw's 1912 play Pygmalion and the 1964 film adaptation, *My Fair Lady*, in which a professor of phonetics, Henry Higgins, bets that he can transform the speech of a cockney flower-seller, Eliza Doolittle, so that she will pass for a duchess. Russell did some of his research for the play at the OU and in the film course materials appear and are discussed.[88]

Gill Kirkup noted that while the play 'purports to show the change in a mature women student who takes an Open University course' it revealed (if it was 'indicative of common beliefs' about the OU) that the OU's teaching system 'seems to be widely misunderstood'.[89] The OU's pedagogy appeared to mimic that of the one-to-one Oxford college tutorial. Rita gains cultural capital through her trips to the theatre, does not mention watching the OU's BBC broadcasts and is dismissive of the possibilities of learning through television.[90] Nevertheless, the text was used to illuminate and support the OU's mission. According to staff tutor Paula James, when students studied *Pygmalion* on the level one Arts Foundation course, A103 (1998–2008), they regularly put on an *Educating Liza* sketch for the arts event evening during residential school week. 'So Rita in one version or another has long been part of the OU fabric and culture!'[91]

To celebrate forty years of the OU, The Open University in the South East and Pitchy Breath Theatre toured a version of the play. Director and actor David Heley said of a performance in HMP Swaleside that the audience there was 'totally engaged' and that 'many of the prisoners said how they recognised themselves within the play's action and meaning' (Plate 8).[92] In 1983 the play was deployed for marketing by the OU, which produced a flyer to accompany a professional performance:

EDUCATING RITA. YOU COULD BE A RITA TOO!

As you watch Rita's intellect developing throughout the play you might be tempted to ask 'Could this really happen in everyday life?'

The answer is 'Most definitely yes' as thousands of adults have proved during the last thirteen years of The Open University. So far more than 57,000 have graduated with a BA degree and very many more have taken single one-year courses. There are no educational qualifications for The Open University, admission is on a first-come, first-served basis, and study mainly involves working at home. Of 5,945 students who graduated last year 17 per cent are housewives, 8 per cent are clerical and office staff and 8 per cent are technicians. 9 per cent had left school at 15. Nearly half of the graduates were women.[93]

Figure 4.5 The BBC kept Alexandra Palace open as a production centre for the OU, and the location of the OU's headquarters in Milton Keynes was selected in part because of the proximity of radio and television studios. Instead of being held on a campus or civic site, as was conventional for many universities, the OU's first degree ceremony was screened live from Alexandra Palace in 1973. On this occasion Walter Perry told the first graduates – there were over 900 of them: 'We have come up with what is undoubtedly the most difficult way of obtaining a degree yet devised by the wit of man. [You] have exhibited not only the necessary intellectual capacity but also qualities of staying power and determination.'

Figure 4.6 University Secretary Joe Clinch and *Rita* star Julie Walters demonstrating that the OU could still use old-fashioned 'chalk 'n' talk' for teaching.

At this time of increasing emphasis on students as active learners, one of the key components of the OU's course-production system came under scrutiny. Course teams were accused of being expensive and time-consuming because, although originally they consisted of between nine and sixteen people, within a few years some were two or three times that size.[94] A report based on a study of the OU in 1972–73 noted that 'ideally there are 18 to 20 academics on each course team, although in practice the number is likely to be considerably smaller'.[95] They were also said be slow to respond to the demand for new materials, so that teaching material was unable to be made topical.[96] Despite being contractually obliged to attend summer schools, and initiatives such as that of 1976 when the Maths Faculty ran a half-credit course tutored by two central academics, central academic staff were considered by some to be remote from students.[97]

In 1974 two staff members produced a critique which focused on the OU's structure:

> Like most organisations of our age, the Open University has a production-line system. Many different people help create the teaching material: authors, educational technologists, editors, designers, illustrators, photographers, television producers. All these work in separate departments, often quite uncoordinated one with another, and all too often mutually suspicious rather than co-operative.[98]

Training was formalised through the lengthy *Course Team Chairman's Handbook*, the first version of which was condemned as 'a total disaster'.[99] Although a series of courses for prospective chairs were established, criticism continued. It was argued that teams felt constrained by rigid timetables and focused on meeting production deadlines and that they allowed practical matters to dominate proceedings because pedagogy was considered a matter for individual authors.[100] A number of studies noted that while course teams often started with enthusiasm, as deadlines approached so collaboration and engagement were reduced. In addition, some team members did not offer criticism, either through a sense of ignorance of the subject matter or because they did not wish to receive criticism by way of reciprocation.[101] Some felt constrained or intimidated. Managing the teams was often stressful. This matter was raised at Senate.[102] George Low recalled that 'within course teams there was very vigorous debate, and sometimes it was well managed'. He also mentioned one debate which 'went on for twenty-four hours or forty-eight hours; it went on forever and, I think, in some cases people had to seek therapy on that one'.[103] On occasion:

> there develops a destructive environment which by the end of the life of the CT [Course Team] has become a punitive one. Course material is produced but usually by a very small residue of the original CT.[104]

Joan Whitehead recalled attempts to belittle women team members when tea was brought: 'they expected you to stand up and, and pour out the tea ... we had a little argument about that'.[105] In 1975 the Professor of Materials Science at the OU assessed his own time as a course team chair and concluded that 'I would want to experiment with ways of structuring the course team'.[106] Although Perry spoke of how the team system 'evolved', by 1979 one Dean felt that the course team had become 'a cancer' within the university.[107] He was rebutted.[108] However, addressing the question 'Do we really need course teams?' Malcolm Tight suggested the need for significant reform of teams a few years later.[109] Over the next few years faculty and university guidelines narrowed. There was a reduction in the number of members of a course team and the time spent on the production of materials. Educational technologists and editors played a reduced role while tutors and students were given new roles within course teams.[110] The aim was to ensure that the problems of course teams being cumbersome and fissiparous would be countered if there were fewer members from across the OU. These changes might also reduce stress and ineffective critiques. Inviting the participation of students and the part-time tutors whose teaching was based on the course materials and who assessed the assignments of the students helped to reduce the sense that OU materials were written with insufficient sense of who the students were.

These changes to structures within the OU illustrate a notable feature of the OU: its use of evaluation and research to improve its methods. The Planning Committee recognised that the innovative teaching methods of the OU would lead to new areas of research into distance teaching, which could occur without disrupting the teaching. Decades before the practice was introduced to the conventional sector, it was decided to assess teaching, student views and assessment on an annual basis. The OU both sought to study the effects of its own teaching (principally through the IET) and to present this research to its students. In 1977, in an OU television programme asking how open the OU was, Dr Ken Jones drew on his own research in order to demonstrate that education was perceived as middle class.[111] He proposed study centres in industrial premises and the offer of guaranteed places for industrial workers. The OU sought to use its research findings in order to challenge elitist assumptions: 'to explode the degree mythology; the impression that only a very small proportion of the population, the seven or eight per cent who go to university are capable of degree work'.[112]

Although some academic staff, the part-time tutors, did not have research in their contracts, the OU nevertheless encouraged them to engage in action research with a view to improving the effectiveness of teaching and learning. This aided their integration within the OU. Walter Perry noted that 'it was the intent of the new university to promote the research activities of its academic staff, an intent from which the Open University has never wavered'.[113] The idea that collating and evaluating data could support learning was developed by, among others, Paulo Freire. He argued that 'participatory' action research could challenge students, the subject being taught and the wider society.[114] The modular design of the teaching at the OU, whereby students could register for one course of either 30 or 60 credits at a time. They were advised not to study more than 120 points at any one time. For their part the 7,000 specialist part-time staff might teach on only one course. Students could take a break from their studies before resuming later, having banked their credit. This led to problems of progression towards a degree, and necessitated an approach to recruitment markedly different from face-to-face universities, where students were recruited once for a degree, not many times for separate courses. It also placed a large burden on the tutors, who, for many students, were the face of the OU. They assessed a student's course work (generally 50 per cent of the final marks, the other 50 per cent being assessed through a conventional examination) and, along with the counsellors, provided individual support for students. Some tutors engaged in research into the most effective teaching practices, and, as well as being published, their conclusions helped to promote the idea, adopted by government, that teaching practices were both important and could be improved.[115]

Along with evaluation of teaching methods, the content of learning materials was also appraised. Initially OU broadcasts reflected the BBC's modernist sensibilities, which led to an emphasis on progress, higher standards, greater knowledge and the spread of control over nature and society. These ideas are reflected in the influential BBC series *Civilisation: A Personal View by Kenneth Clark*, which established the benchmark for educational broadcasting of the era.[116] Despite the title, the focus of this television series was on the history of Western art, architecture and philosophy. The script and the best-selling book which accompanied the series were written by the presenter, art historian Kenneth Clark. The series was aired in colour, initially on BBC2 and subsequently all over the world. George Howard, Chairman of the BBC, called the series 'entertaining and educative as well as being informative'.[117] Walter Perry saw Clark's account of Western societies, and also the BBC's weekly documentary series *Panorama*, as 'crucial' to the development of the Open University.[118] Senator William Benton's publications were also influential. His series *Great Books of the Western World* connected commerce to an account of cultural heritage which he hoped could enlighten citizens and act as a bulwark against communism. Walter Perry noted that the effect of the OU having limited access to broadcasting meant that the media needed to be used strategically. He impressed on the OU the need to use television and radio 'not as gimmicks but to provide the kind of teaching that we cannot provide in any other way'.[119]

The *Civilisation* model was soon adapted. In the Science Foundation Course programme a presenter called fluorine 'the Tyrannosaurus Rex of gases' and thus triggered an animated cartoon form of a roaring dinosaur in a crown, while a colleague employed the phrase 'going down the scale' and then played a recorder on screen. It was difficult to strike an appropriate balance between academic and presentational ambitions. The depth of intellectual engagement displayed in, for instance, a programme for *Comparative politics*, D232 (1979–86), *Madhopur and social change*, and one for *Systems performance: Human factors and systems failures*, TD342 (1976–83), led them to be described as on a par with *Einstein's Universe*, and at the same time two other programmes were deemed 'slickly professional'.[120] A scene in *Understanding space and time* (1983) of ice skaters in period costume was cited as an example of the OU being 'dangerously close' to being unduly influenced by the mainstream's 'cosmetic tricks'. One critic noted that 'it really is quite hard to overcome the feeling today that watching entertaining coloured television programmes is just an excuse for not getting down to some hard work'.[121] Paddy Maguire was irritated by the 'self-conscious didacticism, tinged with aspiring populism customarily adopted by Open University or schools programmes' producers, wherein an adoption of the familiar second person is presumed to serve as an aid to historical imagination'.[122] Conrad Russell claimed that the Humanities television material was 'extremely bitty' and that 'the television programme on the Yorbas [Yoruba], in sharp contrast to the correspondence material, sounded as if it had been put together by a competent travel agent'.[123] The approach taken by television production teams could run counter to the intentions of the academic staff. An example of this is in a course where social scientists sought to convey that unemployment was not necessarily the fault of the individual unemployed person; the way in which television framed the issue, by focusing on case studies of unemployed people, undermined this point.[124]

The OU also had to negotiate with the BBC over broadcasts. The partnership had its successes and there were examples of a symbiotic relationship between BBC and OU staff. Colin Robinson had 'very good relations with colleagues' and recalled that 'a course team would turn to me and say ... what do you think? Is there a film here or not?'[125] Dave Elliott presented the relationship in terms of strength: 'You needed a strong producer who was certain what he wanted, and an academic with a clear view of what he was trying to say. If either was weak, it didn't work. You got the best programmes with the two of you arguing over every line – but with respect for what the other was trying to do.'[126] Donald Grattan called Walter Perry 'a practical fellow [who] understood the nature of the broadcasting'.[127] Perry recalled that the relationship between senior staff at the BBC and the OU was 'always a happy one'.[128] The first agreement with the BBC (there have been six over the years) referred to how 'a reasonable degree of flexibility on both sides is essential'.[129] It was clear that the OU would, 'except for cogent academic reasons, accept the advice of the Corporation on the preparation and presentation of such programmes'.[130] Most of the directors had a degree in a relevant subject and some had taught within further or higher education.[131]

However, the responsibility for the teaching and the integration of the material lay with the OU.

Translating the collective enterprise into practical outcomes generated frequent debate and argument. There were disputes about how to present information, with producers being accused of 'superficiality' by Conrad Russell and of having a desire 'to mix teaching and entertainment' by John Sparkes.[132] There were discussions over the principal audiences for programmes.[133] The Controller of BBC2, Aubrey Singer, had Jarry's *Ubu Roi* and Büchner's *Woyzeck* (plays made for *Drama*, A307) rescheduled to less popular times of day, and he wanted some controversial scenes from Genet's *Le Balcon* (translated by Bernard Frechtmann) re-shot. The OU refused to remake the scenes and so the play was not broadcast, though it was shown at summer school. Press coverage of the resulting row in the *Observer*, *Guardian* and *The Times* was sympathetic to the OU. There was also support for the OU from other academics.[134] The Chancellor rebuked the BBC at a degree ceremony for its decision not to broadcast the play.[135] There was also acrimony over the coverage provided in the BBC's listing magazine, *Radio Times*, and the announcement of forthcoming programmes.[136] On a more day-to-day level there were disputes about the sets, the clothes presenters wore and presentation skills. Michael Drake, once summoned from Milton Keynes to Alexandra Palace to adjudicate when a BBC producer objected to the colour of politics lecturer Mike Barber's shirt, openly speculated about the OU working with ITV

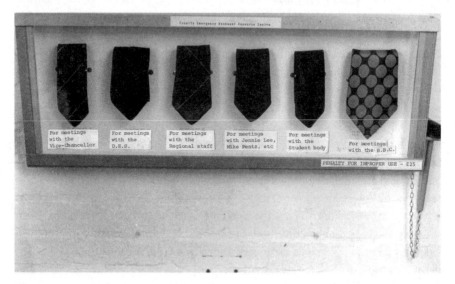

Figure 4.7 The appearance of those OU staff who presented on television was the subject of considerable comment, but at Walton Hall dress codes were often more informal.

instead (Figure 4.7).[137] Hilary Perraton noted that 'there are real conflicts of interest between producers and academics [and] not enough contact between the people on the two sides of this particular fence'.[138]

It was not only the cultural framing of OU broadcast materials which caused concerns. The volume of broadcast output also presented a difficulty for the OU. The number of OU broadcasts rose as the number of modules being presented rose. In the first year of broadcasts, 1971, 124 programmes were made for the four foundation courses, *Basic mathematics*, *Understanding science*, *Understanding society* and *Literature and civilisation*. There were to be 30 hours a week of OU television broadcasts for 36 weeks of the year, 'together with supporting programmes as may be mutually agreed'.[139] In subsequent years there were more courses and a need to repeat the programmes associated with the existing courses and so the number of programmes was increased in 1972. Within a few years there were over 1,000 hours of OU BBC radio and television broadcasts. There was a similar competition for airtime on the radio. A total of 1,500 radio programmes, equalling 26 hours' broadcasting a week, were transmitted in 1978 when the university was producing about 300 new television and about 300 radio programmes every year.[140] In 1979/80 the BBC produced 274 OU programmes and during the academic year 1979 it transmitted 1,502 programmes, using over 35 hours a week of transmission time, at a cost of £7,017 million.[141] If that had continued then there would have been up to 1,900 programmes to be transmitted each year by 1983. In fact the BBC reduced the number of hours allocated to the OU and changed the times of transmissions. In 1983 only 500 OU programmes (12 hours per week) were transmitted.[142]

Although Jennie Lee initially campaigned for BBC2, launched in 1964, to be devoted entirely to education, the idea was rejected. Subsequently the OU student body campaigned for 'an educational television network' but to no avail.[143] However, the issue became of less significance because the use of television for education began to decline. In the USA interest in educational television for adults fell during the 1960s.[144] During the 1970s other countries did not develop their use of television.[145] The OU noted that the number of viewers and listeners fell.[146] The OU did not wish to be tied to one medium but to present ideas and support the construction of knowledge through a variety of media. Surveys indicated that women tended to find their opportunities to watch OU programmes on the television constrained by household and childcare duties, and that social sciences and educational studies students attached a lower priority to watching OU television than science students. In 1986 those studying *Health and productivity in dairy cattle*, P690, found the four thirty-minute television programmes too elementary.[147] Recordings of programmes were made available in study centres, and loans of playback equipment were made as few students had access to such equipment.[148] Some programmes were made for summer schools where tutors could pause the programmes, and live programmes, which caused some anxiety to producers and presenters, were reduced in number.[149] In addition, in line with other open universities, the OU began to 'move from broadcasting'.[150]

Although colour TV sets did not outnumber black-and-white sets until 1976 in Britain, OU programmes began to be made in colour. Soon the cost of making programmes accounted for over 20 per cent of the OU budget. However, the cost of producing television programmes did not result in significant pedagogic benefits. Professor David Murray recalled that 'one of the difficulties with television programmes was that we only had enough money basically to do one programme that included any film and one programme that was talking heads'.[151] *Themes in Wittgenstein's philosophy*, A402 (1976–82) and *Differential geometry*, M334 (1976–90) did not use television, and there did not appear to be any apparently detrimental results.[152] Moreover, there was academic distrust of non-print media, inadequate coverage (television reception was poor in some areas of the country), poor time slots, and disputes between broadcasters and academics. Television showcased, for all viewers, both the OU and university teaching in general. However, OU programmes were expensive to make, the relatively few transmissions made repeated viewing difficult, which reduced their pedagogic value, and the transmissions were increasingly at unpopular times.

Cassettes

Technological developments were employed to aid the personalisation of learning. When audio cassettes replaced radio transmissions, Tony Bates proclaimed that the 'greatest media development during its [the OU's] twelve years of existence has been the humble audio cassette'. They were relatively inexpensive, there was felt to be greater academic control over content than was the case with BBC broadcasts and they could be more easily integrated with other material. Initially, audio cassettes were used to store radio programmes. They later came to be used for commentaries on other media, enabling students to listen to recorded conversations accompanied by commentary as well as specialist lectures.[153] In 1978, 40,000 audio cassettes were distributed, a number that rose to 500,000 by 1983. Sold at 75 pence each, they were popular with students who liked their informality and flexibility. Some felt a personal link to the recorded voice. A popular brand of audio cassette player, the Sony Walkman, was being advertised as a symbol of a freedom, youth and portability.[154] Cassettes were deemed more helpful than transmissions, and by 1988 the OU was using less than a quarter of the radio transmission time that it had used in 1978.[155] Using a cassette a listener could stop and start and rewind at will, and students could use their senses and be active, or at least more active than when watching television. When a commentator asked the student to turn to a specific page and then restart the recording, or when there was commentary on a diagram, the student became the locus of interaction between different media.

Learning together

The creation and maintenance of an OU student body has been addressed by sociologists associated with the OU and can also be understood in relation to more generic theories. The student body, made up of people who differed widely in age, background and previous qualifications and who connected to one another only through the OU, can be understood as a series of new communities of learners who met in new spaces, creating new knowledge. Through a system of mutually reinforcing reciprocity this has bolstered the OU and helped it to become naturalised within the British landscape. The OU student body did not rely on locality. In the 1960s case studies of social groups understood them within networks of local social relations. Examples of such work include Michael Young and Peter Wilmott's *Family and kinship in East London* (1957) and *Family and class in a London suburb* (1960).[156] These indicated the importance of particular localities through the generations. Having argued that 'the old style of working class family is fast disappearing' they sought to study the changes through a local case study.[157] Their conclusion was that in their narratives people retained links to a specific heartland. There are similarities to Dennis Marsden and Brian Jackson's 1962 narrative study of Huddersfield, *Education and the working class*.[158]

By contrast, the 1966 'University of the Air' White Paper was 'influenced by MacKenzie's visionary ideas'.[159] Norman MacKenzie, a lecturer in sociology at Sussex, emphasised the value of technology and multi-media tools for education, expression and communication. He formed a committee on new methods of teaching and learning at Sussex and in 1967, funded by the Rank Organisation, became the Founder-Director of the Centre for Educational Technology there. The work carried out there influenced the OU.[160] MacKenzie joined the OU Planning Committee and was a founder member of the OU Council. To MacKenzie's perspective, which envisaged communities transcending locale, was added a new way of understanding and eliciting the participation of OU students within the institution. Naomi Sargant (later Lady McIntosh) studied sociology, worked within market research, was an associate of Michael Young on the National Consumer Council and joined the OU in 1970, becoming Pro-Vice-Chancellor (Student Affairs, 1974–78) and a Professor of Applied Social Research. Through sample surveys and interviews she 'brought the disciplines of marketing to education before anybody else did ... the voice of the students, fronting the on-air Open Forum and developing a programme of research on their needs, patterns of participation and achievement'.[161] Although 18-year-old students might be categorised in relation to their fathers' social class, Sargant argued that this was a less satisfactory definition of class when used to define people who were considerably older and who had careers of their own; they could be addressed as respondents in their own spaces. This was the approach adopted at the OU. Individual students were not automatically located within families, and class was abstracted from previous ways of understanding it in terms of local social relations.

This was a period associated with the expansion of new industries, the growth of white-collar work for the welfare state and the rise in status of expertise and planning; it foregrounded technical, formal education as a route for social mobility.[162] People had begun to create new identities for themselves. They were no longer embedded in their childhood landscapes but instead based their identities on where they chose to put down roots – on where they elected to belong.[163] They felt able to 'locate themselves outside of place, able to fix on, and choose, where they want to live. This is a discourse of strangers.'[164] When, in 1963, Harold Wilson argued that Labour, with its 'white heat' of technological revolution agenda, would be able to reverse the economic decline, he made the idea of a 'university of the air' central to his thesis. Wilson linked the distance education proposal to the aspirant, emerging, technocratic, scientific intellectuals who had a 'nascent technical identity'.[165] Identities could be strengthened when scattered strangers such as these were connected to one another through the OU. They could be helped to form new epistemic communities. The combination of mass literacy, mass access to broadcasts and a university which recognised that knowledge could be constructed through educational dialogue and activity enabled geographically dispersed OU students to create the networks that are central to the student body.

The OU's collection of data for evaluation, which was then used to refine and reshape its methods, indicates how a centralised system could rely on feedback from its dispersed population and how social science apparatus and quantitative data became central features of modern governance. It was an exemplar of the circularity whereby 'the idea of the modern nation, which could be subject to rational planning, was itself dependent on the mobilisation of sampling methodology'.[166] In 1972 Naomi Sargant argued: 'it is important that this new educational system be adequately evaluated both at the level of effect on the individual student and at the level of total impact on the country as a whole'.[167] This challenged previous ideas of a student body as limited to those registered at a given institution. She went on to stress the active role of students:

> Given the scattered nature of the population under study and its commitment, heavy reliance has so far been placed on self-administered questionnaires. We have been fortunate in having the goodwill of the students. Good communication with them, our respondents and customers, is as important as good communication with our clients.[168]

Naomi Sargant's team, by revealing the student body to be at home in many places, strengthened the wider movement to conceptualise social relations without recourse only to households and localities.

Michael Warner has argued that a new 'a space of discourse' can be formed when texts, circulated among strangers, enable those people, through those texts, to organise together and to have experiences in common.[169] The OU provided the texts, home experiment kits, correspondence materials, television broadcasts, tutorials in study centres and attendance at residential schools which enabled a distinctive student body to be created (Figure 4.8). To learn science no longer required specialist laboratories and students did not have to be on a campus. The home could become a place for university-level study. In the home experiment kits mailed to the first students were over 8,000 tiny (5in × 3in × 1in), cheap (£15 each), lightweight microscopes designed

Figure 4.8 A selection of teaching materials mailed to each of the students who studied P554.

Figure 4.9 Two of the technologies that the OU used in the 1970s: the television and the McArthur microscope.

by Dr John McArthur (Figure 4.9). McArthur conceived the idea of the lightweight microscope in the 1930s and sold his first one in 1957. It enjoyed sales of about 1,000 in its first decade.[170] The OU recognised that many of its students would be unfamiliar with delicate scientific mechanisms or would find it difficult to keep their study materials safe from other family members and ordered a new, simple, robust version with no delicate rack and pinion system for focusing and an objective lens which was very difficult to damage. The inclusion of the microscope in the kits showed the OU's commitment to using technology to support active learning and encourage students to collate and compare results (Figures 4.10 and 4.11). Subsequently, the OU's virtual microscope was developed, enabling students with internet access to explore digitised slides and thin sections and gaze upon images which leading scientists and academics were also examining. These are examples of the ways in which evolving technologies have been used to overcome physical separation.

The university encouraged collaborative learning and helped people to improve their skills, confidence and motivation, to strengthen their identities as learners and to gain a clearer sense of the relationship between learning and the wider world. Tutors were urged not to concentrate only on imparting the canon of accepted knowledge but rather to encourage students to question the assumptions underlying the canon. The significance of self-esteem to

Figure 4.10 Some home experiment kits required the preparation of materials by OU technicians, in this case rock samples.

learners was recognised, and there was encouragement of the respect of the life experiences of other adults. In addition, the OU promoted the development of student-directed learning groups.

These temporary communities could be in specific localities. In 1971, Technology Foundation students formed a self-help group in Beaconsfield 'to discuss their mutual problems, to interpret the course work questions – but, above all, to get that personal feel for what was really expected of them'.[171] Inspired by her students, counsellor Olga Camm recalled joining a similar group which she felt aided her studies and her social connections. Other groups were encouraged by the OU and by 1974 there were over 1,000 self-help groups.[172] Many others recalled the social and intellectual benefits of working with other students.[173] Pauline Swindells met a fellow student who lived near her on a foundation course and they formed a bond: 'We did everything together, our tutorials, our TMAs, summer school and had a very good time.'[174] Ernie Barnhurst, a student in the 1980s, remembered that the

Figure 4.11 Home experiment kits enabled students to learn about science in their own kitchens. The man is using the McArthur microscope.

students 'met in pubs to discuss particular elements of what we needed to do'.[175] Diana Purcell, a tutor-counsellor who taught in the 'H' Blocks of the Maze Prison, Belfast, remembered prisoners helping one another: 'nearly all of them but particularly the IRA, they set up the system if they arranged to do an OU course then they had to give a talk about what they were studying each week to the rest of the guys in that section ... they were extremely good students ... encouraged each other too, which was very good'. [176] The idea of collective self-help was integral to the community education schemes run between 1977 and 1985. These included a system of voluntary local coordinators who put students in touch with one another.[177]

The engagement with the OU changed these locations, be they prisons or pubs, into sites that were part of society but that were also, when used for studying, located outside the mainstream of day-to-day reality. At the university's foundation, Geoffrey Crowther, the first Chancellor, called the OU 'disembodied'. He collapsed the dichotomy between the public and the private and recognised that university studying could occur in locations which had not previously been used for such purposes (Figure 4.12). To study in the home,

Figure 4.12 For some students finding a place at home for all their teaching materials was a problem.

the workplace, the study centre, the residential school was to be in, to employ Michel Foucault's term, a heterotopia – that is, a 'place which lies outside all places and yet is localizable'.[178] These locations were both isolated and penetrable, their focus and meaning unfixed. Students in front of the television set or on a ship (Foucault's examples of heterotopias, with their own rules and practices, included prisons and ships) could rearrange the conventional uses of space, creating a laboratory, lecture theatre or seminar room and juxtaposing 'in a single real space, several spaces, several sites which are themselves incompatible'. These heterotopias were not utopias, which were imaginary, but 'other places' in which existing arrangements were 'represented, contested and inverted' and individuals could be apart from the larger social group.[179] While the literal meaning of utopia is 'no place', an OU-topia could be almost any place. Through students' engagement with texts, broadcasts and other learners, spaces in which the social order could be made and remade were created (Figure 4.13).

Even when physically isolated, an OU student, when engaged in studying, could be part of the OU student body through being involved in learning through dialogue. Assessing the teaching of history at the OU Arthur Marwick noted that 'the emphasis throughout is not upon the teacher offering some kind of performance ... but on encouraging the student to do the discussing, to develop the skills ... We attempt, in our correspondence texts, not to purvey facts and opinions but to encourage the student to argue over

Figure 4.13 Students took the opportunity to study in many places.

and discuss various ideas.'[180] Marwick himself 'loved pontificating in his typically combative Scottish way that provoked a few frights'.[181] The *Daily Telegraph* called him 'a boisterous, pugnacious Scot who enjoyed a good academic scrap'.[182] Bernard Harrison worked for the National Extension College and taught on the London external degree. As a tutor-counsellor on three OU courses he argued that tutors and students were 'fellow-travellers on the outside rim of the Open University wheel' and he sought to encourage 'independent, self-directed, critical thinking'.[183] Another tutor-counsellor described how, because she was unable 'to integrate' a student with disabilities 'into the group as a participating member', she became 'concerned for his development as an effective learner' and sought to develop 'mutual trust and respect between us' so that he could become 'a confident independent learner'.[184] This concept was promoted at the OU. John Ferguson contrasted the style with that of other universities where:

> Many students would pass through their whole student career without any effective personal confrontation with individual members of staff. In Buber's language there was no I-Thou encounter.[185]

It was difficult for the OU to be personal when addressing the 70,000 people who studied with it in the first decade. Its structures, its fragmentation of tasks, mass production, assembly-line manufacture techniques for mass consumption, 'lines of study' and 'production' of 'units' of teaching materials indicate some of the aspects of the OU which could impede personalisation. As a Dean, John Ferguson 'resisted any tendency towards a departmental organisation'.[186] A means of reaching students personally was provided not through central academic teams, but through its system of providing counsellors and tutors. In this way the OU integrated the process of learning and the personal experience of learning. Indeed, 'considerable emphasis is placed on individualising the instruction. Study centres, summer schools and self-assessment exercises are all attempts at such personalisation.'[187] The OU also offered opportunities for students to reflect on their strengths and weaknesses and review their motivations. Students received computer-generated letters but also personal telephone calls. While recognising the need for consistency and the mass production of course units, the OU sought to engage students by encouraging them to build communities. It promoted dialogue as an aid to intellectual development and learning.

The OU student body was also constituted through engagement. Students were required to demonstrate their involvement by participating in the continuous assessment element of their courses and frequently through attendance at residential school. Students studying *You, your computer and the net,*

T171 (1999–2005), were required to take part in online discussions. Over 100 of the earliest students on *Art and environment*, TAD292 (1976–85), helped to remake the module for subsequent presentations. The reciprocity between those defined as learners and those paid as teachers indicates how the OU student body was connected to the texts through students' interactions.

The OU also used television to help strangers find connections and form themselves into the student body. It spread knowledge through its support for the integration and synthesis of information with prior learning. In 1972 the intention of a psychology course film of children talking and teachers at work in schools was for the student to hear 'not the analysis of a lecturer but the actual voices of teachers, children and parents ... the filter of the lecturer's personality has been effectively removed'.[188] David Boswell's sociology film, made in a hostel for 'the mentally subnormal' according to the parlance of the time, showed the group relationships through the use of a hidden camera. There was little editing as the aim was that students could form their own opinions and use these as a starting point for discussion. The BBC producer explained that the programme 'represented slowed down reality upon which the student can wreak his sociology'.[189] Marwick's aim was 'to leave each piece of film to speak for itself without being overlaid by an intrusive commentary'.[190] Television was also said to engender a sense of community by acting as a bridge between the academy and the popular and enabling students to feel closer to academic staff. Of the first 310 people to appear in OU television programmes, 150 were students, and Walter Perry suggested that the television programmes 'probably have a subtle effect in fostering a spirit of comradeship among distance learners'.[191] He recognised that television could be a way of helping 'to develop a sense of corporate identity for students and staff' and went on to compare *Open Forum* (an OU television programme) to *Sesame* (an OU newspaper) in that both played 'an important role in our informal communications system'.[192] The OU saw television as a means by which people could be encouraged to form their own understandings. The OU also encouraged students to use computers to support learning through promoting interaction and dialogue. The dichotomy between impersonal mass production and distribution and a student's personal relationship with learning shifted as the technology developed in a way that could be deployed to support collaboration.

The OU did not take a linear journey from passive to active learning. Rather, having been founded in an era when it was assumed that knowledge could be transmitted to students rather than built by them, the university moved through a process of debate and experiment towards the promotion of dialogue as central to study. While ideas spread unevenly, learner-centred education gained increasing influence in the OU's pedagogy. The university came to perceive its students not as deficient in terms of understanding the accepted canon but as former strangers building knowledge and communities through participation and shared experiences. Students had a sense of belonging, activity and membership and could organise themselves to constitute an unstable, changing public of OU learners. The OU's relationship with its students developed through this circularity. Evidence about how learners made their own meanings based on what they knew and what they sought to achieve accrued, becoming the basis for further developments which in turn enabled the OU's texts to have a greater impact.

'Education is a wonderful thing'

In *Educating Rita*, as the play's title implies, Rita is both being educated and educating others.[193] Throughout the play there is a debate about the nature of learning and knowledge and the extent to which Rita is transformed by her own efforts compared to the influence of her tutor, Frank. Initially Rita feels that her mind is 'full of junk' and that a 'good clearing out' is required and that what she learns from Frank 'feeds me inside'.[194] She admits that she nearly wrote 'Frank knows all the answers' across her exam paper. In addition, she dismisses as 'crap' *Howards End*, a novel which involves co-operative learning between practical people and intellectuals. She expresses scepticism of the approach favoured by theorist Jean Piaget. She describes how at school the pupils would be having 'a great time talkin' about somethin' and the next thing [the teachers] wanna do is to turn it into a lesson'.

One reason she changes is to fit into the academic world. She alters her accent from Scouse to what the stage directions call a 'peculiar voice' but is then dismayed that she has become, in her words, a 'freak' and a 'half-caste'. Echoing this, Frank refers to himself as Mary Shelley, author of a novel about the creation of a man-made person, *Frankenstein*. Having assessed the notion of learning as transmission, Rita then takes control of her own learning and makes only the changes that she requires. In addition, she is able to teach her tutor as well. Just as he asks questions, so does she. Asked why she did not attend a conventional university following her compulsory education she answers with a question: 'What? After goin' to the school I went to?' Once Frank has suggested to her that 'you'll have a much better understanding of something if you discover it in your own terms', she claims to have 'begun to find me' and she reverts to her previous name. She changes, but not into a typical student, at Frank's 'Victorian-built university'.

For her last appearance she does not, as she did before, unpack her notebook and pen. Instead she picks up some scissors and draws on her own skills, which she employs within the learning environment. She starts to cut hair. Neither Delilah nor Sweeney Todd, when Rita returns to hairdressing she wields the scissors in a more knowing fashion than at the beginning.[195] This framing device indicates Rita's circular route, her return to her roots, offering reassurance that, while learning changes people, the effects are likely to be positive. Rita, by taking flight from the humdrum, paradoxically took the university from where Geoffrey Crowther had placed it in his speech at its foundation, as 'disembodied and airborne', and brought it down to earth. In summarising its activities as 'degrees for dishwashers' Russell's character domesticated the OU and placed it, reassuringly, if counter-intuitively, in front of the kitchen sink.

Conclusion

Those aspects of the OU summarised by two of its deans in 1971 as anti-elitism and a systems approach maintained their importance throughout the 1970s and 1980s. When they worked symbiotically and in balance with the needs of students a participatory ethos flourished. However, the relationship between the different elements was complex and fluid. At first the emphasis tended towards the mechanistic. Enthusiasm for television and centralised production was well established. The OU intended to use the methods of mass production in order to provide the materials to train the 'technologists who perhaps left school at sixteen'. It was their reskilling that Harold Wilson saw as central to the creation of a new Britain 'forged in the white heat of this revolution'.[196] Industrial production methods were used to ensure that masses of learner-centred material were swiftly and effectively delivered and tens of thousands of learners could engage with the materials and their tutors in order to create new meanings. Work tasks were fragmented, materials standardised and processes for assessment were made consistent across the country. The logic of manufacture for a mass market helped to ensure rapid growth of the OU. It was as if there was a production line making sacks, each one of which was unable to stand up if the interactions between learners, tutors and course materials were excluded.[197] By contrast, face-to-face universities appeared largely to be serving a limited pedagogy to a narrower social group. There was recognition that the OU set a public standard for pedagogy in higher education. For example, Cambridge University began to teach themes which crossed disciplinary boundaries and to make use of European television satellite links, team teaching, and the modification of lectures so that students were permitted to interrupt and discuss.[198]

At the same time as the OU was being established, the logic of high-volume mass production was beginning to be challenged. Lean, flexible, post-Fordist systems were promoted, accompanied by deindustrialisation and the creation of more work in the service industries.[199] Unskilled labour was becoming less important than teams of relatively skilled workers. Notions of independent learners and teamwork among both staff and students were not inherent within the inherited model. New ideas about collaboration were deeply influenced by the OU's first honorary graduate: Paulo Freire argued that transmission-focused teaching prevented students from renewing cultural knowledge through thoughtful conversations. At the OU it was made clear that 'more attention needs to be given to what learners actually do with the material', that there were many readings of any course text and that students resisted, rationalised and managed material in a variety of ways.[200] Learners, it was increasingly argued, needed to make their own meanings. The new knowledge they constructed was based on what they already knew and what they were trying to achieve. An identification of the importance of the cultural background of students led to surveys being carried out and efforts made to listen to and understand the lives of learners. Many of those within the wide range of learners felt marginalised and anxious. The design of courses and assessment could make use of sophisticated available technologies only if amended to respond to learners' needs.

Course teams, which devised the teaching materials on a module-by-module basis, lay at 'the heart of this particular university': they exemplified both the systems and egalitarian elements of the OU.[201] There was some degree of standardisation and a division of labour, and the teams were part of a chain of production and distribution with a global reach which enabled tens of thousands to study through the OU. Initially including academics and non-subject-specific members, notably BBC staff and educational technologists, these teams produced distinctive, robust and much-valued material through working intensely, and sometimes acrimoniously, together.

As a distance-teaching institution, the OU could have been associated with the isolation of correspondence tuition and the passivity associated with watching either trivia or talking heads on television. Instead it created a student body which was formed and reformed as texts (including broadcasts) circulated in ways which promoted shared, reciprocal experiences. Students' homes were where the pedagogy rendered the unfamiliar – university life – familiar while the habitus of domestic life was re-contextualised (Figure 4.14). The OU's central organisation and regionally and nationally based staff members developed practices which bolstered involvement. They used tutorials, television, print, computers, cassettes and videos to encourage learners to collate data and work in groups. This enabled members of the student body to buttress the OU and together engage in sociable sensemaking.

Figure 4.14 This image of a student, relaxed in a tidy home, complete with wedding photograph on display and quiet child, may have helped to reassure potential students that studying did not necessarily lead to a lack of attention to domestic matters.

Part III

The OU since the 1990s

5

Convergence and divergence

From the early 1990s onwards the OU became both more and less like the rest of the higher education sector. It was no longer directly managed by the Department of Education but instead shared in the evolution of the national funding councils. Where once it had been the only public UK university to charge for its education, the rest of the sector incrementally introduced fees. The focus of funding shifted away from government and towards individual learners and external partners.[1] This trend was exacerbated when, in 2010, teaching budgets were cut by 80 per cent and the UK government formally withdrew all funding for the arts, humanities and social sciences.[2] The OU had pioneered industrial organisational techniques in the creation and delivery of its teaching. Now higher education as a whole began 'functioning increasingly as an industry'.[3] A 'quasi-market' developed within an increasingly 'hollowed out' state sector.[4] Universities and polytechnics had to bid for funds for student teaching purposes from their respective funding councils, student fees were raised, grants were frozen and top-up loans introduced. Although there was little private capital involved and the state remained the principal funder and regulator, there was a sustained interest in corporate management structures, in encouraging competition between universities for resources and in promoting a market orientation. Some priorities changed (see Plate 9). At the same time, as we shall see in this and the following chapter, the digital revolution enabled the university to renew and extend its role as an innovator in large-scale higher education, delivering an increasingly global service that transcended the divide between formal and informal learning.

The first of the two sections in this chapter focuses on how governments sought to deploy versions of the market across the higher education sector.[5] The binary divide between universities and polytechnics was abolished and the harmonisation of curricula and qualifications was promoted when new standards for the quality of the learners' experiences were set. The performance of universities was audited. As the OU escaped direct ministerial intervention by coming under the control of the funding councils, so the councils themselves became more vulnerable to political influence. Various new bodies and market-like apparatuses for funding were developed, resulting in increasing similarity between the research aims and internal, fee, degree and pedagogic structures of all UK universities including the OU. In 1999 a series of international agreements initiated the Bologna Process, which promoted the standardisation of higher education qualifications across Europe. At the same time some universities began to formally stratify themselves and to compete for students.

The second section is an assessment of the OU's work in widening and internationalising what was increasing seen as a marketplace for higher education. During this period the OU both led change in the sector and was embraced by it. Within its established territory the university was exposed to increasing competition. By the early twenty-first century virtually every UK university delivered some kind of part-time course and had gained a competence in techniques of teaching at a distance. The OU's support for learning among older people, those with disabilities and those without prior qualifications was echoed elsewhere.[6] As distance education moved from the margins of policy and practice, the 'distance education tradition' became less distinctive.[7] Interest in widening participation spread across the sector. Where the OU had international partners queuing up in Walton Hall almost as soon as its doors were opened, now the sector as a whole looked to a range of overseas ventures as a means of compensating for the pressure on domestic revenues. The university responded to these challenges by participating in a more complex dialogue with other institutions and taking part in sector-wide innovations in quality review and enhancement. It also engaged in more direct competition with conventional higher education.

Mandatory grants and the centralised administration of university applications had been in existence since before the OU was opened.[8] However, these services had not been available to OU students. Open to learners without prior qualifications, the OU handled its own applications; some students received local authority grants or support from their employers. Following the acceptance of the recommendation of the 2010 Browne Report that part-time students should be eligible for loans for their fees, the OU agreed to enter the Universities and Colleges Admissions Service (UCAS) for both full- and part-time students from 2013. UCAS included information about the OU in its materials. However, in order for students to be eligible for loans from the Student Loans Company the OU's offerings had to fit into the same framework as that of other universities. Faculties needed to identify pathways for each undergraduate qualification. They began to be reorganised so that the focus was on qualifications, rather than individual modules. Student loans were offered for those who committed to study for a qualification or award, not a module, and the loans could only cover strictly educational costs, not, for example, accommodation at a residential school. Under the Browne proposals those studying 30-point modules were eligible for grants, but not those whose studies only amounted to 10-point (later called credit) modules. The OU created its own OU Student Budget Account loan scheme for those for whom the Student Loans Company (SLC) loans were not suitable or who were ineligible for an SLC loan. The OU also provided information, advice and guidance on loans. Students could study full time with the OU, which led to changes in the timings and procedures relating to module presentation. The curriculum was also shaped by the move, initiated in 2000, from a course, or module, to an award- or qualification-based curriculum. The intention was to continue to support students interested in personal development but also to increase the professional and vocational curriculum. While some curricula were designed to serve an occupational purpose (for example the Masters in Business Administration and the modules in nursing and social work), the intention was that the entire curriculum should be career-enabling, and that employability should be explicitly clear to students and employers.

At the OU the initial emphasis on older students has been qualified. Increasing numbers of younger applicants have studied through the OU. A policy review in 2008 concluded that there should be a greater focus on this market, as the university no longer saw 'mature leisure learners as a high priority segment'.[9] However, a further impact of the increase in fees associated with the new loans regime was that the OU's Young Applicants in Schools and Colleges Scheme (whereby about 25,000 school students studied OU modules) was closed in England, Wales and Northern Ireland when the fees were raised. It was retained in Scotland where the fees remained the same.

Change from without

British universities had long been both advised and audited by the state. From the late 1980s onwards, governments became more interested in greater efficiency within the sector. They sought to raise money through fees, to promote graduate employability and to encourage commercially relevant research. New national structures were introduced which gave politicians greater control over the universities. Planning increasingly tried to align student demand with the need for a skilled labour force.[10] Universities began to focus on the competencies required for a society in which wealth-generation was becoming associated with a knowledge economy.[11] Selective cuts in funding were used to steer universities towards a common path. 'British universities,' it was argued, 'could be autonomous provided they marched to the same drummer.'[12] One sign of the changes was that when the University Grants Committee was replaced in 1988, academics were a minority of the membership of the new Universities Funding Council (UFC). The UFC answered to an education minister capable of intervention whereas the old UGC had been, in essence, a Treasury committee. Funding was henceforth provided on an annual rather than triennial basis. There was a centralised assessment of performance and detailed and frequent reviews of the work of universities.

In 1992 the Polytechnics and Colleges Funding Council was merged with the UFC. The polytechnics were granted university status and competition between institutions in this new, larger pool of universities was encouraged. Although forty-two new universities were recognised between 1992 and 1994, in 1993 British higher education became less of a weakly connected, single continent and more like an archipelago of islands. This was because separate agencies were created for England, Scotland, Wales and Northern Ireland.[13] The new councils allocated funds based on the number of students who completed specified amounts of study.[14] As the boundaries of the OU's operations were not coterminous with those of the funding councils, this created some administrative difficulties. It was, and has remained, the only British university answerable to different funding councils and their political masters. However, the changes also 'enabled the OU to play a central and active role in each of the nations and to be regarded as a full member of the sector in each case'.[15]

In this new landscape, the OU was still allocated a distinctive role. 'Its general UK mission' was seen by the Department of Education and Science in 1991 as the provision of higher education through distance learning.[16] This echoed a 1985 White Paper, *The Development of Higher Education into the 1990s*, which envisaged that the OU would 'continue to be the main provider, as it is at present, of part-time education by distance means'.[17] However, competition within this sector increased with the redesignation of former polytechnics as universities and the exposure of older institutions to pressures to promote access.[18] During the latter part of the 1990s the number of higher education students grew by 13 per cent, with part-time growth more than four times larger than full-time.[19] By 1997, 37 per cent of study across the HE sector was part-time. The growth continued into the next decade. Between 2004 and 2006, 30 per cent of all HE qualifications obtained in the UK were obtained by part-time students, who also constituted 28 per cent of those who were awarded undergraduate degrees.[20] Conversely, full-time students were themselves more often attempting to combine study with employment. A study of final-year, full-time home undergraduates in seven UK universities, carried out partly by the OU's

Centre for Higher Education Research and Information (CHERI), found that over 50 per cent of the students were working between twelve and fourteen hours a week in term time.[21] Competition to the OU was also provided by further education colleges. Many of these offered part-time degree-level quali-fications, some validated by the OU, which in 1993 had acquired the functions previously performed by the Council for National Academic Awards (CNAA). An OU study of those who had considered studying at the OU but then selected another institution found that the 'missing market' was the older population and women returnees.[22] Although, in 2001, 16 per cent of the UK population was aged over 65 and there were more people aged over 60 than aged under 16, this study, OU's Academic Board concluded, 'did not see mature leisure learners as a high priority segment'.[23] The OU had a distinctive market role, but it was also part of the new mainstream.

The OU was initially a beneficiary of the reformed funding system. The first grant allocated to the university under the new funding regime was £98 million for teaching and research for the period August 1993 to July 1994. This represented what appeared to be an increase of £11.5 million (later revised to £10 million) on the equivalent sum for 1992.[24] The OU was also permitted to compete for additional funded places.[25] There was a 9 per cent increase in student full-time equivalent numbers during the first full year and a 3.5 per cent rise the following year. In 1994 the university received the largest grant and the largest percentage increase in funding of all the UK universities. Students at the OU were funded at a lower rate than students at other institutions due to their part-time status. As Martin Watkinson recalled, 'the public cost of an FTE student in science at the OU was 60 per cent of the average cost of a full-time student elsewhere. The figure for engineering and technology was 55 per cent and for arts and social sciences it was 45 per cent and 42 per cent respectively.'[26] The OU's teaching model ensured that any additional income could be used very efficiently. The funding was based on the assumption that the costs for each student would be the same, but the OU had economies of scale built into its structure. As the investment in cur-riculum and delivery systems had already been made, the cost of accepting each additional student was relatively low, amounting to the cost of student support, assessment and tuition. The OU's finances improved accordingly.[27] Despite the lower rate of funding for its students, the university had accumu-lated reserves of £37 million by the end of the 1993/94 financial year. Within a decade it had built up very significant funds.[28]

In 1971, 41,000 people applied to study for undergraduate degrees, 32,287 were offered a place and 24,220 accepted. Over the next decade the OU student numbers grew in line not with applications but with funding of places.

There were 61,000 undergraduates by 1980 and about 66,000 by 1983, with some 6,000 people graduating each year. There were over 72,622 students by 1990. The OU, in common with other institutions, was required to cap its student numbers. The OU received funding to increase its student numbers by 3.5 per cent in 1994/95 and by 1.3 per cent in 1995/96. However, as there were already a large number of students within the institution, in effect the university, despite protests, had to reduce intake by 3,000 places in 1995/96. In 1996/97 the OU's baseline grant was trimmed by £2 million in real terms when expenditure on higher education was reduced by 7 per cent.[29] By 1998 there were over 200,000 OU graduates.[30] The OU's worldwide student population was 200,000 individuals by 2005.

Fees, grants and Dearing

The OU had been initially conceptualised in national terms. Between 1972 and 1992 students registered within the UK, irrespective of where they lived, paid standard fees. Members of the armed forces in Germany and Cyprus and their families also paid these fees (Plate 10). Those students registered in Europe (there were schemes in the Benelux countries and Ireland) paid higher fees.

In 1997 the National Committee of Inquiry into Higher Education, chaired by Ron Dearing, considered students' contributions to the cost of their tuition. It recommended that 25 per cent of the cost of higher education come from fees.[31] Unlike full-time students, part-time students in higher education received no maintenance grants, loans, payment from access funds, tax relief on the payment of fees, or tax incentives for employers to pay their fees. Some local educational authorities provided some financial support.[32] Many part-time students also paid tuition fees. A third of students were studying part-time and Dearing concluded that 79 per cent of part-time students 'had their fees paid by their employer'.[33] However, this figure collapsed those who had all their fees paid and those who only received a contribution. It was based on a sample of 573 students at 11 institutions when, in 1996/97, there were almost 2 million students on part-time courses. Although the OU taught 30 per cent of part-time undergraduates it was excluded from the calculation. Phil Willis, the Liberal Democrat higher education spokesman, argued that 'the Dearing committee was misled'. Dearing apologised and the figure of 79 per cent of part-time students who were employer-funded was revised down to 33–40 per cent across the country.[34] It was 16 per cent at the OU. By the end of the first decade of the twenty-first century this had dropped to 23 per cent of all students (51,000) who were fully or partly sponsored by their employer, and 9 per cent of OU students (29,000) were directly and fully funded by employers. OU graduates were also left out of a survey about the impact of a degree on employment. Dearing did not act on the OU's submission that mature part-time students not only paid their own tuition fees, but in effect subsidised full-time students through their taxes. The report presented education as an investment in human capital and referred to the externalities accruing to higher education.[35] This spoke only to some parts of the OU's ethos. In considering all universities alike, the report encouraged the OU to adopt strategies which were similar to those of the rest of the sector.

A Labour government was elected in 1997, committed by leader Tony Blair to an emphasis on 'education, education, education'.[36] The new Prime Minister argued that the US domination of the international rankings was 'inescapably due to their system of fees'.[37] His 1998 decision to introduce means-tested fees across all the universities was the 'supreme fulfilment of my mission to ... modernise the nation'.[38] In regard to new funding regimes the OU was categorised with the other universities of the UK. By the measure of the new funding formula the OU had been underfunded in the past. However, students outside the UK (even those in the EU and HM Forces) were ineligible for funding and so the OU did not receive significantly more money.[39] It was over a decade before the fees were equalised and the OU was able to recoup the higher costs of operating in Europe.[40]

Some of Dearing's assumptions were echoed in Education Minister David Blunkett's 1998 Green Paper, *The Learning Age*. This emphasised the value of a flexible part-time student population, able to enter and re-enter education and training. A discretionary fee-waiver scheme for part-time students was run between 1998 and 2003, and in 2004 means-tested grants became available for the first time. The policy was part of wider plans for reform which aimed to change 'the monolithic nature of the service; introducing competition; blurring distinctions between public and private sector'.[41] The OU students, most of whom paid fees, had not had access to grants. In the late 1990s part-time undergraduates studying 60 credits or more who were on benefit or low incomes became eligible for fee grants and study cost loans. Part-time students who were registered as disabled could now receive disabled student allowances on the same basis as full-time students. These included resources for educational assessment, specialist equipment and non-medical helpers. When, in 1998/99, powers over education and training were devolved to the Scottish Parliament, the National Assembly of Wales and the Northern Ireland Assembly, Scotland reintroduced Individual Learning Accounts to provide support for part-time learners.[42] Those with an income of less than £18,000 per annum could claim £500 a year. In Wales, fee and course grants were introduced. England decided to treat part-time students on the same basis as full-time ones, requiring them to pay their fees following graduation if their income exceeded £21,000. In 2001, the OU was able to offer free places to 18,750 students on benefits and low income and to give Disabled Student Allowances to 2,200 students with disabilities. In 2005 the fee income of the OU was £123.1 million, about a third of the OU's total income of £375.8 million. It also received funding council grants of £212.1 million.[43] In 2007 the government decided to phase out funding for the majority of students in England studying for a qualification that was equivalent or lower than a qualification they already held. The 2010 Browne Report into the funding of higher education and student finance proposed that part-time students be exempt from paying tuition fees in advance. It also wanted the different funding streams for widening access (which included discrete funding for improving access and provision for disabled students) to be merged into a single fund. This was partially accepted. The government agreed that there should be extra support offered to universities to cover the cost of recruiting and supporting students from disadvantaged backgrounds.[44] However, the student loan rules and the overall increase in tuition fees deterred many potential part-time students. The number of Britons starting part-time undergraduate degrees fell by 40 per cent between 2010 and 2013.[45]

In other ways, the OU's development as an institution in this period was influenced by prevailing management trends in higher education. One of the last acts of the DES before it ceased to fund the OU was to commission a wide-ranging review of the university.[46] The Visiting Committee was instrumental in encouraging the review, and the OU provided considerable factual, statistical and costing information to it. Overall, the review was favourable to the OU's ability to provide for part-time degree students and it found it to be highly cost-effective. It concluded that while the priorities of the OU had shifted, further work was required regarding 'priorities and costed strategies'.[47] John Daniel, who became Vice-Chancellor in 1990, sought to address these concerns.[48] The OU was, once again, faced with a DES grant which was inadequate and there was little idea of what the final sum would be when announced less than a month before the beginning of the financial year. This made planning difficult, but the OU sought to 'secure cost efficiencies and increase net income'.[49] A Strategic Planning and Resources Committee was established and the Operational Planning and Budget Committee briefed to focus on implementation of the new committee's priorities. Two Pro-Vice-Chancellors took responsibility for strategy and operational planning and resources. There were a number of internal reviews including a joint one with the BBC of the OU Production Centre, intended 'to avoid significant future costs and provide recurring annual savings'.[50] There was also a review of the processes by which the OU planned academic provision and a review of planning and management information systems, and a hierarchy of trend information and performance indicators was developed. Working in teams, co-ordination and consultation remained important. As a complex and integrated organisation, a change in one part of the OU often had unanticipated effects upon other parts.[51] This meant that implementation proved difficult and in subsequent years the plan was revised. Nevertheless, the intention to run the OU along business lines was clear. A Professional Certificate in Management was launched and there was a stress on the importance of modern languages in 'political and industrial terms' and in terms of the 'market'.[52] When the case was made against the greater integration of Community Education with academic programmes the concern was raised that this would lead to a blunting of the programme's 'entrepreneurial edge' and the Vice-Chancellor referred to how academic units could become 'more entrepreneurial in their activities'.[53] In addition, attention was paid to customer services. In order to offer 'a speedier, more direct response' to potential students, regional centres began to receive and process applications for some short courses and were provided with a 'welcoming "front office"' and educational advisors.[54] There was also further integration within the higher education sector. The number of credit transfer agreements with other universities grew to twenty-six. An agreement with the polytechnics had been agreed at national level. There were also schemes involving studying by OU students in fifteen other universities.

In 1998, amid concerns inside the institution about the growth of a dependency culture and an over-reliance on senior managers, the OU established a Leadership Development Programme. The focus was on those with the potential to become senior post-holders. They were to be equipped both to support the OU's leaders and to enhance teams and links between different parts of the OU and different categories of staff. While this was presented as an effort 'to change the culture by identifying "rising stars"', the promotion of a distributed leadership reflected both management practice of the period and the OU's tradition of supporting adult learners, including staff. The role of Senate was reduced and over five years seventy-five people followed a Senior Leadership Programme. Many were promoted soon after completion.[55]

Ideas derived from the OU's distinctive teaching model spread and it began to change its model. The post of tutor-counsellor, a member of staff who offered support and advice on a personal basis throughout the university career of an OU student, was abolished in 1997. Many tutors combined their OU work with employment at other universities. Links between tutors of different universities were also formed through academic disciplines: in 1985 it was noted that many academics 'see their academic discipline as more important than the long-term well-being of the university which houses them'.[56] Moreover, the concerns of academic staff about the effects of audits and accountability contributed to their sense of being members of a besieged community. One OU professor noted:

> The introduction of markets and contracts, of private finance and entre-preneurial managers, of business values and public private partnerships into the public sphere is one that tends to produce responses rooted in nostalgia for the social democratic state.[57]

One of the effects of the new norms which framed academia was to reduce the sense of the differences between distance and face-to-face educators.

Bridges were also built with learning outside higher education. Research was carried out at the OU into the effectiveness of teaching by non-academic organisations, such as British Telecom (which used interactive video to train managers dispersed throughout the UK) and Price Waterhouse (which used a videodisc-based training programme to acquaint employees with poten-tial computer security risks). An 'Alternatives to print for visually impaired students: feasibility project report' was produced for the Mercers' Company and Clothworkers' Foundation.[58] A team from IET worked with Rank Xerox EuroPARC in order to design effective computer-based support for collabo-rative learning where people were located at different physical sites and con-nected via various forms of technology.[59]

The OU also continued to assess its own teaching in the light of the spread of new forms of educational technology in all levels of learning. In 1990 the Programme in Learner Use of Media (PLUM) was established within IET. It was intended to investigate students' use of and learning from various edu-cational media. PLUM superseded the Audio Visual Media Research Group, which had been created in 1970, and covered a wider range of devices, notably audio, audio-vision, audio-CAL, video, broadcast TV, interactive video, com-puters, CD-ROM and subsequent developments. PLUM assessed the teaching potential of video-cassettes and videodiscs and the implications of their mass usage for OU broadcasts. It also addressed questions raised by course teams and provided the evidence as to the impact of teaching through the use of com-puters. The reports indicated both gaps and achievements. Diana Laurillard employed a new methodology to assess the effects of educational television and found that only half the students in her sample who watched a social science television programme achieved the intended learning outcomes. She diagnosed the problem as being with programme structure rather than presentational quality.[60] Research at the OU drew the attention of the sector to how learning could be efficiently and effectively supported through a variety of media (Figure 5.1). In 2002 John Brennan, OU Professor of Higher Education Research, won an external grant to investigate 'What is learned at university'.[61]

There was also an increased interest in commonalities in syllabi and curricula across national boundaries and in the development of a global knowledge system.[62] Under the Bologna Process, the aims of universities were agreed to include the support of a democratic political system, a view endorsed by the World Bank.[63] In 2007 the Council of Europe stressed the value of 'Universities as Sites of Citizenship and Civic Learning'.[64] These were familiar notions at the OU. They were reflected in its first curriculum plan (approved in 2000) and in the revised versions produced in 2001 and 2003 and subsequently.[65]

John Brennan noted in 2008 that 'higher education institutions are increasingly encouraged to opt for institutional strategies led by institutional rationales'.[66] The OU had, from the outset, been a defining case of practice led by purpose. The encouragement given to other institutions from 1992 to specify their distinctive social and economic purpose brought them closer to the kind of enterprise that the OU had always been. As the OU, through its processes of internal review and external environment scanning, sought better to understand how its mode of education could serve the employment market and exploit the evolving media context, so higher education institutions around the world began to emphasise transferable skills in their teaching and knowledge transfer to industry in their research.[67] A succession of government initiatives qualified the status of universities as self-regulating autonomous institutions. They were more closely monitored and their academic integrity was more actively scrutinised. However, beyond the frequently short-lived regimes of individual ministers, universities, including the OU, were shaped by their interactions with each other, and by their shared exposure to the demands of a post-industrial economy. The OU can be seen to be part of the process of change, pioneering a range of practices including the modularised curriculum, research into student behaviour, fees for learning and the commitment to what came to be termed widening participation. In turn it shared in the currents of institutional reform which led to more professionally managed universities with more informed relations with external stakeholders. The extent to which it preserved its capacity for innovation and leadership in British and global higher education, will be considered in the following section.

Figure 5.1 Media development and learning at the OU.

1970s		1980s		1990s		2000s	
Broadcasts of module-related television	Interactive print media	Broadcasts of module-related television	Interactive video-cassette	Non-course-related television (outreach)	Interactive video-cassette	Non-course-related television (outreach) Mobile technology	Audio-visual digital media
Broadcasts of module-related radio	Tutors • face-to-face tutorials • telephone tutorials • postal correspondence • residential schools	Broadcasts of module-related radio	Interactive audio-cassette	Interactive integrated multi-media	Interactive audio-cassette	Social media	Web 2.0 and beyond
		Interactive print media	Support media • conferencing • email	Print media	Support media • conferencing • email	Support media • conferencing • email	Virtual worlds
		Interactive integrated multi-media	Tutors • face-to-face tutorials • telephone tutorials • postal correspondence • residential schools	Internet Web 1.0	Tutors • face-to-face tutorials • telephone tutorials • postal correspondence • residential schools	Tutors • face-to-face tutorials • telephone tutorials • postal correspondence • residential schools	Print media

This representation of the journey from reliance on broadcast, personal and postal delivery towards an increased use of disk-based media and online delivery is based on Josie Taylor, 'Learning Journeys: the road from informal to formal learning – The UK Open University's approach', *Journal of Interactive Education, Autumn*, 2013, accessed 15 October 2013, http://jime.open.ac.uk/jime/issue/view/2013-Autumn

1. The Open University in London
   Camden
2. The Open University in the South
   Oxford
3. The Open University in the South West
   Bristol
4. The Open University in the West Midlands
   Birmingham
5. The Open University in the East Midlands
   Nottingham
6. The Open University in the East of England
   Cambridge
7. The Open University in Yorkshire
   Leeds
8. The Open University in the North West
   Manchester
9. The Open University in the North
   Newcastle
10. The Open University in Wales
    Cardiff
11. The Open University in Scotland
    Edinburgh
12. The Open University in Ireland
    Belfast
13. The Open University in the South East
    East Grinstead

The Open University

11 Edinburgh
9 Newcastle
12 Belfast
7 Leeds
8 Manchester
5 Nottingham
4 Birmingham
6 Cambridge
10 Cardiff
2 Oxford
3 Bristol
1 Camden
13 East Grinstead

Plate 1 Regional and national centres of the Open University.

Plate 2 From the start the OU had to deal with a vast number of students and huge data sets. Staff soon became familiar with maintaining complex and sensitive data.

Plate 3 Finding a space was often a problem. In the East Midlands the extramural department of Nottingham University loaned the OU two rooms until a suitable office was found. David Grugeon, the first Regional Director for East Anglia, initially had a desk and a secretary. They shared a little room and utilised nearby space, including the local pub.

Plate 4 In Wales there was no office for over six months after Harford Williams was appointed as the Director in Wales. The University of Wales helped out by providing accommodation.

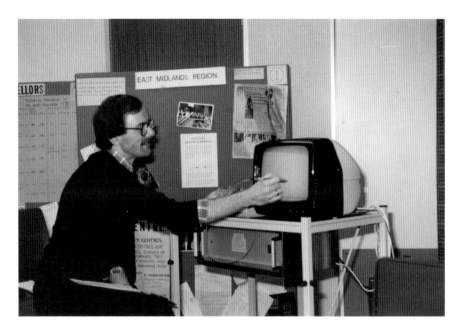

Plate 5 In 1982 a telewriting system was trialled in some study centres in the East Midlands. Telephone lines were connected to TV monitors so that drawings made on a screen in one location could be seen in other locations.

Plate 6 Professor Colin Pillinger, who led the European Space Agency's 2003 Mars Express mission.

Plate 7 Lifelong learners do not stop their engagement with the OU, even after graduation.

Plate 8 In 2009 real-life tutor David Heley and OU student Lisa Hubbard played Rita and Frank in a production of *Educating Rita* presented by the Open University in the South East with Pitchy Breath Theatre. This was part of the celebrations of The Open University's fortieth birthday. The production toured the UK, playing in theatres, schools, community centres and prisons. In the written programme to accompany it there was information about the OU and links to the website. The Regional Director explained that although 'Willy Russell's play is not a very accurate presentation of Open University tutorials it does capture the excitement of learning with the Open University and the life changing experience which our courses can bring.'

Plate 9a and b The Open University Students Association ran a number of campaigns to try and ensure that OU students received a fair deal. Many students found it difficult to access university libraries.

Plate 10 The OU had always been available to service personnel. It flew tutors out to Cyprus in the 1970s and permitted examinations to be sat on a Polaris submarine. Vice-Chancellor John Daniel further developed the links through an agreement with the RAF.

Plate 11 Elluminate was web-conferencing software which enabled students to meet via their computers and for tutorials to take place online.

Plate 12 Mavis Nkwenkwana, a teacher at Isithsaba Junior Primary school in Mdantsane, the largest township in East London, South Africa was one of those who studied through the Teacher Education in Sub-Saharan Africa programme. This took the OU's ideas about open learning and helping people to gain new skills into new directions.

Plate 13 In 2004 in Cape Town, Nelson Mandela accepted an honorary doctorate from Vice-Chancellor Brenda Gourley and Chancellor Betty Boothroyd. Brenda Gourley was born in Johannesburg and became South Africa's first female Vice-Chancellor. The OU has been teaching in South Africa since 1997. In 2005 it created the Teacher Education in Sub-Saharan Africa programme (TESSA) as a resource bank of teacher education materials. In 2011 it launched the accelerated and scalable Healthcare Education and Training programme for frontline healthcare workers in Africa, providing them with vital healthcare skills and the potential to save millions of lives.

Plate 14 Professor of Sociology at the OU, 1979–97, Stuart Hall retired to become an Emeritus Professor.

Plate 15 Martin Bean moved from Microsoft, where his work had been to harness technologies to improve teaching, to become Vice-Chancellor at the OU. Soon after his appointment he addressed a meeting in the virtual world of *Second Life* where the OU owned some virtual property. There is teaching material about this virtual world in *Understanding global heritage*, AD281 (2009–20).

Plate 16 OU students paid fees but, unlike other students, were not eligible for grants.

Plate 17 PhD student Rebecca Ferguson's poster about Schome, an informal collaborative learning project with teenagers in virtual reality. The project was sponsored by the National Association for Gifted and Talented Youth.

Plate 18 A tutorial in the 1990s. Tutors were encouraged to arrange the furniture so as to facilitate discussion and the co-construction of knowledge.

Plate 19 23 August 1985 was the last day of the final *Art and environment*, TAD292, summer school. Some of the students held a ceremonial bonfire of the course materials. David Ayres recalled, 'I finally went home on Monday night. Life was never the same again.'

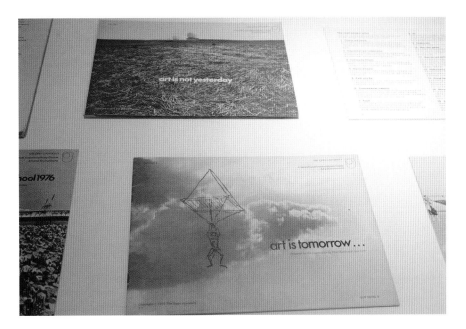

Plate 20 Olivia Plender's art installation, *Rise Early, Be Industrious*, which toured the country in 2012 drew on the OU course *Art and environment*, TAD292.

Plate 21 Discussion in a tutorial. Social and collaborative learning have long been important at the OU.

Plate 22 Learning together has long been encouraged by the OU.

Plate 23 Finding the time for both weeding and reading could be difficult.

Plate 24 While students learnt at home, many also attended field trips, often as part of their residential school experience.

Make a new start with The Open University

The Open University

Studying with The Open University

A guide for learners in prison

2013/2014

INSPIRING LEARNING

Plate 25 In 2006 the Prison Service called OU study 'a vital part of resettlement and a route to reducing re-offending'.

'From the start it will flow all over the United Kingdom': the spread of OU innovations[68]

The overseas student market exemplifies the extent to which the OU made a distinctive response to a common set of pressures and opportunities. Changes during the early 1980s compelled UK universities to charge overseas students what were known as 'full cost' fees, rather than the same fees regardless of where they were domiciled. As successive administrations from the early 1990s onwards drove down the unit of resource for domestic students, so all institutions, including the OU, sought to maximise non-governmental sources of income by engaging in the overseas market. However, unlike its full-time competitors, the OU was, and has remained, legally forbidden to recruit part-time overseas undergraduates. Of all the barriers between the OU and the rest of the sector, this has remained perhaps the most rigid and significant. It meant that as other universities sought to charge high fees to increasing numbers of overseas students recruited to UK campuses, the OU had to find ways to delivering its product into the countries where the students lived. Although a Dutch Open University was founded in 1984, in 1990 the OU opened a study centre in the Netherlands and registered 700 students based in Europe. In 1992 the Singapore Ministry of Education chose the Singapore Institute of Management and the OU to run the country's only distance-taught university degree programme. The university also began to offer courses through a partner institution in Hong Kong. In 1994 an OU office was opened in Brussels and the university offered education courses to managers in Bulgaria. Soon there were 2,000 OU students within the European Community, 6,000 in eastern and central Europe studying in Hungarian, Slovak and Russian, and a total of over 20,000 overseas students.

Between 1993 and 1998, under the direction of the Humanities Programme Committee of the European Association of Distance Teaching Universities, four universities, led by the OU, offered a course on European identity, *What is Europe?*, to over 4,000 students in different formats and languages. The first book was a Dutch–Danish collaboration; a second emanated from Germany, though one of the authors was British; a third was a French product with Italian, British and German contributions; and the fourth one came from the UK. In 1994 the course was awarded a prize for its contribution to an understanding of European educational systems. It became the focal point of a conference sponsored by the European Cultural Foundation and its core texts were published for sale to undergraduates. There was no international course team, fixed product or standard method of presentation. Instead there was a decentralised, flexible arrangement which recognised differences between the cultures of different institutions. The agenda was set by the Humanities Programme Committee of the European Association of Distance Teaching Universities which agreed the draft material from each of the partner institutions. These drafts became the basis for the core academic materials. However, the format and languages in which these were produced varied between partners. The presentation, teaching, assessment and certification arrangements also varied between partner institutions. The materials could be exploited in different ways by different partners and the product was praised for its European, rather than national, flavour. However, there was no move towards a widespread repetition of this production method. The course cost the OU more than a comparable in-house product and to obtain the English-language version involved the translation of almost half the materials. Intellectual property rights and copyright clearance were complicated and, over its lifespan at the OU, 1993–98, only 400–500 students registered each year, which was below the average for a comparable OU course. Moreover, although the Danish and Dutch partners used the English version, the German partner also had expensive translation costs. In addition, when computer conferencing and virtual seminars grew in popularity, new possibilities for collaboration arose and universities started to look towards a different model: joint presentation and teaching.[69]

In 2000 the OU opened the United States Open University (USOU), an independent, private, not-for-profit higher education institution which initially ran seven courses. A year later, following an OU feasibility study, it created another non-profit organisation, the Arab Open University (AOU), in collaboration with the Arab Gulf Programme for the United Nations Development Organisation. The OU element of the AOU was managed through the Open University Worldwide, a wholly owned trading subsidiary which was created in 1996 and sold and licensed OU resources. The OU was not financially responsible for the AOU but was awarded the sole contract to supply the curriculum, quality assurance and other infrastructural services. The AOU had a headquarters in Kuwait, which donated a site and provided temporary accommodation, and branches in Kuwait, Lebanon, Egypt, Bahrain, Jordan and Saudi Arabia. A branch was opened in the Sultanate of Oman in 2008. Teaching began in 2002 and the first students graduated in 2007. A comparison of these two ventures indicates that while the OU was capable of providing new pathways for exporting UK higher education, it could not always transcend larger economic and cultural frameworks.[70]

In the US the plan was to recruit 2,000 students in the first year and 6,000 in the second. However, the USOU opened at the moment when the dot.com bubble burst.[71] Many online universities found it difficult to find funding for online courses.[72] Some left the field.[73] John Daniel, who had promoted the USOU, left his post as OU Vice-Chancellor in order to serve as Assistant Director-General for Education at UNESCO and in June 2002, after the USOU had enrolled only 1,500 students, with funding concerns in the UK and costs which had risen to an estimated US$20 million, it was closed.[74] Reliance on tuition fees for much of its working capital placed it in competition with over 3,800 US institutions of higher education.[75] There were difficulties marketing online courses to a national market when there were virtually no national media vehicles for marketing. As a result the USOU focused on regional and local communication and on working through partners. In 2001 the University of Maryland-Baltimore County partnered with the USOU to offer an online MSc in Information Systems.[76] The USOU was presented as a 'sister institution' and 'part of a multinational network of institutions'.[77] The phrase 'a confederation of partners' was also used and yet the relationship between the UK and the US was often more paternal than fraternal.

Across the USA recognition of the OU brand was low.[78] One advertisement made the connection to the UK overt by referring to a playwright with a high transatlantic profile, claiming that if 'your interest lies in the meaning of Shakespeare's plays, the … USOU has a course to satisfy your quest for knowledge. There is something for everyone.'[79] The failure of the USOU was, it was argued by the Chancellor, Richard Jarvis, due to the 'queen and cricket problem' – that some OU courses could not easily be adapted because 'they had a distinctly European slant on things'.[80] He also noted that 'we should have done an MBA or Americanized the OU MBA first'.[81] Jarvis was English (though he was deeply familiar with the US system), the learning management system was imported from the UK and the author of an influential text (on e-moderating) was OU graduate and staff member Gilly Salmon.[82] However, being connected to the UK did not appear to help the USOU to establish a reputation for high-quality materials.[83] As USOU courses failed to gain rapid accreditation (apart from that of the Distance Education and Training Council in mid-2001) so US companies would not reimburse employees who studied them. The length and depth of course differed between the continents. The OU's UK model of open access could not be applied in a standard way, as some partners required higher prior qualifications than others.

In contrast to the competitive HE sector in the US, the Arab world had a high unmet demand for university places: only 50 per cent of high school leavers with appropriate qualifications were able to gain access to other universities. The age profile of the Arab market was quite unlike the OU's domestic cohort. Over a third of the AOU students were aged under twenty-one and almost two-thirds were aged under twenty-four. The AOU required students to have a general secondary school certificate and had funds to support some students in need. In 2006/07, 611 students received financial assistance.[84] By contrast, in the USA financial support for many distance education students did not exist until 1998 and even then the USOU was excluded because of the absence of accreditation.[85] The AOU's provision increased as the need for a qualified workforce grew. It also offered in-service teacher training for teachers and opportunities for women.

At the AOU students received an OU-validated qualification in addition to a local AOU award. The OU assisted in the creation of an online student environment and e-library and continued to provide consultancy and training services. The OU's materials were adapted for a variety of qualifications and from 2003 the AOU's undergraduate programmes were accredited by the OU as well as in the Arab countries. There was tutored independent learning supported by a 'delivery methodology ... based on programmed and progressive course lectures'. There was a blend of components 'including tutorials of around 20 students in Learning Centres, a dedicated integrated satellite network and use of the internet'.[86] In common with many OU modules, exams were weighted at 50 per cent of the total grade for the course, with the remaining 50 per cent assigned to term work including TMAs and quizzes. Partly because the young students were unfamiliar with university education, 25 per cent of study hours were face-to-face whereas only a few of the USOU modules included a face-to-face or residential element.[87] Having learned important lessons about venturing abroad the OU was able to provide a model for online and international teaching.

By 2012 the AOU had 30,000 students and 12,000 graduates. By supporting the creation of a distance-education university the OU claimed that the AOU offered the 'democratisation of education in the Arab World' and enabled 'Arab citizens, irrespective of age, gender, income, geographic location and employment to gain access to higher education'.[88] Antony Gribbon, the former managing director of Open University Worldwide, has emphasised that 'The mission of AOU is to reach out to minority peoples and people in remote regions who would not otherwise have access to higher education. There is no sense of a conflict in this, it is about helping the individual, rather than helping any political cause.'[89] Each branch of the AOU has elected student councils, and students are represented on the branch and university councils. Two students are members of the AOU council. A survey and discussions with 324 students indicated their 'pleasure for learning and performing democratic activities in the university'.[90] Through electronic forums students could interact across national boundaries with men and women. These features mark the AOU as different to other universities of the Arab states.

For the AOU the OU was prepared to adapt learning materials 'for all territories to meet cultural and religious requirements'.[91] The importance of this approach was emphasised by the experience of another venture with which the OU was associated. In February 2000 the government promised £62 million to fund the e-University or UKeU. Rather than building on the OU's established systems, it was decided to create a new eLearning platform to which institutions were invited to contribute courses. This initiative connected several British universities, including the OU, to a technology company. The aim was to market online degrees from British universities to students around the world. The first programme opened in 2003 with two courses, one from the OU. By 2004 there were 25 courses but there was little interest from potential students and the scheme was closed.[92] In his subsequent assessment, the Minister for Higher Education, Kim Howells, noted:

> We have learned from The Open University that … you have to, as the jargon has it, engage with students and, if one lesson came out of this lot, it probably is that they should have been much more sensitive to those needs of students the world over.[93]

The experience of the OU made it clear that to teach online required more than simply a transfer of materials developed for face-to-face teaching to a website (Plate 11).

In 2002 Singapore Institute of Management became an accredited institution through Open University Validation Services, and then, in 2006, a private university, Singapore Institute of Management University, UniSIM was created. It awarded its own degrees and continued to license OU content to form part of its own degree programmes.[94] Over thirty organisations without their own UK degree-awarding powers had their higher education and vocational qualifications validated by Open University Validation Services and overseen by Open University Worldwide. Partner organisations selected the OU material to be translated, adapted or both. They were offered advice about teaching, systems and methodologies and then took responsibility for examining and assessing students and the qualification received. By 2003 the OU had 26,000 overseas students directly taking OU courses and over 25,000 studying OU courses in collaborative teaching programmes. These involved the use of adapted OU materials in programmes offered by overseas universities with at least 25 per cent of tuition being face-to-face.

The OU expanded its international outreach to provide opportunities not just for individual students, but for communities. In 2005 it created programmes for Teacher Education in Sub-Saharan Africa, (TESSA), building on its familiarity with teacher training (Plate 12).[95] Working in countries with substantial numbers of working but unqualified teachers, it developed a curriculum that could be delivered into the classroom rather than requiring periods of study in distant towns. Instead of exporting a completely packaged curriculum, the donor-funded project committed resources for adapting the core materials to the language and pedagogic needs of the partner countries. The OU also nurtured a concept of stakeholdership, forming partnerships with the Nelson Mandela Foundation and University of Fort Hare's Unit for Rural Schooling and Development in order to run projects to support the teaching of numeracy, literacy, science and citizenship, Health Education and Training and English in Action (Plate 13). These partners, together with the Open University of Tanzania, the Open University of Sudan and other partners in Bangladesh and Egypt[96] joined the OU in the Digital Education Enhancement Project (DEEP). This was a research and development programme in which the OU made use of information and communications technology for teaching and learning in schools serving disadvantaged communities in different parts of the world.

Where the OU had little choice but to develop innovative methods of engaging with overseas learners and partners, other UK universities gradually began to explore similar possibilities for internationalising their product.[97] Some developed franchising, validation and distance and online teaching. A handful took the radical step of establishing international branches to teach full-time students. The University of Nottingham opened campuses in Malaysia and China, engaged in research with Chinese scholars and appointed the President of Fudan University as Chancellor.[98] In 2006 the University of Liverpool and Xi'an Jiaotong University established a new autonomous institution, the Xi'an Jiaotong-Liverpool University.[99] For the OU the journey was one of exploration, at its most successful delivering a combination of high-quality, technical sophistication and effective adaptation to local circumstances. Over the two decades it fulfilled the university's mission to bring the opportunity of learning to all who hungered for it, irrespective of location and circumstance. At the same time it supplemented rather than transformed the OU's business model. In 2010, on the eve of the introduction of the new funding structure in England, the university's budget, which was now approaching half a billion pounds a year, was still dominated by a combination of UK government grants and student fees. Funding-body grants represented 52 per cent of all OU income, with tuition fees and educational contracts forming the next largest source of funding at 34 per cent. The remainder was made up of research grants and contracts at only 4 per cent, endowment and investment income at 4 per cent and 6 per cent from other sources (including sales of materials).[100]

Equal opportunities

During the first phase of the OU's history there were legislative changes which aimed to improve equal opportunities: notably, the Sex Discrimination Act, 1975, the Race Relations Act, 1976 and the Equal Pay Acts, 1970 and 1983. After 1990 there was a further set of reforms including the Disability Discrimination Act, 1995, the Human Rights Act, 1998, the Special Educational Needs and Disabilities Act, 2001 and the Disability Discrimination Act, 2005. In compliance with legislation, universities across the UK began to treat staff and students in similar ways. In 1976 the OU was advised that its admissions policies might be discriminatory against men. There was a quota system in operation as there were so many applicants: 52,000 in 1975 of whom 17,000 were successful. In 1971 the proportion of successful women applicants across all universities was 32 per cent compared with 26 per cent in the very early days of the OU. By 1975 the OU's figure was 42 per cent, outstripping the conventional sector, which stood at 37 per cent.[101] There was increasing concern about how staff appointments were made, and incentives were introduced for individuals to identify themselves with the new discrimination categories.[102] In 1987 Senate called for 'an equal opportunity employment policy and its implementation as soon as possible'.[103] It was the first time that a UK university had devoted resources to a comprehensive review. The OU also wanted the collection of data on students' ethnic origins and policies to 'increase the recruitment of and provision of services for students from racially, socially and economically disadvantaged groups'. An equal opportunities team was created and an action plan was agreed. At the OU a black academic, Stuart Hall, 'made a telling set of comments about the insidious nature of indirect discrimination within so-called liberal institutions, such as universities' (Plate 14).[104] Some of the members of a group which examined discrimination at the OU concluded that 'the liberal model can be said to be limited'. It was also noted that 'few wished to alter the University's fundamental "first come, first served" principle ... Some felt that this compromised the University's openness.'[105]

The OU in Yorkshire ran a Race Equality Project, 1999–2002, and an Equal Opportunities office was created within the OU. It collected data and ran targeted recruitment campaigns. Elsewhere, widening participation in higher education was increasingly framed in terms of compliance with equal opportunities legislation. By the early 1990s most universities, polytechnics and colleges had equal opportunities policies and were developing action plans.[106] What remained distinctive to the OU was the sheer scale of its engagement with equal opportunities for learners, most notably in the field of disability. In 2003 the Institutional Disabled Students Strategy and Action Plan was launched, having been developed in the context of both Quality Assessment Authority guidelines and the Disability Discrimination Act. Although data collated about students refers only to those who have self-declared as having disabilities, by 2013 there were over 17,000 UK-based students with disabilities, health conditions, mental health disabilities or specific learning difficulties (such as dyslexia) studying at the OU.

In addition to its overseas activities the OU also pioneered many elements of the industrial model of central control, uniform products and economies of scale which were adopted by the growing number of overseas universities with over 100,000 students – the 'mega-universities', as OU Vice-Chancellor John Daniel called them.[107] Within the UK, a combination of growing volumes and a falling unit of resource ushered in the massification of higher education. Between 1994/95 and 2009/10 the number of students within the UK increased by 59 per cent to almost 2.5 million and the number of higher education institutions fell from 182 to 165 as 30 per cent of them, 55 in total, were involved in mergers. Larger universities had to find ways of teaching more undergraduates for less money. Methods of delivering learning designed for small elite institutions had to be reformed.[108] In this process some of the OU's solutions to its particular task of distance education began to become relevant to the sector as a whole. As numbers grew so the national and regional offices of the OU took on new roles. The work of co-ordination of students in much of Western Europe was done by one region, another dealt with students in Ireland, a third with postgraduate courses. Devolution in the United Kingdom and regionalisation in England resulted in different foci of new legislative bodies and regional agendas. There was recognition that the growth of contact with students via the web reduced the need for some of the activities previously carried out through the regional offices, and in August 2011 the role of Regional Director in the English Regions was abolished.

In 1991 the Committee of Vice-Chancellors and Principals of the Universities of the United Kingdom (CVCP, later Universities UK) issued a paper which set out the benefits of the 'Modular Curriculum and Structure'. Many universities adopted the curriculum model that had been in use at the OU since its foundation.[109] The direction of change generated fierce criticism.

This kind of reform on an institutional basis restricted the long-established freedom of individual academics to control their own courses. Mary Henkel argued that modularisation was

> frequently seen as compounding the difficulties consequent on massification. It signified a transfer of power from academics and departments ... most academics felt that modularisation had been imposed upon them by the senior management of their universities and for political and administrative, rather than educational reasons.[110]

As we saw earlier, the OU had wrestled with its own difficulties in balancing the rigour of institution-wide systems with the creativity of small academic teams, and in an uncoordinated fashion the rest of the sector now had to engage in a similar journey.

The OU proffered a second set of solutions to the task of high-quality teaching at scale. Many universities began move towards e-learning as a way to develop students' skills in finding, analysing and evaluating information. Work on retention within the OU suggested that it is higher among students with supportive kinship or other networks and when tutors made personal contact. John Daniel said of the OU that it was

> Both very big and very small. From the student's point of view the OU is a small organisation. With study centres all over the country and a local, personal tutor for each course, the student gets an individual service ... The small-scale nature of the teaching makes for learning effectiveness.[111]

Online learning could help to overcome geographical isolation if it also supported a focus on knowledge construction, problem-solving and both collaborative and autonomous learning (Plate 15). When carefully designed, this application of communication technology enabled teaching to be tailored to individual needs irrespective of the size of the total student cohort. Traditional institutions began to move into the space that the OU had previously dominated. As face-to-face academic departments began to experiment with educational technology, the need for a separate organisation to manage distance education was reduced. During the 1990s the 'defining characteristics of distance education were confronted by technological changes that made them potentially available for educators everywhere to replicate'.[112] One analysis concluded that 'On-campus delivery has become more like distance education and – in so doing – undermined the distinctive contribution to overall provision of ODL [Open and Distance Learning] practitioners.'[113] Whatever the quality of the pedagogy offered elsewhere, online educational provision was a potential rival to the OU's status, identity and function. As the new century opened the university faced the challenge of demonstrating that the scale of its investment in e-learning and the quality of its associated pedagogy continued to set it apart from the rest of the sector.

Open for business

In 1977–79 there was widespread acceptance of the OU degree by employers. By 1980 graduates were seen as mature, serious, determined and self-motivated; most employers felt that studying with the OU was acceptable for employees as it improved their work.[114] In 1982 the Manpower Services Commission – a government body created in 1973 – sponsored an OU 'women in technology' scheme which consisted of a bursary for women with engineering qualifications who had taken a career break. This enabled them to study an OU course, attend a 'return to study' weekend at Loughborough and, in most cases, also attend a summer school. A further survey of employers in 1992 reflected similar views on the acceptability of OU graduates.[115] By this time over 7,000 employers directly sponsored employees on OU undergraduate and postgraduate courses. Partners included both the public sector – notably the Prisoners Education Trust, the Youth Justice Board, the NHS and the Ministry of Defence – and also the private sector, including BAE Systems, Ford Motor Company and Pfizer International. Later a partnership was forged with Unionlearn, the learning and skills organisation of the Trades Union Congress.

The OU delivered Higher Apprenticeship programmes to Visa, O2/Telefonica and Capgemini. Building on its expertise in communicating at a distance, the OU became the only higher education corporate member of Intellect, the Technology Trade Association.[116] In addition, it helped to deliver the e-Skills Professional Programme for e-Skills UK. It was also its partner in the Vital IT 70 Continuing Professional Development programme for specialist IT teachers in schools and developed modules through collaboration with it.[117] Over seventy continuing professional development modules were developed at the OU, which became the first higher education provider to be approved by the National Skills Academy for IT. It developed links with professional bodies including the Chartered Institute for IT, the Institute of Engineering and Technology and the Institute of Telecoms Professionals.

When Lord Browne reported on the future of higher education in 2010 he framed his conclusions in terms of personal economics: 'On graduating, graduates are more likely to be employed, more likely to enjoy higher wages and better job satisfaction, and more likely to find it easier to move from one job to the next.'[118] The potential economic benefits of the OU had long been recognised by its students. Recalling their time with the OU many students mentioned new work, increased pay, or as Ernie Lowe called it, an 'immediate return on the OU investment!'[119] The OU, unlike most distance education providers, offered careers advice from the 1970s with 'the materials designed as an aid to self-help [which] increases the learner-centredness'. Its advertising materials stressed the value of an OU degree to those seeking to improve their job status.[120] In the 1980s over 70 per cent of students had career-related goals when they started and 74 per cent experienced an occupational benefit related to their studies.[121]

During the 1990s OU students' earnings increased more than those of the general population.[122] A third of Lunneborg's case studies of male OU students of the 1990s changed their careers completely and a third were promoted as a result of their degrees; they generally agreed that their qualification 'gives a man an extra edge within any organisation'.[123] It was a period when there was a growth of interest in universities providing graduates with skills which would add to their employability. Building on its engagement in the field since its foundation, the OU formed partnerships and offered modules focused on professional development. There was wider interest in graduates' employability following the publication in 1995 of the European Commission's paper 'Education and Training, Teaching and Learning: Towards the Learning Society'. An OU academic, Fiona Reeve, noted that, during this period, 'Policies to support lifelong learning were presented as being essential to enable society to meet the challenges which it faces, and among these challenges the ones associated with economic changes are most strongly emphasised.'[124] A further sign of the importance of this focus to government was that in the UK over fifty-five OU courses and study packs, which were used by around 3,000 learners, attracted tax relief.[125] Expenditure on work-related training incurred by an employer, or a third party, could be claimed against tax. In 1990 the lobbying for tax relief on fees for self-funding part-time students was rewarded when a concession was made in regard to courses for NVQ levels 1–4 (Plate 16).[126] Before 1997/98 an extra-statutory concession provided relief from tax if certain conditions were met.

Environmental practice: Negotiating policy in a global society, D833, a postgraduate module, was an exemplar of these ideas about engagement with the real world. It sought to build communities of learning, challenging the notion of teachers as active and students as passive. Presented in 2002, it used synchronous and asynchronous conferencing software so that people could both communicate with one another at the same time and also have conversations spaced over a number of days. This technology was becoming familiar across the OU. In 1994 2,000 OU students met via internet conferences and 110,000 did in 2005. Active, experiential learning was encouraged and opportunities provided for reflection and learner autonomy. Students following D833 were invited to represent different specific countries attending a virtual United Nations.[127] They were given the problem of constructing a shared agreement through virtual UN negotiations. Negotiation was presented as an interactive, dynamic, social activity and mutual learning process. Students were encouraged to understand both negotiation and how practitioners deploy theory through engaging in reflection on the simulation. They were also invited to keep non-assessed negotiation journals.[128] An evaluation of the first presentation suggested that they appreciated the sense of community engendered and the support for reflection.[129] Some of them said that they used the negotiation skills they had acquired in other situations and that they felt empowered by the course. While this module simulated a workplace, the United Nations General Assembly, other courses written for practitioners overtly tied their practical workplace activities to their studies.

The university continued to make the most of learners' experiences and to motivate by situating learning in a meaningful, often real-world, context. *Children's learning in the early years*, E124 (2004–11), was open only to those who were working in an early years setting. This was because, as the information about the course made clear, 'during the course, you will need to be working in the setting for a minimum of five hours a week in order to carry out the practical activities'. Between 2005 and 2010 the Practice-Based Professional Learning Centre for Excellence in Teaching and Learning (PBPL) was funded by the Higher Education Funding Council. This, one of the OU's four Centres for Excellence in Teaching and Learning, involved collaboration between four units: Health and Social Care, Education and Language Studies, the Business School, and the Institute of Educational Technology. It focused on learning about effective practice from study and in the workplace.

While students could still study for an 'Open' degree, consisting of a wide variety of subjects, they could also follow specific pathways to qualifications comparable to those offered elsewhere. In addition to the general degree, prescribed programmes of courses for named degrees were introduced in 1999. This helped to trigger an expansion of the curriculum to fourteen subjects within a framework of twenty-three programmes, each of which offered awards and courses. Other factors behind this shift included the focus of the

UK government and the devolved administrations on skills development in the workplace. There was the introduction of foundation degrees in England in 2000 and an increased demand for a customised curriculum, delivered flexibly, to suit different purposes and legislative areas and a growth in the OU's international activity.[130] In 2003 Foundation Degree Forward was created to support and promote high-quality foundation degrees. The OU helped to develop the National Information and Communications Technology Foundation Degree. The introduction of the pre-registration nursing programme was agreed in 2001.[131] Diplomas of Higher Education in Adult Nursing and Mental Health Nursing were offered, and students could also register as qualified nurses with the Nursing and Midwifery Council. In 2006 the project broadened from foundation degrees towards workforce development and partnerships between higher education and employers across all qualifications. Undergraduate certificates and diplomas which permitted subject-specific profiles within degrees were also devised.

Given the nature of its creation and development, the OU could claim to be the most pedagogically conscious institution in the sector. As earlier chapters have demonstrated, its approach to teaching was from the outset a matter of constant internal and external debate. Staff were trained and evaluated, and students were the subject of research into the effectiveness of teaching methods. This approach continued through the second phase of its development. Associate lecturers assessed and improved their practices through considering specific issues. These included an analysis of the effectiveness of initial contact practices and an assessment, through the use of a questionnaire, of students' project skills both before and after they undertook a research project.[132] However, the university was now becoming part of a national process of debate and innovation. During the 1990s the sector as a whole began to display a more extensive and formalised interest in approaches and outcomes. There was a shift towards teaching through guidance and assistance rather through the management of knowledge.[133] Increasingly educators sought to understand the interests of learners, and, based on this information, to incorporate relevant learning activities. Disciplines collaborated at many universities, echoing the OU's long tradition of inter-disciplinary modules.

It was many years after the OU had started to provide detailed advice on teaching for its staff that two national agencies were established to increase the professional competencies of teachers and to ensure that degrees could be compared against national standards and specified outcomes. Following a recommendation in Ron Dearing's *Higher Education in the Learning Society* report, the Institute for Learning and Teaching in Higher Education was founded in 1999.[134] Its first chief executive was Paul Clark. He joined the OU in 1972, became Dean of Science and Director for Teaching and Learning at the Higher Education Funding Councils for both England and Scotland, and the OU's Pro-Vice-Chancellor (Learning and Teaching). He retired in 2008.[135] The Quality Assessment Authority was established in 1997, combining the functions and staff from the Higher Education Quality Council and the quality-assessment divisions of the higher education funding councils for England and Wales. It created a system of subject reviews based on a national quality-assurance framework and institutional audits designed to assess the management of academic standards and quality.[136] One impact of these changes was that universities began to appoint staff to administer the quality and research procedures. The academic hold on strategy and policy formation weakened in the face of the arrival of a large number of non-academic colleagues. Estimates made for 2005, 2009 and 2010 suggested that 20–30 per cent of the total higher education workforce comprised managerial staff.[137] This shift in the organisational culture was less dramatic at the OU than in many other universities. The sense of change lay in the extent to which it was now more formally engaged in a process of dialogue and improvement with the rest of higher education. In one sense it had come in from the cold. Through its extensive use of external examiners and assessors it had always sought to maintain parity of standards with other institutions. Now it was formally embraced by the sector-wide quality-assurance and enhancement systems.

To ensure compliance with new regulations and audits, new data was collated. Academic and other staff became involved in the implementation of new procedures as they were both inspected and were, in some cases, inspectors.[138] The idea of benchmarking subjects so that degrees offered by different universities could be compared was a familiar one to those who worked at the OU. This is because any one module was taught by a large number of tutors for as long as a decade. Methods had previously been devised to ensure that the assessment of the material was consistent over space and time. Nevertheless, disciplines at the OU (later called departments) had to be organised in ways which rendered them easier to audit. Evaluation had been accepted at the OU since before its opening because it offered a way to establish if it had delivered on the promises of access and openness. There had been developmental testing of the first courses before they were launched and studies of those people who had enrolled on the National Extension College preparatory courses.[139] Even before the first students arrived there were staff engaged to support course development and institutional research. In 1970 the Applied Educational Sciences Unit (AESU) and Survey Research Department were merged to form an Institute of Educational Technology.

The Head of the AESU, David Hawkridge, became the first Director of the Institute. He built on the experiences that he had gained at the Center for Research into Applications of Technology in Education in the American Institute for Research in the Behavioral Sciences where he had worked before he joined the OU. He also built on ideas developed at the University of London's Institute of Education. The IET set out to explore and understand new possibilities for teaching and supporting learners. It gathered data about courses from students and staff and collated information about all aspects of courses. Drawing on this vast evidence base it produced ideas about pedagogic design and the students' learning experiences. The OU had peer review and the external assessment and examination of modules. Prior to the presentation of any module a large number of leading academics had checked the teaching and assessment standards. The OU's long-term efforts to be self-critical and open-minded and its experience of collecting and analysing data about its teaching and having systems for making amendments made it easier to be compliant with the new demands of external evaluation agencies and accreditation bodies.[140]

Conclusion

To characterise the OU as simply Harold Wilson's 'pet', as some of his political colleagues reportedly did, is to miss the importance of the development of its relationships with the state and the private sector.[141] Two socialist commentators made this point when they noted that while the OU 'contributed significantly to the advance of a socialist education policy for higher education' it was also 'always within the parameters of a capitalist system'.[142] The OU's streamlined, administrative rationality and standardised procedures may have worked only on an individual level to narrow the gap between incomes, ameliorate inequality or provide improvements in jobs. Education tends to maintain and recreate, rather than create, societies. In some respects the OU may have shored up and reproduced differences because 'as the state has become much more involved with higher education it also became increasingly entwined with corporate capitalism'.[143] Since the 1990s there has been a shift in the balance between autonomy and accountability as well as between developing the 'general powers of the mind', as Robbins proposed, and treating students as customers who select the skills required for knowledge management. In the year that the OU opened Shirley Williams, then Junior Minister at the DES, and her officials spent a day with selected members of the UGC and CVCP in order to consider funding issues. Since then, the idea of politicians, civil servants and university academics and administrators exploring common problems together has been replaced by distant relationships, formal structures and a sense that universities are part of a larger public sector, not always distinctive or necessarily deserving of institutional autonomy.

As funding methods, student numbers and access policies changed there was greater rivalry between universities for resources and students, and a more market-oriented approach towards students as customers. Changes at the OU which have led it to appear to be more like other universities are partly due to a general political shift away from overt state control and towards giving greater opportunities to private companies within regulated parameters. For example, a private non-university was permitted to award degrees in 1996 and FE colleges could do this from 2004. Further support for the private sector was offered from 2011 and there was a greater emphasis on fees, while universities have increasingly been seen as valuable if they produce graduates who make money.[144]

The OU was the subject and the partial architect of these developments. It both contributed and adapted to the new parameters. The university modelled some of the important developments within the higher education sector, notably the promotion of the effective use of technologies to communicate collaboratively in order to construct and share knowledge. In so doing it has maintained its commitment to the idea of education as a process of dialogue and of symbiotic relationships between and within communities of learners. In terms of its social role the OU was initially unusual in seeking to support those marginalised by many universities. Many of those who sought to study through the OU, for example mature students, people with disabilities and prisoners, were peripheral to the central concerns of most universities, which focused on young adults with A-levels. However, by 2009 the National Higher Education conference was eager to stress how universities 'play a key role in promoting social mobility and enabling disadvantaged young people to access the professions'.[145] This shift also echoed a new focus on students as consumers and a qualification as a commodity, rather than a signifier of the attainment of particular knowledge and skills. The familiarity of the OU to many people within the UK, coupled with the OU's experience with fees and its emphasis on real-life relevance, may have helped to normalise ideas about new roles for universities. The OU was subject to change, and also helped to shape trends during the period when the post-war welfare state was coming under increasing challenge.

6

Pedagogies promoting participation

The Open University has always faced the task of balancing independent study with collaborative learning. Stephen Brookfield observed that 'all learning exhibits some independence' and survey evidence suggests that many students at the OU favour working by themselves.[1] At the same time the trend across the university has been towards encouraging forms of social interaction. Since the 1990s the OU's pedagogy has aimed to enable students to build their own mental structures through transformative dialogue. The intention has been that they can be helped to construct knowledge with fellow students and tutors. Independence and collaboration were not mutually exclusive. Rather, students were emboldened to develop new relationships between the interpretation of ideas and the construction of meaning. While OU production methods may have resembled factory assembly lines, academic study itself was far from a uniform experience. The individual nature of the learning experience became more pronounced as technologies were deployed to enable the OU provision to become increasingly decentralised, adjustable and personalised.[2]

The first of this chapter's three sections outlines the OU's continued development of self-directed, student-centred learning. The preferred pedagogic framework emphasised discursive interactions between teacher and student. From the outset the university challenged the views that knowledge was a possession contained within individual minds taught only through transmission, that maintaining the conventional division between the teacher and student was the best way to learn, and that access to information should be limited and controlled. There needed to be both experience and reflection through experimental activity, fieldwork and projects. The employment of these component processes – the discursive, adaptive, interactive and reflective – will be illustrated by reference to some of the modules presented at the OU from the early 1990s onwards.

In the second section the university's support for informal learning is assessed. The recollections of learners in extra-mural communities created after they have completed formal OU studies illuminate another element of the impact of the OU and the experiences of life-long learners. Developments in this area were related to technological changes. Broadcasting became used less for the delivery of specific, module-related materials and more to support informal learning. Technologies enabled students to build relationships and formalise their informal knowledge while extending their structured learning into *ad hoc* activities and networks (Plate 17).

The third section considers changes in the work of tutors. Each student is allocated to a local part-time tutor (also called an associate lecturer or AL) who provides them with general learning support, specific tutorial activities (either face-to-face or electronic) and grades, and provides feedback on completed assignments (Plate 18).[3] The tutors are supported in their work by a monitoring system through which senior staff (sometimes this can include fellow tutors) provide advice on their tuition and marking. They are line-managed by staff based in the nations and regions and there is also provision for staff development. The course (or module) team responsible for the teaching and assessment strategy of each course provides tutors with detailed marking guidelines and sometimes specimen solutions (Figure 6.1). As the media evolved, new structures, activities and approaches were developed. Research on how best to support learning was made available to tutors. It was argued that knowledge could be gained by actively seeking meaning from events and that teaching should make provision for social learning spaces, employing technology to create and support them. Further efforts were made to enable tutors to contribute to generative relationships from which learners could emerge with an expanded potential for effective learning. While many tutors were well suited, well trained and diligent, in 2003 a survey of students who had withdrawn from OU courses indicated that, for them, tutorials were among the least highly rated items provided by the OU.[4]

Learning through discourse

The OU presented discussion and debate as the means of fostering learning and recognising different perspectives in the discovery of new ideas. Its enthusiasm for creating structures to support collaborative study was reflected in a programme to support the career development of open learners.[5] David A. Kolb proposed a four-stage, repeatable cycle. His experiential learning model has been summarised as sensing/feeling, watching/reflecting, thinking and doing. This student-centred and outcome-based approach encouraged students to construct personal portfolios, to create their own pathways through the materials provided and to keep a 'learning file' to facilitate

The Open University

COPY 1

TMA FORM (PT3)

CENTRAL RECORD

NOTE: Please use a ball point pen and rest on hard surface when completing this form - carbon paper is not required
Ensure all three copies are legible and that the complete assignment is sent with the form.

SECTION 1 STUDENT TO COMPLETE

Name

Address

Postcode/Country

Regional Code: O 2   Date Sent to Tutor: 17 09 98

Telephone

Personal Identifier

Course Code: M 261   TMA No.: 0 4

TAKE CARE TO ENTER THESE NUMBERS CORRECTLY

SECTION 2 TUTOR TO COMPLETE IN BLOCK CAPITALS

Date from Student: 18 09 98

Date to Centre: 25 09 98

Tutor's Name

Telephone

Tutor's No.

Contracting Region

Use this space to indicate permission, and reason, for late submission, or to affix TMA regrading label:

FOR OFFICE USE ONLY

Assignment Handling Office Date: 28 9

Question Grades/Scores

1	2	3	4	5	6	7	8	9	10	11	12	13	14	15	16	17	18	19	20
1,5	1,4	27	20	1,4															

Overall Grade/Score: **90**

TUTOR'S GENERAL SUMMARY

Another high quality TMA.
You lost a couple of marks in Q2 / Q5 for relatively minor omissions and errors in your induction arguments. However, you have grasped the method and its intricacies extremely well.
It was Q4 that threw you - specifically how to get negation-free deductions for 7 (a ⇒ d). You worked backwards, but not successfully, since you tried to use multiple cancellations - this does not work in general ! See on your script for full details of the proof that all cows are called Daisy ! ! !
Overall, an excellent grasp of some technically demanding ideas. You should do well in the examination

- all the best,

Alex

Figure 6.1 a, b, c and d Tutors completed separate Tutor Marked Assignment forms for each assignment they assessed. They were offered advice as to how to teach through these forms and a sample of the forms of each tutor was monitored to ensure that marking and advice to students was consistent.

The Open University

COPY 1

TMA FORM (PT3)

CENTRAL RECORD

NOTE: Please use a ball point pen and rest on hard surface when completing this form - carbon paper is not required
Ensure all three copies are legible and that the complete assignment is sent with the form.

SECTION 1 STUDENT TO COMPLETE

Name

Address

Postcode/Country

Regional Code: 0 5   Date Sent to Tutor: 7 04 99

Telephone

Personal Identifier

Course Code: K 257   TMA No.: 0 1

TAKE CARE TO ENTER THESE NUMBERS CORRECTLY

SECTION 2 TUTOR TO COMPLETE IN BLOCK CAPITALS

Date from Student: 8 4 97

Date to Centre: 22 4 97

Tutor's Name

Telephone

Tutor's No.

Contracting Region: 0 5

Use this space to indicate permission, and reason, for late submission, or to affix TMA regrading label.

FOR OFFICE USE ONLY

Assignment Handling Office Date

Question Grades/Scores

1	2	3	4	5	6	7	8	9	10	11	12	13	14	15	16	17	18	19	20
42																			

Overall Grade/Score: 42

TUTOR'S GENERAL SUMMARY

TERRY: This is marked as a "bare pass" for two main reasons: (a) you make only very limited direct use of the course materials and therefore don't demonstrate your knowledge of them clearly; and (b) much of your essay is essentially description or narrative rather than presenting analysis and discussion of reasons why "some people" object to the term "mental illness". This means that you don't demonstrate your understanding of the reasons clearly.

This is not to suggest you lack knowledge and understanding — rather that you've not presented them in this TMA as effectively as you could. Don't be too downcast: TMA 01 (with 10% weighting) is intended as an opportunity to make mistakes and learn lessons with little penalty! Read my notes and suggestions on your TMA itself. I hope they are helpful, and remember you are welcome to discuss them with me — give me a call.

Best wishes

Anwar

PT3 5-97

Figure 6.1 b

The Open University

COPY 1

TMA FORM (PT3)
CENTRAL RECORD

NOTE: Please use a ball point pen and <u>rest on hard surface</u> when completing this form - carbon paper is not required
Ensure all three copies are legible and that the complete assignment is sent with the form.

SECTION 1 STUDENT TO COMPLETE

Name

Address

Postcode/Country

Regional Code: **0 5**   Date Sent to Tutor: **21 03 99**

Telephone

Personal Identifier

Course Code: **U 210**   TMA No.: **0 1**

} TAKE CARE TO ENTER THESE NUMBERS CORRECTLY

SECTION 2 TUTOR TO COMPLETE IN BLOCK CAPITALS

Date from Student: **23 3 99**

Date to Centre: **2 4 99**

Tutor's Name

Telephone

Tutor's No.

Contracting Region: **0 5**

Use this space to indicate permission, and reason, for late submission, or to affix TMA regrading label:

FOR OFFICE USE ONLY
Assignment Handling Office
Date

Question Grades/Scores

1	2	3	4	5	6	7	8	9	10	11	12	13	14	15	16	17	18	19	20
78																			

Overall Grade/Score: **78**

TUTOR'S GENERAL SUMMARY Well done, Chris; you've managed to achieve a good first essay under heavy pressure. I hope this convinces you that you'll survive the rest of the course! You've managed the step up from first to second level very capably. This is a thoughtful discussion of a complex issue; you have devised a sound structure, linking Ramson's points to a survey of three forms of colonization and their effects on English. You offer a careful analysis of the course material, especially of the readings which discuss other colonial varieties of English. You gain particular credit for the comparison which points out how local languages can affect English at the more fundamental levels of grammar and syntax, as well as vocabulary. I've suggested ways of extending and developing your argument; in particular, build up the element of evaluation, which you start to discuss in your conclusion. e.g. does Nigerian or Guyanese English have a stronger claim than Australian English, to be considered as a distinctive variety, because it has undergone more changes, at levels other than just vocabulary? How far is Ramson's case based on a desire for national identity, and how far has he got a wide range of linguistic evidence - is he making the most of what he has? This is good, promising work. Give me a ring if you need to discuss your work at any time.

PT3 5-97

Figure 6.1 c

The Open University

COPY **1**

TMA FORM (PT3)

CENTRAL RECORD

NOTE: Please use a ball point pen and <u>rest on hard surface</u> when completing this form - carbon paper is not required
Ensure all three copies are legible and that the complete assignment is sent with the form.

SECTION 1 STUDENT TO COMPLETE

Name

Address

Postcode/Country

| Regional Code | O 6 | Date Sent to Tutor | 19 | 4 | 98 |

Telephone

Personal Identifier

| Course Code | S103 | TMA No. | 0 4 |

TAKE CARE TO ENTER THESE NUMBERS CORRECTLY

SECTION 2 TUTOR TO COMPLETE IN BLOCK CAPITALS

| Date from Student | 21 | 04 | 98 |
| Date to Centre | 03 | 05 | 98 |

Tutor's Name

Telephone

Tutor's No.

| Contracting Region | O 6 |

Use this space to indicate permission, and reason, for late submission, or to affix TMA regrading label:

FOR OFFICE USE ONLY

Assignment Handling Office Date

Question Grades/Scores

Overall Grade/Score

1	2	3	4	5	6	7	8	9	10	11	12	13	14	15	16	17	18	19	20
23	05	17	1	3	03														

Overall: 61

TUTOR'S GENERAL SUMMARY *This is a good mark for a much longer and more demanding assignment, so I hope you won't be disappointed after the high mark you received for TMA 03. You continue to demonstrate a good grasp of the course material, but lost marks in a few places for insufficient detail or the use of the wrong method in a calculation.*

Q1 – excellent calculations – no further comments needed!

Q2 – I'm afraid you lost a lot of marks for not using the correct method of finding the gradient of a graph. Work through Box 10.1 in Block 3 again, to see the correct method, and read pp 105–107 where it describes how we find P-wave speeds.

Q3 – A good answer, just a few marks lost for minor details omitted from your account.

Q4 – some mistakes on the table, and again a lack of detail in the 'types of place' column

Q5 – your analysis was rather brief – have a look at the outline answer enclosed for an idea of the sort of detail required.

Do phone me if you are not clear about anything in the outline answer, or in my comments on your script.

Best wishes, Pat.

PT3 5-97

Figure 6.1 d

reflective study.[6] For Kolb, 'learning is the process whereby knowledge is created through the transformation of experience'.[7]

An experiential and reflection-orientated approach was employed for *Learning through life: Education and training beyond school*, EH266 (1993–99), in which students completed a learning log and a reflection section for the assignments. The titles of the two main study texts, *Learners' experience* and *Frameworks for learning*, indicated the course's emphasis on the process of learning, 'with learners invited to define their own goals, plans and learning contracts'.[8] Senior counsellor Anne Vickers explained that 'the programme itself acts as facilitator as well as providing the raw materials for learning'.[9] A pilot version led to extensive amendments of the programme in the light of comments from tutors, counsellors and students. In addition to the tutors, students were also offered support by 'enterprise counsellors' and a mentor who they found for themselves. The module *Communicating technology*, T293 (1997–2001), integrated the shared process of learning with the student's personal experience. It offered opportunities for students to reflect on their own strengths and weaknesses and review their motivations. The course put unusual demands on tutors as well as students. Guidance was provided for both groups and, after the first presentation, was amended for subsequent presentations.[10]

The use of computers in learning at the OU evolved from an initial limited availability. On the first mathematics foundation course, 7,000 students were given access to the OU's mainframe computers via 109 Teletype terminals in study centres and four terminals available at summer schools. Access was limited by the scarcity of terminals. One student recalled making a forty-mile round trip 'to set up a simple query in Basic and then wait ages for the response to clatter back'.[11] Over 10,000 hours were logged by students who learned, through a dial-up service, how to write programmes in BASIC. The OPUS computer supplied for *The digital computer*, TM221 (1975–82), had no operating system or non-volatile storage. Students could programme using switches on it byte by byte. For *The digital computer*, TM222 (1983–91), students could experiment with both software and hardware using the (H)ome (E)lectronic (K)it compu(TOR) – HEKTOR. By 1980 there were 35 courses using some aspect of the terminal access system and trials began of the OPTEL system, which was later made available via dial-up from home, and then Telnet.[12] Gradually, opportunities for computer use by OU students were developed. These were framed by the premise that knowledge is socially constructed and that learning may be accomplished through reciprocity. To ensure that learners could exchange information and develop a common space where helpful encounters could

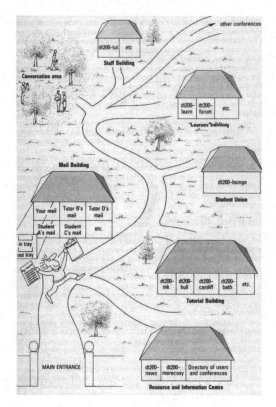

Figure 6.2 *Information technology: Social and technological issues*, DT200 (1988–94), introduced many students to computer conferencing with this electronic map of a virtual campus.

occur, the OU developed a Canadian computer-mediated communication system called CoSy. This asynchronous text-based communication application was first used in 1986 for a second-level module. It was soon integrated into the Master of Business Administration award. In 1988 *Information technology: Social and technological issues*, DT200 (1988–94), used computer conferencing (Figure 6.2).[13] This was the year that the OU introduced some courses which required students to have access to a desktop computer. By 1990 about 2,000 students were using CoSy to communicate with tutors and with other students.[14] *Programming and programming languages*, M353 (1986–99), required a home-computing facility, while *Matter in the universe*, S256 (1985–92), provided computer-assisted learning for home computers and employed interactive videotape. Students were given opportunities to buy or rent computers. In 1995 twenty courses, with a total of almost 21,000 students, required undergraduates to have access to an MS-DOS machine. Conferencing enabled students to select a time which was convenient to them to respond. This did not offer the immediacy of quick-fire debate but it did provide opportunities for reflective dialogue. The large-scale use of this facility on *Information technology*, DT200, helped to shift the focus within the OU away from the individual learner towards consideration of how best to support social interaction. Individual students were encouraged to construct personal meaning and to contribute to their own learning and that of others through online discussion.

A new text-based conferencing system was developed. In 1994 FirstClass was provided for undergraduate courses following successful trials, 'particularly of the collaborative learning activities' that it supported.[15] It was 'much more intuitive a system than CoSy'.[16] A year later 5,000 students were conferencing; by 1996 there were 13,000 and soon 50,000.[17] Initially the conferencing was used for interactions previously carried out by phone or letter.[18] Tutors offered advice and responded to requests via FirstClass. This was considered to be particularly valuable to house-bound students and those based in Europe. Moreover, conferencing was used to aid swift global exchanges and reduce costs. A short course, aimed at teachers who were based all over the world and who wanted to receive multi-media attachments, capitalised on FirstClass, as did a course which consisted of a workbook and conferencing. It permitted students to submit assignments electronically. A module in *Renewable energy technology* provided opportunities for groups of students distributed over several different countries to use computer conferencing to collaborate on report writing, information selection and other activities.[19]

Having pioneered conferencing for educational purposes, the OU continued to assess and experiment in order to stimulate and monitor interactions among learners. When students worked among themselves they found it 'valuable', concluded Robin Mason and Paul Bacsich, 'to create the kind of community usually only found on campus'.[20] It was clear that online elements required structuring. Leaving students alone rarely resulted in significant educational outcomes. In addition, conferencing worked better when linked to assessment. It was also noted that awareness of others was enhanced by explanations about messaging style ('netiquette'), the use of digital photographs of users, the creation of student-only conferences and the provision of synchronous 'chat' opportunities.[21] One of the course team responsible, Chris Bissell, argued that *Information technology*, THD204 (1995–2001), used computer-mediated conferencing and internet resources which could be accessed via a CD-ROM, 'to encourage construction and dialogue, not simply to expose students to new concepts'. He also noted that 'old power relations' might need to be renegotiated. The old model of the university teacher as an expert in a given subject area cannot continue to hold when students have immediate access to information – and other experts – throughout the world.[22]

A survey of tutors on the module found that many hoped to increase their IT skills through the process of tutoring.[23]

Students did not immediately shift from individual studying, and conferences needed to be actively supported by tutors. The university began to devise guidance for tutors on conference moderation.[24] Ideas about conferencing were developed for an online course *You, your computer and the net*, T171 (1999–2005), which enrolled around 10,000 students in its first year and had 12,500 students by 2000. In addition to access to an extensive website, students received a CD-ROM of software and set texts. Narrative was used in the module to provide a coherent structure to the web material, to supply students with the skills to use new technologies as tools for learning and 'to act as a means of enculturation to bring students into the general culture of ICT'.[25] Learning was integrated with practice rather than pursued through 'time out' from practice.[26] Students were required to submit their work electronically, as HTML documents. They communicated not only with the central computing facility but also with one another and their tutors. Groups of about fifteen worked collaboratively on projects in their own conferences. Each of these groups was moderated by a tutor. As part of the assessment students could reflect on the process and comment on their contributions. The intention was to use the new delivery modes to ensure that the OU's environment remained congenial and supportive of the creation of knowledge by learners.[27] Students were required to provide evidence of participation in online discussions. There were both embedded conferences and a number of tutor-led group activities. While students were allocated to a tutor based in their region they were also directed to national conferences to discuss issues relating to the material they read either in the book or on the website. Many students found these convenient ways to interact with tutors and peers. There was some flexibility as to when and how students engaged in text-based discussions. The 'social, interactive discussion-based' format helped some to reduce their sense of isolation.[28]

Videos

The number of television transmission slots available to the OU did not grow at the same rate as the number of OU broadcasts and, by 1978, about 20 per cent of OU television broadcasts had only one transmission.[29] The percentage of students watching the broadcasts fell and the Video-Cassette Loan Service was introduced in 1982. As only about 8 per cent of OU students had a VHS player at home, machines were distributed to the regions.[30] By 1986 60 per cent of OU undergraduates had a video player in their homes.[31] Britain had the highest ownership of video-cassette recorders in Europe, and OU students' access to such technology was 'well above the national rate'.[32] A survey found that only 14 per cent of OU undergraduates could not arrange access to a machine.[33] In 1992, 90 per cent of OU students surveyed had a VCR and 80 per cent of them recorded OU programmes.[34] From 1993, instead of mailing video-cassettes to students, the OU arranged for the night-time broadcast of programmes for students to record.[35] Video-cassettes liberated students from a fixed viewing schedule. OU Professor John Sparkes argued that 'it was a mistake to try to teach conceptually difficult material by broadcast TV. It goes too fast and cannot be slowed down to allow for thinking time.'[36] Using video, students could skim, pause, rewind, fast forward and search. They could integrate reflection on other teaching media. By contrast, a third of students who watched television material focused on the details and failed to draw out the general principles.[37] For courses with fewer than 650 students each year it was cheaper for the OU to distribute returnable video-cassettes than to broadcast the material.[38] The OU began to produce course-specific, non-broadcast materials (for group viewing at residential schools, for example). It made a number of videos as part of its Continuing Education activities. A video for *Talking with young people*, P525, included forty-three sequences. Students were invited to watch in groups and consider their reactions. The constraints inherent in a 23-minute broadcast slot did not apply to a video-cassette with a number of independent sections of varying lengths. For *Social psychology*, D307 (1985–95), students were invited to analyse a drama by referring to letters in the corner of the screen and a grid provided in the video notes. The presenter explained:

> watch the excerpt straight through first time, even if you can't get it all down in your notes, you'll have a chance to replay this section of the tape later on. Doing this analysis in real time will be good practice for when you do your own observation.[39]

Similarly the, video associated with *Matter in the universe*, S256 (1985–92), included the instruction that viewers should watch it more than once and that they should address questions related to the numbers in the corner of the screen. For *Engineering mechanics: Solids and fluids*, T331 (1985–2004), students were expected to measure the time period of an oscillating pendulum, and then stop the tape and apply the data to an equation. The impersonal broadcast to an infinite crowd had been adapted to enable personal use by members of the OU's student body.

Tutors and students acknowledged that learners benefited not only from well-constructed teaching materials but also from tutors, fellow students and supportive social networks.[40] Simone Siddle, an associate lecturer, asked students to telephone one another to encourage tutorial attendance and reported that this was very successful. She also asked a student who had completed the module to attend the first tutorial of the next presentation in order to give 'a student-centred view of the highs and lows of OU study – this worked really well'. Another associate lecturer, Gillian Leighton, noted that students had created an online self-help group and concluded that 'student-only internet groups seem a good way forwards to promote identity, community retention and progression'.[41] While student Catherine Smith mentioned the 'devoted support' of her spouse and her mother, she added that 'what often kept me going was reading [of] other students in much worse situations' and that she 'had a whale of a time' at summer school thanks to the company of a fellow student.[42] Hayley Staniforth recalled that as she 'sat alone each night at my kitchen table I was buoyed by the knowledge that thousands like me were also sitting with a cold cup of coffee at 1.30am!! I felt a shared isolation! I loved it.'[43]

For *Studying family and community history: 19th and 20th centuries*, DA301 (1994–2001), students wrote short theses about local history based on primary sources. This was one attraction of the module.[44] In addition, there was engagement with the work of other students across time. The students' research was collated on CDs, which were issued to subsequent students who then wrote their own theses. By the final course presentation there were hundreds of earlier studies to which students could refer. Subsequently the students' reports were made available more widely. Michael Drake, a member of the course team, suggested that 'the student is no longer a passive recipient of historical knowledge, but a creator of it … he or she has become a real and not just a token member of the community of scholars.'[45] The course also encouraged students to develop their transferable skills by making audio and video recordings. Other collaboration was encouraged, such as completing a form readable by a computer. Their individual information was collated and collective data generated. This element of the module was not formally assessed.

Participating in projects

By encouraging students to learn from one another and participate in data collation the OU challenged the idea that learning was merely a matter of gathering information over many years and then becoming an expert. For *Decision-making in Britain*, D203 (1972–82), students were asked to interview local industrialists. Prior to this they could watch a programme in which students talked about their experience of doing this. Science students were encouraged to contribute data. They gathered readings of atmospheric pollution from all over the country, which were collated and discussed. The first technology module, *The man-made world: A foundation course*, T100 (1972–79), included a home experiment kit with a simple binary computing device, a logic kit, a control/analogue kit and a noise measurement meter. Using the last of these items, students contributed towards the production of a national noise map. They also learned to build their knowledge using more than one medium.[46] On one of the module's television broadcasts the results were presented and assessed.[47] As the leader of a project to promote such data collection noted, 'the distance in distance learning is generally regarded as an obstacle that must be overcome. But this can turn that distance into a pedagogical asset.'[48] Much of *Historical sources and the social scientist*, D301 (1974–88), was devoted to supporting students to engage in historical projects of their own devising. By 1976 there were at least ten modules which included a project element.[49] In that year and also in 1984 and 1992 a quarter of assessed OU modules contained or consisted of projects.[50] Those who studied *Science: A foundation course*, S101 (1979–87), collected data about the peppered moth near where they lived, building up a collective picture of the whole. The information was incorporated into a peer-reviewed article.[51] In 1984 a stand-alone pack guided groups to engage in independent learning about local history.[52] The OU encouraged its own students to engage in research and experiments, including calculating the distance to the moon and analysing popular culture in Blackpool. It has also called on other students: a survey sponsored by the Department of the Environment of non-residential buildings in the UK involved students from the universities of Manchester and Sheffield Hallam recording data, directed by OU academics.[53]

In 1998 Pro-Vice-Chancellor Diana Laurillard stressed that 'multimedia must be an active medium for the user, creating opportunities for the learner to make decisions, formulate and test hypotheses, make choices, construct interpretations'.[54] Reflecting this view, *Applications of information technology in open and distance education*, H802 (1998–2005), concentrated on collaboration. This module was completely online and, in order to encourage students to contribute to group discussions and collaborations, it offered relatively little prepared content. Instead, it structured online interactions in order to help users feel comfortable and encouraged students to use extracts from online discussions in their assignments. Professor of Educational Technology Robin Mason explained that 'the approach is largely constructivist and collaborative, the emphasis being on online activities and peer learning'.[55] It soon became apparent that while many students became 'total converts to the value of collaborative learning', many others suffered from 'collaborative fatigue' as they found it so overwhelming.[56] She also noted that tutors were liable to suffer from 'interaction fatigue'.[57] In 2001 an assessment of online collaboration indicated that while students valued it, particularly in the early stages of a course, it could over-emphasise the social at the expense of individual flexibility of study. Laurillard suggested that an effective strategy would be to 'offer collaborative learning as a support at the beginning of the course and then reduce it towards the end, as students become more independent, and need more control of their own schedules'.[58]

The idea that encouraging students to support each other and learn co-operatively could improve attainment, student cohesion and retention received support from the Higher Education Funding Council for England in 2001. In most universities the focus was on face-to-face meetings but at the OU, where from 2006 all courses had some ICT-based activities, the focus was on making the best use of online opportunities.[59] By 2008 around 10 per cent of OU courses were 'almost completely online'.[60] A postgraduate course launched in 2006, *Team engineering*, T885, made considerable use of audio-visual conferencing and wikis in order to aid the development of teams among the students.[61] Students could access the conversations of other students, the responses of tutors and formal online tutorials. The students also contributed to the development of the content of their module. There were three project options and they worked in online teams of five to seven members to produce joint reports. This reflected the experience of the workplace for many of the students.[62] Moreover, the students replayed their online interactions in order to aid reflection on the process of team working. The technology informed as well as supported the pedagogy.

Digital photography: Creating and sharing better images, T189 (first presented in 2007), aimed to 'teach you how to critically evaluate your own and others' work in the spirit of continuous technical and artistic improvement'.[63] The idea that learning was a social phenomenon was reflected in the module guide of this short, first-level module, which stated: 'this is the very first online digital photography module provided by a university anywhere in the world that is structured around online collaborative photo sharing'.[64] The module was moderated rather than tutored, and although moderators offered guidance it was explained that 'You will also find lots of help and support from your fellow students in the forums and in OpenStudio.'[65] 'OpenStudio' enabled students to upload non-assessed photographs to a shared online site. Dave Philips, the co-chair of the module team, felt that the moderators provided a 'huge range of knowledge' and that 'because we have got moderators rather than tutors it's actually given us a bit more freedom to choose who they are'.[66] The focus was on supporting rather than directing learning, with students taught to peer-review. A number of students appreciated the value of moderators who steered them towards peer review.[67] One student noted that 'as a novice it's a bit intense at times, but the tutors [i.e. moderators] and some of the more experienced students help you through'. Another posted that 'through viewing and commenting on fellow students' work and receiving their comments I have developed greater awareness of what makes a good photograph'.[68] The format was partly derived from commercial sites which permitted sharing. Students were directed towards one of these, Flickr, which enabled users to 'store, sort, search and share ... photos online'.[69] As access to new technologies spread, the OU remained committed to the principle that in order to solve problems, learners, even if physically isolated individuals at a distance from one another, needed to work together to construct and maintain shared concepts.

In addition to using new technologies to aid communication the OU also saw the possibility of new ways of providing resources. *Homer: Poetry and society*, A295 (1993–2004), supplied a CD-ROM containing exercises, activities and other resources which could be accessed and employed in less formally structured ways. Students could search poems using key words. An electronic notebook enabled them to move text around, add comments and construct their own knowledge base of material. Compared to previous OU courses they had greater choice over which materials to use, and how to sequence the content and control the pace of moving through it. Students used the texts and resources to take part in 'investigation activities'. The resources were not structured by a narrative but could be accessed at any point.[70] Although there were initial operating difficulties, a structuring device in the form of an analytic map helped to overcome these problems.[71] In 2003, when the OU introduced the world's first online postgraduate music course, the materials included a specially created online 'music research environment' that contained a bank of musical and other databases, full-text articles and audio clips.[72] Through practice, reflection and amendment of its teaching the OU developed ways of supporting learning through participation in dialogues.

Incrementally, by testing ideas against the experiences of students, it found ways of supporting learners within hypermedia learning environments.

Students on *Materials: Engineering and science*, T203 (1994–2003), were able to learn basic aspects of the subject through correspondence texts and then practise their skills through an interactive programme which prompted the student through questions. The programme was written in the form of a game with students able to attain grades ranging from 'applicant for apprentice metallurgist' to 'works metallurgist'.[73] This course sought to overcome the difficulties associated with interpreting diagrams representing physical phenomena. Its description referred to 'exploring the relationships between structure, properties and processes', adding that 'for this exploration you will need a scientific modelling "toolkit"'. On *Computing: An object-oriented approach*, M206 (1998–2005), students were guided though an interactive practical environment which included integrated web resources, video, interactive multi-media and print materials. The module won the British Computer Society (BCS) Gold Medal in 1997, the BCS IT Award in 1998 and the Design Council Millennium Innovation Award in 1999.

Discovering science, S103 (1998–2007), offered students multiple-choice options with video-clip explanations and an online quiz to enable them to check their understanding. Ideas regarding natural selection were not taught directly. Rather, students were introduced to fieldwork observation and note-taking skills in relation to Charles Darwin's work in the Galapagos Islands. They were encouraged to make systematic notes and choices about where to observe, identify and categorise finches using a field guide. The virtual trip indicated which species would be observed and the conditions that Darwin faced.[74] Other virtual field trips followed. Those who studied *Environmental science*, S216 (2002–14), could use DVD technology to travel on virtual field trips to the Teign Valley in Devon and the Sevilleta wildlife reserve in New Mexico.[75]

Courses became less print-dominated as the use of a variety of media grew. At the same time there was a shift from materials to communications-based learning and from complete materials delivery to greater exploitation of proprietary or publicly accessible digital resources. The major objective of *Keeping ahead in information and communication technology*, T324 (first presented in 2007), was to equip 'students with the skills to enable them to "keep ahead in ICTs" in a critically informed manner'.[76] It made extensive use of third-party resources. This kept the learning materials up-to-date and also supported the teaching of skills in research and evaluation, enabling students to learn how to use vast databases in an effective, critical fashion. *Technologies for digital media*, T325, followed two years later. It made such substantial use of third-party material that 'it can be seen to be embedded in the "outside world" in a way which would have been impossible a few years previously'.[77] Topicality and authority were significant in a module designed to help learners understand the rapidly changing field of digital media. Presenting timely materials was also aided by changes in the ways in which modules were created. Instead of making integrated whole modules, some teams began to create smaller units which could be reused. These were electronically tagged so as to make them searchable and relatively easy to update. The approach offered flexibility in the construction of courses and in the range of audiences that could be served. In 1999 a project promoted the wider re-use and re-versioning of module materials. Sharing was made easier by the use of a central resource bank and the digital production of materials. For example, the Faculty of Technology and the Business School used the same material to teach systems. *Learning in the connected economy*, H806 (2002–08), was versioned as *Understanding eLearning*, T186. The *Postgraduate certificate in learning and course design in HE*, H850 (1999–2005), was also re-used. The material was subsequently made available for the OpenLearn and OpenChina projects.

The OU's emphasis on reflective learning did not develop in isolation. The OU, in common with other UK higher education institutions, was required to offer students what the Dearing Report of 1997 called 'a structured and supported process ... to reflect upon their own learning performance and/or achievement and to plan for their personal, educational and careers development'. Informed by the Quality Assurance Agency's *Framework for higher education qualifications*, the OU produced an undergraduate-level framework, which, after revisions, was approved in 2005. The aim of this generic levels indicator, which focused on the development of knowledge and understanding, cognitive skills and key skills in an OU context, was to support curriculum design and development and to inform students about study expectations. A statement of graduate aims and abilities, intended to describe the overall attributes of the OU graduate, was also produced, as were links to personal development planning. The intention was to help students identify personal goals through their OU studies.[78] The key skills national standards, defined by the Qualifications and Curriculum Authority, provided reference points for six key skill areas: improving own learning and performance, communication, information technology, application of number, problem solving and working with others. An additional key skill area of information literacy – focusing on identifying, finding and critically evaluating information – was developed by the Information Literacy Unit in the OU library.

Exploring how to make the best use of developments in communications has long been of importance to the OU. It sought not to deliver lecture notes that left students isolated but to provide supported open learning that enabled learners to acquire information and discover how to construct knowledge together. The modules outlined in this section illustrate some of the ways in which the OU has sought to co-ordinate reflection on experience and negotiation within a community and to allow people's interests to help frame their learning. They also indicate how the view that learning was not a possession of individuals but found in dialogue informed OU teaching. More generally this approach to teaching exemplifies the OU's interest in helping learners to build a sense of confidence and offering them realistic objectives and opportunities to share ideas and learn new skills. Buttressing the relationship between learning and social connections took different forms over the years but remained a central tenet of OU teaching.

The development of the teaching materials and the curriculum did not always proceed smoothly. There were examples of courses being cancelled or drastically amended after a few, or even one, presentation, of the technology being insufficiently flexible or robust, and of the pedagogy being flawed. Sometimes implementation of new procedures was delayed or hindered because of resistance from staff and students. There was resentment when the OU's focus moved towards eLearning, when different technologies were adopted and when the financial model was not premised on growth. There was not a universal welcome for the end of compulsory residential schools and the shift away from the model of a course in which six assignments constituted half the overall marks and a three-hour unseen exam constituted the other half (Figure 6.3). By 1992 the OU was, as the Vice-Chancellor noted, 'a large institution and large institutions often find it difficult to adapt to change'.[79] However, the OU was, to quote the title of the access course it produced that year, *Living in a changing society*, and, in the circumstances of recessionary economic conditions, a closer relationship with the rest of higher education and the evolution of the partnership with the BBC through a series of agreements, new projects and goals were set. The variety of awards available grew with the introduction of the BSc. The number of credits to gain a degree was set at 360 credit points, with Honours requiring 480 credit points. Much time was spent in debate of these matters and *Open House* claimed that the decisive meeting at Senate

> will go down in history as the one that ... made more fundamental and far-reaching changes to the OU than it has previously taken during the first two decades.[80]

The introduction of an electronic system for submitting, recording and returning assignments (800,000 were handled every year by 2000) and the new

Figure 6.3 One of the occasions when students could meet other students was in the examination. Most students sit their examinations in centres around Britain and Northern Ireland, but exams have also been held in many other countries, as well as at home, in hospitals and on a Trinity House lightship.

integrated student records system, introduced in 2001, also led to expressions of concern. There was also some opposition to a variety of other decisions, notably the interest in raising funds to ensure that the OU could engage with Africa, the introduction of scenario planning about the external environment as a key element of strategic planning and change processes, and the decision in 2002 to employ over 150 staff to work with a branding consultant so that the OU's mission statement could be renewed and ten strategic priorities be defined.[81] Although the overall commitment to supporting dialogue between adult learners was maintained and extended, the development of the OU was uneven because of external constraints and also because structural, pedagogic and political developments, which disrupted routines and challenged accepted aims, routes and systems, met with internal resistance.

Environment at the OU

By 2009 the OU had produced almost 1,800 modules, of which almost 100 were environment-related modules.[82] Topics covered included oceanography, biology, environmental engineering and systems. Structured to be able to produce multi-, trans-, cross- and inter-disciplinary modules, to merge disciplinary traditions and to promote experiential, collaborative learning, the OU was well placed to engage with the development of modern environmentalism in the 1960 and 1970s. *Art and environment*, TAD292 (1976–85), for example, sought both to merge disciplines and encourage students to learn through their experiences (Plate 19).[83] On *Environment*, S2–3 (1972–82), students were offered material about geological and biological processes and international environmental politics. It included the 1972 *Stockholm Declaration* of the United Nations Conference on the Human Environment.

In 1974 the OU launched the first university module in ecology (*Ecology*, S323 (1974–85)). This unified, in one 30-point module, a wide range of subjects, including population, physiology, ecosystems and paleoecology. There was a project element enabling students to follow their own interests. Students also carried out group activities.[84] Students selected a project, sent a plan to the tutor who commented upon it and, following negotiation, the student then carried out the practical work and collated the data.

A further idea developed at the OU was the use of current ideas and prominent contributors to debates to promote understanding of the issues. On *Man-made futures: Design and technology*, T262 (1975–82), the teaching materials included an interview with the advocate of alternative technology, E. F. Schumacher. Popular BBC science and current affairs programmes had foregrounded concerns about population growth, the subject of material on *The man-made world: A foundation course*, T100 (1972–79).[85]

The OU encouraged students to move into new disciplinary areas by introducing modules which were foregrounded as available to all students by the use of the letter 'U' in their code. John Daniel's first annual report as Vice-Chancellor indicated that he sought 'to build on the University's contribution to environmental education … across a number of faculties'.[86] *Environment*, U206 (1991–2002), integrated social sciences, science and technology. It too had a project element. Indeed, as geographer Philip Sarre noted, 'the pedagogy of the course aimed to give students as active a role as possible [and a] substantial student project'.[87] A science pack, PS621, produced in the late 1980s encouraged learners to consider 'cutting edge issues ahead of broad public debate'. *Environment*, U206, was 'extremely current' and the presentation of the debate over genetic engineering of crops in *Science matters*, S280 (1993–2005), was 'way ahead'.[88]

U206 was replaced by a module covering similar territory, *Environment*, U216 (2003–13). In 2003 the first online inter-disciplinary module, *The environmental web*, U316 (2003–14), was presented. This also had a project in which students shared data. A report noted that they offered one another considerable support.[89] *Neighbourhood nature*, S159 (launched in 2009), built on iSpot, the OU's social networking website, which enabled users to share data about nature.[90] People could upload photographs with location-based tags and comment on the images of others. In 2010 a partnership with Earthwatch, an organisation which arranged for volunteers to collect data in the field, enabled OU students to count Earthwatch volunteering towards a BSc in Natural Science. Both *Environmental policy in an international context*, DT210 (1995–99), and *Environmental policy in an international context*, DU310 (2000–06), involved the sharing across national borders of teaching resources and methods and the latter gave ALs an enhanced role.

The teaching of environmental matters at the OU received recognition when in 2012 Mark Brandon, Senior Lecturer in Environmental Science, won 'Most Innovative Teacher of the Year' at the *Times Higher Education* Awards. He contributed to the most popular OU unit of all time, which was the first chapter of *The frozen planet*, S175. It was made available free online via OpenLearn.[91]

Informal learning

Television, with its set times and speeds for broadcasts, was frequently dismissed as liable to induce passivity and an intellectually lazy approach. Nevertheless, the OU has, since its inception, worked with the BBC to broadcast educational resources freely for non-commercial use and adaptation.[92] Programmes were designed to have a wide audience appeal, as well as being of value to students studying specific modules. Television has aided recruitment to the OU. A 1991 survey of viewers who were not OU students found that 73 per cent of the drop-in viewers were motivated to do some kind of follow-up activity by OU programmes. It was also noted that women preferred community welfare programmes, psychology and art/literature, and men tended to favour science, technology and mathematics.[93] Interest in general, rather than module-specific, viewers of the OU's BBC programmes grew when teaching materials began to be supplied via cassettes, videos, CDs, DVDs or in electronic format. As broadcasting became even less significant in regard to formal teaching and assessment, co-productions by the OU and the BBC began to emphasise the general benefits of participation in lifelong learning. There were a variety of formats used but the overall effect was to showcase the possibility of study through the OU. *Someone to Watch Over Me*, a series looking at the work of Bristol's childcare social workers, was first broadcast in 2004. It aided recruitment to train for social work and parts of it were used as teaching materials on *Critical practice in social work*, K315 (first presented in 2008), a module which was integral to the OU's social work degree. *Bang Goes the Theory*, a science magazine series, was first broadcast in 2009. It was supported by a website, interactive resources and free events designed to encourage interest in science. It was not linked to a specific module. *The Money Programme*, made in conjunction with the OU Business School, was, in 2007, the first full BBC programme to be broadcast inside the virtual world of *Second Life*. *Empire*, screened in 2012, attracted up to 2.96 million viewers per programme and another 1.2 million iPlayer views. In addition, 53 per cent of respondents to a BBC survey reported they had 'learned a lot' from watching the series. By March 2013, 63,700 hard copies of the associated printed poster had been requested and there had been 2,811 downloads of it by July 2013. Related to the series were six 'Selling Empire' online lectures with an annotated and hyperlinked bibliography. There was also an online 'Empire Game', which was available throughout the screening of the series.[94] Links were made to the OU module *Empire: 1492–1975*, A326.

OU programmes were initially broadcast on BBC2 but as the number of BBC channels grew so did the reach of OU programmes, which have been broadcast on all of the BBC's TV channels, including the digital channels BBC3 and BBC4. The form and content of co-productions related to the priorities identified by the faculties which could use the material for teaching and learning. Bespoke content, such as additional or extended interviews, was commissioned for the use of OU module teams. An agreement allowed reciprocal use of the BBC Archive from which additional material could be identified for educational use. All programmes encouraged viewers to learn more about the broadcast material by ordering a free print item or visiting the OpenLearn website, where themed interactive learning materials were provided. Television, once used to delivery teaching materials for specific courses, had become the vehicle for more generic encouragement for learning.

In addition to television, the OU used the internet to create and disseminate open educational resources. In 2005 the OU obtained a $10 million grant from the William and Flora Hewlett Foundation to launch OpenLearn, an initiative designed to make about 10 per cent of the OU's educational resource freely available. This large-scale experiment in open content attracted one million unique visitors in the first year, rising to six million by 2013. The platform supplied not just teaching notes but structured units of learning. In addition a range of social tools were provided to encourage discussion and collaboration among users.[95] The content had a Creative Commons licence, which enabled users to change and develop the material.[96] The site became an effective channel for the conversion of enquirers into registered students – that is, it enabled people all over the world to move from informal to formal learning. Nevertheless, the idea of providing teaching materials for free, through OpenLearn and later through FutureLearn, met with scepticism about the lack of a clear income stream. It was, one Pro-Vice-Chancellor argued, akin to giving away the crown jewels.[97] Features incorporated into OpenLearn included forums and learning journals. These were 'supplemented by custom-developed tools for nurturing and supporting social presence, instant messaging, video conferencing and building knowledge maps'.[98] OpenLearn was a major contributor to the work of the Open Door scheme to provide online teaching and electronic materials for free to Africa and to the Teacher Education in sub-Saharan Africa programme (TESSA). The OU also provided LabSpace, a platform which provided tools for academic re-use of Creative Commons licence material. This enabled new versions of the available content, or entirely new material, to be uploaded and built upon to form online courses. It offered additional tools, notably Compendium (which allowed users to connect together internet resources which could be shared) and FlashMeeting (which offered recordable, low-cost communication using web-cam, audio and text chat). There was also guided, peer-facilitated learning through the LearningSpace platform. Learners could join discussions, write blogs, contribute to wikis and add material. In 2012 *China on four wheels*, two BBC2 broadcasts, had over a million viewers and over a third of those who went to the associated OpenLearn site then went to the 'Study at the OU' web pages. The total number of iTunesU downloads between 2008 and 2013 was almost 65 million. Only 18 per cent of the visitors were from the UK, with more coming from the USA. In 2013 there were over 5.2 million unique visitors to OpenLearn and 2.4 million to the OU's YouTube channels.

In 2007 the OU started to use an open source management system, Moodle, for its modules, and in the same year, in order to address the question 'if we were to start a new university from scratch, harnessing the very best of new technologies – what would it look like?', the OU began to develop SocialLearn.[99] It was recognised that learners could benefit not only from access to information but also from structures which could help them to connect with others and develop bonds of mutual support and affirmation. This could enable them to move beyond their assumptions and towards learning which stretched them. SocialLearn was intended to support existing social learning websites and to improve teaching- and learning-related ideas and designs. The tools, resources and discussions were openly available online. This was part of a wider trend. The government commissioned, and largely accepted, an independent study which promoted open access for users of university research.[100] Massive open online courses (MOOCs) were developed and large-scale projects were launched in the United States. The challenge of teaching tens of thousands of people online led to debates about the best ways to develop effective pedagogical approaches and assessment strategies, and the role of open source material. In 2012 the OU formed its own company in this field, FutureLearn.[101] Building on the availability of blogs, chat forums, wikis and group assignments the OU sought to apply and develop its social learning practices, which emphasised engagement and interaction.

The development of peer-to-peer pedagogies has not been straightforward, as OU undergraduates study modules in a variety of sequences and speeds. Some have taken many years to graduate and some did not complete a degree. Fellow students encountered on a particular module might never be met again. Nevertheless, groupings which can be classified, to employ educationalist Etienne Wenger's term, as 'communities of practice' have been formed by OU students. In such communities members build relationships that enable them to learn from each other because they share interests and competencies and engage in activities and discussions together, helping one other and sharing information.[102] One such community was created after OU staff encouraged former students on the family and community history module, DA301, to join a group they had started, Open Studies in Family and Community History. Some of these students also studied for a BPhil for which they collated and exchanged local historical records. In 1999 a new body, the Family & Community Historical Research Society, was founded at a meeting held at the OU. Initially the Society's journal was co-edited by three OU academics. While a number of those involved in FACHRS felt that the OU had fostered their confidence and skills, it was separate from the university.[103] It was former students who developed the structure of the body and decided on the topics to study together. The results were published in books and papers.[104] The Society developed a range of self-help strategies to sustain its informal communities and began to run its own courses. These former students, many of whom had never met one another prior to joining the Society, identified common aims and created informal, voluntary, convivial, educational communities of practice based on their OU studies. These networks have enabled these learners to achieve what they could not have done individually.

The OU had encouraged students to engage in local research prior to DA301. *Great Britain: 1750–1950: Sources and historiography*, A401

(1974–82), involved students in projects using local documents and other materials. *Historical sources and the social scientist*, D301 (1974–88), also supported students who engaged in historical projects of their own devising. Many of them, it was noted, 'cope competently with the project without resorting to the telephone or letter'.[105] Students were asked their views about the course design and as a result more material about Scotland was offered. In addition, a newsletter was provided when one was requested. Some of the students on this course established their own day school outside of the formal OU system. This was attended by nine OU staff members on a voluntary basis. Four unofficial weekend schools were also held. The East Anglian Studies Resources pack, PA730, was available from 1984 to 1997. Developed with the Norfolk Federation of Women's Institutes, it was a stand-alone pack sold to the public. It included facsimiles of primary sources and recordings of older local people's personal testimonies. These gave learners opportunities to interpret material for themselves. There were ideas for activities, readings and visits. The pack was used as a resource and as a guided approach to independent learning by local groups.[106]

Charles Booth and social investigation in nineteenth-century Britain, A427 (1997–2004), enabled students to conduct research on a question of their own devising. They were sent the OU's first interactive research CD-ROM, which provided maps, structured databases of census records, copies of original documents and guided 'visits' to locations of especial historical interest.[107] Student researchers have also been aided by the development of an online library which has enabled them to access electronically journals, e-books, databases and resources. FirstClass was used to guide students, and there were monitored seminars and discussion threads. *The oral history project*, A422 (1994–2001), had a project in place of an examination, as did *The Roman family*, A428 (1997–2004), and *Art, society and religion in Siena, Florence and Padua 1280–1400*, A354 (1995–2006). Together, these modules provided models of how student researchers could be supported.

Former students on the digital photography module, T189, established their own online groups and maintained contact with one another after completing the course. A co-chair of the module team joined the first of these groups to be formed but soon left the students to engage with each other.[108] These groups mimicked the module in that those involved uploaded photographs and then commented on the pictures. Members sought and provided advice, offered ideas about a Royal Photographic Society qualification, ran competitions and met to take pictures together. Through T189 they learned to offer, request and accept advice and supportive criticism from others in their online groups. One person said that he had purchased additional books on photography, joined a local camera club and used the T189 materials as the basis for a booklet that he wrote for fellow club members. Another recorded events at a local industrial museum and soon became involved in this volunteer-run establishment.[109] These photographers echoed Tony Whittaker of the Tadpoles, a society created in the 1980s by students who had studied TAD292. He felt that:

> It is very interesting that actually there is still quite a focus on learning and skills in the same way as there was in the summer schools. The society, it could have drifted to another purpose, but it seems to have retained quite a focus on learning.[110]

The evidence of these organisations of former students suggests that the OU explored ways in which learning and research could become active personal endeavours, socially mediated through supportive groups (Plate 20). In demonstrating that students can be encouraged to contribute to scholarship, that knowledge can be produced in many places beyond the academic realm and that a variety of media can be employed to enable learners to access open resources, the OU has continued to reconfigure understandings of the roles and impacts that a university can have.

Tutors

The original model for tutorials was that tutors taught small groups of students, face-to-face, in study centres (Figure 6.4). Course materials were delivered to the students via print, radio and television, and tutorials were based on these. Sometimes tutorials were spent watching television programmes associated with the course. Tutors were encouraged to relate concepts, values and lines of enquiry to specific situations, mediating between materials produced in Walton Hall and the individual student (Plate 21). The tutors also assessed students' assignments and taught through the critique they offered of the assignments. By 1995 the university had over 200,000 distance learners, of whom more than 100,000 were studying one or more of the 140 undergraduate modules, and there were about 7,700 tuition and counselling staff throughout Europe.[111] In the face of pedagogic and technological developments, it appeared that the tutorial model needed adaptation.

Tutor-counsellors

When the OU first opened each OU undergraduate was assigned a personal tutor-counsellor, who offered support and advice to that individual as long

Figure 6.4 Desks rearranged for a tutorial.

as the student remained at the university.[112] The idea of counselling students had been raised by the Planning Committee in 1969 and developed by the first Director of Regional Tutorial Services, Robert Beevers. Walter Perry felt that it was 'fundamentally correct to offer students counselling throughout their studies' and the post of counsellor, later tutor-counsellor, was created.[113] Tutor-counsellors were responsible for all first-year tuition (they assessed assignments) and counselling on the broader educational needs of the student. Student counsellor Peter Grigg remembered the first years of the OU and how 'One student had to be helped to the examination hall, his state of mind being such that his grip on the stair rail had to be forced free to get him to the room.'[114] When the student moved on to a second-level course, the tutor-counsellor retained their advisor role, providing an element of stability and continuity. Students came to rely on these staff members for a variety of forms of support. Although a training document was introduced in 1976 and revised in 1977, and a handbook soon followed, their development was hampered by the fact that advice on pathways became more difficult to give when the number of courses and awards on offer grew. Furthermore, by 1990 all the regions had online access to a computerised enquiries system. This reinforced the tutor's status as the prime source and access point for personal advice. In 1997 there were 140,000 students, many of them in Europe, Asia and Africa, as well as the UK. It was difficult for part-time, locally based staff to be conversant with all aspects of the OU. In addition, specialist advice about careers (60 per cent of students said that they had an interest in changing their job) and disabilities (5,500 students had logged that they had special needs) and a range of other matters had become available.[115] Line-managed, full-time, dedicated staff members were appointed to support students. Moreover, face-to-face contact with students had fallen as there were, by that time, 20,000 students studying online. There were fewer opportunities for sustained personal contact. A former tutor-counsellor argued that the role 'stopped being effective. The OU is now much too complicated for one person to know about all aspects of the university.'[116] There was not much evidence that tutor-counsellors performed a clearly beneficial role.[117] A review of the role in 1996 concluded that the policy of employing tutor-counsellors had no evidence base. As Perry had acknowledged, many academics felt this to be a 'relatively peripheral and minor activity', and in 1997 there was a 'significant change' to this 'core concept'. The work of tutor-counsellors was shifted to tutors and student advisors, who were available to offer advice on the telephone.[118]

Counselling continued and its effects have been recalled by many students. Ian Glynn mentioned his 'long term friendships with both tutors and students' and Rebecca Hodson referred to her tutor's ability to 'secure additional software and funding'.[119] Like many others she referred to gaining self-confidence. Christine Smith, another student, recalled that 'the evening before the exam I panicked and phoned my tutor and said I couldn't do the exam – I just couldn't revise – I knew nothing. Very patiently she talked me through what I had to do and convinced me of how much I did know and gave me the confidence to take the exam. I passed.'[120]

Susan O'Donnell studied with the OU while a single parent with a part-time job. She found the tutors 'encouraging' and the learning materials 'inspirational'. Other students also recalled the support they received from tutors and fellow students.[121]

One of the earliest developments of tutorials was when tutors began to use other methods of communication. Despite initial complaints from the GPO, which ran the UK telephone system at the time, telephones had been used for tutorials since 1973 (Figure 6.5).[122] To support the physically isolated, the itinerant, the housebound and the shiftworkers who were often unable to attend tutorials, expertise was developed and a pack produced.[123] To be useful, telephone contact had to be planned and structured. Strategies for telephone counselling and group telephone tutorial were developed and evaluated.[124] Suggestions were made not only that that students and ALs prepare the books and papers needed for the conversation but also about the tone of voice and the need for the student to review and summarise the session. Advice was offered to tutors about encouraging students to gather around a loudspeaker telephone for self-help activity 'with the added bonus of you taking part from a distance – like an academic Cheshire cat'.[125] Audio-conferencing, which could involve up to eight people on telephones in different locations, was also employed as were faxes, personalised audio-cassette messages and video-conferencing. It was emphasised that whatever the technology, the pedagogic principles remained unchanged.

On *Discovering science*, S103, computer-mediated communication was optional for students but a requirement for ALs. They used FirstClass to access a national conference at least once a week and they could also exchange messages using conferences designed for the localities in which they were based. ALs were provided with guidance as to how to teach in the interactive seminars and offered practical advice which reflected the ethos of OU teaching practices. It was suggested, for example, that they 'adopt an informal, friendly tone. Start a message with a greeting such as "Hello" ... avoid the more formal "Dear Chris".' In addition, they were told that 'CMC is a medium devoid of warmth and you need to compensate for this'.[126] The use of pictorial representations of facial expressions or emotional states (emoticons) was suggested. The view that 'technology offers many benefits, but it does not have the capacity in itself to help students learn' was echoed through OU materials for many years.[127] However, one tutor pointed to the effectiveness of using the web compared to the telephone:

> Email makes a huge difference to the speed at which you can communicate without being intrusive because you don't want to ring people up all the time ... and also on my own side I have rung people and listened for hours to all their sorrows.[128]

Figure 6.5 Telephone tutorials enabled those who could not attend face-to-face tutorials to receive support. This is a tutor working from home.

Those who tutored a module without face-to-face contact all felt that conferencing enabled them to offer more support than in the past. The module completion rate was significantly higher than that of comparable modules without the online element. The OU developed ways to use the web to reduce the sense of distance between learning materials and learner support. It sought to offer opportunities for more exploratory and independent learning and teaching.[129]

As new ways of providing interactive and individualised support for learners became possible, so the importance of maintaining face-to-face contact declined.[130] The OU study centre had begun life as 'a "Listening and Viewing Centre" with the express purpose of providing access to VHF radio and BBC2'. Used for counselling and other purposes, many initially cost little to rent. However, 'all too often they are in dreary, poorly equipped schools'. The rents rose over the years and once people were more likely to access BBC2 and video recordings at home it appeared, in 1996, as if 'the future for study centres is clear ... extinction'.[131]

Pedagogic developments also had an impact on tutorials. When collaborative learning began to play a larger role at the OU, the notion of learner support changed. More of the content of courses became generated through online interaction and collaborative activities.[132] The role of tutors shifted. They had been 'in a special position: accountable, exposed, experiencing both considerable pressure and unusual liberty'.[133] For *The environmental web*, U316 (2003–14), although ALs marked written assignments, spent time in online conferences (as students' participation in forums was assessed) and there was a day school and supported collaborative activity, there were no tutorials. Being online did not diminish the role of ALs in helping students to negotiate the OU's structures and to progress with their studies.[134] Tutors were still expected to be interested in the process of their students' learning and in 'the discovery of what it is that they need to learn'. They were informed that good tutoring involved 'your ongoing learning about your students' learning and your impact on this ... a key component for good teaching is evaluation'.[135] They were encouraged to focus on promoting meaningful participation within the specialist discourses with which they were familiar.[136]

In 1997 part-time tutors were redesignated as ALs. Rather than being paid on a piece-rate system for each assignment they marked, they were paid as fractional workers. Those who had contracts were given priority for new contracts when new courses came on stream and they were given the right to sick pay and to join the pension scheme. The aim was to offer greater security and engagement with the OU to ALs. Further assimilation of the ALs into the main employment framework occurred in 2004, with the role being designated a single three-point pay spine in 2005. This was later replaced by thirteen salary bands and seven salary points for each band. A further aim was to reduce the number of ALs, with each one doing work equivalent to a 0.4 full-time contract. Between 2011 and 2013 the number of ALs fell from 7,000 to 6,000, but many ALs had difficulties increasing their workload because the cut-off point for assignments on different modules and the dates of tutorials often coincided, leading to peaks of work. More teaching was done online and the amount of local contact with students fell. To stream-line and standardise processes and reduce costs it was proposed to create a single, virtual and distributed UK-wide AL Services team with an integrated management structure.

Although the posts of AL and counsellor were reconfigured, the impor-tance of the AL in reinforcing students' confidence was retained. When, in 2009, the higher education sector faced significant economic pressures, OU Vice-Chancellor Brenda Gourley concentrated on playing to the university's strengths. She pointed to how OU modules were designed to offer an inten-sive level of personal support:

> Right from the start, we've been unremittingly focused on the quality of teaching material and student support ... Some of our students say they've received more personal attention from The Open University than they had when they were at conventional universities.[137]

Four externally funded Centres for Excellence in Teaching and Learning were established, and ALs' views were sought as to how to develop a model of learning support which was affective, reflective, cognitive and systematic.[138] The intention was to dismantle some of the barriers between 'the academic process, the support process and the motivations of the student' and for students to become more confident in their abilities and clearer about their motivations, and to enhance their employability.[139] Further aims were to strengthen their changing identities and to provide scaffolding for problem-solving and reflection so as to enable them to build on their own existing concepts and those of other students.[140]

Although training schemes were implemented, so as to enable tutors to keep apace of the new uses of technology and the new pedagogy, and although tutors' assignment marking was monitored and there were national and region-based and online meetings at which information was exchanged, by the 1990s there were concerns raised about the effectiveness of teaching at the OU. A team from the Committee of Vice-Chancellors and Principals' Academic Audit Unit reported the relative weakness of both quality assurance and the monitoring of the implementation of policies in the regions.[141] Scottish Director John Cowan produced the Quality Tuition Report, which emphasised the need for staff development to support the tutors.[142] There had been a process of accretion. The 2002 publication for tutors had quotations from plans and materials dating back to the 1980s. This emphasised continuity as well as change.[143] Folders with information on how to support open learners were developed, as were 'toolkits' on specific issues (e.g. equal opportunities).[144] A module designed for Level 1 students, *Learning online: Computing with confidence*, TU170 (2001–03), was adapted to support the staff development of a group of tutors who were members of nine different academic faculties but all lived in one region. Some parts of the teaching materials were removed and additional face-to-face tutorials were provided. In addition the tutors completed questionnaires designed to encourage reflection about the module. A few years later Judith Fage, a senior counsellor and later a regional director, felt able to report that that a 'well-developed and comprehensive system' of staff training had been developed.[145]

A further element of staff development was to encourage tutors to learn. Being interested in their own learning was considered to be a sound foundation for facilitating the learning of others.[146] On some modules, notably *Culture and belief*, A205, and *Themes in British/American history*, A317 (1985–94), tutors were encouraged to use conferences to present their own research. Tutors were also encouraged to improve through research into teaching practices. Methods were described, assessed and suggested in OU materials aimed at ALs. Advice on the systematic and collaborative assessment of teaching was offered. ALs defined their research questions, collected evidence, took action designed to improve their teaching and observed the impact of the changes. Many small-scale projects were conducted by ALs. Some used questionnaire and interviews; others used journals and diaries, field notes and representations of learners' social links. They were reminded that 'researching what you do does not always confirm what you do – and learning can sometimes be painful. It is a salutary reminder that this may the case for our students too.'[147]

In 1996 the *Supporting open learners reader* suggested that 'reflection is the core process for effective professional learning'.[148] A study of the tutors who had participated in the module indicated 'the value and effectiveness of engaging in course-related activities as a form of staff development ... Tutors gained considerable insights into being a student.'[149] ALs were also encouraged to learn from students and from one another. As informal feedback was often 'gratifying but imprecise', ALs were invited to ask students to complete questionnaires. This could 'enhance the idea of the tutorial as a collaborative project'. It was also proposed that 'peer observation' was a 'valuable activity' as it could lead ALs to exchange ideas and was evidence of professional development.[150] ALs were also encouraged to seek the advice of their AL mentor. In 2000 a project brought together ALs from a variety of locations for co-ordinated research, and in 2005 a report concluded that tutors who engaged in scholarly practices felt more strongly identified with the OU, felt more valued and gained new skills and perspectives. They also built stronger relationships with their students.[151]

In 2005 tutors Carole Arnold and Norma Rothwell studied the materials which were used to make initial contact with students who did not hand in their first assignment on the Level 1 science course, S103. They then made changes to the letter sent to students and made contact immediately after the deadline for submission had passed. This resulted in improved response rates.[152] In one region four ALs sent out questionnaires about written materials, telephoned students and talked to students during a tutorial. As a result they improved the quality of the comments made on students' work.[153] Veronica Davies, who taught Art History at Levels 2 and 3, told her students about her project on distance teaching of visual material and involved them by asking for specific responses 'in the form of reflective comments, not tick boxes'. She drew attention to the teaching of visual materials in her comments to students and in the course materials. She concluded that making learners aware of the issues raised their interest in these issues and led them to conceptualise themselves as 'taking charge'. As gallery visits were important in the module she worked with students on a list of local gallery resources and incorporated some of her findings into her subsequent teaching.[154]

In 2009, as part of a HEFCE-funded scheme, over 150 'Practitioner Enquiry Reports' were completed by ALs. They undertook short practice-based projects into a variety of pedagogy and student-support topics.[155] Tutor Natasha Sigala investigated the use by second-level psychology students and their tutors of online tutorial group conferences/forums as a teaching tool and a method of learner support.[156] Through questionnaires, telephone interviews and tutorial observations Isobel Shelton assessed the development of map interpretation and data analysis skills among second-level geographers.[157] Frank Lally identified a weakness within a third-level biology module by reviewing assignments and listening to his students. He devised an electronically delivered preparatory study unit to support students who had little prior knowledge of chemistry. He then reflected on the students' assessment of his unit. He spoke with the chair of the module about his conclusions and wrote a report.[158] This enabled his conclusions to be assessed and his generic ideas employed across the university. In 2012 ALs from five different faculties,

Figure 6.6 Tutorial on *Death and dying*, K260 (1993–2016).

all based in the same region, were issued with wifi-enabled iPads and asked to experiment by using them in their teaching, recording their experiences and sharing their findings on a dedicated forum.[159]

Modules are no longer largely print-dominated, materials-based and aimed at individual learners. Many are more multi-media, collaborative and communications-based. Support is offered to enable students to build on proprietary or publicly accessible digital resources. While the media used to facilitate communication has changed and extended, from face-to-face and telephone to a variety of electronic teaching methods, the importance attached to students' interactions with the person assigned to assess and to provide academic help remains significant (Figure 6.6).

Conclusion

The deployment of new technology has been described by Christensen as a central aspect of disruptive innovation.[160] Since the 1990s the OU's use of new technologies to administer student services has been disruptive in the economic sense, which was the area on which Christensen focused, but its increasing categorisation as one of many UK universities has rendered its impact in this area relatively minor. More significantly, its use of technology has also disrupted ideas about the relationship between academics and learners. By enabling students to engage, via online conferences, with each other and with tutors and to become researchers, it has empowered them. They have remained located within the wider society and their own homes and also connected through their mobile and other devices. Learners have been encouraged to generate and process content, publicise their ideas and contribute (in editorial or other capacities) to the open source knowledge repositories.

The promotion of ideas about learning through dialogue and debate, and the encouragement of networks of learners, has not always been straight-forward. The replacement or refinement of one set of pedagogic ideas with other frameworks to support learning has not been an evenly distributed process. The understanding that knowledge can be seen as a co-construction, a relational achievement, the result of co-ordinated action has not been easy to implement because, while some welcomed new conceptualisations and adapted them for the OU, there have also been both students and staff who have challenged change. In addition, sometimes subject fields, administra-tive and production processes and assessment practices have not been easily adapted for the practices of experimental modules. Furthermore, sometimes the technology has not proven to be sufficiently robust to support the aims of enthusiastic educators. Although group work has been encouraged, the OU's assessment systems have remained focused on individuals providing evidence of attainment of a level of knowledge and understanding as measured against pre-defined criteria. There has had to be recognition of the practicalities of studying part-time and away from a campus. There were external quality assurance frameworks to consider, and the interpretation of new ideas by tutors, often the only staff that OU students meet in person, cannot always be predicted or controlled. The interest in bolstering the informal sector and in promoting journeys from it to formal learning, by making use of BBC tel-evision and radio broadcasts, OpenLearn, SocialLearn and FutureLearn, has met with a mixed reception. Much informal learning has remained outside the formal sector, and tutors, teaching materials and delivery system have all been cited by students as the reason they ceased to study through the OU. Nevertheless, despite the constraints and the setbacks there remains a com-mitment to supporting self-directed, learner-centred approaches. Since the 1990s the OU, with its students, has created new spaces for learning. It has also continued to offer a blend of media. For *An introduction to the social sciences: Understanding social change*, DD100 (first offered in 2000), there were books, study guides, CD-ROMs, audiotapes, online information and specially produced television broadcasts. Such a combination was no longer novel but the familiar was well regarded. A record number for a single presentation of a course, 13,000 people, registered for it. Through its promotion of notions of shared repertoire, mutual engagement and joint enterprise the OU positioned itself to be able to meet many challenges, to disrupt education and to remain popular.

Part IV

Half a century of learning

7

Open to people[1]

In his inaugural speech as Foundation Chancellor of the OU, Geoffrey Crowther declared the new institution 'open in many ways, but first of all to people'. The commitment to inclusivity was linked to an aspiration to aim 'higher and wider' than its acknowledged role as an 'educational rescue mission'. The impacts of the OU's strategies were significant at a societal level, but, by meeting needs for higher education, it has also fostered the realisation of individual potential within a diverse constituency: 'There are no limits on persons.'[2] The ways in which OU students assess their experiences indicates both the academic impact of the OU but also of many instances of personal transformations which went far beyond the notion of rescue.

For individuals there were improvements in careers, confidence and contentment. In common with other students, OU graduates often refer to their enhanced personal efficiency and productivity.[3] Overall the university has, in the words of one researcher, 'changed the lives of thousands of its students hugely for the better'.[4] Their journeys have been more dramatic than those of many other students because their travels involved large-scale changes in expectations and understandings. Personal accounts, reflecting on changes in their world and in themselves, reveal the impact of the OU. The narratives indicate how many students moved from a stage of uncompleted secondary education to degree level or beyond. Learning was now a matter of excitement and progress rather than misery and failure. As their own ability to make meanings became more sophisticated, OU students were better equipped to transform their own lives and recognise changes in the lives of those around them. This helped in turn to shape the university and the society in which it was embedded.

The first of the three sections in this chapter focuses on the diversity and number of OU students. Some students had not gained the entry qualifications required by other universities or had disabilities or familial or workplace commitments which prevented full-time attendance at university. Others were living abroad or in remote areas and were looking for accessible higher education. Some were in prison. An unknown number of learners on whom the OU had an impact were not registered students but beneficiaries of the OU's policy of making many educational resources freely available. Many others learned indirectly from OU students. The university also supported former students who wanted to continue to learn together.

Although students who brought such a heterogeneous range of experiences, skills and ideas with them cannot easily be categorised, some patterns can be outlined. Many students presented their success in terms of economic gain due to individual effort. They reported feeling driven by a need to change direction or prove their scholarly credentials or capacity for focused work. They saw how their personal acquisition of new knowledge changed their lives and relationships. They frequently acknowledged that their engagement was initially determined by their peers, families and communities as well as their own expectations and experiences. A number referred to how the OU broadened their horizons, increased their confidence and, by enabling them to form communities of learners, helped them become active citizens who could benefit the wider society.

Fear and laughter

One student recalled her husband's reaction when he discovered that she was studying with the OU by finding her books:

> He threw them all down the rubbish chute (we live on the 7th floor). I get on well with Ted the caretaker so next morning when my husband had gone to work I went to see him and said I had to go through the bins ... there I was with big rubber gloves picking my way through everything but I got it all back and cleaned up. I can leave it at my pal's flat.

Another student nervously attended a day school: 'They all looked a bit posh, some had briefcases ... it was OK until this man at the front asked a question. I hadn't a clue what he was asking me and I wet myself there and then and had to leave.'[5]

Martin Broadhurst, a construction worker from Derby, recalled his experiences of the residential element of an OU module, which was held at the University of Bath. He describes it as

> the closest I was ever likely to get to living the traditional student life – minus the instant noodles, lie-ins and cheap overdraft ... The study

sessions began at 9 a.m. and ran through until 8 p.m. or 9 p.m. with occasional breaks to prevent our minds from overheating ... my tutors were incredibly personable and patient and gave valuable constructive feedback ... Just having peers there to discuss our difficulties with was a real benefit ... I was put in a study group with a great bunch of people meaning the long days were filled with a mix of insightful debate, serious hard work and full-on belly laughs ... The principal benefit of attending the residential school, for me at least, was the realisation that other students were having the same difficulties that I was having. I no longer felt alone in the world of long-distance study.[6]

In the second section the spotlight is on a specific element of the OU which formed an important part of its national image and pedagogic strategy – residential schools. Often held in summer on otherwise largely empty university campuses, these enabled the available resources, such as libraries and laboratories, to be utilised to offer face-to-face teaching. While the role of the residential schools has now shrunk in the face of critical assessment and the rise of alternative means of supporting learners, they retain significance for some qualifications: for example, accreditation by the British Psychological Society requires that students engage in some face-to-face learning. More generally they have informed wider understandings of the impact of the OU.

The focus in the third section shifts from particular aspects of the structures which have supported learning towards a specific group of learners whose access to resources was limited: prisoners. Even more so than many other students, prisoners often started from a position of low self-esteem, often had difficulties studying and often benefited from personal support. Their studies provided at least some of them with a sense of release and equipped them with fresh tools with which to deal with issues of power and politics. In Ireland, through the OU, students in prison addressed overtly political concerns, notably attitudes towards the British and Irish states and towards women. This helped some of them to emerge into positions of community leadership and to promote politically stable structures.

'A great variety of people'[7]

Most UK universities which opened in the 1960s initially catered for a few hundred students.[8] By contrast, on 4 August 1970, when the first round of applications to the OU closed, 42,281 people had applied. This was more than anticipated. In the academic year (October–June) 1970/71 there were 621,000 students in higher education. Although the new minister, Margaret

Thatcher, was said to approve of the OU, her decision not to cut to 10,000 students at the OU (a reported possibility) may have been taken because such a reduction would have saved little of the annual costs of about £3.5 million.[9] Instead the decision was made to permit up to 25,000 people to enrol.[10] The number of students in the country was also expanding: by 1985, 15 per cent of young people in the UK went to university.[11] The OU more than kept pace with this expansion. By 2009, when it was much the largest university in the UK by student numbers, there were nearly 600 courses being offered to 150,000 undergraduates and 30,000 postgraduates.

The student numbers give only a partial insight into the scale of the university's operations. In its first year the OU sent 2.7 million mailings, including 33,000 home experiment kits. The students completed about 320,000 assignments: half of these were marked by tutors (Tutor marked assignments) while the other half were marked by computers (Computer marked assignments).[12] The administration of just one OU social sciences module involved some 22,000 applicants, nearly 8,000 enrolments, 85,000 essays which required assessment by hand, 64,000 assignments marked by computers, 24 summer schools in five different locations, 300 study centres and over 1,000 part-time tutors. The logistical difficulties of supplying a wide range of learning materials to each student is illustrated by Lee Taylor, who recalled that 'we had to scour London trying to find cardboard boxes of a suitable size for sheep's brains. Eventually we found a place where I purchased something like 500 boxes, which said "Chanel No 5" on them.'[13] Early accounts of the OU often noted its sheer size and scope. The first Dean of Social Sciences, Michael Drake referred to 'the numbers that numb'.[14]

Although Jennie Lee demanded a 'university with no concessions', increasing the number of graduates has never been the sole aim of the OU.[15] Far more people have started with the OU than have completed degrees through it. Indeed, the prediction made by a professor of adult education in 1968 that 'it seems improbable that the Open University will produce an output of graduates greater than a medium-sized university' initially looked as if it might prove accurate.[16] The OU stressed that its purpose was not simply to create more graduates, but to extend the concept of learning. Harold Wilson envisaged a university for 'housewives who might like to secure qualifications in English Literature' and opportunities for non-vocational courses, for people who sought to improve their language skills before travelling abroad and also material for those who did not formally register but sought to 'enrich themselves by a more passive participation in the educational programmes'.[17] In 1972 the founding professor of systems at the OU, John Beishon, reiterated this theme, stating that 'we do not believe that the Open University should stand or fall on the number of its graduates'. He went on to explain the hoped-for impact of the OU on its students: 'Our aim is not everybody to be a BA but what new learning opportunities could mean in their lives, in terms of renewal, change in occupation, refreshment, intellectual stimulation, new skills.'[18] The OU continued to be committed not to formal qualifications alone but to offering 'high-quality distance learning for all'.[19]

Some students did not intend to study for a degree but sought to achieve the qualifications they required through specific courses and packs. Some took modules but had no intention of sitting an exam; some transferred to other institutions after a few courses.[20] At most universities students graduated after a specific number of years, often three. At the OU it took longer for the number of OU graduates to build up. Students progressed between modules at a pace that suited them. Lindsay Ring started at the OU in 1978 when she had one small daughter, paused in her studies and resumed them after the birth of a fourth child. Michaela McNeill noted that 'It took me fourteen years to complete my Open University degree. That is the joy of the OU! You can take your time!'[21] The OU's modular system was endorsed by Susan Morris, who on graduation (aged 25 in 1974) concluded: 'having studied with the Open University actually gave me a great advantage over some of the other candidates. I had accumulated substantial and relevant work and voluntary experience.' Most OU students completed the modules they started but it could take them many years to finish a degree, studying for only a few hours each week. Some have taken far more modules than is required for a degree. Philip Sully has made studying a way of life. He started with the OU in 1973 and has taken at least 56 modules.[22] The completion rates could reflect that those studying on a part-time basis have less invested in their identity as students than those studying full-time.[23]

Within the first few years approximately 75 per cent of those who registered for an OU course succeeded in getting credit for it. In 1981, of the 150,000 students who had been admitted to the OU over the preceding decade, only 45,000 had graduated. In regard to the rest, 45,000 had left without graduating and 60,000 were still at the university.[24] There were over 200 graduates in 1974, almost 1,000 in 1977 and 1,800 by 1992. Following a change in the requirements for graduation there was a peak year in 1994 when 7,800 degrees were awarded. After this the OU awarded between 6,000 to over 7,000 degrees each year.[25] The number of new students had grown to 47,000 in 1991 and to over 80,000 by 2009, a high percentage of the OU's total in that year of around 150,000 undergraduates and 30,000 postgraduates.[26]

It was not only the popularity of the OU which attracted attention but also the breadth of its appeal: 'Open university chancellor and window cleaner among 5,800 latest graduates' ran one headline above an article which noted that 1 in 14 of all UK graduates came from the OU, that almost 25 per cent of graduates had not achieved the usual entry requirements, that over 10 per cent were in manual or routine office and service posts, and that almost 40 per cent were women.[27] In 1976 *The Economist* concluded that 'the university was serving a different population from traditional universities'.[28] Many OU students rarely met with staff as tutorials were relatively infrequent, compared to contact hours of full-time students, and often students found it difficult to attend due to constraints of time or distance. As summer schools were – at least initially – compulsory, it was there that the distinctiveness of the students of the OU could be seen. Dr Ian Flintoff recalled how:

> You can never go to an OU summer school without seeing this amazing cross-section of society. The first time it brought tears to my eyes, the beauty of it ... I was in an all-male college at Oxford which was mainly Etonians who were charming people, but I can't kid myself for a moment that Trinity had anything on the majesty or poetic brilliance and imagination of the Open University. The Open University is a century or two ahead of Oxford.[29]

Part of a tutor's list of those attending one summer school also demonstrated the range of students:

> company directors and city councillors, pilots and priests, housewives and hairdressers, pregnant mothers and men from the Pru, social workers and salesmen, journalists and Justices of the Peace, doctors and dog breeders.[30]

Gary Slapper illustrated the different circumstances of OU students when he recalled some of the reasons given for requests for extensions on tutor marked assignments:

> the commander of a major British submarine who was called into military service. Someone who had been shot in the course of duty ... it was a police officer while trying to stop a bank being robbed. Someone who had gone out to insert a pacemaker in an emergency roadside operation.[31]

Since the Second World War entrance to UK universities, although not based on A-levels alone, was increasingly determined by an applicant's prior qualifications. The OU bucked this trend and offered places initially on a 'first come, first served' basis and then using a quota system based on regions and professions. In 1971 over 7 per cent of OU students had no formal educational qualifications and fewer than 9 per cent of entrants had an A-level or equivalent. In 1971 43 per cent of the new OU undergraduates were teachers and 67 per cent of all the undergraduates were in high-status occupations (administrators, managers, professions and arts, qualified scientists and engineers). Those in medium-status occupations, in the armed forces, or working as technicians, clerical and sales, accounted for a further 28 per cent. People in lower-status work accounted for 5 per cent. The percentage of teachers who started at the OU fell to between 30 and 37 per cent for the next four years, and the overall percentage of higher-status workers fell to 53 per cent by 1975. The percentage of lower-status workers attracted to the OU rose to 10 per cent, and the percentage of medium-status workers rose to 38 per cent.[32] During the 1970s the number of OU students with an A-level or equivalent qualification was never greater than 1,400. This changed in the 1980s, as the number of OU students who started with an A-level or equivalent almost tripled, then tripled again in the 1990s. Despite this rise, students with an A-level remained a minority in the OU student body. In the 1980s 8 per cent of OU students had no formal qualifications (compared to 1 per cent at other universities and 7 per cent at the polytechnics), and 16 per cent had O-level or equivalent (compared to 2 per cent at other universities and 12 per cent at the polytechnics).[33] In 2009 almost a half of new OU students had lower qualifications than the usual requirements of UK universities.

Individual stories behind the statistics of students with few or no prior qualifications emphasise the transformation of these students' attitudes towards education and their own abilities. Richard Baldwyn recalled 'the dreaded [OU] exam' which led him to be 'transported back some fifty years'.[34] Judith Hudson was given a rather backhanded recommendation of the OU by her Workers Education Association tutor, who told her, 'they take anyone!'[35] Michael Hume felt that the OU helped him to overcome 'the huge mental blocks A levels were giving me'. Emma referred to 'my biology teacher's absolute hatred of me'. She added that on her graduation: 'I will pay my Mum to put an advert in the local paper just as my friend's mother did [after the award of her daughter's PhD from the OU]'.[36] After her head teacher told her that she was unsuited to university, Vida Jane Platt recalls being 'distraught but obedient'. She nevertheless went on to study with the OU:

When I heard that I'd got a First Class Degree I drove into town. The shopping centre turned into the multicoloured set of a musical. It took me all my time not to break into a song and dance act. Finally I could look everyone I met in the eye. I felt equal for the first time since that day in my headmistress's study.[37]

Some students gave positive accounts of their OU experience without specific reference to past humiliations. Jenny Millns compared 'how nervous, how uncertain' she felt on starting her degree course compared to how, aged 58, when she completed her degree, she felt 'for the first time in my life, a real sense of achievement'. She added that through her studies 'my mental health has remained stable, I don't have time to fret over my physical health and I'm keeping my brain active'.[38] Ian Ellson recalled opening his first course results letter: 'The amazing thing was that an hour and a half later I was still looking at this letter expecting it to say "Fail" when in reality it still stated "Passed".' He went on to be awarded a degree.[39]

The absence of entry requirements for the OU was balanced against the insistence by its founders that open access should not equate to lower standards. In 1965 Jennie Lee told the Commons, 'I am not interested in having the next best thing, a poor man's university of the air, which is the sort of thing that one gets if nothing else is within reach. We should set our sights higher than that.'[40] She was adamant 'that the most insulting thing that could happen to any working class man or woman was to have a working class university'.[41] 'It is a fallacy', she said, 'that the Open University was intended to be a working man's university. It is not a university of the working class, or the middle class or white man or black man or men or women. It is just a university.'[42] However, although she stressed that 'the last thing in the world that we wanted was a proletarian ghetto!', the OU became associated with the working class.[43] Terry Lewins, one of the first OU students, reflected that the university was 'a personal opportunity for me but I knew it was an opportunity for working class people, because it was not elitist'.[44] Former Conservative Education Minister William Van Straubenzee went even further, arguing that funding should be directed away from the OU when it did not attract as many working-class students as he deemed was an appropriate figure.[45] Tyrell Burgess claimed that the original Planning Committee of the OU had a sense of 'egalitarian idealism' and Ray Woolfe suggested that it set out 'to attract the under-educated and working-class cohorts in the population'. Such formulations were explicitly denied by a member of the Planning Committee, John Scupham.[46] The Open University was designed to offer support to a wide range of applicants rather than a single socio-economic group.

Whatever the planners' intentions, the OU reached lower socio-economic groups. If students are defined by the social class of their fathers (which was often the measure used to assess the social status of eighteen-year-old students) then the percentage of working-class OU students has always been higher than at the institutions that gained university status before 1992. Many OU students had already climbed several rungs up the social ladder prior to starting their studies and it made relatively little sense to classify them by reference to their fathers. During its early years the OU asked applicants to self-code themselves. Approximately 10 per cent were in routine and semi-routine jobs, a third in lower-level white-collar jobs and just over half were professionals, managers or administrators. Initially, teachers (many with teaching certificates but not degrees) were the biggest single occupational group.[47] One of the practical ways in which the OU fulfilled the need identified by government to produce the human capital required by a highly skilled, science-based economy was to provide places for teachers at a time when their training was being shifted from teacher training colleges to the universities. By 1975 teachers constituted 60 per cent of all OU graduates. *The Economist* marked a decade of the OU by saying that it had 'become a cheap mechanism for turning the teaching profession into an all-graduate body' and that it was also a 'boon to the economy of the new town of Milton Keynes'. It called for the OU to have higher fees, to end its postgraduate teaching and to obtain funding from private sources.[48] Once the bulge of teachers had graduated, the percentage of those starting their studies at the OU with previous experience of higher education fell. The class profile remained similar: surveys in both 1976 and 2005 indicated that about half of OU students would categorise their parents as working class.[49] Even though there has been a rise in the number of students from lower socio-economic groups across the UK sector, class remains a strong indicator of likelihood of obtaining a university education. By the 1990s the wealthiest quarter of young people had approximately a 50 per cent chance of attending a university while the poorest quarter had only an 11 per cent chance.[50] During the period 1995–2005, those from middle-class homes were 50 per cent more likely to stay in education after 16 compared to their working-class counterparts, and, by 2005, 10 per cent of those entitled to free school meals left school with no qualifications at all.[51] The expansion of higher education had not seriously challenged the hierarchies and social exclusiveness of universities.[52]

Universities, it was argued in 2004, had 'disproportionately benefited children from relatively rich families' and the middle class. In 2010, 60 per cent of entrants to the twenty-four members of the Russell Group of universities were from professional backgrounds, compared with 49 per cent among other pre-1992 universities and 39 per cent among post-1992 institutions.[53] In 1996 the comparable figures had been 72 (Russell), 63 (pre-1992 universities) and 49 per cent (post-1992 universities) respectively.[54] It was notable that the OU continued to attract the 'socially and educationally less privileged'.[55]

A survey of UK universities in 2002 reported that 'many students, especially working-class students, never get to the position where they can contemplate HE'. Many exclude themselves or avoid certain institutions, because they are concerned about 'who they might become and what they must give up'.[56] Unlike isolated working-class students at elite universities, OU students did not need to move away from their familiar surroundings in order to study. As one tutor noted, 'If our own students tend to be isolated from their teachers, at least they remain sturdily themselves, which might not be so easy for the bright working-class lad from Rochdale who "gets through" to Cambridge.'[57] In 1960 Lord James expressed concern about the children of clerks and technicians who came 'from homes which are culturally pretty dim' and went to university to find they had to negotiate 'the struggle between the home or the sub-culture and the life that you are trying to make him [sic] lead and the values that you are trying to give him'. These students needed 'positive guidance' and a greater 'emphasis on personal relationships'.[58]

Sarah Burge felt that being able to study in a similar way to other OU students (at home, part-time) meant that she was able to avoid the 'psychological drain of being the odd-one-out all the time' and that she felt 'happier and more fulfilled'.[59] Such accounts indicate how the intention to promote a classless university was experienced by those who studied with it. A certain consciousness about class was evident at the OU. However, much of the awkwardness felt by isolated young working-class students who attended face-to-face universities was avoided.

In 1971 the university made its first foray into the international arena, with twenty students taking their exams overseas, including one on a weather ship in the North Atlantic with the ship's captain as invigilator. By 1972, eighty-nine students stationed in Cyprus were registered for courses by special arrangement with the Ministry of Defence. In January 1974 the university opened its North American office, which enabled US colleges to offer complete OU courses. Later the British Open University Foundation took over the work.

From 1982 the OU, with British Council support, offered courses to British nationals resident in Brussels. The scheme was expanded in 1983 to include more courses and non-nationals and then other EU countries.[60] Tutor John Kirkaldy reported: 'I have met every profession from casino croupier to cowman, and from millionaire to the unemployed'. He also noted that the students came from France, Germany, Holland and Spain and that he had 'received essays dispatched from service personnel in Iraq and Afghanistan and from an ocean-going sea tanker somewhere between Japan and Australia'.[61] Often the Armed Services supported personnel in their studies. Ian Price was stationed in Bagram, Afghanistan, on the day he had to take a German oral exam. The Ministry of Defence permitted him to make a call and he did his oral examination over the phone. Despite the telephone being cut off twice, he passed.[62] During the 1990s OU courses became available to residents of the European Union countries. The OU, by enabling access to the materials that it had produced in the UK, created international networks of transnational learners. Both universities and the English language have been credited as engines of globalisation.[63] The OU, with its vast international reach, played a part in this development.

At the time that the OU opened to students there had already been a quarter of a century 'of unprecedented growth and expansion' for higher education in the UK.[64] There were 400,000 students in the UK in the 1960s, a figure rising to two million by the turn of the twenty-first century, most of them aged under 25.[65] In 1965 about 10 per cent of students were aged over 25, primarily medical students who already had a first degree.[66] Concerns about the ability of adults to learn had diminished by this time. Between the wars Edward Thorndike demonstrated that while the ability of an adult to learn differed from that of a child, adults had the capacity to learn, something that had previously not been substantiated by research.[67] After the war Donald Hebb argued that 'learning is not the same at all stages in development, but changes with experience. The infant is not at all capable of learning in the same way as an adult.'[68] Subsequently, magnetic resonance imaging has been used to map the brain from early childhood into adulthood, and reveals that the frontal lobes, responsible for reasoning and problem solving, tend to develop when a person is in their twenties. This may have alleviated concerns about the abilities of OU students, 91 per cent of whom were aged over 25 in 1971. This percentage fell slowly, reaching around 75 per cent by 2006.

Some people with disabilities were particularly attracted to the OU. Mohanty concluded that, 'As there is no basic qualification for entry to the OU and most of its students are deprived or handicapped in some way or other, this University is the most socialistic in nature and spirit.'[69] In 1972, long before legislation encouraged other universities to accept students with disabilities,[70] the OU appointed a Senior Counsellor with special responsibility for this field. In 1973 there were 554 students with disabilities identified in the rest of full-time higher education; by comparison the OU had about 1,200. In 1975 it specifically undertook to 'continue to take all possible practical steps to enable full participation by disabled students in all aspects of University life', and a study concluded that students with disabilities had higher success rates than achieved by their non-disabled counterparts, and

Figure 7.1 The 1978 Students Association (OUSA) study tour to Rome.

a drop-out rate markedly lower than for the general student population.[71] Maggy Jones reported that she had to leave another university because of lack of wheelchair access, adding that 'for the severely handicapped the Open University is proving to be their first real educational opportunity' (Figure 7.1).[72] Leslie Hayward lost his hearing at the age of nine, had little schooling and counted bottles at a factory for a living. He received his OU degree in 1975 because he could read materials, rather than having to listen to lectures.[73] One student said her choice had been made because 'due to ill health I couldn't take up the unconditional offers I had received from traditional universities' and that her studies dovetailed with her work as 'a full time Mum'.[74] A further reason for the relatively high number of students with disabilities might be because, on average, OU students were ten to fifteen years older than conventional, full-time students.[75] John Cowan concluded that the students felt that within the OU they 'had a community experience in which they cared for students with disabilities'. He recalled one summer school when, at about one o'clock in the morning, on seeing a severely disabled student arriving in a vehicle adapted to take his wheelchair, he asked the student, 'How is it going for you?' And he looked at me and said, 'I've just been to a party, and I've never been to a party in my life. And it was absolutely wonderful.'[76] Students with multiple disabilities continued to be attracted to the OU because, even though legislative changes improved access to other institutions, the OU continued to offer support across a range of disabilities. These included audio recordings and 3D diagrams for the visually impaired.[77]

Educating housewives

Within a few days of the first OU TV broadcasts one newspaper noted the comic potential of women studying by watching television: 'The whole idea of the Open University must be a cartoonist's as well as a student's dream. Just imagine the problem there may be in some homes when Dad wants to watch one channel, the kids a second and Mum is adamant that she must study for her degree.'[78] Even *Sesame*, the OU's magazine, indicated concerns about women adult learners. One illustration showed a woman, complete with curlers and irritated expression, listening to the radio at just after 6am while her husband sleeps. Another wife foregrounds lack of self-confidence and the contents of home experiment kits when she tells her husband 'Looks like a tough course – the kit is a set of worry beads.' A man is reading his newspaper while his wife fails to multi-task, as so distracted is she by her text (a theoretical approach to power and heat) that the ironing has caught alight. She is labelled as 'the housewife'. A housewife watching television, eating chocolates and drinking addresses her spouse, saying 'When do we eat? When do we eat? – You just can't get used to being married to an intellectual, can you!'[79] Michael Drake drew attention to another way in which the OU disrupted expectations about gender roles when he assessed the impact of summer schools. These

> transformed the lives of women more than any other feature of the Open University. I think women who had often never left their home, either their parents' home or the marital home, were suddenly meeting other people in a similar position.[80]

One of benefits of the popularity of the eponymous heroine of the play and film *Educating Rita* was that, by literally being on stage, Rita helped to take the OU off the metaphorical stage and make it a safe place for those who, as Betty Friedan argued in *The Feminine Mystique* (1963), suffered from the problem with no name – housewives.

Among those questioned, the single most remarked upon attainment of OU students was an increase in self-belief.[81] Adult learners' enthusiasm for their engagement in learning has long been linked to their feeling of self-confidence.[82] A report on a post-war scheme to encourage adult learners, many without the minimum entry requirements, to attend university concluded that such students on the scheme 'left university or college with an enhanced sense of self-esteem and a new ability to engage with political, economic and cultural life'.[83] In 1984 Jan Hobbs recalled that she was 'over the moon' to be offered a place at the OU as 'it was the first institution which wanted me for myself'.[84] Following her graduation she improved both her job and her self-esteem. Her remarks about confidence were 'repeated by women all over the country'.[85] One of the first students was Jacqueline White. She studied for three years at the OU before becoming a full-time student in London:

> I found the work agreeably hard. It is bliss when you've grappled with a maths problem for days and then it comes out right. My difficulties were social ones ... I was always frightened they [the other students] were cleverer than I. However, I soon discovered that we were all equally shy and equally insecure and then everything was alright.[86]

The engagement of OU students (who have often been physically isolated from their fellow students) can also be connected to the support provided by their existing networks. As one of the first graduates noted, 'students need sympathetic families'.[87] Asked to rate the importance of sources of external support, OU students placed family and friends at the top of the list. Although some represented their decision to become OU students as individual, often accounts refer to a recommendation from a family member.[88]

Figure 7.2 Sources of external support (students could give more than one source)[89]

Source	per cent
Family and friends	32
Tutors	29
Other students	21
Employers	19
The institution	17

Once studying began, the support of families remained important.[90] George Saint believed that 'My wife's support was responsible for my success more than my determination.'[91] Ernie Lowe joined the first intake in 1971. His children were born in that year and in 1973. He felt that his wife 'shielded me from the demands of a young family'; he chose not to study for Honours because 'my wife deserved a rest and I wanted to enjoy my children'. Emma's comment reveals both a realisation of the unhelpfulness of a poor self-image and a changing relationship with a spouse:

> Shouting 'I'm fat and stupid' at your husband will not make you understand the equations needed to calculate the emissions from an incinerator (though speaking to him nicely means he might just sit with you and talk it over in a very calm and patient manner).[92]

When providing materials for learners the OU had to take into account that these were not necessarily self-assured people with control over when and where they studied. Some of the OU's advertising reflects its ideas about potential students. In its second and third years the OU concentrated such advertising resources as it had into attracting 'women' and the 'working class'. An advertisement featuring a student changing a nappy with a home experiment kit in the background attracted attention but also caused some fury.[93] Perhaps it was because the novelty of learning through the OU was deemed to be disruptive of the familiar conventions about gender roles that the image of the housewife student was evoked in the OU's 'Guide to the Associate Student Programme' leaflet. Next to the words 'Put the Open University at the top of your shopping list' was a picture of the contents of a supermarket shopping basket. Items in and around the basket were labelled 'Social Work', 'Genetics' and, in the case of a sardine tin, 'Oceanography'. One item had a label reading 'Control of Education in Britain' and another 'Control of Technology' (Figure 7.3).[94] This suggested that the OU was emphasising that students could have some influence and that although a modular course structure might appear to be 'the ultimate supermarket model of total freedom of choice', there was still scope for staff and students to work in collaboration (Plate 22).[95]

As the percentage of women students across the country rose, so did the percentage of women who studied through the OU. In 1971 over 72 per cent of the 18,357 new OU students were male, the highest percentage for men of any year. Gradually the percentage of women increased. In 1970 there were 10 per cent more mature women students than in 1969, and the figure continued to rise during the 1970s.[96] In the late 1970s, when women formed 33.7 per cent of university students in the UK, they represented 42.2 per cent of the finally registered OU students.[97] Within the UK older and female students increased: by 1980, 34 per cent of students were 25 and over, and 40 per cent were women. The percentage of women within the OU student population rose to 50 per cent by 1987 and over 60 per cent in 2003. Moreover, at the OU 'women achieved

Figure 7.3 A learner could be conceptualised as both a student and a consumer.

higher grades than men'.[98] Widening access to higher education has tended to benefit middle- and upper-class young women.[99] The rise in the proportion of women students might reflect a broader social change exemplified by the passage of the Equal Pay Act, 1970, and the Sex Discrimination Act, 1975.

The role of the OU in women's increasing participation and achievement in higher education was used by some critics to marginalise both the university and its female students. The BBC publication *Radio Times* introduced the first broadcasts of OU materials by asking:

> New hope for education-hungry adults, or just a new hobby for middle-class housewives? A radical new learning process or an ill-considered muddle of television, radio and correspondence course? An important educational breakthrough or a jaded, semi-political gimmick?[100]

The OU was alleged to be a 'haven for housebound *Guardian* housewives'.[101] It was suggested that the OU might act as a 'consciousness-raising stimulus' for female students.[102] Women were such a threat to *The Spectator* that it collapsed the range of learners who could access the OU into a dismissive categorisation: 'a useful instrument of middle-aged housewives with nothing much to do of an afternoon … it seems quite impossible for it to provide any alternative to a university education … it is certainly no university and in all probability not open'.[103] Others echoed the theme, calling the title of the OU paradoxical in that 'Open' implies opportunities for the educationally disadvantaged while 'University' suggests academic standards comparable with other universities.[104] In 1983 the OU started to present *The changing experience of women*, U221, which, with its successor, *Issues in women's studies*, U207, ran for seventeen years until 1999. Over 8,300 students studied the modules, 94 per cent of them women. A crèche was arranged for the residential schools associated with the module.[105] The course's objectives were apparently lost on a reporter at *The Times*. A report on the OU's women students in 1984 included an interview with Jan Hobbs, who left school at 16, received her OU degree while aged in her mid-40s and was by this point studying for her Honours. The reporter noted that while Jan said that she was happy, the garden was 'a confusion of weeds and piles of unmatched socks sit jumbled in a chair' (Plate 23).[106]

Some students found that their studies disturbed previously held expectations about relationships and lifestyles. Those who offered accounts which affirmed that studying strengthened familial ties were perhaps recognising that education can disrupt, that learning with the OU changes lives, and that while for them education was the lighting of a fire which provided warmth, others felt burned. While many women felt supported by their families and friends, such buttressing could not be assumed. Despite being married to 'a sympathetic husband', Jill MacKean ('housewife with five children') felt guilty about the time that she spent studying, noting that 'most working mothers suffer to some extent from domestic and maternal bad conscience: I started baking my own bread and doing my own laundry at the same time that I started my OU course.'[107] To be successful, teaching at the OU had to recognise that its students were likely to have conflicting calls on their time and to have anxieties which full-time students may not have shared. It could not treat them as passive, genderless recipients if it was to have an impact on their lives.

Alex Richards studied two foundation courses in 1980 and 1983, and her husband was also an OU student. Despite this familiarity with the OU she felt challenged when he started to study *Art and environment*, TAD292. She recalled that it was 'very strange for me and a little bit threatening because it was so unusual'. It was

> a course that really provoked your thinking and it was a course that made you re-evaluate things and in a way that can be quite tricky in a relationship, you know somebody starts doing very different things

and mixing with very different people ... a lot of relationships got a bit sunk by TAD[292]. It did cause a lot of ripples ... it was about people's thinking differently and being open to different things and I think that is quite threatening. I experienced it as very threatening.[108]

Others mentioned ways in which the demands of study at the OU challenged household structures and conventions. Matt Kendall felt it was reasonable to utilise the table in the spare room but recalled that a 'matrimonial' resulted from his experiment involving suspending a brick in the airing cupboard.[109] One child is reported to have remarked, 'Mummy, that university is sending you silly. All you say is "um".' Susan Swete said, 'it upsets my husband some-times ... We argue, well debate sometimes. He thinks I've gone left-wing ... I live differently ... I have less social life by choice.'[110] A number of approaches were taken when explaining the ways in which OU studies challenged conven-tional family structures. A summer-school counsellor recalled talking with a woman who said, 'Well you know what? My husband rang me up and he was up to his neck in it with the kids and I can't believe I laughed.' She continued, 'And I don't miss my *Mr Sheen* a bit.'[111] Clare Burdett wrote, 'When I joined the Open University it became a way of life, not just a spare time activity', and Doris Lawrence observed that the OU 'transformed my way of thinking'. Another student captured the welcome disruption the OU can cause when she sum-marised her experience thus: 'It messes up your whole life, but it's worth it.'[112]

For some the egalitarian principles of the OU involved changes within exist-ing relationships. *The Times* reported the case of a woman who, while eight months pregnant with her third child, left her children with her husband while she attended summer school.[113] When Alan Gordon's wife Sylvia became both an OU student and active within student representation, he stayed at home with four sons aged 4–11 years old.[114] While male students were often relieved of childcare and household duties and received help from their part-ners, women found that the demands on their time increased. Some felt the need to compensate for their studies by being better mothers and partners.[115] In an article about housewife students, Margaret Powers reflected, 'perhaps I listen more intently to the children's tales and troubles than full-time mothers. I have to convince myself they don't suffer because of the way of life I have chosen.' The piece concluded that 'help with the washing up is fine, but far more [was the support of husbands to provide] constant reassurance to assuage your built-in guilt for not warming his slippers'.[116] In 1992 a national survey found that full-time working women (that is, about 80 per cent of women undergraduates at the OU) had 3.3 hours of free time on weekdays compared to 4.5 for men, and 10.3 at weekends compared to 12.1 for men.[117]

Learners as teachers: *experty tadpoleous*[118]

Art and environment, TAD292 (1976–85), crossed disciplinary boundaries. It sought to promote both a better understanding of the environment (as noted in the 'Environment at the OU' box in the previous chapter) but also the self-esteem of learners. In 1977 Professor of Adult Education Roby Kidd argued that 'the deepest foundations for learning are self-confidence, trust, belief and love'.[119] At the OU there has been recognition that the reinforcement of feelings of confidence often aided academic success.[120] TAD292 sought to develop 'strategies for creative work'. It dealt with 'the processes and attitudes of art not so much as these were evidenced in products of art but as they underlie the very act of doing art. This can be seen already from the titles which were given to some of the units in the course: "Boundary Shifting", "Imagery and Visual Thinking", "Having Ideas by Handling Materials".'[121] TAD292 students were offered a range of projects. One was that the students cease their activities in order to engage in listening. Another was to compose a score for sounds made from differently textured papers and a third was to enumerate the household's activities and categorise these in terms of role and sex stereotyping. The aims of the course were attitudinal, sensory and subjective rather than cognitive, relating to feeling rather than knowledge. They were 'more phenomenological than conceptual in nature'.[122] Assessment involved a student submitting not only the product, such as a self-portrait photograph, but also notes describing the process and rationale behind its creation. The criteria were not specific but involved formulations including enthusiasm, imagination and authenticity. Former TAD292 student Dale Godfrey concluded that 'the ethos behind the TAD course was you built your own hoops and then decided whether you wanted to jump through them or not'.[123]

Some TAD292 students, fresh from its summer school, organised a camp at which they developed the learning and activities associated with the OU summer schools.[124] Soon an annual camp was instituted and the Tadpole Society developed. Tadpoles, members of the society created by former students of the module, 'share skills, experiences, ideas and knowledge of creativity and personal growth'.[125] One member called it 'a lovely way of spending time, growing and learning'.[126] When Tony Whitaker sought to conceptualise the relationship between TAD292 and his subsequent learning, he said TAD292 'opened a door that said "There is another world out there" and the Tadpoles allowed me to go out there and play for the last 20 odd years'.[127] Alex Richards used a similar metaphor. She said: 'what it did was open up to me the possibilities for us as human beings and our capacity for kindness and compassion and creativity and to actually achieve things as a group that I didn't know about before'. John Leach also spoke about gaining control, noting that TAD292 'changed me completely because I actually stopped looking for results and was looking at the process of what I was doing and if I didn't want to do something I wouldn't do it. It just freed me up from the constraints of expectation.' Edwina Nixon found that TAD292 led her to gain a 'perspective that was very different on creativity and people consciousness'.[128]

Having gained a sense that further learning through the OU was possible and pleasurable, the students formed their own communities. Members offered accommodation to one another, held weekend events at their own homes and travelled abroad together.[129] Alex Richards recalled that

> it was just being in another reality for a weekend when you went away. We'd all go and meet in each other's houses and it was like so much of ordinary life was suspended ... There was always an element of creativity.

She said that, from being a Tadpole, 'I think I learnt everything ... I learnt what I needed to learn' and that being a Tadpole was a way of 'trying to serve'. She connected this to her understanding of TAD292, where she felt 'absorbed in being creative and having your thinking ignited'.[130] One Tadpole called the experience 'a re-familying. My family I am very fond of but I have a much wider family [and with] some of the people I have enjoyed deeper relationships.'[131]

Female OU students were more likely than their male counterparts to involve their families and fellow students in their studies.[132] Students reported that through studying they became better able to help their children to learn.[133] Joanne Pye was 'inspired' by her mother's studies with the OU. Soon afterwards she realised 'I needed to be proud of myself too'.[134] Deirdre Nelson, born in 1971 to parents who were both OU students, also came to the university through parental involvement. She felt that her studies led her children to gain a sense of the value of education. Pam Jarvis studied with the OU, became an OU tutor and then completed three other degrees.[135] This activity 'created some of the background' for her son, who went on to study for a PhD.[136] In framing their studies and their achievements in terms of families these students reinforced the role attributed to families within society and helped to integrate the OU within people's lives and the wider society. The idea spread that learners benefited not only from well-constructed teaching materials but also from tutors, fellow students and sportive kinship and social networks. Other universities and the government funding body recognised that by encouraging students to support each other and learn co-operatively, attainment, student cohesion and retention could be improved.[137]

The OU's profound impact on students' relationships stemmed from the deeply personal motivations for study. While many undertook study in order to improve their career prospects, others were driven by more personal reasons. The explanatory category which was most popular with those who had not received funding from an employer was 'enjoyment'.[138] In 2007 the most commonly reported reason for study was 'progression and personal development'.[139] Ron Sambell started at the OU because he felt 'a desperate need to have a more fundamental understanding of science and technology'.[140] Jackie Diffey felt that when mailings arrived it was 'like getting a Christmas present'.[141] Vida Jane Platt wrote, 'Oh the bliss of waiting for the new year's course material to drop through the letter box and the pleasure in doing those TMAs.'[142] Elinor Ashby remembered how 'I was often so excited by the arrival of my units that I would stand over the cooker stirring home-made soup whilst avidly reading.'[143] Audrey Moore, who started her studies in 1974, recalled that the television programmes were often on early in the morning and she was 'frequently rather tired going to work', but that one programme, on the Cuban revolution, 'inspired me to want to sing and dance all the way to work'.[144]

There was previous experience in the higher education sector of instruction at a distance, of teaching mature students and those with disabilities, and of provision for part-time students and those without prior qualifications. Nevertheless, to bring all these ideas together and launch a vast new university using a range of communications technologies, distinctive notions of distributed learning and offers of personal support for independent learners was a bold idea. It dramatically shifted the scope, range and pedagogies of higher education. The generic structures of the OU enabled students in different countries and at different times to study the same material and be assessed according to the same criteria. Yet this process was experienced by individual students as a deeply personal one. Since at least the early nineteenth century, when the Society for the Diffusion of Useful Knowledge published inexpensive educational texts aimed at encouraging the auto-didactic, there have been learners who have demonstrated great perseverance in overcoming barriers of disability, social class and educational classification. The OU can be seen as part of this tradition of encouraging individuals to transform their prospects, self-understanding and relationships.

'Short-haired students keen to work': experiencing summer school[145]

OU summer schools have, for better and worse, become mythic.[146] Their timing coinciding with the 'silly season' for the national press, and being run on university campuses largely empty of full-time students, made them a gift to newspaper journalists eager for salacious copy.[147] *The Times* reported the case of Carol Park, who left her husband and children to live with David Brearley after the pair had met at summer school.[148] Stuart Hall recalled that 'I've never been anywhere else in the academic world where a husband turned up and said, "My wife's going home ... She's coming home with me. I'm not leaving her in any longer."'[149]

Before the OU opened, the residential element of its teaching had been endorsed by Crowther, Young, Jennie Lee's White Paper and the OU Planning Committee.[150] The use of university property in the vacations for residential group-learning programmes for adults had significantly grown in popularity since the war. The OU schools were intended to enable students to make use of the laboratories and other facilities and to attend lectures and seminars led by experts in the field. These aims, together with the mutual support offered by students, feature in Sally Ford's recollection of her experiences of *Exploring the molecular world*, SXR205, in Nottingham:

> The first day of activities was so hectic, I thought I would be left behind at times, but on voicing my worries to my fellow students I realised that everyone was in the same boat, and more importantly, we were all helping each other and working as a team instinctively. Over five-and-a-half days, I had written over 80 pages in my lab notebook. More importantly, I had put an awful lot of theory into practice, and got vital laboratory experience that I would not have been able to gain otherwise. [Figure 7.3][151]

Students frequently concluded that residential schools transformed their understandings (Figure 7.5).[152] Tutor Sue Danks pointed out: 'The students' lack of experience with even basic equipment can hinder understanding at the beginning, but being mature students and working in the laboratory for a whole week means they learn very quickly' (Figure 7.6).[153] Residential schools were staffed by academic course team members and tutors, and ran for several weeks on many sites, though any one student would attend one campus for only one week.[154]

Many students, worried about their intellectual capacities and grateful for the opportunity to be away from everyday chores, worked diligently

Figure 7.4 Residential schools provided an opportunity to engage in lab work.

Figure 7.5 OU students often study alone. Residential schools provided opportunities to meet with other students.

Figure 7.6 At residential schools student experimentation sometimes involved other students. Those attending the *Biology: Brain and behaviour*, SD206, summer school at the University of York in the mid-1990s (the module was presented 1992–2001) had the opportunity to measure nerve conduction velocity – how fast information travels along a nerve cell. A volunteer wore shorts to the class and allowed other students to administer a small electric shock to a nerve in his leg and record how long it took to reach a point further down his leg. Other practicals on SD206 involved teaching a rat to press a lever, counting the number of cheeps a day-old chick made and investigating woodlice in a maze.

and enthusiastically (Figure 7.7). Nevertheless, there was press ridicule and outrage.[155] John Kirkaldy remembers that a journalist he escorted around a Bath summer school was disgusted when he found 'No nookie and no pot!'[156] *The Times* headlined an account of the 'University where a lecture begins with a beer', while the BBC ran a story about 'bizarre games and happenings' including OU students who 'made bare bottom prints ... dragged rubbish through the streets [and] appeared to be aimlessly kicking a giant rugby ball about'.[157] It was not only students who were accused of taking advantage of the intense atmosphere generated at summer schools. One professor was recalled by Barbara Vowles as being 'unfailingly kind, courteous' but also 'a hazard' to female students.[158]

The OU's monthly magazine for students and staff, *Sesame*, fanned the flames. The September 1974 edition, for example, carried a number of post-summer-school messages. One read, 'A. I will never forget York. The spark

Figure 7.7 As part of a summer school in design there was an evaluation of the Sinclair C5. This battery-assisted tricycle was produced in 1985. There were few sales. The rider was exposed to the weather and the tricycle had no gears to assist when it was being pedalled uphill.

of affinity still glows bright. H.' Another declared, 'I loved you for a week, a week to fit uncrowded in an hour of normal life. Now I know there are no separate compartments in the mind because I cannot lock you out. And you refuse to go.'[159] References to summer schools were later banned from the personal advertisements of *Sesame*. The press coverage had other effects as Stuart Hall recalled.[160] During the first summer schools there were press reports which criticised the summer schools and the OU.

The idea that it was through working together that problems were resolved was reflected in the teaching materials. These took an 'integrated approach' and were 'creative, formative and very influential'.[161] This co-operative model was developed further when, in 1978, instead of discussing course choices on an individual basis with students, a tutor and a tutor-counsellor in London encouraged a cohort of students to study the same course together. The tutor involved in this activity stressed that 'students of mathematics must meet other mathematicians, they must talk to one another and with one another and try out the concepts involved in mastering the subject without being afraid to make naive statements'.[162] The result was that the module enjoyed a greater than expected retention rate. Moreover, the OU retained a high number of women and people with few academic qualifications.[163]

The strategy of enabling learners to construct meanings together continued to be of importance. When in 2000 the Vice-Chancellor attended the OU's first Spanish summer school, held at the University of Santiago, he noted that 'local and OU tutors formed a cohesive team and the activities had been carefully and imaginatively designed to maximise the time that students spent speaking Spanish in a variety of situations'.[164]

Students at residential schools found that they benefited from the opportunities for clarification and consolidation of knowledge. They also spent long periods studying and revising, and enjoyed meeting course team authors and having the opportunity to learn from specialised tuition.[165] Professor of History Arthur Marwick argued that

> The Summer Schools enable students who are having difficulties to get to grips with the problems of the study of primary sources and ... have the opportunity to enter into a much more detailed study of individual film items ... by careful use of the media we can enable students to share in experiences not possible for the conventional university student ... it is the imaginative use of media which gives a special quality to Open University education.[166]

Students could also access places they might not otherwise have visited, including academic libraries and art galleries. Student Maggie Donaldson recalled that a summer school trip around the National Gallery led by Charles Harrison 'was such an exciting experience, and made me feel like I was a "real" student for a while, being taught by an inspirational expert on the subject. He was a class act in every way.'[167] When surveyed in 1972, students ranked residential schools as the most helpful teaching component – ahead of correspondence tuition, television, tutorials, counselling and radio.[168] Subsequent studies also found them to be seen as educationally beneficial.[169] A student account from 1972 offered a balancing perspective: 'We all had the most marvellous time at the summer School at Keele with late-night parties after the classes had finished for the day.'[170] Former Labour minister Richard Crossman, who had been sceptical about the OU before it opened and remained so after a trip to Walton Hall, returned from observing summer schools at Bath full of praise for the 'remarkable' teaching. 'I'd never seen people working with such intensity and also enjoying themselves', he noted.[171] *The Times* reported that it was a 'hard week's work' for students and that while there were 'films, discos – yes discos – and parties' it was doubtful that there would be 'the family breakdowns predicted by the *News of the World*' (Figure 7.8).[172]

Figure 7.8 Poster from a residential school held at Sussex, 2009.

In 1975 Christine Saxton wrote in *Sesame*: 'Until summer school, never was so much adrenalin manufactured in 1 week. Never did so few hours sleep suffice over such intense activity. Never had a profusion of profound thoughts been mulled over and revelled in. Never did I realize what the old brain was capable of.'[173] Her conclusions are echoed in Cheryl Markosky's recollections, written in 1997: 'I've taken in a lot of information and spent too many late nights staying up and talking. Bob Wilkinson's sage parting advice to all is: "When you get home, and you're looking completely exhausted, remember to have a good story." My story is that I've had a good time.'[174] Tilly Bud's account, written six years later, also echoes the memories of those who attended many years before her. She was so nervous of attending summer school that she planned an exit strategy 'if it was all too much for me. It wasn't. I had a fabulous time … a week of being a "real" student … it's in my Top Ten List of Best Experiences Ever.'[175] Some students found considerable pleasure in intense study and the sudden reduction of intellectual isolation.

Mark Youngman, who attended summer school in 2000, recalled both the intensity and the differences from his home life:

> During the week we were kept very busy from 9 am often to 8 or 9 pm with only an hour for lunch and dinner ... I couldn't believe how quickly the week had gone by ... The most satisfying thing of all was that I had been able to talk about my course with like-minded people, people who knew what I was talking about and had the same problems, fears and assignment deadlines as myself. I could never have talked to my wife or anyone else in the same way.[176]

Residential schools were seen to boost motivation and progression. Attendance might have added a few percentage points to a student's final exam score. Tutor Joan Christodoulu said that they offered opportunities to provide remedial support and advice on exams and that the student benefited from 'the intellectual discussion and sitting up all night talking'.[177] Summer schools were said to provide an opportunity to receive peer reassurance at a time when students were part way through an individual course and many were 'floundering', as Professor Michael Drake put it. He added that 'a lot of students thought they were the only ones who were not coping and everyone else knew more than they did'.[178] Tutor Sean Cubitt argued that the *Popular culture*, U206, summer schools provided 'spaces where students can air their problems with the course and pursue their learning in new directions'.[179]

Stirling efforts

In 1976 Mike Hey started to tutor at Stirling summer schools. He recalled:

> After dinner, things began in earnest. The 'set book' for the Maths Foundation Course (M100 at that time) was Polya's 'How to solve it', and the first session was to be a group problem-solving exercise involving the well-known problem of the number of areas formed by n intersecting lines, extended to n intersecting planes. There were some impediments to my success in this venture:
>
> a) I didn't know the answer
> b) I wasn't at all sure that I understood the question
> c) All the other tutors appeared to have mastered both a) and b), and
> d) I had little hope that any of my group of students would know what to do either.

My expressed fears in this area were dismissed by the Course Director with a wave of the hand and a comment to the effect that 'it's much better if you don't know what to do; the students can follow your problem-solving processes better'. (This was my one point of disagreement with OU philosophy throughout my summer school career – I did not, and still do not, believe that the interests of the students are best served by the fuddled machinations of tutors who don't know what they're doing.) To cut a long story short, my fears were realised. I talked a lot, wrote a lot on the blackboard, came out in hot and cold sweats, and at the end of the hour neither I nor the students were any the wiser as to a) or b) above.[180]

Problem-solving as pedagogy was put to use more successfully by John Mason, who designed and implemented the first OU mathematics summer school. It involved 5,000 students over eleven weeks on three sites. Mason instituted active problem-solving sessions, which later became investigations. He also developed project-work for students.[181]

The teaching staff also recalled the intensity of residential schools (Plate 24). Sir John Daniel, later the Vice-Chancellor, recalled his first summer school:

that summer of 1972 in the UK was a conversion experience. I saw the future of higher education and wanted to be part of it. Everything was hugely impressive and stimulating. First there was the scale: the Open University already had 40,000 students in its second year of operation. Second came the idealism: here were people who walked the talk on access and student-centred pedagogy. Third, there was palpable love of learning: the students were unbelievably motivated by the opportunity presented to them. I went to one of the residential summer schools where students spent a full day in labs, seminars and field trips and then most of the night in the bar; continuing the academic discourse. Fourth, I was captivated by the media and technology: my key task was to help develop computer-marked assignments that tested advanced cognitive skills, but I spent every spare moment viewing the brilliant BBC television programmes. This exposure to the future of higher education infected me with the virus of open and distance learning.[182]

In 1973 Peter Montagnon noted the enthusiasm of the students to talk with academics.

And talk to them these students do – from breakfast-time to bedtime non-stop. This is an exhilarating experience for them all but, I suspect, particularly so for the lecturers from the more conventional universities. It is the reversal of the situation that is to be found on so many of our campuses ... The students not only want to hear what their lecturers have to say, they pursue them – almost hunt them down – until they have said it.[183]

A reporter claimed that 'it wasn't the students who complained about hard work but the tutors who were apparently unused to such keen students'.[184] Another noted that older OU students provided 'a highly critical audience' for A. J. P. Taylor's lecture about the Second World War.[185] Former tutor Christopher Harvie, who married a tutor who he met at a Norwich summer school, argued that 'summer schools altered the whole demography of Britain'. He also recalled 'teaching for three weeks instead of the statutory two at the Stirling summer school, of which some tabloid – I think it was probably the *News of the World* – remarked, "Cool it, telly dons are told!"'[186]

Changing times, changing methods

From the outset the OU subjected every part of its teaching to continuing scrutiny, up to and including the summer schools which were so salient a part of its offering. While those who attended them attested to the intellectual engagement and motivation of students and saw a positive correlation between attendance and recruitment, retention and results, their value for money was questioned from the early 1970s. Although an early Senate resolution made attendance at residential schools compulsory, that decision was questioned by the Faculty of Technology soon after it was created. In 1974 Hilary Perraton noted 'euphoria' gained 'within the social situation in which students can learn together' but then asked 'whether it's as valuable as the amount of money you spend on it'.[187] In 1975 a paper addressed the question as to which OU students were deterred by the prospect of a summer school of the OU before concluding that 'probably nobody would argue against foundation course summer schools remaining compulsory'.[188] During the 1990s the Mathematics Faculty decided to rewrite its foundation course without a residential school. Studies sought to quantify the gain of OU residential schools.[189] One considered the records of 1,500 students and concluded that 'the value of traditional teaching components of courses taken by thousands of students each year was shown to be overestimated'.[190]

Evidence accumulated that the residential element had little bearing on the measured achievement of students. Residential schools were expensive for students. In 1994 21,000 students paid over £4 million to attend the week-long events. The *Guardian* reported that 'online tutorial groups are replacing the legendary summer schools. They're simply cheaper' (Figure 7.9).[191] General shifts in lifestyles made it difficult for many students to attend. Some students felt that their families were resentful of this use of annual leave and found being away stressful. Writing in 2001, one student noted that attendance could 'be a problem for some people who have to take time off work or find someone to look after the kids'.[192] Alternative learning experiences had to be created. These aimed to deliver the same core learning outcomes through a variety of methods. These have included

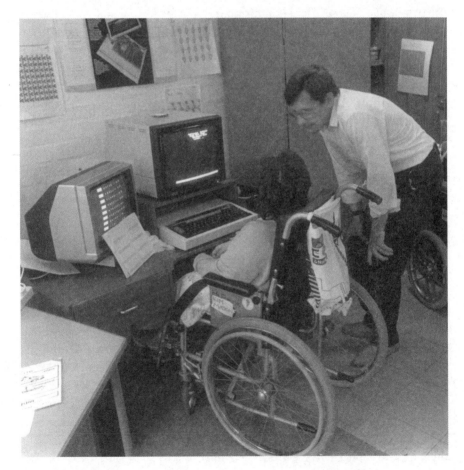

Figure 7.9 Tutorial support could involve using technology to support learning.

a written assignment, an online project and computer conferencing. While these may not have delivered the breadth of learning opportunities offered by residency, they undermined the distinctiveness of the pedagogic benefits of the residential schools. Different means of supporting learners such as the virtual microscope and other forms of online communications became accessible to students. These online activities sought to recreate aspects of the residential experience and offer an alternative to the intensive experience of face-to-face teaching.[193] New media, the virtual reality of *Second Life* for example, became more popular and enabled people to exchange ideas and work together without being in the same room at the same time.

Residential schools continued to be an integral element of some modules. In 2012 there were business schools, day schools and summer schools for over thirty modules. These offered opportunities for intellectual and social mixing and for students to gain practical skills and to develop their communication and group-working abilities and examination techniques. However, residential schools were no longer a compulsory element on first-level modules (formerly Foundation courses) and were less frequently featured in the press. The need for the OU to prove that it offered a comparable experience to fully residential universities had diminished. The requirement that students gain hands-on experiences rather than virtual ones had, in the globalised online world, been reduced.

Learning inside

The OU's role in educating prisoners divides opinions. One MP described the OU's offer of higher education to students in prisons and secure environments as an 'example of gold-plated rights for convicted criminals at the expense of their victims and the law-abiding majority'.[194] The OU argued that its work in prisons was 'a key part of its mission to widen participation in higher education especially by those groups who are traditionally excluded', while the Prison Service conceptualised OU study as 'a vital part of resettlement and a route to reducing re-offending' (Plate 25).[195] Among the first OU students who started in January 1971 were twenty-two serving prisoners.[196] In 1985, 150 prisoners in thirty-one establishments were registered as OU students, and by 1989 the OU was the main provider of university-level study to prisoners. Prisons teams were established in each of the OU's regional and national centres. By 2006 there were over 1,200 OU students in prisons, and by 2011 there were around 1,800 OU students in more than 150 prisons across the UK and Ireland.[197] They were studying over 200 courses across all faculties.

Johnny (to maintain anonymity, some of the students in prison are identified here only by their first names), who studied for his first degree and his
PhD through the OU while in prison, said, 'I got hooked on education with
The Open University. And I study now for knowledge, for knowledge's sake,
and I love it ... The single most important thing that education in prison has
given me is a sense of self-worth.' Barry also emphasised the change in his confidence, the importance of his tutor and how he had come to realise that 'you
make your own light at the end of the tunnel'.[198] It was not just the prisoners
who felt that there was a benefit. Katla Helgason, who played an important
part in the creation of the Scottish Prison Scheme, felt that the work of the OU
was clear: 'we are delivering education'.[199] The first Dean of Arts recalled that

> One of the more moving letters I have received came from a tutor in the
> Isle of Wight to say what a therapeutic effect the Socrates units had had
> on long-time prisoners in Parkhurst gaol.[200]

In the early 1980s two modules based on the OU course *The pre-school child*
were developed for use by prisoners (only prisoners whose offences do not
relate to children are allowed to study on courses which include any material
on children). One prisoner in Barlinnie felt that his relationship with his wife
and children had dramatically improved, saying, 'They get more out of me
and I get more out of them.'[201]

Prisoners were motivated by interest and felt that success aided their confidence. The conclusion of Linda of HMP Morton Hall might have been
expressed by any OU student: 'At first I thought I would not meet the
requirements ... my results give me joy and hope.'[202] Robert recalled that his
success with assignments 'boosted my self-belief in my capabilities, which
prior to that were a little bit low'.[203] John mentioned the development of
a sense of self-worth, Trevor felt that 'the OU has built my self-esteem up'
while James also stressed the previous lack of confidence and how education
could help prisoners to 'pay something back to society'.[204] John L. wrote that
having spent much of the period since the age of 15 in prison he had low self-
esteem. However, he met a helpful tutor, studied *Astronomy and mechanics
of the universe* through the OU and, having previously been classified as a
danger to the prison population and to the community, began work as a peer
tutor, helping people learn how to read and write.[205] Others also spoke of the
transformative effects of study. Tony, HMP Wymott, said that 'OU study
has completely changed me as a person. As well as being more knowledgeable about social issues, I am much more confident and optimistic about the
future.' Ben, HMP The Wolds, felt that 'learning has widened my outlook

and interests', while Nigel, HMP Frankland, found his studies to be a 'practical, life-affirming endeavour'. Edwin, HMP Chelmsford, felt that he gained 'a new perspective on [his] life'.[206] Several of those who were interviewed while in prison expressed the hope that study would improve their intellectual, psychological and career prospects. Trevor commented, 'education has rehabilitated me', and Conor said, 'It keeps me sane.'[207]

These comments echoed the information provided for prisoners by the OU. This refers to the value of 'constructive and worthwhile' activities, how some people 'gain confidence and belief in their own abilities', and notes that some prisoners have gained 'opportunities for a new start after release'.[208] Prisoners also echoed some of the remarks made by non-prisoners about the sense of release and of change found through study. John started to write while in prison and discovered: 'You really don't feel like you're in prison, it's just everything disappears in the background ... when I have the story sort of set up and lined up in the direction I want to go ... I'm in with my characters in the story and just the prison's not there.' An OU student from a middle-class background felt that his studies while in prison were 'An expression of an alienation I already felt. I applied so that for just a few hours a week I could get away from the obscenities, the prison gossip, the scheming. A lot of us are alienated before we start this sort of thing.'[209]

The Home Office paid each student's fees, and provided the necessary equipment in terms of set books, projectors, tape cassettes and films, but acceptance of students in prison on to OU courses has always been at the discretion of the governor. There were additional hurdles to study. Modules which involved the use of home experiment kits were excluded and the prisons' tutor organisers were appointed counsellors.[210] Some prisons did not permit access to CDs, or the use of PCs. There is a paucity of books. In the early part of the new century access to the internet was uneven within the wider population (41 per cent of households in Northern Ireland had access compared to 53 per cent in England, and while 84 per cent of those aged 16–24 were users, only 15 per cent of those aged over 65 were).[211] The problem was more acute for students in secure hospitals or prisons (and indeed for some students in the armed forces) who often found it difficult to access the internet. This made it hard to peruse materials only published via the course website and to take part in online discussions. Reading, updating and commenting on blogs and wikis was difficult, as was watching online videos and podcasts, performing online searches, completing quizzes, writing and submitting assignments, visiting the online library and receiving module news posted online. Some prisoners made use of an intermediary, a family member or tutor, but this was not always straightforward. A sample of ninety-one students suggested that most wrote their assignments by hand and then typed them up during the brief periods of access to a computer.[212] Katla Helgason felt that tutors 'had to be very proactive and very positive'.[213] Some tutors downloaded online conference messages for prisoners and one brought in pictures for a student studying astronomy.

A virtual campus for Offender Learners was tested at HMP Wormwood Scrubs in 2008, and HMP Whitemoor ran Offline Moodle, an offline version of the virtual learning environment software which the OU used to deliver its teaching systems. After funding and security issues were addressed, POLARIS, the Programme for Offender Learning and Resettlement Information Services, was trialled in Wormwood Scrubs and Latchmere House, an open prison, and then in five other prisons in London. Services using it included LearnDirect, Meganexus and Jobcentre Plus as well as the OU. There were ten workstations for offender access installed at each site. The aim was to provide a secure internet which would give students in prison access to a wider range of OU courses and help solve some of the study problems which arose when prisoners moved from one prison to another.[214] The Centre for Open Learning in Mathematics, Science, Computing and Technology (COLMSCT) project developed online aspects of courses for use in prisons, starting with the first-level mathematics module, M150. This project introduced a new wiki and forum for OU prison tutors and was trialled in a number of prisons. Similar developments to POLARIS were tried in Swedish prisons and then in HMP Swinfen Hall (West Midlands) and HMP Blundeston (East of England). None of these developments mean that students in prison will be able to access teaching materials or ALs in the ways that other students can (for example the addresses and names of tutors are not provided to students in prison).

Sally Jordan pointed out, 'it is difficult for a Category A prisoner to set up an outdoor rain gauge and check the water level each day when he has to be handcuffed to a prison officer'.[215] At HMP Maghaberry, County Antrim, prisoners studying with the OU were allowed three days per week study time but this was not the case elsewhere.[216] One interviewee (Student 4) said that the prison officers were 'very resentful'. He was studying mathematics and claimed that when he was spotted writing algebra, 'they wanted to know why I was writing in code'. Student 36 offered an explanation for the behaviour of some officers: 'they work hard – horrible hours – and they see you on a laptop getting a degree'.[217] Despite the attention given to overcoming the difficulties faced by learners in prisons, the disparities in resources offered to prisoners (when compared to other students) remain.

Although in 1974 Wakefield prison produced the first OU prisoner graduate, Walter Perry pointed out in 1979 that 'prisoners tend to have a relatively high rate of withdrawal from courses before the examinations ...

Nevertheless, for those who actually sat the examinations, the results are reasonably good.'[218] By the new century things had changed. A study of retention between 2002 and 2008 found that a higher percentage of prisoners than other students completed modules. The percentage of those who complete a module was approximately the same for prisoners and non-prisoners.[219] Norman Woods, Regional Director of the East Midlands, recalled one of the results of these studies, the graduation ceremony in a local prison: 'You used to put on your glad rags and go and hand them their diploma and certificate, whatever. And their families used to come in. You know, it was quite good. And the prison would provide some cakes and cups of tea.'[220]

There have been some high-profile prisoners. Myra Hindley has been called 'the Open University's most famous graduate'.[221] Even after her death in 2002 newspapers continued to link her to the OU.[222] John McVicar, sentenced to twenty-six years, took an Open University degree in sociology and was awarded a BSc first class. He was paroled in 1978; his studies were perhaps important in helping him to leave criminal activity behind. Former addict and armed robber Graham Godden studied criminology and social sciences through the OU while in prison. On his release he worked with young people at risk of offending.[223] John Hirst, who won his case after he took the government to the European Court of Human Rights over voting rights for prisoners, spent thirty-five years in prison. While there he studied with the OU and claimed, 'I was transformed from a law breaker into a law-maker.'[224] Erwin James Monahan went to prison with, in his own words, 'massive failings to overcome'. He completed an OU degree, wrote a newspaper column while still a prisoner and, on his release, published a number of books and became a full-time freelance writer.[225] When Jason Warr went to prison he had a few low-grade GCSEs. On release, twelve years later, he had enough credits from Open University philosophy courses to get an unconditional offer for a degree place in the subject at the London School of Economics.[226] Bobby Cummines, now an OBE, said that 'what changed my life was the OU'. After he left prison, he set up a charity, sat on the Rehabilitation of Offenders Act Review Management Advisory Group and worked with government ministers and civil servants on matters related to prison.[227]

In late 1960s there were about 600 people in prison in Northern Ireland. The outbreak of 'the Troubles' resulted in a significant increase in the prison population. Internment without trial was introduced in 1971, and within four years 1,981 people had been interned.[228] Most were held in the Maze, a prison built at a former military air base, RAF Long Kesh. They wore their own clothes, rather than prison uniforms, had free association and had some control over their own order, in that they maintained their own structures within the gaol, complete with Officers Commanding, who dealt directly with the prison authorities. They did not carry out prison work. In 1972 the British government assumed responsibility for security measures in Northern Ireland and trials for 'scheduled offences' (such as the illegal possession of firearms) started to take place in jury-less courts in front of a judge. By 1975 the prison population of Northern Ireland had quadrupled over five years.

In 1973 the OU's Regional Director, Gordon Macintyre, visited Long Kesh Internment Centre. There he met the Officers Commanding of the Provisional Irish Republican Army, the Official Irish Republican Army, the Ulster Volunteer Force and the Ulster Defence Association. Different communities, including the Provisional Irish Republican Army, the Official Irish Republican Army, the Irish National Liberation Army and the Ulster Defence Association, had their own, almost self-contained, compounds. Although in some there were lectures given by prisoners, the leaders met by Macintyre testified to the need for educational facilities. Soon afterwards arrangements were made for two prisoners from the Ulster Volunteer Force/Red Hand Commando, two from the Ulster Defence Association and two from the Official Irish Republican Army to study with the OU.[229] Ten men were designated 'serious students'. Initially they lived in different compounds. Most of those in prison in Northern Ireland came from Northern Ireland. They were less likely than prisoners in mainland UK to have their studies disrupted by being moved to other gaols. There were, however, additional difficulties for the OU's 'most isolated group of students' and their tutors.[230] Due to the restrictions imposed for security reasons, access to 'the OU's oddest study centre', a study hut, was difficult. Eventually, most of the students were moved together. OU tutor-counsellor Diana Purcell, who had initially taught prisoners through a scheme established by a criminologist at Queen's University, Belfast, went on to teach OU students in the H-Blocks of the Maze prison.[231] She recalled that initially, as part of their protest, the prisoners associated with the Provisional Irish Republican Army 'wouldn't take part [in educational courses] because they were not co-operating in anything ... finally the Provisional IRA took a decision to join in'.[232] Those in the compounds retained Special Category status until 1986. However, those sentenced after 1 May 1976 were placed in the H-Blocks and were not granted Special Category status. In response, there was a 'dirty protest' and a hunger strike by prisoners. Those who protested were not permitted to sit together or hold classes, so they shared information by shouting. This had a levelling effect among the prisoners. Eventually what was, in effect, political status was granted, with a variety of different paramilitary groups in charge of the H-Blocks. One effect of this disruption was to undermine the convention that learning occurred when a teacher explained to a group. This method was replaced by greater debate, discussion and active learning.[233]

In 1979 there were ten OU students in the compounds and seven in the H-Blocks. After 1984 there were eighteen students in the compounds and twenty-six in the H-Blocks. In the H-Blocks the number of OU students rose to forty-nine by 1986. The maximum number of students in the compounds was twenty-one in 1985, including one who was a postgraduate. It was argued that in the prisons of Northern Ireland, between forty or fifty prisoners a year studied with the OU.[234] The first of a number of informal 'graduations' took place in the Maze prison in April 1981; one of the graduates was a Republican and the other a Loyalist. Their parents, the prison governor, Diana Purcell and Gordon Macintyre attended. There was an elaborate afternoon tea and then the Regional Director presented each graduate with a home-made scroll to commemorate the occasion, a few words were said and photographs were taken. By 1984 from among these prisoners there had been fifty-six passes, eighteen with distinction, and only one fail.[235] In 1986 seventeen former OU students who had been released from prison were in full-time university education, and there had been ninety-six OU degrees awarded to prisoners in Northern Ireland. The following year a further five students graduated, all from the Ulster Volunteer Force compound. Many of the OU graduates went on to hold positions of authority in a variety of community organisations.[236] One study concluded that 'more prisoners enrolled in higher education at the Maze than at any other prison in the British system. Ten times more took university degrees.'[237]

Loyalists who studied in the H-Blocks at the Maze often took pride in studying from individual choice rather than as part of a group, while the Republicans developed their own education programme. Those who received OU teaching materials used these not only to learn for themselves but to teach other prisoners. Diana Purcell explained:

> nearly all of them, but particularly the IRA, they set up the system [in the H-Blocks]. If they arranged to do an OU course then they had to give a talk about what they were studying each week to the rest of the guys in that section ... they were extremely good students ... encouraged each other too, which was very good.[238]

There was interest in modules which drew on the work of Paulo Freire, notably *Education for adults*, E355. Laurence McKeown, who spent sixteen years in the H-Blocks, became interested in Freire's notions of non-hierarchical, dialogue-based education.[239] He felt that his writing was 'absolutely brilliant'.[240] Another hunger striker, Jackie McMullan, felt 'exhilarated' by the idea of education as a revolutionary force, and Patrick Magee, who wrote a PhD while in prison, argued that 'there was an element of personal development in education in jail. You worked to be able to articulate better your political perspective and I saw education as a means to an end.'[241] McKeown recalled an example of peer learning. After some men had studied the OU's 30-point course *The changing experience of women*, U221 (1983–91), a class of 'over 200 men took part in the women's studies class over a two-year period' supported by OU tutor Joanna McMinn. In common with other courses of the period, its design was influenced by the principles associated with Freire. The formation of self-help groups was encouraged, as was the view of staff as resources rather than pedagogues. The course team sought – argued one of its members, Gill Kirkup – to ensure that material was not abstract but could be tested against learners' experiences and that students 'value each other's experience and examine it supportively'.[242] Despite the atmosphere in the men-only Maze (Diana Purcell's first impression was of 'the maleness of it all'), McKeown felt that through the course 'men became aware of the power they held. Power they held over their female relatives and loved ones [and] over women in general.'[243] Gordon Macintyre, the tutor who assessed Laurence McKeown's double assignment, recalled that it was 'an essay full of feminist insights'.[244] A further study concluded of Republican prisoners that they were keen 'to move away from the hierarchical notions of knowing teacher and passive students' and that they felt that 'reading and studying in jail involved self-improvement overlaid with political commitment'.[245]

The violence within Northern Ireland had other impacts on the OU. Regional Director Gordon Macintyre recalled how on one day he marked an assignment which had been written 'with undeniable intelligence, sensitivity and wit' by a Republican in the Maze prison, and on the following day, due to a series of IRA bombs and hoaxes, his journey home took him three times longer than usual.[246] Although visits were time-consuming, due to the security checks, Macintyre felt that it was a duty: 'we all saw the work as a professional responsibility, analogous with that of a doctor present at the scene of a terrorist incident, who would do his best to treat the injuries of the perpetrator as well as those of the victims'.[247] There was also an attempt to kill the Chancellor of the OU, 1973–78, Gerald Gardiner. Selected to be Lord Chancellor by Harold Wilson in 1964, Gardiner retired from the post when Labour lost power in 1970. In 1972 he was appointed to investigate the alleged abuse of interrogation procedures in Northern Ireland. His minority report condemned the use of 'procedures which were secret, illegal, not morally justifiable'.[248] As chair of another committee on Northern Ireland in

1975 he approved the continuation of detention without trial. In 1981 the IRA argued that Gardiner was responsible for the H-Blocks and the criminalisation of the Republicans.[249]

One of the effects of the OU's work in prisons was that cross-border links were strengthened. After some Republicans from Northern Ireland who were imprisoned in the Republic requested access to OU courses, Diana Purcell helped to set up an arrangement to enable them to study.[250] The scheme grew to involve 'about eight prisons'.[251] Staff tutor Rosemary Hamilton noted that, whereas prisoners and prison officers in the Republic became eligible to study through the OU, others in the Republic were not permitted to study with the OU,[252] and *The Times* reported this discrepancy.[253] In 1985, in addition to the ninety-eight OU students in prison in the Maze, Armagh, Crumlin Road and Magillan, twenty-nine prisoners became OU students in Limerick, Portlaoise and Cork. While the OU claimed back from the British government the costs associated with the work of tutors who taught in prisons in Northern Ireland, the university did not receive payments from the Republic of Ireland.[254]

A number of those who became Republican political leaders took OU courses. In 2012 five Sinn Féin Assembly members, a Member of the European Parliament and others in a number of civic roles were OU graduates.[255] Peter Smith, who taught Sinn Féin Member of the Legislative Assembly Martina Anderson when she was a prisoner, said that it felt 'surreal to be holding a politics tutorial with a member of the IRA, in the chapel of the prison'.[256] Some former prisoners felt that they owed their political and organisational skills to studying with the OU. Diana Purcell argued that OU courses proved to be 'amazingly successful' within prisons, and pointed out that the prisoners were 'part of our community and they're going to come out ... and it's important that they have some skills, this is particularly with the political ones'.[257] The effect of studying through the OU on those people who became active and useful citizens was mentioned by the *Times Higher Education Supplement*:

> The extraordinary role of Open University degrees in furthering the peace process in Northern Ireland is acknowledged throughout the Republican sector as well as by the smaller Loyalist political parties whose support for the Good Friday agreement of 1998 and for the 1999 Northern Ireland Executive is vital.[258]

Popular Unionist Party Assembly members, the late David Ervine and Billy Hutchinson were both Long Kesh Compound prisoners who completed OU degrees.[259] They felt that their degrees gave them political confidence and an understanding of methods other than violence.[260] Both were elected to Belfast City Council in 1997 and to the Northern Ireland Assembly in 1998.

Based on their prior experiences of schooling, many OU students, both inside and outside prison, start their OU studies with a sense of trepidation and alienation from formal education. Those who have succeeded often gained not only knowledge but the confidence and social and intellectual equipment which enabled them to cope better with, and sometimes take active roles in shaping, their communities and the wider society. A report by the OU's Offender Learning Steering Group in 2008 found that module completion rates for prison students were higher than for non-prison students and much higher than for students with disabilities or additional requirements or students in receipt of financial support.[261] Although the OU's role in prisons was not on the agenda during its creation, through its support for these developments the OU has strengthened civil society in ways which reflect its founders' ambitions.

Conclusion

Encouraged by the Wilson government's Industrial Reorganisation Committee a new car company, the British Leyland Motor Corporation, was formed in 1968. Within a year it employed 250,000 people at the largest car plant in the world. The OU, opened in 1969, deployed some of the methods of mass production in order to provide the materials to train the 'technologists who perhaps left school at sixteen'.[262] Industrial production methods were applied to the creation and distribution of course materials to ensure that students received the thousands of OU learning resources that were posted out. Work tasks were fragmented, materials standardised and processes for assessment were made consistent across the country. The logic of manufacture for a mass market helped to sustain the vast size and scope of the OU. It was not only to be for technologists (indeed, it did not initially have a Faculty of Technology). Rather, the university was to bring together a range of learners including mature students, people with disabilities, women and those from lower socio-economic backgrounds.

Over the decades the OU expanded its physical and human infrastructure – the necessary logistical operations, warehousing, tutors and study centres – but increasingly sought to combine its scale with a capacity to meet the specific needs of different categories of students. It helped to shift education away from an emphasis on production and transmission as the best means of teaching and towards the notion of renewing cultural knowledge through thoughtful conversations. Many saw in the OU the possibility of going beyond creating an educated workforce and strengthening cross-class engagement in civil society. Former Labour minister Richard Crossman cited the 'housewives doing physics and a lorry driver deep in sociology' to suggest that there was a 'vast reservoir' of working-class intellectual ability going to waste which, once tapped, would lead to a 'social explosion'.[263] Informed by this ethos the OU enabled many people from a wide range of backgrounds and previous experiences to build understandings together. Surveys of OU graduates between 1975 and 1989 indicated that over 70 per cent felt that they derived 'great' or 'enormous' benefit from their time as students, that over 80 per cent felt that it had had a good impact on them 'as learners' and 'as a person', and that more than 50 per cent noted the beneficial effect on their careers and on them as 'members of society'.[264] Subsequently, OU students have credited their studies with helping in the development of their self-esteem, careers and familial relationships. Their accounts narrate dramatic changes to beliefs, thoughts and tastes. Many have concluded that their OU studies provided them with intellectual stimulation, pleasure in learning and what has been termed 'cultural capital'.[265] Since the inception of the National Student Survey in 2005 the OU has consistently outscored almost every other university in the level of student satisfaction with the quality of its teaching.[266]

Numerous graduates have recognised the positive impact of university on their lives. However, for many OU students their studies dramatically changed their life trajectory. Pride in their achievements often came after a serious fall. Adult learners embarking upon distance education after a range of life experiences tend to hold distinctive culturally and contextually dependent conceptions of learning, seeing it as critical thinking and as personal development, rather than being simply about increasing one's knowledge.[267] In addition to the possibility of personal redemption through education, the OU had an impact on the lives of those around the principal learners. For the state, families have long been a key formal means by which citizenship has been legally conferred. The OU built on that connection between identification with the nation and kinship by offering education which OU students could take into their homes and which could be built through communication within their networks. Even though the OU also offered opportunities to those separated from their families because they were in prison or for other reasons, its bolstering of learning through collaboration helped to give communities new roles and strengths. Just as it is said that it takes a village to raise a child, many OU students recognised that completion of an OU degree was a shared experience achieved when students extended their networks and also

Figure 7.10 Some of them appearing both nervous and proud, OU students congregate at Ely Cathedral in order to receive their qualifications.

drew upon and strengthened the communities they inhabited. Graduation for such OU students was not the marking of an apparently seamless, individual intellectual journey from school to degree but was the culmination of collective support and commitment from family, tutors, colleagues and friends. Students did not arrive at the OU assuming that a university education was a birthright determined by their class position, previous educational qualifications or age. The whoops and cheers that can be heard at any OU graduation ceremony give voice to the collective transformations that the OU has helped to shape (Figure 7.10).

Awards

If heaven is indeed a place on earth, I'd put money on it being an Open University graduation ceremony. There's nothing quite so electrifying as watching families jump to their feet when mum, dad, or even great-gran takes to the stage. The years of juggled childcare, jobs and family finances melt away as the graduate beams down from the stage, amazed that their moment has come. And in the audience you see the cavalry: the proud partner who poured endless cups of tea, the parents who babysat, the children who hugged mum the morning of her exams and almost made her cry when they said: 'We love you whatever'. This is the stuff that makes The Open University great.[268]

The OU has travelled a long way since the time when it was a highly contested innovation. It has become an institution valued for its contributions to higher education, research and the wider societies that it serves. The university has adapted its focus, strategies and methods on the basis of its original values and ethos. Walter Perry felt that the OU could 'change the face of education not only in Britain but in the world'.[269] In fulfilling that ambition, it has also become secure in the affections of the nation. At an individual level, because it inspired their thinking, strengthened their minds and connected them to learning communities, it has found a place in the hearts of over two million students. Harold Wilson introduced his idea of a 'University of the Air' during a period when notions of Keynesian stability and prosperity dominated. In the years since the OU was conceived, education has come to be more commonly conceptualised less as a relationship and more as a product that can be bought in a globalised market. Many costs and responsibilities have shifted from the government to individuals. While the OU has played a role in these transformations and also felt their impacts, the broad vision outlined at its foundation by its first Chancellor, of being open to people, places, ideas and methods, has been maintained. The OU has been given many identities. It has been called Wilson's 'pet scheme' and is said to be marked with his 'personal imprint'.[270] Wilson's press secretary called it his 'monument'.[271] The description is an apt one if the reference is to the words written for Christopher Wren, *lector si monumentum requiris circumspice* ('Reader, if you seek his monument – look around you'). By engaging with the passions and pleasures of learning, the OU's two million plus learners have formed a wide range of fluid, emergent communities, have changed themselves, and have contributed to the transformations that we see all about us.

Select bibliography

Annual reports of the Vice-Chancellor to the council, Milton Keynes: The Open University (various years).

Ashworth, Mandy, *The Open University in Wales: A Charter celebration* (Milton Keynes: The Open University, 1994).

Atkins, Pat, Chris Baker, Sue Cole, Judith George, Maureen Haywood, Mary Thorpe, Nora Tomlinson and Sue Whitaker, *Supporting open learners reader: A staff development reader for Open University associate lecturers*, 3rd edn (Milton Keynes: The Open University, 2002).

Bell, Robert E. and Malcolm Tight, *Open universities: A British tradition?* (Buckingham and Bristol: Society for Research into Higher Education and The Open University, 1993).

Beloff, Michael, *The plateglass universities* (London: Secker and Warburg, 1968).

Briggs, Asa, *Michael Young: social entrepreneur* (Basingstoke: Palgrave, 2001).

Briggs, Asa, *The history of broadcasting in the United Kingdom*. Volume V. *Competition 1955–1974* (Oxford: Oxford University Press, 1995).

Christensen, Clayton M., Sally Aaron and William Clark, 'Disruption in education', in Maureen Devlin, Richard Larson and Joel Meyerson (eds), *The internet and the university: Forum 2001* (Boulder: EDUCAUSE and the Forum for the Future of Higher Education, 2002).

Dalgleish, Tim (ed.), *Lifting it off the page: An oral portrait of OU people* (Milton Keynes: The Open University, 1995).

Dearing, Ron (Chair), *Higher education in the learning society: Report of the National Committee of Inquiry into Higher Education* (London: Stationery Office, 1997).

Ferguson, John, *The Open University from within* (London: University of London, 1975).

Henry, Jane, 'The course tutor and project work', *Teaching at a Distance*, 9 (July 1977).

Hollis, Patricia, *Jennie Lee* (Oxford: Oxford University Press, 1998).

Hollister, Geoff S. and Michael J. Pentz, 'Science and technology at "The Open"', *Vestes: The Australian Universities Review, Journal of Federation of Australian University Staff Associations*, 14 (1971).

Holloway, Les (ed.), *The first ten years. A special edition of Sesame to mark the tenth anniversary of the Open University, 1969–1979* (Milton Keynes: The Open University, 1979).

Horlock, John, *An open book: A memoir* (Weardale: The Memoir Club, 2006).

Hoult, David A., 'The Open University: Its structure and operation' (Dip. Ed. thesis, University of Hull, 1971).

Lunneborg, Patricia W., *OU men: Work through lifelong learning* (Cambridge: Lutterworth, 1997).

Lunneborg, Patricia W., *OU women: Undoing educational obstacles* (London: Cassell, 1994).

Macdonald-Ross, Michael, 'Janus the consultant: Educational technology at the Open University', *British Journal of Educational Technology*, 1:7 (January 1976).

MacKenzie, Norman, 'Genesis: The Brynmor Jones report', *British Journal of Educational Technology*, 36:5 (2005).

Mason, Robin and Anthony Kaye (eds), *Mindweave: Communication, computers and distance education* (Oxford: Pergamon Press, 1989).

Perry, Walter, *Open University: A personal account by the first Vice-Chancellor* (Milton Keynes: The Open University, 1976).

Pimlott, Ben, *Harold Wilson* (London: HarperCollins, 1993).

Ponting, Clive, *Breach of promise: Labour in power 1964–1970* (London: Hamish Hamilton, 1989).

Review of the Open University, conducted by the Department of Education and Science and the Open University (Milton Keynes: The Open University, 1991).

Riley, Judith, 'Course teams at the Open University', *Studies in Higher Education*, 1:1 (1976).

The Robbins report, *Higher education: Report of the Committee appointed by the Prime-Minister under the chairmanship of Lord Robbins*, Cmnd. 2154, and five appendices (London: HMSO, 1963).

Russell, Willy, *Educating Rita*, ed. and annotated Albert-Reiner Glaap (Frankfurt am Main: Verlag Moritz Diesterweg GmbH, 1984).

Simpson, Ormond, 'This door is alarmed: 35 years of attempting to widen participation in the UKOU', *Journal of Access Policy and Practice*, 3:2 (2006).

Tunstall, Jeremy (ed.), *The Open University opens* (London: Routledge and Kegan Paul, 1974).

Young, Michael, 'Is your child in the unlucky generation?', *Where?*, 10 (Autumn 1962).

Notes

Preface

1 David Hencke, 'How open is open?', *Studies in Higher Education*, 1:1 (1976), 91.

2 Clive Ponting, *Breach of promise: Labour in power 1964–1970* (London: Hamish Hamilton, 1989), p. 133.

3 W. A. Campbell Stewart, *Higher education in postwar Britain* (London: Macmillan, 1989), pp. 116–17.

4 David Sewart, Review, *Open Learning*, 10:2 (June 1995), 62.

5 Hilary Perraton, *Theory, evidence and practice in open and distance learning* (BIS-Verlag der Carl von Ossietzky Universitaät Oldenburg, 2012), p. 9. Available as an e-book at www.mde.uni-oldenburg.de/download/ASFVolume14_Ebook.pdf, accessed 1 September 2013.

6 Clayton M. Christensen, Sally Aaron and William Clark, 'Disruption in education', in Maureen Devlin, Richard Larson and Joel Meyerson (eds), *The internet and the university: Forum 2001* (Boulder: EDUCAUSE and the Forum for the Future of Higher Education, 2002), pp. 19–44, 26–32; Michael Warner, 'Publics and counterpublics', *Quarterly Journal of Speech*, 88:4 (November 2002), 413–25, http://knowledgepublic.pbworks.com/f/warnerPubCounterP.pdf, accessed 16 April 2014.

7 Etienne Wenger, *Communities of practice* (Cambridge: Cambridge University Press, 1998), p. 96. This theory has been developed in a number of subsequent texts.

8 J. F. C. Harrison, *Learning and living 1790–1960: A study in the history of the English adult education movement* (London: Routledge and Kegan Paul, 1961), p. xi.

9 Texts which have helped to reconfigure the historiography include Tom Woodin, '"Chuck out the teacher": radical pedagogy in the community', *International Journal of Lifelong Education*, 39:5 (2007), 551–67, and David Vincent, *Literacy and popular culture: England 1750–1914* (Cambridge: Cambridge University Press, 1989).

10 Hilary Young, 'Whose story counts? Constructing an oral history of the Open University at 40', *Oral History*, 39:2 (Autumn 2011), 95.

Chapter I

1 www.nocn.org.uk, accessed 1 September 2013.

2 www.open.ac.uk/platform/news-and-features/pm-ou-has-huge-huge-role-play-uk-recovery, accessed 1 September 2013.

3 Bill Bryson, *Notes from a small island* (London: Black Swan, 1996), p. 352.

4 Mary Stuart, the current Vice-Chancellor of Lincoln University, who gained a first class bachelor's degree and a PhD from the OU: www8.open.ac.uk/about/showcase/article/under-confident-student-university-vice-chancellor, accessed 28 September 2012. The phrase 'National Treasure' was also used by actor Kevin Doyle to describe the OU: www8.open.ac.uk/platform/news-and-features/downton-abbey-actor-declares-ou-national-treasure, accessed 2 October 2012.

5 Aristotle, *The politics of Aristotle*, trans. Ernest Barker (London: Oxford University Press, 1971), p. 105.

6 For Wilson's remark, made shortly after his speech in Glasgow on 8 September 2013, see Phoebe L. H. Hall, Hilary Land, Roy Parker and Adrian Webb, *Change, choice and conflict in social policy* (London: Heinemann, 1975), p. 251.

7 The *Guardian* (9 September 1963) reported the speech and carried an editorial ('Higher education outside the walls') calling the idea 'good and welcome'. The front page report in the *Scotsman* (9 September 1963) included a photograph of Wilson delivering the speech.

8 *The Times* (9 September 1963).

9 David Harris, *Openness and closure in distance education* (Brighton: Falmer, 1987), pp. 19, 20.

10 Phyllis K. Hall, 'The Open University: Its origin and development', OU archive WP1/1/1.

11 Les Holloway, 'In the beginning. The founders of the university trace its origins', in Les Holloway (ed.), *The first ten years: A special edition of Sesame to mark the tenth anniversary of the Open University, 1969–1979* (Milton Keynes: The Open University, 1979), p. 2.

12 John Dodd and Greville Rumble, 'Planning new distance teaching universities', *Higher Education*, 13 (1984), 233.

13 Royal Charter (RC 000391) establishing the Open University, 30 May 1969, pp. iv, v. Online at www.open.ac.uk/about/documents/about-university-charter.pdf, accessed 1 December 2012.

14 Hall *et al.*, *Change, choice and conflict*, p. 239.

15 G. Catlin, 'A "university of the air"', *Contemporary Review*, 198 (1960), 358–60. On Wyatt's bill to provide for the establishment of a higher education

service on television see *Commons Debate 7 March 1961, vol 636 cc267–71*, http://hansard.millbanksystems.com/commons/1961/mar/07/television-higher-education-service#S5CV0636P0_19610307_HOC_290, accessed 1 June 2011; The Post Office, *Report of the committee on broadcasting, 1960* (Pilkington Report) Cmnd 1753 (London: HMSO, 1962), pp. 273–84.

16 The Labour Party's Study Group on Higher Education, *The years of crisis: Report of the Labour Party's Study Group on Higher Education* (London: Labour Party, 1963), p. 34.

17 *Times Higher Education Supplement* (4 March 1966).

18 Norman Birnbaum, 'A view from New England', in Jeremy Tunstall (ed.), *The Open University opens* (London: Routledge and Kegan Paul, 1974), pp. 34, 37.

19 Michael Young, 'Education for the new work', in Nigel Paine (ed.), *Open learning in transition: An agenda for action* (Cambridge: National Extension College, 1988), p. 5.

20 Stuart Hall, *New Statesman and Society* (26 November 1993).

21 Interview with Stuart Hall, OU Oral History Project recording, OU Archives, Milton Keynes (hereafter OU Oral History Project). All interviews from The Open University Oral History collection are copyright 2014 The Open University. Stuart Hall joined the OU in 1979 having been at the Birmingham Centre for Cultural Studies, which he helped to establish in 1964. His wife, Catherine Hall, taught at the OU from the early days and contributed to some early course materials.

22 For examples see George Low, OU Oral History Project. George Low was born in 1940, attended Oxford University and then worked in publishing. He worked at the OU 1971–74 and his wife Sally, a teacher, was one of the first OU students. Joan Whitehead, OU Oral History Project. Joan Whitehead attended a comprehensive school, completed a degree in psychology at the University of North Wales and worked as a Research Associate in the OU's Faculty of Educational Studies between 1970 and 1976.

23 *Times Higher Education Supplement* (3 December 1971).

24 Jeremy Tunstall, 'Introduction', in Jeremy Tunstall (ed.), *The Open University opens* (London: Routledge and Kegan Paul, 1974). The Planning Committee was appointed in 1967 to develop the plan for a university as outlined in the 1966 White Paper.

25 Wilson's 1 October 1963 'white heat' speech opened the science debate at the Labour Party conference. The speech was later produced as a pamphlet, *Labour's plan for science: Reprint of speech by the Rt. Hon. Harold Wilson, MP, leader of the Labour party at the annual conference Scarborough, Tuesday, October 1, 1963* (London: Labour Party, 1963).

26 Tony Benn, 'Yesterday's Men at Mintech', *New Statesman* (24 July 1970).

27 Mike Savage, *Identities and social change in Britain since 1940: The politics of method* (Oxford: Oxford University Press, 2011).

28 Samuel Hutchinson Beer, *Britain against itself: The political contradictions of collectivism* (London: Faber, 1982), pp. 111–26.

29 David Edgerton, *Science, technology and the British industrial 'decline', 1870–1970* (Cambridge: Cambridge University Press, 1996).

30 Eric Hobsbawm, *Age of extremes: The short twentieth century, 1914–1991* (London: Michael Joseph, 1994), p. 264. On the role given to technology by politicians see Arthur Marwick, *The sixties: Cultural revolution in Britain, France, Italy, and the United States, c. 1958–c.1974* (Oxford: Oxford University Press, 1998), p. 248.

31 Email cited on www.smalltalk.org/alankay.html, accessed 28 November 2012.

32 *Early Leaving. A Report of the Central Advisory Council for Education (England)* (London: HMSO, 1954).

33 *15 to 18: A report of the Central Advisory Council for Education (England)* (London: HMSO, 1959).

34 *Half our future: A report of the Central Advisory Council for Education (England)* (London: HMSO, 1963).

35 R. Layard, J. King and C. Moser, *The impact of Robbins* (Harmondsworth: Penguin, 1969), p. 13; Michael Beloff, *The plateglass universities* (London: Secker and Warburg, 1968), p. 15.

36 Noel Annan, *Our age: Portrait of a generation* (London: Weidenfeld and Nicolson, 1990), p. 377. The term 'golden age' is also used in Mary Henkel, *Academic identities and policy change in higher education* (London: Jessica Kingsley, 2000), p. 167; Harold Perkin, *Key profession: The history of the Association of University Teachers* (London: Routledge and Kegan Paul, 1969), p. 1.

37 Adrian Jones, *Death of a pirate: British radio and the making of the information age* (New York and London: W. W. Norton, 2010), pp. 238, 225. See also Des Freedman, *Television policies of the Labour Party, 1951–2001* (London: Frank Cass, 2003), p. 73, and Robert Chapman, *Selling the sixties: The pirates and pop music radio* (London: Routledge, 1992), p. 36.

38 Asa Briggs, *The history of broadcasting in the United Kingdom*. Vol. V: *Competition 1955–1974* (Oxford: Oxford University Press, 1995), p. 507.

39 Briggs, *The history of broadcasting in the United Kingdom*. Vol. V, pp. 457, 458, 460.

40 *Saturday Review* (29 April 1972); *The Times* (13 July 1973).

41 *BBC Handbook, 1960* (London: British Broadcasting Corporation, 1961); *BBC Handbook, 1970* (London: British Broadcasting Corporation, 1971).

42 http://news.bbc.co.uk/onthisday/hi/dates/stories/july/20/newsid_3728000/3728225.stm, accessed 1 November 2013.

43 Dolly Smith Wilson, 'A new look at the affluent worker: The good working mother in post-war Britain', *Twentieth Century British History*, 17:2 (2006), 207.

44 Hannah Gavron, *The captive wife: Conflicts of housebound mothers* (London, Routledge and Kegan Paul, 1966).

45 Sue Bruley, *Women in Britain since 1900* (Basingstoke: Palgrave, 1999), p. 143.

46 Ponting, *Breach of promise*, p. 133.

47 *The Economist* (14 September 1963).

48 Editorial, 'Over the air', *The Times* (14 August 1970).

49 *The Listener* (1 May 1969).

50 Norman MacKenzie, OU Oral History Project. Norman MacKenzie, who had worked at the *New Statesman* and the University of Sussex, had spent a year looking at distance education in the US. He was a member of both the Advisory Committee and the Planning Committee.

51 Michael Drake, *Kentish Gazette* (26 November 1971). The phrase was repeated in Michael Drake, 'The Open University concept', *Studies: An Irish quarterly review*, 61:42 (Summer 1972), 158.

52 Greville Rumble, 'Labour market theories and distance education: Industrialization and distance education', *Open Learning*, 10:1 (February 1995), 14.

53 Otto Peters, 'Distance education and industrial production: A comparative interpretation in outline', in David Sewart, Desmond Keegan and Börje Holmberg (eds), *Distance education: International perspectives* (Beckenham: Croom Helm, 1983).

54 G. S. Hollister and M. J. Pentz, 'Science and technology at "The Open"', *Vestes: the Australian Universities Review, Journal of Federation of Australian University Staff Associations*, 14 (1971), 98.

55 Early studies were Börje Holmberg, *On the methods of teaching by correspondence* (Lund: Lund universitets årsskrift, 1960) and Triangle Publications, Radio and Television Division, *The University of the Air: Commercial television's pioneer efforts in education* (Philadelphia, PA: Triangle, 1959). Soon others were collating data, testing approaches and compiling reports on the use of correspondence and broadcasting for teaching adults. See, for example, Hilary Perraton, *Correspondence and television: A report of a small pilot experiment in the teaching of mathematics by television and correspondence; together with a note on some implications for a 'University of the Air'* (Cambridge: National Extension College, 1966); Hilary Perraton, 'Television and the university crisis', *Educational Television International*, 4:3 (1970), 208–12; Hilary Perraton, 'Are satellites for people?', *Educational Broadcasting International*, 5:3 (1971), 155–60.

56 Otto Peters, 'Theoretical aspects of correspondence instruction', in O. MacKenzie and E. L. Christensen (eds), *The changing world of correspondence study* (University Park: Pennsylvania State University Press, 1971).

57 Desmond Keegan, 'On defining distance education', *Distance Education*, 1:1 (1980), 21; N. Farnes, 'Modes of production: Fordism and distance

education', *Open Learning*, 8:1 (1993), 10–20; P. Raggatt, 'Post-Fordism and distance education: A flexible strategy for change', *Open Learning*, 8:1 (1993), 21–31; M. Campion, 'Post-Fordism and research in distance education', in T. Evans (ed.), *Research in distance education* (Geelong: Deakin University, 1990); M. Campion and W. Renner, 'The supposed demise of Fordism: Implications for distance education and higher education', *Distance Education*, 13:1 (1991), 7–28.

58 The chief administrator of the Department for Education and Science Policy at the Ministry of Education in Finland, Mikko Niemi, called the modern mass university a huge production plant which could be used to promote social goals. See Marja Jalava, 'When Humboldt met Marx: The Humboldtian Bildungsuniversität in the Finnish leftist student movement of the 1970s', *The Humboldtian tradition: Origin and legacy, Symposium in Uppsala*, 24–25 November 2010, http://histcon.se/file/90/the-humboldtian-tradition-abstracts-och-schema.pdf, accessed 20 September 2011.

59 Michael Young, 'Announcing the National Extension College', *Where?*, (the periodical of the Advisory Centre for Education) 14 (1963), 16–17.

60 Beryl McAlhone (ed.), *After school English* (Cambridge: National Extension College, 1967), p. 16. Following the NEC's successful course the BBC ran one in 1965 which involved over 1,800 people.

61 Thorsten Nybom, 'The Humboldt legacy: Reflections on the past, present, and future of the European University', *Higher Education Policy*, 16 (June 2003), 141–59.

62 On the positive impact of higher education on economic growth see C. Goldin and L. F. Katz, *The race between education and technology* (Cambridge, MA: Harvard University Press, 2008).

63 The Hadow Committee, *New ventures in broadcasting: A study in adult education* (London: BBC, 1928), p. 87.

64 *The Straits Times* (1 February 1929) http://newspapers.nl.sg/Digitised/Page/straitstimes19290201-1.1.10.aspx, accessed 1 June 2011. For an obituary of Fournier d'Albe, see *Nature*, 132 (22 July 1933), 125–6.

65 Asa Briggs, *The history of broadcasting in the United Kingdom*. Vol. II (Oxford: Oxford University Press, 1965), pp. 218–26; Mary Stocks, *The Workers' Education Association: The first 50 years* (London: Allen and Unwin, 1953); R. Peers, *Adult education* (London: Routledge and Kegan Paul, 1958), pp. 234–5.

66 'Television Group Viewing', *Adult Education*, 29:3 (1956), 143–4.

67 Bernard Hawkins, 'Television in the Australian classroom', *Quarterly Review of Australian Education*, 3:1 (September 1969), 1.

68 Harold Wiltshire, 'The great tradition in university adult education', *Adult Education*, 28:2 (1956). Reprinted in Alan Rogers (ed.), *The spirit and the form: Essays in adult education by and in honour of Professor Harold Wiltshire* (Nottingham: University of Nottingham, Department of Adult Education, 1976).

69 D. L. C. Miller, 'Ontario universities pool their talents for brighter ETV picture', *Canadian University and College* (October 1969).

70 Peers, *Adult education*, p. 235.

71 Marshall McLuhan, *Understanding media: The extensions of man* (New York: McGraw-Hill, 1964).

72 *The Listener* (7 July 1966), 8.

73 Quoted in Robert Rowland, 'Some thoughts on the use of broadcasting in the Open University', *Teaching at a Distance*, 2 (February 1975), 64.

74 Geoffrey Lunn, 'Programmed learning news', *New University* (November 1969), 23.

75 Brian Lewis, 'Course production at the Open University IV: The problem of assessment', *British Journal of Educational Technology*, 3:2 (1972), 108–28.

76 David Harris, 'Educational technology at the Open University: A short history of achievement and cancellation', *British Journal of Educational Technology*, 1:7 (1976), 44, 49.

77 M. L. J. Abercrombie, *Aims and techniques of group teaching* (London: Society for Research into Higher Education, 2nd edn, 1971); Andrew Northedge, 'Learning through discussion in the Open University', *Teaching at a Distance*, 2 (February 1975), 10–19.

78 David Sewart, 'Some observations on the formation of study groups', *Teaching at a Distance*, 2 (February 1975), 2–6; Keith Whitlock, 'Study groups: Some follow-up proposals', *Teaching at a Distance*, 3 (May 1975), 44–7.

79 Roger Watkins, 'Co-operative learning in discussion groups', *Teaching at a Distance*, 2 (February 1975), 7–9.

80 M. L. J. Abercrombie, 'Paths to learning', *Teaching at a Distance*, 5 (March 1976), 12

81 Judith Riley, 'Course teams at the Open University', *Studies in Higher Education*, 1:1 (1976), 61.

82 Charles Newey, 'On being a course team chairman', *Teaching at a Distance*, 4 (November 1975), 47–51.

83 Naomi McIntosh, 'Women and the OU', in Staff Development in Universities Programme, *Women in higher education: Papers from a conference held in London on 29 June 1973* (London: University of London Teaching Methods Unit, 1975).

84 Ken Boyd, OU Oral History Project. Ken Boyd worked for Belfast Education Department until he became the OU's first administrator in Northern Ireland in December 1970. Until 1973 Northern Ireland was run by the North West Region. Ken Boyd was involved in that change, in establishing an OU office in the Republic of Ireland in 1995 and in the transition to OU Ireland. He became Assistant Regional Director in the Open University in Ireland and retired in September 2001.

85   Christensen *et al.*, 'Disruption in education', pp. 19–44, 26–32.
86   www.claytonchristensen.com/disruptive_innovation.html, accessed 1 December 2011. See also Clayton M. Christensen, Michael B. Horn, Louis Caldera and Louis Soares, *Disrupting college: How disruptive innovation can deliver quality and affordability to postsecondary education*, February 2011, pp. 2–4, www.americanprogress.org/issues/2011/02/disrupting_college.html, accessed 24 May 2011. For a critique of Christensen's taxonomy see Constantinos Markides, 'Disruptive innovation: In need of better theory', *Journal of Product Management Innovation*, 23:1 (January 2006), 19–25.
87   Vice-Chancellor Brenda Gourley referred to Christensen's theory at the September 2008 meeting of the OU Council. The thesis has also been applied to Athabasca University. See Walter Archer, D. Randy Garrison and Terry Anderson, 'Adopting disruptive technologies in traditional universities: Continuing education as an incubator for innovation', *Canadian Journal of University Continuing Education*, 25:1 (1999), 13–30.
88   Clayton M. Christensen, Mark W. Johnson and Darrell K. Rigby, 'Foundations for growth: How to identify and build disruptive new businesses', *MIT Sloan Management Review*, 43:3 (Spring 2002), www.biu.ac.il/soc/ec/students/teach/554/data/doc/christensen.pdf, accessed 21 November 2012.
89   Nigel Thrift, Fulbright lecture 2009, 'We can't go on like this: British higher education as it is and as it could be', www.timeshighereducation.co.uk/Journals/THE/THE/14_May_2009/attachments/RSA%20LECTURE.docx, accessed 1 October 2012.
90   Elizabeth Gibney, 'The dambuster', *Times Higher Education* (24 October 2013), 41.
91   www.gov.uk/government/speeches/universities-uk-spring-conference-2011, accessed 23 September 2012.
92   http://blog.universitiesuk.ac.uk/2012/12/14/moocs-digital-higher-educatio, accessed 28 December 2012; *Daily Telegraph* (24 July 2013), www.telegraph.co.uk/education/universityeducation/10198076/David-Willetts-our-privately-funded-university-revolution.html, accessed on 26 March 2014.
93   www.open.ac.uk/choose/ou/rcn, accessed 3 November 2013.
94   M. Hart, A. Nelson, J. Swift and J. Wiggans, 'Widening participation in the workplace: A partnership between the Open University (OU) Aimhigher and unionlearn', Paper presented at the European Association of Distance Learning Universities (EADTU) Conference, Widening participation and opportunities for lifelong open and flexible learning in HE (Tallinn, Estonia, 2006) www.eadtu.nl/proceedings/2006/Presentations%20parallel%20sessions/Hart,%2038Nelson;%20Widening%20Participation%20in%20the%20Work%20Place,%20a%20partnership%20between%20the%20OU,%20Aimhigher%20and%20Unionlearn.PDF, accessed 3 November 2013.
95   www.open.ac.uk/quarterly-survey, accessed 3 November 2013.

96 Martin Trow, *Problems in the transition from elite to mass higher educa-tion* (Berkeley, CA: Carnegie Commission on Higher Education, 1974); G. Neave, 'The future of the city of intellect', *European education: Issues and studies*, 34:3 (2002), 20–41.

97 *Daily Telegraph* (9 April 2008), www.telegraph.co.uk/news/uknews/1584495/ Labour-sticks-to-50-per-cent-university-target.html, accessed 2 October 2012.

98 Thirty polytechnics in England and Wales and subsequently five Scottish Central Institutions were granted university status following legislation in 1992. A further wave of universities followed after legislation in 2004 per-mitted colleges without the powers to award research degrees to obtain a university title. The rationale for this was contained in a White Paper, DfES, *The Future of Higher Education* (London: The Stationery Office, 2003), p. 54, www.bis.gov.uk/assets/BISCore/corporate/MigratedD/publications/F/ future_of_he.pdf, accessed 2 February 2012. Other definitions of universi-ties in the UK suggest that there were as many as 162 by 2010. See Malcolm Tight, 'How many universities are there in the UK? How many should there be?', *Higher Education*, 62:5 (2011), 649–63; *Social Trends 40*, cited by Michael McCarthy, *Independent* (3 July 2010).

99 Roger Brown with Helen Carasso, *Everything for sale? The marketisation of UK higher education* (London: Routledge 2013).

100 PA Consulting Group, *The quiet revolution: How strategic partnerships and alliances are reshaping the higher education system* (London: PA Consulting, 2012).

101 www.distancelearningnet.com/the-history-of-distance-learning, accessed 24 October 2011.

102 Asa Briggs, OU Oral History Project. Lord Briggs was Professor of History and then Vice-Chancellor at the University of Sussex, a member of the OU Planning Committee, 1967–69, and the chair of its working group on students and the curriculum. He went on to become the OU's Chancellor between 1978 and 1994 and he also taught at the OU. Lord Briggs was awarded a Fellowship of the OU in 1999.

103 Obituary, *The Herald* (15 July 2013), www.heraldscotland.com/comment/ obituaries/norman-mackenzie.21440715, accessed 30 July 2013.

104 Mary Thorpe and Roger Edmunds, 'Practices with technology: Learning at the boundaries between study and work', *Journal of Computer Assisted Learning*, 27:5 (2011), 385–98. See also Robin D. Mason and Anthony A. Kaye (eds), *Mindweave: Communication, computers and distance educa-tion* (Oxford: Pergamon Press, 1989).

105 Ormond Simpson, 'A case for coarser courses', *Teaching at a Distance*, 6 (June 1976), 131.

106 Malcolm Chase, '"Mythmaking and mortmain": The uses of adult educa-tion history', *Studies in the Education of Adults*, 27:1 (1995), 53–4.

107 Michael Macdonald-Ross and Robert Waller, 'The transformer revisited', *Information Design Journal*, 9:2–3 (2000), 178. This article was written in 1974, it appeared in *Penrose Annual*, 1976, and a postscript was added when it was published in 2000.

108 John Kirkaldy, 'To Tommy – wherever she is', in *Learn & Live* (Milton Keynes: The Open University, 1994), p. 23.

109 Paulo Freire, *Pedagogy of indignation* (Boulder, CO: Paradigm, 2004), p. 15.

110 Alan Woodley, 'Graduation and beyond', *Open Learning*, 3:1 (February 1988), 16.

111 Alan Woodley and Jane Wilson, 'British higher education and its older clients', *Higher Education*, 44:3–4 (October–December 2002), 329–47.

112 Claire Callender and Rayah Feldman, *Part-time undergraduates in higher education: A literature review. Prepared for HECSU to inform Futuretrack: part-time students*, www.hecsu.ac.uk/assets/assets/documents/research_reports/part_time_undergraduates_in_he_0509.pdf, accessed 3 November 2013.

113 OU Chancellor Betty Boothroyd in the House of Lords, 19 April 2004 www.theyworkforyou.com/lords/?id=2004-04-19a.39.1&s=%28Education %29+speaker%3A10054#g99.0, accessed 1 June 2011.

114 Campbell Stewart, *Higher education*, pp. 116–17.

115 On the importance and influence of the OU's credit system see DES, *Adult education: A plan for development* (Russell Report) (London: HMSO, 1973), p. 296. For precedents see Börje Holmberg, *On the methods of teaching by correspondence* (Lund: Lunds universitets, 1960); Börje Holmberg, *Distance education: A survey and bibliography* (London: Kogan Page, 1977); Charles A. Wedemeyer, 'Independent study', in Lee C. Deighton (ed.), *The Encyclopedia of Education*. Vol. 4 (New York: Free Press, 1971), pp. 548–57.

116 'For richer, for poorer', quoted in Asa Briggs, *Michael Young: Social entrepreneur* (Basingstoke: Palgrave, 2001), pp. 155–6.

117 P. G. Wodehouse, *The Inimitable Jeeves* (London: Herbert Jenkins, 1923).

118 For examples from Kent and York see the *Observer* (2 June 1968); the *Guardian* (26 June 1968).

119 Donald Hutchings, 'Has the student image reached a new low?', *New University* (February 1969), 22.

120 *The Times* (13 August 1970).

121 E. P. Thompson (ed.), *Warwick University Ltd: Industry, management and the universities* (Harmondsworth: Penguin, 1970), p. 155.

122 As reported by the *Observer* (3 February 2002).

123 The University of Sussex accepted a few students who did not have the usual university entry requirements, but they were not mature students. See Edwin H. Cox, '15+ drop-outs', *University Quarterly*, 25:2 (Spring 1971), 169–76.

124 *Education + Training* 14:7 (June 1972), 216; *Education + Training* 12:10 (October 1970), 374–5; AGOU (78) Minutes of the meeting of 9 February 1978, espec. Item 7.4, The National Archives, ED 250/75. There

was opposition from the former Education Secretary and the OU's Vice-Chancellor, and the scheme was deemed to have had limited success. See Alan Woodley and Naomi McIntosh, *The door stood open: An evaluation of the Open University Younger Student pilot scheme* (Brighton: Falmer, 1980).

125 John Ferguson, *The Open University from within* (London: University of London, 1975), p. 94.

126 *The Times* (1 August 1973).

127 Ferguson, *The Open University from within*, p. 156.

128 *Times Higher Education Supplement* (3 December 1971).

129 John Brennan, Jonathan Mills, Tarta Shah and Alan Woodley, *Part-time students and employment: Report of a survey of students, graduates and diplomats* (London Centre for Higher Education and Information, Open University and Department for Education and Employment, 1999); John Brennan, Jonathan Mills, Tarta Shah and Alan Woodley, 'Lifelong learning for employment and equity: The role of part-time degrees', *Higher Education Quarterly*, 54:4 (2000), 411–18; Alan Woodley and Ormond Simpson, 'Learning and earning: Measuring "rates of return" among mature graduates from part-time distance courses', *Higher Education Quarterly*, 55:1 (2001), 28–41.

130 Margaret Salter, 'More of a way of life than a course of study: Fast track to a fitter future', in *Learn & Live* (Milton Keynes: The Open University, 1994), pp. 12, 18.

131 Peter Syme, 'Capitalising on commitment', in *Learn & Live* (Milton Keynes: The Open University, 1994), p. 23.

132 *Open Minds* (19 June 2012), www.open.ac.uk/blogs/History-of-the-OU/?p=2607, accessed 14 June 2013.

133 E. P. Thompson, 'The pursuit of learning', *Teaching at a Distance*, 22 (Autumn 1982), 3.

134 *The Times* (7 June 1968).

Chapter 2

1 Between 1919 and 1989 the University Grants Committee advised on the distribution of state funding among the British universities. Tom Owen, 'The University Grants Committee', *Oxford Review of Education*, 6:3 (1980), 255–78.

2 www.open.ac.uk/blogs/History-of-the-OU/?p=1255, accessed 20 May 2011. On hostility within the Labour Party see Betty Boothroyd, *Betty Boothroyd: The autobiography* (London: Century, 2001), p. 295.

3 *Guardian* (8 January 2010), www.guardian.co.uk/media/2010/jan/08/richard-hooper-itv-regional-news, accessed 20 November 2012. Richard Hooper, 'New media in the OU: An international perspective', in Jeremy Tunstall (ed.), *The Open University opens* (London: Routledge and Kegan Paul, 1974), p. 183.

4 Walter Perry, 'The Open University', in Ian Mugridge (ed.), *Founding the open universities: Essays in memory of G. Ram Reddy* (New Dehli: Sterling, 1997), p. 5.

5 H. J. Perkin, 'The new universities', *Western European Education*, 2:4 (Winter 1970/71), 308–9.

6 Clark Kerr, *The uses of the university*, 4th edn (Cambridge, MA: Harvard University Press, 1995).

7 These included the predecessor colleges, which became the University of Exeter (which received a Royal Charter in 1955), Manchester College of Science and Technology (which was awarded a Royal Charter in 1956 and became the University of Manchester Institute of Science and Technology) and University College, Leicester (which in 1957 was granted a Royal Charter and became the University of Leicester).

8 Geoffrey Price, 'Universities today: Between the corporate state and the market', *Culture, Education, Society*, 39:1 (Winter 1984/85), 43.

9 Simon Szreter, 'Britain's social welfare provision in the long run: The importance of accountable, well-financed local government', in Armine Ishkanian and Simon Szreter, *The Big Society debate: A new agenda for social welfare?* (Cheltenham, and Northampton, MA: Edward Elgar, 2012), p. 47.

10 Fred Gray (ed.), *Making the future: A history of the University of Sussex* (Falmer: University of Sussex, 2011), pp. 4–5.

11 Michael Sanderson, *The history of the University of East Anglia, Norwich* (London: Hambledon and London, 2001), pp. 5–6. The new universities of the period in England were Sussex (1961), York and East Anglia (1963), Lancaster and Essex (1964) and Warwick and Kent (1965). In 1966/67 nine colleges of advanced technology were designated as universities, and Bradford Institute of Technology became the University of Bradford.

12 John Pratt, 'Open University!', *Higher Education Review*, 3:2 (Spring 1971), 10.

13 John Pratt, 'Gone to lunch: A critical look at the Open University', *Education + Training*, 12:10 (October 1970), 375. There were precedents. In 1884 the government provided £2,500 to Aberystwyth for university education.

14 *The Times* (9 September 1963).

15 Wilson, *Labour's plan for science*, p. 4.

16 The phrase 'city of dreaming spires' as a description of Oxford occurs in Matthew Arnold's 1865 poem 'Thyrsis'.

17 Daniel Bell, *The coming of post-industrial society: A venture in social forecasting* (Harmondsworth: Penguin, 1974); Fritz Machlup, *The production and distribution of knowledge in the United States* (Princeton, NJ: Princeton University Press, 1962); Marc U. Porat, *The information economy: Definition and measurement* (Washington, DC: US Department of Commerce, 1977); Alaine Touraine, *The post-industrial society: Tomorrow's social history, classes, conflict and culture in the programmed society*, trans. L. Mayhew

(London: Wildwood House, 1974); Yoneji Masuda, *The information society as post-industrial society* (Washington, DC: World Future Society, 1980).

18 The speech is available at http://er.jsc.nasa.gov/seh/ricetalk.htm, accessed 24 May 2012.

19 Thomas Docherty, *For the university: Democracy and the future of the institution*, Bloomsbury Academic, online at www.bloomsburyacademic. com/view/For-the-University/book-ba-9781849666336.xml, accessed 24 May 2012.

20 www.col.org/SiteCollectionDocuments/Daniel_CROWTHER_Speech _1969.pdf, accessed 24 May 2012.

21 Briggs, *Michael Young*, pp. 198, 201, 372; Peter Laslett, 'Linking universities by TV', *Where?*, 21 (Summer 1964), 21. The follow-up conference in 1964 issued a report, 'Towards an Open University', *Where?*, 18 (Autumn 1964). For the cultural policy context see Janet Minihan, *The nationalization of culture: The development of state subsidies to the arts in Great Britain* (New York: New York University Press, 1977), p. x.

22 Karl Schriftgiesser, *Business comes of age: The story of the Committee for Economic Development and its impact upon the economic policies of the United States, 1942–1960* (New York: Harper and Brothers, 1960) and Sydney Hyman, *The lives of William Benton* (Chicago: University of Chicago Press, 1969).

23 13 November 1961, 16 November 1961 Box 60 File 4, University of Chicago, Special Collections Research Center (hereafter Benton Papers). The Special Collections Research Center, University of Chicago Library, is the owner and source of the Benton Papers material.

24 Benton to Wilson 19 November 1962 Box 374, File 2, Benton Papers.

25 Jeffrey Lustig, *Corporate liberalism: The origins of modern American political thought, 1890–1920* (Berkeley, CA: University of California Press, 1982), p. 7.

26 Robert Griffith, *The politics of fear: Joseph R. McCarthy and the Senate* (Amherst: University of Massachusetts Press, 1987), pp. 159, 163. McCarthy was hostile towards both Benton and Benton's company, Encyclopaedia Britannica.

27 William Benton, 'Television – a prescription: A national citizens' advisory board', *Vital speeches of the day*, 26:8 (15 June 1949), 572.

28 Michael Barker, 'Social engineering, progressive media, and William Benton', refereed paper contributed to ANZCA08 Conference, *Power and Place*. Wellington, July 2008 available at www.massey.ac.nz/massey/fms/Colleges/ College%20of%20Business/Communication%20and%20Journalism/ ANZCA%202008/Refereed%20Papers/Barker_BentonPaper_ANZCA08. pdf, accessed 1 December, 2011. The term 'manufacturing consent' is derived from E. S. Herman and N. Chomsky, *Manufacturing consent: The political economy of the mass media* (New York: Pantheon Books, 1988).

See also Cynthia B. Meyers, 'From radio adman to radio reformer: Senator William Benton's career in broadcasting, 1930–1960', *Journal of radio and audio media*, 16:1 (2009), 17–29.

29   Box 522, File 17 Speech 5 June 1960 'The cold war and the liberal arts', Benton Papers.

30   Harold Wilson, *Memoirs: The making of a prime minister, 1916–64* (London: Weidenfeld and Nicolson and Michael Joseph, 1986); Walter Perry, *Report of the Vice-Chancellor to the council, 1972* (Milton Keynes: The Open University, 1973), p. 30.

31   9 January 1961 Box 60 File 4; 8 September 1961 memo, Box 60 File 4; 12 September 1961, Box 60 File 4; Letter from Marcia Williams, 23 October 1961, Box 60 File 4; Benton to Wilson, 12 January 1962, Box 60 File 4; Handwritten letter Wilson to Benton, 28 January 1962, Box 274 File 3; Wilson to Benton, 7 February 1962, Box 374 File 2; Benton to Wilson, 19 February 1963, Box 274 File 3; Benton to Wilson, 22 April 1963, Box 274 File 3; Benton to Wilson, 27 September 1963, Box 274, File 3; Benton to Dean Rusk, 27 September 1963, Box 274 File 3. All in Benton papers.

32   *The Times* (24 April 1974).

33   *The Economist* (14 September 1963).

34   David Grugeon, OU Oral History Project recording. David Grugeon developed 'a prenatal link with the Open University from August 12th 1963', the day he first met Brian Jackson and Michael Young. They worked on an initiative that became the National Extension College. Enthused about opening up access to educational provision, he made television programmes, lobbied politicians and edited publications. In 1969 he became the OU's first Regional Director for East Anglia and in 1971 he became Assistant Director of Central Regional Tutorial Services. He began to edit *Teaching at a Distance* from 1974 and later became a Pro-Vice-Chancellor and was seconded to the Open College 1987–89.

35   *The Times* (7 February 1972) carried an obituary.

36   Ben Pimlott, *Harold Wilson* (London: HarperCollins, 1993), p. 269.

37   Lawrence Black, 'Whose finger on the button? British television and the politics of cultural control', *Historical Journal of Film, Radio and Television*, 25:4 (2005), 566; Briggs, *Michael Young*, p. 211.

38   Michael Cockerell, *Live from No 10: The inside story of prime ministers and television* (London: Faber and Faber, 1989), p. 125; Austen Morgan, *Harold Wilson* (London: Pluto, 1992), p. 332; Wilson to Benton, 4 December 1962, Box 374 File 2, Benton papers. Charles was William's son and had recently joined the boards of Encyclopaedia Britannica and Encyclopaedia Britannica Films and a recent acquisition, Crompton's. He was a vice-president of the film company.

39   Wilson to Benton, 12 February 1960, Box 60 File 4, Benton Papers. UK Legislation in 1927 required that cinemas show a set percentage of British

films. By 1935, 20 per cent of all films both distributed and exhibited in the UK had to be British, and this rose to 45 per cent after the war. Between 1938 and 1960, in order to encourage bigger-budget films that could compete better internationally, a screen quota was set for feature films and for short films. Quotas were finally abolished in the 1980s.

40 Wilson also promised to help Benton acquire the appropriate papers which would enable him to visit China. Wilson to Benton, 4 February 1962, Box 60 File 4, Benton papers.

41 28 February 1963 broadcast, Box 274 File 3, Benton papers.

42 Benton to Wilson, 21 October 1963, Box 274 File 3, Benton papers.

43 Benton to Maurice Mitchell and John Howe, 24 September 1963, Box 274 File 3, Benton papers.

44 On the political loyalties of Sydney and Cecil Bernstein see interview in 2006 with Sir Denis Forman, www.buzzle.com/articles/112182.html and www.allvoices.com/news/5360202-baron-bernstein-creator-of-granada-tv-a-soviet-informer, both accessed 10 December 2011.

45 30 June 1962; 31 July 1962, Wilson to Benton. Benton expressed his gratitude, 7 August 1962, all Box 374 File 2, Benton papers.

46 Anthony Wedgwood Benn, the Postmaster General, thought it an 'appalling solution' and favoured a joint approach. Tony Benn, *Out of the wilderness: Diaries 1963–67* (London: Hutchinson, 1987) pp. 236, 239. See also The National Archives, Kew (hereafter TNA), PREM 13/735 handwritten note on paper dated 9 February 1965, which had been prepared by the education secretary for the Ministerial Committee on Broadcasting.

47 Peter Gosden, *The education system since 1944* (Oxford: Martin Robinson, 1983), p. 161. Jennie Lee's biographer suggested that starting a university of the air was Harold Wilson's idea. See Patricia Hollis, *Jennie Lee* (Oxford: Oxford University Press, 1998), p. 297. This view is echoed in Jagannath Mohanty, 'The British Open University: A model of distance education', in J. Mohanty (ed.), *Studies in distance education: Concepts and development, need and role. A critical assessment* (New Delhi: Deep and Deep, 2001), p. 65.

48 Ralph C. Smith, 'Developing distance learning systems – the UKOU experiment: some lessons', in G. Ram Reddy (ed.), *Open universities: The ivory towers thrown open* (London: Oriental Press, 1988), pp. 244–5.

49 TNA, T 227/2736 marginalia by Chancellor. His later reflection on this matter was made to the former OU Pro-Vice-Chancellor, David Grugeon, OU Oral History Project.

50 TNA, T 227/3245, 18 March 1970.

51 Bryan was a director of one of the larger TV companies, Granada, and sometime Front Bench spokesman on broadcasting. See Commons Debate, 3 March, 1966, www.theyworkforyou.com/debates/?id=1966-03-03a.1509.10&s=speaker%3A16737, accessed 5 May 2010.

52 Holloway 'In the begining', p. 2. The church was probably the Anglican one of St Mary, Old Town, where Wilson was buried. Harold Wilson subsequently told the story to OU students: see www.open.ac.uk/researchprojects/historyofou/story/harold-wilson, accessed 24 October 2012. He also related it in the foreword to Walter Perry, *Open University: A personal account by the first Vice-Chancellor* (Milton Keynes: The Open University, 1976), p. xi. Wilson's son Robin confirmed his father's account of that Easter: 'I certainly remember being in the Isles of Scilly in 1963, I think it was, when my father had the idea of the Open University', Robin Wilson, OU Oral History Project. Having previously taught at the University of Oxford, Robin Wilson started at The Open University in 1972. He became a Dean and Professor of Pure Mathematics and retired in 2009 to become an Emeritus Professor. He taught 70 weeks at residential schools and also gained a first-class Open University degree in Humanities with Music.

53 Harold Wilson, *The Labour Government, 1964–70* (London: Weidenfeld and Nicolson, 1971), p. 86.

54 Labour Party, *Educational policy*, 1943, cited in Jean Bocock and Richard Taylor, 'The Labour Party and higher education: 1945–51', *Higher Education Quarterly*, 57:3 (2003), 250; Jean Bocock and Richard Taylor, 'The Labour Party and higher education: The nature of the relationship', *Higher Education Quarterly*, 57:3 (2003), 220; Richard Taylor, 'Lifelong learning and the Labour governments 1997–2004', *Oxford Review of Education*, 31:1 (March 2005), 101.

55 The Taylor report, *The years of crisis: The report of the Labour Party's Study Group on Higher Education* (London: Labour Party, 1963). Briggs dates Labour's interest in educational broadcasting to this report: see Briggs, *The history of broadcasting in the United Kingdom*. Vol. V, p. 491n.

56 *The Times* (5 October 1963).

57 David Marquand, *The progressive dilemma* (London: Heinemann, 1991), p. 157. Labour's majority of 4 in the Commons in 1964 increased to one of 96 in 1966. 'The New Britain', Labour's manifesto, www.labour-party.org.uk/manifestos/1964/1964-labour-manifesto.shtml, accessed 19 April 2010.

58 Richard Crossman, *Diaries of a cabinet minister*, Vol. I (London: Hamish Hamilton and Jonathan Cape, 1974), p. 9.

59 Holloway (ed.), *The first ten years*, p. 24.

60 *The Times* (9 September 1963).

61 Briggs, *Michael Young*, p. 75. Young called the years 1945–51, when he was head of the Research Department of the Labour Party, 'the most exciting period of my life'; Michael Young, 'Education for the new work', in Nigel Paine (ed.), *Open learning in transition: An agenda for action* (Cambridge: National Extension College, 1988), p. 3.

62 Briggs, *Michael Young*, pp. 193, xvi.

63 Quoted in Briggs, *Michael Young*, p. 198.

64 David Grugeon, OU Oral History Project.

65 Michael Young, 'A tribute to Brian Jackson', *Where?*, 191 (September 1983).

66 Geoffrey Crowther, *Schools and universities*, a lecture at the LSE 1961, cited in Briggs, *Michael Young*, p. 196. This echoed H. G. Wells' speculation in the late nineteenth century that university laboratories could be used in the vacations. See Norman MacKenzie, 'Genesis: The Brynmor Jones report', *British Journal of Educational Technology*, 36:5 (2005), 714.

67 Michael Young 'Is your child in the unlucky generation?', *Where?*, 10 (Autumn 1962), 3–5.

68 There were precedents. In Finland from 1912 courses were held for adult learners utilising universities during their summer vacations: see Nina Halttunen, 'Changing missions: The role of open university education in the field of higher education in Finland', *Scandinavian Journal of Educational Research*, 50:5 (November 2006), 503–17.

69 Young, 'Announcing', pp. 16–17.

70 Young 'Is your child?'

71 Laslett, 1915–2001, was a Third Programme producer who went on to become a Fellow and Reader in politics and the history of social structures at Cambridge. See Humphrey Carpenter, with research by Jennifer Doctor, *The envy of the world: Fifty years of the BBC Third Programme and Radio 3, 1946–1996* (London: Weidenfeld and Nicolson, 1996), pp. 263–4. 'Recalling the real founding fathers of the OU', *Independent* (4 February 1999), www.independent.co.uk/news/education/education-news/open-eye-recall ing-the-real-founding-fathers-of-the-ou-1068517.html, accessed 30 March 2014; Briggs, *Michael Young*, pp. x, 3.

72 Briggs, *Michael Young*, pp. 194–5. The phrase 'the invisible college' was employed by Young. See *The National Extension College* (London: National Extension College Trust, 1990), p. 2.

73 Pye HDT Limited supplied a 'language bus' (complete with booths and tape recorders) and special instructional radio sets, which were assembled by long-stay hospital patients. Rediffusion made *Towards 2000, the Britain we make* (which was about the social implications of technological change) to which the National Extension College added a twelve-part correspond-ence course. See *Where?*, 18 (Autumn 1964). The National Extension College incurred the opposition of the BBC because it gained support from Rediffusion and Anglia Television.

74 Broadcasts were made by the Hull University Department of Adult Education, residential courses were held at Keele and the GPO was to grant licences until, following consultation with the BBC, the Post Office concluded that a radio service run from the University of Hull would 'be regarded as an experiment in local sound broadcasting' and it refused to do this. See Briggs, *Michael Young*, pp. 201–2.

75 Brian Jackson, 'University of the Air', *Guardian* (22 June 1965).

76 Letter to Kit Hardwick from Shirley Williams, 15 November 1996, quoted in Kit Hardwick, 'The life and works of Brian Jackson' (PhD dissertation, University of Huddersfield, 1997), p. 46.

77 Leader, *Guardian* (18 September 1964).

78 Jo Grimond, *The liberal future* (London: Faber and Faber, 1959), p. 127. In the *Times Higher Education Supplement* (10 December 1971) Laurence Edwards claimed of the OU that 'the idea owes its inception to a meeting at the Liberal Party Council at least a year earlier as any Liberal pamphlet for the year 1962 can amply demonstrate'. However, the British Library list of Liberal Publications Department pamphlets issued between 1956 and 1976 indicates no publication which deals with the question of university, adult or further education.

79 A Conservative MP who had worked in news and current affairs for both ITN and the BBC, Chataway issued the pamphlet *Educational Television*, which advocated the use of closed-circuit television systems for educational purposes.

80 Commons Debate, 2 April 1965 http://hansard.millbanksystems.com/commons/1965/apr/02/university-of-the-air#S5CV0709P0_19650402_HOC_37, accessed 19 April 2010.

81 *Daily Telegraph* (17 February 1969). For another example of disdain see *The Times* (15 February 1968).

82 Charles A. Weyermeyer, 'The birth of the Open University: A postscript', *Teaching at a Distance*, 21 (September 1982), 25.

83 Perry, *Open University: A personal account*, pp. 28, 30.

84 The request came from Sir Hugh Greene, see 14 June 1968 Box 194-1 'The Open University: policy', BBC Written Archives Centre, Caversham Park (hereafter BBC) File R78/654/1.

85 MacKenzie, 'Genesis', p. 721.

86 House of Lords Debate, 4 June 2009, c392, www.theyworkforyou.com/lords/?id=2009-06-04a.379.3&s=Open+University+speaker%3A13699#g392.0, accessed 19 April 2010.

87 *Times Higher Education Supplement* (3 December 1971).

88 *Daily Telegraph* (31 August 1971).

89 *Education + Training*, 12:10 (October 1970), 374–5. Edward Pearce's obituary of Ted Short (Baron Glenamara) proposed that he 'took charge of the final stages of creating the Open University', *Guardian* (10 May 2012), www.guardian.co.uk/politics/2012/may/10/edward-short-lord-glenamara?newsfeed=true, accessed 11 May 2012. In the House of Lords on 14 June 2004 Edward Graham, Lord Graham of Edmonton (who left school aged 14 and was one of the first students at the OU) attributed the creation of the OU to Harold Wilson, Jennie Lee and Ted Short: www.publications.parliament.uk/pa/ld200304/ldhansrd/vo040614/text/40614-16.htm, accessed 11 May 2012.

90 Albert Mansbridge, *An adventure in working class education* (London: Longmans Green, 1920). In Glasgow, Independent Labour Party member Alexander Lindsay was the University of Glasgow Chair of Moral Philosophy 1922–25 and Hector Hetherington, who succeeded him in the chair, was a WEA lecturer. See Robert Hamilton and Robert Turner, 'Hegel in Glasgow: Idealists and the emergence of adult education in the West of Scotland, 1866–1927', *Studies in the Education of Adults*, 38:2 (Autumn 2006), 195–209.

91 Hollis, *Jennie Lee*, p. 14.

92 Commons Debate, 2 April 1965, www.theyworkforyou.com/debates/?id=1965-04-02a.2007.4, accessed 19 April 2010.

93 Aneurin Bevan, *In place of fear* (Ilkley: EP Publishing, Scolar Press, 1976), p. 86.

94 Holloway, 'In the beginning', p. 3. Jennie Lee connected her late spouse to the OU, ceremonially hanging his cap and portrait in the Milton Keynes campus cellar bar which was funded from the Trust Fund established in his name. Hollis, *Jennie Lee*, p. 335.

95 Norman MacKenzie, OU Oral History Project.

96 Holloway (ed.), *The first ten years*, p. 24.

97 Stuart Hood, 'Dangers of educational television', *The Times* (22 September 1967). He was the controller of the BBC television service, 1961–63, and the article is an extract from his book, *A survey of television* (London: Heinemann, 1967). Bevan's formal adult education amounted to two years at the Central Labour College, London, funded by the South Wales Miners' Federation.

98 Michael Young, *The story of the National Extension College*, typescript. Cited in Hollis, *Jennie Lee*, p. 305.

99 Ponting, *Breach of promise*, p. 133.

100 Scottish Parliament debate on motion S3M-5328 www.theyworkforyou.com/sp/?id=2009-12-16.22243.0, accessed 17 August 2012.

101 Geoff Mulgan, 'Culture: The problem with being public', in D. Marquand and A. Seldon (eds), *The ideas that shaped post-war Britain* (London: Fontana, 1996), p. 196.

102 Asa Briggs, *Special relationships: People and places* (London: Frontline, 2012), p. 232.

103 Hollis, *Jennie Lee*, pp. 305–6.

104 Editorial, *The Economist* (1 June 1946).

105 Quoted in Hollis, *Jennie Lee*, p. 306. The Department of Education and Science (DES) was created out of the Ministry of Education, which itself had been formed in 1944 from the Board of Education. The DES became the Department for Education in 1992 and the Department for Education and Employment in 1997. Other iterations followed.

106 Wilson, *Labour's plan for science*, p. 4.

107 Holloway, 'In the beginning', p. 3.

108 TNA, ED 181/180; ED 188/104.

109 House of Commons debate, 2 April 1965, www.theyworkforyou.com/debates/?id=1965-04-02a.2007.4, accessed 11 May 2012.

110 *A plan for polytechnics and other colleges*, Cmnd 3006 (London: HMSO, 1966) and *A university of the air*, Cmnd 2992 (London: HMSO, 1966).

111 The *national plan*, para. 23, p. 198. Cmnd 2764 (London: HMSO, 1965). The figure of 60,000 included sandwich students.

112 Public lecture delivered at the University of Central Lancashire on 19 January 2007, www.socialisteducation.org.uk/robinson_lecture_March07.htm, accessed 1 November 2010.

113 *New Statesman* (11 March 1966), p. 326.

114 Asa Briggs, OU Oral History Project.

115 Hardwick, 'The life', pp. 45, 55.

116 MacKenzie, 'Genesis', p. 721.

117 Donald Grattan, OU Oral History Project. Donald Grattan taught mathematics in a school before he joined the BBC School Television department. He became BBC Head of Further Education Television, Controller of Educational Broadcasting and a member of the OU Planning Committee (1968–69). In 1970 he became the Head of the Open University Production Centre at Alexandra Palace. He retired in 1984.

118 *A university of the air*, Section 8, para 8, p. 6. The OU's first Vice-Chancellor, Walter Perry, claimed that had Jennie Lee 'attempted to start with a scheme offering education through the media to adults at school or pre-university level, I think the concept would have disappeared', Perry, *Open University: A personal account*, p. 24.

119 This is reported in John Scupham, 'The original brief for the Open University', *Teaching at a Distance*, 2 (February 1975), 67.

120 Quoted in Ormond Simpson, 'This door is alarmed: 35 years of attempting to widen participation in the UKOU', *Journal of Access Policy and Practice*, 3:2 (2006), 185–99.

121 Briggs, *Michael Young*, p. 211.

122 House of Commons debate, 2 April 1965, www.theyworkforyou.com/debates/?id=1965-04-02a.2007.4, accessed 1 October 2010.

123 Perry, *Open University: A personal account*, p. 24.

124 *A university of the air*, Section 4, p. 3.

125 This is a reference to the television broadcasts *Midnight Oil*, which were made with Queen's University, Belfast, and *Dawn University*, made by Anglia in 1963 and followed by *College of the Air*. Anglia Television operated a closed-circuit link between UEA and Cambridge University.

126 Commons Debate, 2 April, 1965, www.theyworkforyou.com/debates/?id=1965-04-02a.2007.4, accessed 5 May 2010.

127 Crossman, *Diaries*, Vol. XI, pp. 470–1. To ensure that the meeting about the manifesto was swift and conclusive, Wilson arranged a press confer-

ence on the same day: see Dennis Kavanagh, 'The politics of manifestoes', *Parliamentary Affairs*, 34:1 (Winter 1981), 18–19.

128 Holloway, 'In the beginning', p. 2.

129 Christopher Pollitt, 'The Public Expenditure Survey 1961–72', *Public Administration*, 55:2 (Summer 1977), 127–92.

130 TNA, PREM 13/740 letters Lee to Wilson, 13 August 1965; Diamond to Bowden, 3 February 1966; Lee to Wilson, 3 February 1966; Lee to Bowden, 7 February 1966.

131 Cabinet Minutes Discussion of the Open University, 8 February 1966 TNA, CAB 128.41. See Des Freedman, *Television policies of the Labour Party, 1951–2001* (London: Routledge, 2003), p. 57.

132 Sir Martin Roth, Obituary of Lord Goodman, *Psychiatric Bulletin*, 20:60 (1996), 60.

133 Lord Maybray-King, *House of Lords Debate, 23 May 1974*, http://hansard. millbanksystems.com/lords/1974/may/23/the-open-university-1, accessed 1 December 2011. Both Hollis, *Jennie Lee*, and Brian Brivati, *Lord Goodman* (London: Richard Cohen Books, 1999), indicated that Goodman's role was of importance.

134 Low estimations as to costs continued. When Goodman recommended the use of the new BBC2 TV channel, which starting to broadcast in 1968, he suggested that ten hours a week would initially cost £1 million, and the running cost would be £3.5 million annually.

135 Three days later, on 14 March 1966, Malcolm Reid, who worked in the PM's office, wrote to Peter Litton, who was at the DES, to note that Benton had linked Britannica's 200th anniversary, in 1968, with the University of the Air project but that the two issues were to be treated separately. TNA, ED181/179.

136 TNA, PREM 13/3070.

137 http://thatllteachemtoo.co.uk/second-series/background/education-manifesto/index.shtml, accessed 1 December 2011.

138 MacKenzie, 'Genesis', p. 715. See also Tony Becher and Richard Lyne, 'Review', *Education + Training*, 10:12 (December 1968), 494–5.

139 Norman MacKenzie, OU Oral History Project.

140 Briggs, *Michael Young*, p. 211. The same phrase, 'whose backstairs role was as important as Wilson's', is employed in Briggs, *Special relationships*, p. 126.

141 Holloway, 'In the beginning', p. 3. See also Hollis, *Jennie Lee*, p. 306.

142 MacArthur, 'An interim history', p. 5; Hollis, *Jennie Lee*, p. 353.

143 Asa Briggs, OU Oral History Project.

144 *A university of the air*, para 3; Planning Committee Report, para 16; 'Vice Chancellor's Guide to spending units', Senate Minutes, S/22/3 April 1971. These are available through The Open University Archive, see http://library. open.ac.uk/find/specialcol. Peter Venables, *The Open University: A report*

of the Planning Committee to the Secretary of State (London: HMSO, 1969) (henceforth Planning Committee).

145 Asa Briggs, OU Oral History Project.

146 Planning Committee, Education Sub-Committee Meeting 1; Planning Committee R McLean, unnumbered notes on Minutes of Ways and Means Sub Committee Meeting 1, filed with the papers of Meeting 3.

147 Weyermeyer, 'The birth', p. 26.

148 Ian Donnachie, OU Oral History Project. In 1970, soon after completing his history doctorate (studied part-time while working), Ian Donnachie was appointed as a staff tutor based in Edinburgh. Initially much of his work involving the recruitment of tutors and finding suitable study centres but he also engaged in research on distance education in Australia and served on the OU's University Council. He has been an assessor with the QAA and the Scottish Funding Council, and a reviewer for the Arts and Humanities Research Council. After a career at the OU Ian retired as an Emeritus Professor in History.

149 John Horlock, *An open book: A memoir* (Weardale: The Memoir Club, 2006), p. 65. Sir John Horlock was the Vice-Chancellor at Salford University before he became the OU Vice-Chancellor, 1981–91. An enthusiast for science and engineering, he oversaw the introduction of a taught postgraduate programme, the opening of the Open Business School and the expansion of the OU into western Europe.

150 Letter from the DES to the OU, 12 August 1970, cited in Leslie Wagner, 'The economics of the Open University', *Higher Education*, 1:2 (May 1972), 159. On Thatcher's views see Margaret Thatcher, *The path to power* (London: HarperCollins, 1995), p. 166; Robert Stevens, *University to uni: The politics of higher education since 1944* (London: Politico's, 2004), p. 38. See also memo cited in Hollis, *Jennie Lee*, p. 328; Hugo Young, *One of us: A biography of Margaret Thatcher*, revised edn (London, Sydney and Auckland: Pan, 1991), p. 70.

151 Brian Simon, *Education and the social order: 1940–1990* (London: Lawrence and Wishart, 1991), p. 79; Education Group (CCCS), *Unpopular education: Schooling and social democracy in England since 1944* (London: Hutchinson, 1981); Beloff, *The plateglass universities*, p. 24; Ken Jones, *Education in Britain: 1944 to the present* (Cambridge: Polity Press, 2003), p. 39; Harold Silver 'Higher technological education in England: The crucial quarter century', *Journal of Vocational Education & Training*, 59:3 (2007), 308.

152 *The* [Zuckerman] *Report on scientific and engineering manpower in Great Britain*, Cmnd 902 (London: HMSO, 1959). Zuckerman was the chief scientific adviser to the Ministry of Defence 1960–66.

153 The Robbins report, *Higher education: Report of the Committee appointed by the Prime-Minister under the chairmanship of Lord Robbins*, Cmnd 2154, and five appendices (London: HMSO, November 1963).

154 Richard Layard, John King and Claus Moser, *The impact of Robbins: Penguin education special* (Harmondsworth: Penguin, 1969), p. 26.

155 Carol Dyhouse, *Going to university: Funding, costs, benefits*, www.history-andpolicy.org/papers/policy-paper-61.html#funding, accessed 1 December 2011.

156 Margaret Jones and Rodney Lowe (eds), *From Beveridge to Blair: The first fifty years of Britain's welfare state, 1948–98* (Manchester: Manchester University Press, 2002), p. 113. Briggs, *Michael Young*, p. 186; Tessa Blackstone, 'Education', in Nick Bosanquet and Peter Townsend, *Labour and equality: A Fabian study of Labour in Power, 1974–79* (London: Heinemann, 1980), p. 229.

157 Arthur Marwick, *British society since 1945*, 2nd edn (London: Penguin, 1990), p. 178.

158 James Mountford, *Keele: A historical critique* (London: Routledge and Kegan Paul, 1972). Michael Young suggested that Keele's foundation year courses be broadcast, but, despite support from the Vice-Chancellor, George Barnes (a former station Controller of both BBC Radio and BBC Television), the scheme was not implemented. Briggs, *Michael Young*, p. 202.

159 In 1963–64 Southampton created seven new chairs and made about fifty new appointments. The following year a further 135 staff joined four departments. Sally Nash and Martin Sherwood, *The University of Southampton: An illustrated history* (London: James and James, 2002), p. 68. Durham doubled its intake in 1937–51 and opened a new college in 1959. Nigel Watson, *From the ashes: The story of Grey College, Durham* (London: James and James, 2004), pp. 16, 20.

160 M. Blaug, 'An economic interpretation of the private demand for education', *Economica*, 33:130 (May 1966), 166.

161 See Beloff, *The plateglass universities*, pp. 15, 23, 44, 151, 154, and Briggs, *Michael Young*, pp. 160, 185.

162 Briggs, *Michael Young*, p. 160. Commons Debate, 19 November 1963, http://hansard.millbanksystems.com/commons/1963/nov/19/science-and-education, accessed 5 May 2010.

163 Gerry T. Fowler, 'May a thousand flowers bloom: The evolution of the higher education system and of institutions within it', *New Universities Quarterly*, 36:2 (Spring 1982), 142.

164 Commons Debate, 19 November 1963, http://hansard.millbanksystems.com/commons/1963/nov/19/science-and-education, accessed 5 May 2010.

165 By 1964 over half of local authorities had plans to open comprehensive schools, implicitly recognising the inadequacy of making decisions about children's futures at the age of 11. Jones and Lowe (eds), *From Beveridge*, pp. 113, 114.

166 Suzanne Hodgart, 'Courses at the new universities', *Where?*, 14 (Autumn 1963), 20.

167 This notion of openness echoed back to the attitude taken by the universities at Oxford and Cambridge, which would, in the nineteenth century, set aside their minimal entrance requirements in some circumstances. Robert E. Bell and Malcolm Tight, *Open universities: A British tradition?* (Buckingham and Bristol: Society for Research into Higher Education and Open University, 1993), pp. 16, 22, 26; N. A. Jepson, *The beginnings of English university adult education, policies and problems: A critical study of early Cambridge and Oxford University extension lecture movements between 1873 and 1907* (London: Michael Joseph, 1973).

168 *Higher technological education: Statement of government policy*, Cmnd 8357 (London: HMSO, 1951). See also James Jackson Walsh, 'Higher technological education in Britain: The case of the Manchester Municipal College of Technology', *Minerva*, 34:3 (1996), 241–3.

169 Tyrrell Burgess and John Pratt, *Policy and practice: The Colleges of Advanced Technology* (London: Allen Lane, Penguin, 1970). See also E. G. Edwards, 'Colleges of Advanced Technology in Britain', *Nature*, 199:4899 (1963), 1131–6.

170 *The Times* (9 September 1963).

171 Charles A. Wedemeyer and Robert E. Najem, *AIM: From concept to reality. The Articulated Instructional Media Program at Wisconsin. Notes and essays on Education for Adults, No. 61* (Syracuse, NY: Syracuse University Press, 1969). See also A. D. C. Peterson, 'A University of the Air?', *Universities Quarterly*, 18:2 (1964), 180–1.

172 G. Selman and P. Dampier, *The foundations of adult education in Canada* (Toronto, ON: Thompson Educational, 1991).

173 Börje Holmberg, *Growth and structure of distance education* (London: Croom Helm, 1986).

174 John C. Scott, 'The mission of the university: Medieval to postmodern transformations', *Journal of Higher Education*, 77:1 (January/February 2006), 10.

175 M. Boucher, *Spes in Arduis: A history of the University of South Africa* (Pretoria: University of South Africa, 1973).

176 J. L. Garcia Garrison, 'The Spanish UNED: One way to a new future', in R. Reddy Ram (ed.), *Open universities: The ivory towers thrown open* (London: Oriental University Press, 1988), p. 214.

177 Burton Paulu, 'Europe's second chance universities', *Educational Television International*, 3:4 (December 1969), 270, 266.

178 Doug Shale, 'Innovation in international higher education: The open universities', *Journal of Distance Education*, 2:1 (1987), Table 1, p. 8; Boucher, *Spes in Arduis*; Ramesh C. Sharma, 'Open learning in India: Evolution, diversification and reaching out', *Open Learning*, 20:3 (November 2005), 227–41.

179 L. S. Domonkos, 'History of higher education', *International encyclopedia of higher education*, Vol. V (San Francisco: Jossey-Bass), p. 2037.

180 Glen Creeber, '"Hideously white": British television, glocalization, and national identity', *Television & New Media*, 5 (2004), 28–9; Paddy Scannell and David Cardiff, *A social history of British broadcasting*, Vol. I: *1922–1939. Serving the nation* (London: Basil Blackwell, 1991), pp. 163, 168. The *BBC Yearbook* 1933 defined the audience as the 'national community'.

181 Marina Moiseeva, 'Distance education in Russia: Between the past and the future', *The Quarterly Review of Distance Education*, 6:3 (2005), 219.

182 M. Young, H. Perraton, J. Jenkins and T. Dodds, *Distance teaching for the Third World: The lion and the clockwork mouse* (Boston, MA: Routledge and Kegan Paul, 1988).

183 Beloff, *The plateglass universities*, p. 23.

184 MacArthur, 'An interim history', pp. 3–17.

185 Williams also wanted a new residential university near Guildford 'but built into its foundations should be the concept of using television for education by extramural courses'. He suggested: 'We should give everybody really equal opportunities for education – everybody no matter what their background and then make sure all those able and willing to take advantage of it have the opportunity of higher education.' See R. C. G. Wilson, 'A television university', *Screen Education*, 13 (March/April 1962); Robert C. G. Williams', *Electrical Journal*, 23 (February 1962), 434–6.

186 Letter 24 February 1966 from William Benton to C. A. Thompson, Acting Consul-General in the British Consulate in New York. OU archive WP1/1/1.

187 Alexander King, 'Higher education, professional manpower and the state: Reflections on education and professional employment in the USSR', *Minerva*, 1:2 (Winter 1963), 182, 185.

188 L. I. Tul'chinskii, 'Economics of higher education', *Soviet Education*, 7:1 (November 1964), 49.

189 Stuart Hood, 'Dangers of educational television', *The Times* (22 September 1967).

190 Alan Tait, 'What are open universities for?', *Open Learning*, 23:2 (2008), 89.

191 Commons Debate, 2 April 1965, www.theyworkforyou.com/debates/?id=1965-04-02a.2007.4, accessed 5 May 2010.

192 Young, 'Education for the new work', p. 9.

193 Børje Holmberg, *On the methods of teaching by correspondence* (Lunds: universitets årsskrift N. F., 1960).

194 Editorial, *The Times* (3 April 1965).

195 D. Freedman, 'Modernising the BBC: Wilson's government and television 1964–66', *Contemporary British History*, 15:1 (Spring 2001), 35–6.

196 Catlin, 'A University of the Air', pp. 358–60. Brian Jackson, *Education and the working class* (London: Routledge, 1962); Young 'Is your child?', pp. 3–5. Young popularised the term 'open university' in Michael Young, 'Towards an open university', *Where?*, 18 (Autumn 1964), 26–33.

197 Asa Briggs, OU Oral History Project.

198 Ruth Weinstock, 'Chicago TV College: Twenty years on old and still innovating', *Planning for higher education*, 4:2 (2/5 April 1975), no page numbers.

199 David F. Noble, 'Digital diploma mills: The automation of higher education', *First Monday*, 3:1 (5 January 1998).

200 *The Economist* (6 July 1946). The phrase referred to the engineering and pilot training school that Hawker Siddeley ran from 1931 until 1960. It was sometimes called Britain's Air University.

201 John Ohliger, 'The listening group', *Journal of Broadcasting & Electronic Media*, 13:2 (Spring 1969), 156.

202 Box 522, File 17, Benton Papers.

203 J. F. Kett, *The pursuit of knowledge under difficulties: From self-improvement to adult education in America, 1750–1990* (Stanford, CA: Stanford University Press, 1994), p. 186. See John Ohliger, 'Adult education television in the United States: The current scene', *Educational Television International*, 3:4 (December 1969), 262–3; William Bianchi, 'The Wisconsin School of the Air: Success story with implications', *Educational Technology & Society*, 5:1 (2002), 141–7.

204 Asa Briggs, *The BBC: The first fifty years* (Oxford: Oxford University Press, 1985), pp. 54, 116.

205 *Radio Times*, 3:38 (June 1924). For a reference to 'the wireless university' which would 'require no fixed standard of entrance [and] the students would be of all ages and conditions', see Stobart to Reith, 8 October 1926, OU archive WP1/1/1. John Stobart, of the Board of Education, was appointed Director of Education at the BBC in 1924.

206 Hooper, 'New media'.

207 Peter S. Richards, 'The establishment of evening classes in Wallasey: The work of the local technical instruction committees from 1893 to the early years of the twentieth century', *Journal of Educational Administration and History*, 19:1 (January 1987), 19–26; Stuart Marriott, 'Adult education in England: The history of an administrative contrivance', *Journal of Educational Administration and history*, 32:1 (2000), 23–37; Andrew Saint, 'Technical education and the early LCC', in Andrew Saint (ed.), *Politics and the people of London: The London County Council 1889–1965* (London and Ronceverte: Hambledon Press, 1989), pp. 71–92.

208 J. Burrows, *University adult education in London: A century of achievement* (London: University of London, 1976); Jepson, *The beginnings*.

209 Two years' study at a distance was deemed to be equivalent to one year on campus and the idea spread so that by 1905 attendance at Huddersfield Technical College could shorten a degree course at the University of Leeds to two years. Some universities developed from the teaching institutions which arose because of the extension system. Bell and Tight, *Open universities*, pp. 19–20.

210 J. H. Sadler, 'William Temple, the WEA and the Liberal tradition', *Journal of Educational Administration and History*, 18:2 (July 1986), 37; Stuart Marriott, 'From university extension to extra-mural studies: Conflict and adjustment in English adult education 1917–1939', *Journal of Educational Administration and History*, 30:1 (January 1998), 17–34.

211 Tait, 'What are open universities for?', p. 87; Negley Harte, *The University of London 1836–1986: An illustrated history* (London: Athlone, 1986), p. 25.

212 Peter Montagnon, a member of the BBC Schools Television Department who produced the first television language-speaking series, *Parliamo Italiano*, became Head of Open University Productions nine months before its first year of operation. See Hans Birkrem, Fred Rainsberry and Peter Montagnon, *The media and educational development: A seminar held in Dublin, 21–22 February 1973* (Dublin: RTE Education, 1974), p. 56; Jennie Lee, Commons Debate, 2 April, 1965, www.theyworkforyou.com/debates/?id=1965-04-02a.2007.4, accessed 19 April 2010; Principal's Report, ULC 1968–69, pp. 142–3, cited in Bell and Tight, *Open universities*, p. 97. It took The Open University a very long time to overcome the resentment which resulted from this exclusion.

213 Bell and Tight, *Open universities*, p. 50.

214 P. Northcott, 'The tyranny of distance and proximity', in K. Smith (ed.), *Diversity down under in distance education* (Toowoomba: ASPESA/ Darling Downs Institute Press, 1984), p. 42; M. White, 'Distance education in Australian higher education: A history', *Distance Education: An International Journal*, 3:2 (1982), 256; S. A. Rayner, *Correspondence education in Australia and New Zealand* (Melbourne: Melbourne University Press, 1949), p. 12; Elizabeth Stacey, 'The history of distance education in Australia', *The Quarterly Review of Distance Education*, 6:3 (2005), 253–9.

215 Twelve were commercial, with only a few hours of educational programming, eleven were operated by land-grant universities, nine were run by agricultural schools or state agricultural departments, two by church-affiliated educational groups and one by a high school. In 1938 some FM channels were reserved for educational broadcasters and in 1951 some television channels. See Christopher H. Sterling and John M. Kittross, *Stay tuned: A concise history of American broadcasting* (Belmont, CA: Wadsworth Publishing, 1978), pp. 158–60; 'Around the world', *Educational Television International*, 1:4 (December 1967), 333.

216 For further details see Sterling and Kittross, *Stay tuned*, pp. 69–70, 111–12, 267–9, 299, 301, 332, 333, 389. For an outline of the post-war use of television in US colleges see Doyle D. Smith, 'An evaluation of the effectiveness of television instruction at Midwestern University', *Journal of Educational Research*, 62:1 (September 1968), 18–24.

217 Stanley K. Derby, 'Continental classroom: An experiment in educational television', *School Science and Mathematics*, 59:8 (November 1959), 651–9.

218 Peter Laslett, 'Teaching by television', *Where?*, 15 (Winter 1963), 4–5. The Advisory Centre for Education helped finance Laslett's trip.

219 Diane Mirth, 'Corbett and radio at the University of Alberta extension', *Canadian Journal for the Study of Adult Education*, 10:1 (May 1996), 49.

220 John Nicol, Albert A. Shea, G. J. P. Simmins and R. Alex Sim, *Canada's farm radio forums* (Paris: Unesco, 1954); W. F. Coleman *et al.*, *An African experiment in radio forums for rural development* (Paris: Unesco, 1968). UNESCO projects were started in France, Japan, India, Italy, Puerto Rico, Pakistan and several countries in Africa. See 'Around the world', *Educational Television International*, 1:4 (December 1967), 333–4.

221 Henry R. Cassirer, 'Audience participation, new style', *Public Opinion Quarterly*, 23:4 (1959), 529–36.

222 Elihu Katz and Paul Felix Lazarsfeld, *Personal influence* (New York: Free Press, 1955). Katz went on to work with Eberhard George Wedell, whose work on broadcasting and education influenced the development of the OU.

223 Paulu, 'Europe's second chance', pp. 264–71; 'Around the world', *Educational Television International*, 332; Georg Rückheim, 'The radio science course "Science of education"', *Western European Education*, 2:2–3 (Summer/Fall 1970), 176–91; 'A history of distance education in Mexico', *The Quarterly Review of Distance Education*, 6:3 (2005), 227–32.

224 James Donald, *Sentimental education: Schooling, popular culture, and the regulation of liberty* (London: Verso, 1992), p. 123.

225 Jacqueline Kavanagh, 'The BBC's written archives as a source for media history', *Media History*, 5:1 (June 1999), 84.

226 Brian Groombridge, 'Broadcasting', in R. Fieldhouse and Associates, *A History of Modern British Adult Education* (Leicester: NIACE, 1996), p. 360.

227 E. C. Thomasson, 'The use of films and television in the education of mechanical engineers', *Education + Training*, 8:9 (September 1966), 406–8; R. C. G. Williams, 'Industrial and professional applications of television technique', *The proceedings of the institution of electrical engineers*, 99 Pt IIIA (Television), 20 (1952), 651–64.

228 John Cain and Brian Wright, *In a class of its own … BBC Education 1924–1994* (London: BBC, 1994), p. 34.

229 CAB/129/46, Report of the Broadcasting Committee to Cabinet, 27 June 1951, p. 41 Section 12. http://filestore.nationalarchives.gov.uk/pdfs/small/cab-129-46-cp-51-183-33.pdf, accessed 17 December 2012.

230 The Ministry of Agriculture provided agricultural advice, www.bbc.co.uk/news/entertainment+arts-10634844, accessed 5 May 2010. See also Colin Fraser and Sonia Restrepo-Estrada, *Communicating for development: Human change for survival* (London: I. B. Tauris, 1998).

231 Janet Coles and David Smith, 'The Fifty-One Society: A case study of BBC radio and the education of adults', *Studies in the Education of Adults*, 38:2 (Autumn 2006), 218, 222.

232 Briggs, *Michael Young*, p. 202.

233 Groombridge, 'Broadcasting', pp. 374–5.

234 J. Langham, *Teachers and television: The IBA Educational Fellowship Scheme* (London: John Libby, 1990), pp. 40–1.

235 Wilson to Benton, 12 November 1962, Box 374 File 2, Benton Papers.

236 Southern TV screened programmes for doctors, Westward for teachers and Border for farmers. In 1963 the first Professor of English at the University of Sussex, David Daiches, gave lectures on English literature via Southern. See William Baker and Michael Lister (eds), *David Daiches: A celebration of his life and work* (Eastbourne: Sussex Academic Press, 2007).

237 Harold Wiltshire and Fred Bayliss, *Teaching through television* (Nottingham: University of Nottingham, Department of adult education, 1965); Harold Wiltshire, *Viewing and learning* (London: WEA, 1964).

238 Universities Council for Adult Education, *Proposals for a Centre for Broadcast Adult Education*, mimeograph, 1965.

239 Laslett, 'Linking', p. 20.

240 Michael Young and Christine Farrell, 'Who uses correspondence colleges?', *Where?*, 14 (Autumn 1963), 12–14.

241 Norman MacKenzie, Richmond Postgate and John Scupham (eds), *Open learning: Systems and problems in post-secondary education* (Paris: Unesco, 1975).

242 Briggs, *The history of broadcasting in the United Kingdom*. Vol. V, p. 935.

243 MacKenzie, 'Genesis' p. 721; University of the Air, Commons Debate 2 April 1965. http://hansard.millbanksystems.com/commons/1965/apr/02/university-of-the-air, accessed 5 May 2010.

244 W. E. Syler, 'Training through television', *Adult Education*, 41:5 (January 1969), 294.

245 Sanderson, *The history of the University of East Anglia*, pp. 115–16; *Guardian* (11 June 1965); TNA University of the Air, Miss Jennie Lee's Working Party, UGC/7/8925.

246 Brian Jackson, 'Dawn University', *Where?*, 17 (Summer 1964), 19.

247 Chaired by Herbert Bowden MP, 1905–94, Lord President of the Council 1964–66, the members included Anthony Wedgwood Benn and Jennie Lee, the Chief Whip and the Home Secretary. Benn was in charge of broadcasting, telecommunications satellites and information technology. *The Times Educational Supplement* (22 January 1965), p. 186.

248 MacArthur, 'An interim history'; Young and Farrell, 'Who uses correspondence colleges?', pp. 12–14. On Young's connection of his work in Bethnal Green to The Open University see Annan, *Our age*.

249 Börje Holmberg, 'Open and distance learning in continuing education', *International Federation of Library Associations Journal*, 17:3 (1991), 274–82; Barry Willis (ed.), *Distance education: Strategies and tools* (Englewood Cliffs, NJ: Educational Technology, 1994), p. 5; C. Latchem

and L. Xinzheng, 'China's higher education examinations for self-taught learners', *Open Learning*, 14:3 (1999), 3–13. On the spectrum between face-to-face and distance forms of education see Malcolm Tight, 'London University external developments', *Open Learning*, 2:2 (1987), 49–51.

250 B. F. Skinner, 'Teaching machines', *Science*, 128 (1954), 969–77.

251 Young, 'Announcing', p. 16.

252 Universities Grant Committee, *Report of the Committee in University teaching methods, Chairman Sir Edward Hale* (London: HMSO, 1964). See also D. Rowntree, 'Two styles of communication and their implications for learning', in J. Baggaley, G. H. Jamieson and H. Marchant (eds), *Aspects of educational technology 8: Communication and learning* (London: Pitman, 1975), pp. 281–93.

253 Tony Babb, 'The West Riding Programmed Learning Project', *Technical Education* (January 1967), 24–32; Hooe Primary School Log Books, www. hooeprimary.co.uk/community_detail.asp?Section=201&Ref=130, accessed 5 October 2010.

254 Michael MacDonald-Ross, 'Programmed learning: A decade of development', *International Journal of Man-Machine Studies*, 1:1 (January 1969), 73–100.

255 www.labour-party.org.uk/manifestos/1966/1966-labour-manifesto.shtml, accessed 5 October 2010.

256 Debate in the House of Commons, 3 March 1966, http://hansard.millbank-systems.com/written_answers/1966/mar/03/teaching-machines, accessed 5 May 2010.

257 'How the universities are using programmed learning', *New University* (December 1967), 21–4.

258 *Education + Training*, 14:7 (June 1972), 216.

259 David A. Hoult, 'The Open University: Its structure and operation' (Dip. Ed. thesis, University of Hull, 1971), p. 55. See also W. Gordon Lawrence and Irene Young, *The Open University* (London: Tavistock Institute of Human Relations, 1979), p. 2; Greville Rumble, *The Open University of the United Kingdom: An evaluation of the innovative experience in the democratisation of higher education*, Distance Education Research Group, Paper No 6 IET (Milton Keynes: The Open University, 1982), p. 86; Perry, *Open University: A personal account*, p. 77. In common with the OU, the Dutch Open University, Deakin University, Australia, the Allama Iqbal OU in Pakistan, amd the distance universities in Thailand, Korea, South Africa and Taiwan all developed course teams.

260 David Hawkridge, 'Next year, Jerusalem! The rise of educational technology', *British Journal of Educational Technology*, 7:1 (January 1976), 7–30; see also David Hawkridge, 'Challenging educational technology', *Educational and Training Technology International*, 28:2 (May 1991), 96–102; M. MacDonald-Ross, 'Behavioural objectives: A critical review', *Instructional Science*, 2 (1973), 1–52.

261 Alan Woodley, OU Oral History Project. Born in 1947 Alan Woodley attended a grammar school and the University of Birmingham before he became a research assistant in the Institute of Educational Technology soon after graduation. He spent his working life at the OU engaged in research.

262 Perry, *Open University: A personal account*, p. 269.

263 P. T. Maileny and R. L. Ison, 'Appreciating systems: Critical reflections on the changing nature of systems as a discipline in a systems-learning society', *Journal of Systemic Practice and Action Research*, 13:4 (2000), 563.

264 Bob Bell, '"Education for adults" (E355): An Open University case study', *Open Learning*, 4:1 (February 1989), 39; Tony Bates, 'Transforming distance education through new technologies', in Terry Evans, Margaret Haughey and David Murphy (eds), *The international handbook of distance education* (Bingley: Emerald, 2008), p. 224.

265 Nicholas Valéry, 'Students of the air', *New Scientist*, 52:775 (23 December 1971), pp. 208–9.

266 G. O. M. Leith and C. C. Webb, 'A comparison of four methods of programmed instruction with and without teacher intervention', *Educational Review*, 21:1 (1968–69), 30. See also D. Wallis, K. D. Duncan and M. A. G. Knight, *Programmed instruction in the British armed forces* (London: HMSO, 1966).

267 Michael Young, Brian Jackson and Peter Laslett, 'On the air: The end of a phrase', *Where?*, 53 (1971), 5–7.

268 *A university of the air*, Section 8, para 7, pp. 5–6.

269 Albert Mansbridge, *University tutorial classes: A study in the development of higher education among working men and women* (London: Longmans Green, 1913), p. 37.

270 *Address by Lord Geoffrey Crowther, Foundation Chancellor. At the formal inauguration of The Open University. July 1969*, www.col.org/SiteCollectionDocuments/Daniel_CROWTHER_Speech_1969.pdf, accessed 20 April 2014.

271 In 1985 Dr Ian Donnachie reviewed off-campus and distance teaching in Australia for the OU and compiled a report. Copy in the OU Archives.

272 J. S. Coleman, E. Campbell, C. Hobson, J. McPartland, A. Mood and F. Weinfeld, *Equality of educational opportunity* (Washington, DC: US Government Printing Office, 1966).

273 Quoted in Hollis, *Jennie Lee*, p. 321.

Chapter 3

1 Hollister and Pentz, 'Science and technology', 98.

2 Samuel Brittan, *The treasury under the Tories 1951–1964* (Harmondsworth: Penguin, 1964), pp. 204–45.

3 John Campbell, *Edward Heath: A biography* (London: Jonathan Cape, 1993), p. 163. On the wider notion of the decline see Jim Tomlinson, 'Inventing "decline": The falling behind of the British economy in the post-war years', *Economic History Review*, 49:4 (November 1996), 731–57.

4 Brian Abel-Smith and Peter Townsend, *The poor and the poorest: A new analysis of the Ministry of Labour's family expenditure surveys of 1953–54 and 1960* (London: Bell, 1965).

5 Robert Anderson, 'The "idea of a university" today', www-histpol.hist. cam.ac.uk/papers/policy-paper-98.html, accessed 24 October 2011. For the view that this 'research/teaching schism' has roots in the 1960s see Malcolm Tight, 'The golden age of academe: Myth or memory', *British Journal of Educational Studies*, 58:1 (2010), 109.

6 A. J. Kim, *Community building on the web* (Berkeley, CA: Peachpit Press, 2000); Diana Laurillard, *Rethinking university teaching: A framework for the effective use of learning technologies*, 2nd edn (London: Routledge Falmer, 2002); G. Pask, *Conversation theory: Applications in education and epistemology* (Amsterdam and New York: Elsevier, 1976).

7 Douglas Jay, *The socialist case* (London: Faber and Faber, 1937). Jay was a Labour MP 1946–83 and a minister.

8 www.lancs.ac.uk/users/gap/GAP2007/Charter-Statutes-Ordinances.pdf; www.york.ac.uk/media/abouttheuniversity/governanceandmanagement/ documents/charter_statutes_apr11.pdf; www2.warwick.ac.uk/services/gov/ calendar/section2/charterstatutes; www7.open.ac.uk/gsh/Charter/Charter. pdf; all accessed 1 March 2013.

9 Cited in Ernest Stabler, *Founders: Innovators in education, 1830–1980* (Edmonton: University of Alberta Press, 1987), p. 249.

10 The first Chair of Milton Keynes Development Corporation, Lord Campbell of Eskan, sought to attract the OU to Milton Keynes. His role was acknowledged at the first OU graduation ceremony, when he became an honorary graduate.

11 Harold Wiltshire, cited in Planning Committee, MC 5/1. OU Archives.

12 Mark Clapson, *A social history of Milton Keynes: Middle England/edge city* (London and Portland: Frank Cass, 2004), pp. 154–5.

13 *Open House*, 63 (14 June 1972); George Low, OU Oral History Project. Milton Keynes Corporation offered council housing to new staff recruits.

14 *Report of the Vice-Chancellor to the Council 1972* (Milton Keynes: The Open University, 1973), p. 30; Peter Waterman, OU Oral History Project. Peter Waterman was the Social Development Manager for the Milton Keynes Development Corporation, 1972–88.

15 *Report of the Vice-Chancellor, January 1969–December 1970* (Milton Keynes: The Open University, 1971); *The early development of the Open University* (Buckingham: The Open University Press, 1972), p. 20.

16 The story of the slippers was one of the most frequently told tales. See Young, 'Whose story counts?', p. 102.

17 Joan Christodoulou, OU Oral History Project. Joan Christodoulou was born in India, educated in England, studied at Oxford and taught in schools. She married the Secretary of the OU, became a tutor, assistant staff tutor and assistant senior counsellor, and did a lot of assessment.

18 Harold Lowndes, OU Oral History Project. Harold Lowndes started work at the OU as a Physics Technician in 1969 and retired in 1996.

19 Christopher Harvie MSP, Scottish Parliament debate on motion S3M-532816 December 2009 www.theyworkforyou.com/sp/?id=2009-12-16.22243.0, accessed 17 August 2012.

20 *The Times* (3 August 1970).

21 Stephen Potter, OU Oral History Project; Roger Moore, OU Oral History Project. Stephen Potter joined The Open University as a PhD student in 1974 and rose to become Professor of Transport Strategy in the Department of Mathematics, Computing and Technology; Dr Roger Moore joined OU in 1981 as an analyst programmer in Academic Computer Servicies. He became the Quality Assurance Manager and subsequently a Service Team Manager based in Learning and Teaching Solutions.

22 Tony Tompkins, OU Oral History Project. Tony Tompkins worked in the computing department at Southampton University and when his boss, Bruce McDowell, became the first OU data processing manager Tony Tompkins followed him. He joined the OU on 1 December 1969 and helped to create a vast application system. When Bruce MacDowell left, in 1979, Tony Tompkins moved to operations as Computer Centre Manager. He remained at the OU for 40 years and both his wife and daughter worked there.

23 Norman Woods, OU Oral History Project. Norman Woods left school in 1945 aged 14 but later studied for an London external degree and became a senior lecturer in law. One of 11 people appointed as the first OU Regional Directors (Northern Ireland and South East of England were added later) he recalled that an allocations solution created in his region became the model for the UK after an administrative assistant was seconded to Walton Hall to help devise a nationwide computerised system.

24 Planning Committee Report, para 71. The Planning Committee was dissolved in 1969 when responsibility for the government of the OU fell to the newly created Council and Senate.

25 Hoult, 'The Open University', p. 55.

26 Robert Rowland, 'Some thoughts on the use of broadcasting in the Open University', *Teaching at a Distance*, 2 (February 1975), 64.

27 *Report of the Vice-Chancellor*, 1971, p. 13. The term 'course', as employed at the OU, is synonymous with the term 'module' as used at many other universities. As to employ the term module anachronistically might confuse, the terms are here used interchangeably.

28 Thatcher, *The path to power*, p. 166; Stevens, *University to uni*, p. 38; Pimlott, *Harold Wilson*, p. 515.

29 House of Commons debate, 13 November 1973. http://hansard.millbank systems.com/search/comparatively%20generous%20support?speaker=mrs-margaret-thatcher&type=Commons&year=1973, accessed 5 May 2010.

30 *Guardian* (12 November 1970); *The Times* (12 November 1970).

31 John Pemberton and Joyce Pemberton, *The university college at Buckingham: A first account of its conception, foundation and early years* (Buckingham: Buckingham University Press, 1979), pp. 170, 84, 167, 183.

32 G. K. Shaw and M. Blaug, 'The University of Buckingham after ten years: A tentative evaluation', *Higher Education Quarterly*, 42:1 (Winter 1988), 76.

33 Charter article 15 (1) and Planning Committee Main Committee 3/1. An Academic Advisory Committee was created by the Privy Council in October 1969 to review the standards of the education provided and the degrees awarded. An interim committee was formed and then the substantive one met in 1970.

34 M. R. Gavin, *Report of the Group to the Department of Education and Science and to the Council of the Open University*, June 1975. Gavin helped to establish Britain's first chair in Science Education at Chelsea College.

35 Charter article 13; Planning Committee, Main Committee, 4. OU Archive.

36 Senate Minute 2.1; Senate Minute 36.1. OU Archive.

37 Colin Robinson, OU Oral History Project. Colin Robinson was a trainee film editor with the BBC in 1969 when he started to work with the OU at Alexandra Palace. He was involved in the production of a variety of technology and mathematics programmes. He went on to be the Head of The Open University Production Centre at Milton Keynes. He retired in 1996.

38 *Report of the Vice-Chancellor*, 1971, p. 92. Hoult, 'The Open University', p. 38.

39 John Horlock, OU Oral History Project. The size of Senate was one reason Horlock gave for forming a General Purposes Committee.

40 Hoult, 'The Open University', p. 37.

41 David Murray, OU Oral History Project. Professor David Murray joined the OU in September 1969 as Professor of Government. He chaired and was a member of several main OU committees before being seconded to the University of the South Pacific between 1975 and 1978. In 1980 he was made Chair of the Examinations and Assessment Committee. Between 1983 and 1988 he was a Pro-Vice-Chancellor. He then helped to set up The Open University of Hong Kong before becoming a Pro-Vice-Chancellor again in 1990–91. He subsequently worked with the Higher Education Quality Council (which became the Quality Assurance Agency for Higher Education) and retired in 1999.

42 The Planning Committee had used the term 'faculty' but also 'line', and Senate decided both terms were acceptable. Senate Minute 30.18 (3rd meeting). OU Archive.

43 Senate Minute 67.2 (6th meeting). OU Archive.

44 Senate Minute 38.1 (4th meeting). OU Archive.

45 *Report of the Vice-Chancellor, 1984* (Milton Keynes: The Open University, 1985), p. 5; *Report of the Vice-Chancellor, 1985* (Milton Keynes: The Open University, 1986), pp. 9–11.

46 Christopher Harvie MSP, Scottish Parliament debate on motion S3M- 532816.

47 David Murray, OU Oral History Project.

48 Horlock, *An open book*, p. 57. In 1980, shortly before Horlock took up his post, the University Secretary Anastasios Christodoulou left to become Secretary of the Commonwealth Universities.

49 8 July 1982 S/71/M Appendix II; Horlock noted in S/70/3, 'Organisational issues: A progress report from the Vice-Chancellor'. OU Archive.

50 Charles Cleverdon, OU Oral History Project. Born in 1953 Charles Cleverdon joined the OU on 3 September 1971 as establishments clerk. After six months in finance he moved into distribution as a junior technician, spent four years in print and then returned to distribution. He rose to become manager of the distribution site in Wellingborough.

51 The block grant was £45.1 million in 1980 and £70.3 million in 1989, a decrease of 8 per cent in real terms while the full course equivalent student numbers rose by 12,000. The grant covered about 78 per cent of the costs of the undergraduate programme. *Review of the Open University, conducted by the Department of Education and Science and the Open University* (Milton Keynes: The Open University, 1991), p. 57.

52 *Report of the Vice-Chancellor to the Council 1972*, p. 73. The Universities Grant Committee funded on a five-yearly basis.

53 Asa Briggs, OU Oral History Project.

54 Horlock, *An open book*, pp. 68–70.

55 Horlock, *An open book*, p. 65.

56 Horlock, *An open book*, pp. 59–60.

57 Sir John Daniel speech at the retirement party of Joe Clinch, 15 December 2012, www.open.ac.uk/johndanielspeeches/JoeClinch.html, accessed 17 October 2012.

58 Martin Watkinson, 'Funding and strategy'. Paper for the History of The Open University Project, October 2011.

59 Michael Sanderson, *The universities and British industry, 1850–1970* (London: Routledge and Kegan Paul, 1972); Sheldon Rothblatt, *The revolution of the dons: Cambridge and society in Victorian England* (London: Faber and Faber, 1968); Martin Weiner, *English culture and the decline of the industrial spirit* (Harmondsworth: Penguin, 1981).

60 Sir Alexander Jarratt CB served during the war, was a civil servant 1949–70 and was then a successful businessman. He was Chancellor of the University of Birmingham, 1983–2002.

61 Alexander Jarratt, *Report and national data study*, Steering Committee for Efficiency Studies in Universities (London: Committee of Vice-Chancellors and Principals, 1985).

62 *Into the 1990s: The role of the Open University in the national provision of part-time higher education* (Milton Keynes: The Open University, 1986), pp. 9, 41.

63 Austin Bide was a member of the University Grants Committee 1985–87 and a former part-time student at Birkbeck. He also chaired Glaxo Holdings and was a member of the British Leyland board from 1977 and then its chair. In 1990 Bide was replaced on the Visiting Committee by Sir Kenneth Dixon, who had joined Rowntree in 1956 and chaired it 1981–89. In 1993 new funding councils were established for all UK universities, including the OU, and the Visiting Committee was abolished.

64 *Report of the Vice-Chancellor, 1989* (Milton Keynes: The Open University, 1990), p.1.

65 Horlock, *An open book*, pp. 68–70. See also *Report of the Vice-Chancellor, 1980*. Nevertheless, it took 113 applications to external funders to produce 65 successful outcomes in 1983 and 206 to produce 79 in 1984. Moreover, there were costs to these grants. £1.5m implied £600K in overheads. Only 1.6 per cent of the total income of the OU was derived from research grants compared to an average of 4 per cent for universities funded by the University Grants Committee.

66 There was subsequently an extension of baseline funding. See OU Visiting Committee, *Report to the Secretary of State on the Open University's Plans for 1993 and on its entry into the new funding system for HE*, Department for Education, August 1992, p. 20; *Report of the Vice-Chancellor, 1992* (Milton Keynes: The Open University, 1993), p. 4; and *Report of the Vice-Chancellor, 1993* (Milton Keynes: The Open University, 1994), p. 3.

67 *Review of the University Grants Committee: Report of a committee under the chairmanship of Lord Croham, GCB*, Cmnd 81 (London: HMSO, 1987).

68 Stuart Maclure, 'England's Open University: Revolution at Milton Keynes', *Change*, 3:2 (March–April 1971), 62–8.

69 'The open university', *Convergence: An International Journal of Adult Education*, 2:3 (1969), 22. This was abstracted from Planning Committee. Zvi Friedman, a systems analyst in Walton Hall, argued that the hierarchy should be reasserted, while Walter Perry was accused of referring to the regions as 'glorified post boxes'. See the staff newspaper, *Open House*, 110

(29 August 1974). The account of Perry's view is from Christopher Harvie MSP, Scottish Parliament debate on motion S3M-532816.

70 Eric Newman, OU Oral History Project. Eric Newman was a mature student and teacher before he became a regional secretary of the OU in the north-west, in 1970. He was active in the Association of University Teachers and retired in 1984.

71 Cited in *Report of the Vice-Chancellor, 1970*, p. 15. Two further regions, Northern Ireland and the South East, were later created. Scotland and Wales were later designated as nations.

72 David Murray, OU Oral History Project.

73 Robert Beevers, 'Revised Student Support System for 1976', *Teaching at a Distance*, 1:1 (1974), 72.

74 *Report of the Vice-Chancellor, 1970*, p. 18.

75 *Scottish Educational Journal*, 25 June 1971, p. 525. Transferability was not assumed. It was only in 1983 that Senate approved that OU students could spend a year at Warwick studying courses full-time. These would count towards their BA (Open). See S/76/2 Appendix 10.

76 The Campaign for Social Justice in Northern Ireland was inaugurated in 1964; Plaid Cymru won a seat in Westminster in 1966 and the Scottish National Party in 1967.

77 Perry, *Open University: A personal account*, p. 63.

78 Winnie Ewing, *Stop the world: The autobiography of Winnie Ewing*, ed. Michael Russell (Edinburgh: Birlinn, 2004), p. 269.

79 J. G. S. Shearer, 'The universities and adult education in Scotland', *Studies in Adult Education*, 1:2 (October 1969), 140–56 (p. 142).

80 David Alexander, 'The education of adults in Scotland: Democracy and curriculum', *Studies in the Education of Adults*, 26:1 (April 1994), 31–49 (p. 34).

81 John Nisbet, 'A forlorn aspiration? The story of SUCSE', *Scottish Educational Review*, 35 (2003), 60–4.

82 Allan Macartney, 'Angus Calder, Obituary', *Independent* (27 August 1998), www.independent.co.uk/arts-entertainment/obituary-allan-macartney-1174297.html, accessed 15 October 2012.

83 Bob Glaister and Ronnie Carr, 'The Open University in Scotland', in T. G. K. Bruce and W. M. Humes (eds), *Scottish education* (Edinburgh: Edinburgh University Press, 1999), 650–4 (pp. 651–2).

84 Macartney, *Independent*.

85 Phillip Whitehead, 'Crisis at the Open University?' *The Listener* (10 May 1984), 7–9 (p. 8).

86 Obituary of Roger Carus, *Scotsman* (7 October 2009), www.scotsman.com/news/obituaries/roger-carus-1-777460, accessed 22 June 2013.

87 For example there was *Handbook on the use of telephones* (1976), *Tutoring by telephone: A handbook* (1982) and *Supporting students by telephone* (2003). Handouts and a CD of conversations were also created.

88 There were others working on the use of the telephone to support adult learners. The OU organised a conference on this subject in July 1975. See for example the work of a senior counsellor in London, Ben Turok, 'Telephone conferencing for teaching and administration in the Open University', *British Journal of Educational Technology*, 6:3 (October 1975), 63–70, and Ben Turok and Teresa Daniuk, *Teleconferencing: A bibliography* (Milton Keynes: The Open University, 1977).

89 Judith George, *On the line: Counselling and teaching by telephone* (Milton Keynes: The Open University, 1983). In 1997, with John Cowan, she wrote *Tutoring by phone: A staff guide* (Milton Keynes: The Open University, 1997).

90 Mandy Ashworth, *The Open University in Wales: A Charter celebration* (Milton Keynes: The Open University, 1994), p. 14. See also *Scotsman* (9 October 2009), www.scotsman.com/news/education/ordinary-guy-who-dedicated-life-to-education-1-1220691, accessed 22 June 2013.

91 Gordon Macintyre, *Directing a trouble region*, Edinburgh, July 2011, notes written at the request of Peter Syme; obituary of Roger Carus.

92 Norman Woods, OU Oral History Project.

93 Head of OU Productions Peter Montagnon. Memo to Don Gratton 25 October 1972, B194-4, R03/218 Open University General, BBC Archives.

94 Perry, *Open University: A personal account*, p. 109.

95 These included Gordon Macintyre, Rosemary Hamilton, Judith George, Peter Syme and John Cowan.

96 Graham Hill and Robin Lingard, *UHI: The making of a university* (Edinburgh: Dunedin Academic Press, 2004), p. 171.

97 David I. Gibson, 'Profile: H. Harford Williams', *Systematic parasitology*, 29:3 (November 1994), 237–88.

98 Ashworth, *The Open University in Wales*, p. 6.

99 Ashworth, *The Open University in Wales*, p. 16.

100 D. T. Thomas and Paul A. S. Ghuman, *A survey of social and religious attitudes among Sikhs in Cardiff*, mimeograph (Cardiff: The Open University in Wales, 1976). Thomas contributed written and broadcast teaching materials on this subject to *Man's religious quest*, AD208 (1978–85) and other modules.

101 Gordon Lammie, OU Oral History Project. Gordon Lammie joined the OU in 1970 as the Assistant Regional Director in the East Midlands. He became the Director of The Open University in North America, worked as Deputy Director of Regional Academic Services 1983–86 at Walton Hall and was a Regional Director in both the North West and the East Midlands.

102 David Grugeon, OU Oral History Project. Harford Williams was appointed as the Director in Wales in October 1969, but as he had no physical OU office until April 1970 when the OU's office was opened, he spent much of his time Aberdeen and made use of an office provided by the University of Wales.

103 Ken Boyd, OU Oral History Project.

104 Sue Cole and Maggie Coats, 'The role of the regions in the OU', *Open Learning*, 4:1 (February 1989), 27–32 (p. 30).

105 Joan Christodoulou, OU Oral History Project.

106 Naomi Stinson, OU Oral History Project. Naomi Stinson (née Irwin) started doing secretarial and clerical with the OU in Belfast in February 1971. Apart from a two-year gap she remained there until her retirement, taking on many tasks: 'we literally had to do everything – typing, clerical work, and you did all things across the board. There was no such thing as Student Services and exams and tutors, it was just you did everything ... I used to go to students' homes to do invigilation.' Through part-time study she became a member of the Institute of Administrative Management, which helped her to 'appreciate where students are coming from ... I have some understanding what it's like to get all this stuff through the post coming at you and getting your TMA done'.

107 There are recollections of this strike in the testimony of Ken Boyd, Rosemary Hamilton, Naomi Stinson and Norman Woods. OU Oral History Project. Rosemary Hamilton became an OU tutor in 1970, then a staff tutor, and from 1992 was the Regional Director of The Open University, Ireland. See also www.independent.co.uk/student/news/the-televised-revolution-1679156. html, accessed 20 May 2011.

108 Email to author, 10 August 2011. David Sewart was Director of Student Services at the OU and later President of the International Council for Distance Education.

109 C. Brook, 'Something strange in our regions', *Teaching at a Distance*, 25 (1984), 77–83.

110 David Sewart, 'Distance teaching: A contradiction in terms?', *Teaching at a Distance*, 19 (1981), 8–18.

111 *A university of the air*, para 8 (12) d. OU Archive.

112 Perry, *Open University: A personal account*, p. 109.

113 Planning Committee, Ways and Means Sub-Committee, 10; 'The Open University', *Report of the Vice-Chancellor, 1971*, p. 7.

114 Ken Boyd, OU Oral History Project.

115 Aldwyn Cooper, 'Computer-based learning at the Open University and the CICERO system', in R. Lewis and E. Tagg (eds), *Computer assisted learning: Scope, progress and the limits* (Amsterdam: North-Holland Publishing, 1980).

116 Stephanie Clennell, *Teaching for the Open University* (Milton Keynes: The Open University, 1982), p. 58.

117 The project was directed by Tony Bates. Mike Sharples and David McConnell worked on it as research fellows.

118 Norman Woods, OU Oral History Project. In 1990 the timing of OU programmes moved from evening and weekend slots to the BBC's overnight Learning Zone. Students were expected to record material.

119 John S. Daniel, 'Independence and interaction in distance education: New technologies for home study', *Programmed learning and educational technology*, 29:3 (August 1983), 156.

120 A credit course structure was developed to enable students to leave time between courses. See W. James, 'Not a solution but a start', *New Academic*, 2:13 (May 1971), 1.

121 As reported in *Times Higher Education* (23 April 2009), www.timeshighereducation.co.uk/story.asp?storyCode=406249&sectioncode=26, accessed 24 July 2011.

122 Maureen Barrett, 'The attitude of industry to the Open University', *Teaching at a Distance*, 18 (Winter 1980), 66.

123 Naomi E. McIntosh, 'The response to the Open University: Continuity and discontinuity', *Higher Education*, 2:2 (May 1973), 187–8.

124 On the use of OU teaching materials in other institutions see C. D. Moss, 'The influence of Open University distance teaching in Higher Education', *Teaching at a Distance*, 14 (1979), 14–18. See also B. Glaister and R. Carr, 'Education open to all', *Open Learning*, 1:3 (1986), 50–2.

125 www8.open.ac.uk/researchprojects/historyofou/memories/tutoring-mathematics-some-reflections, accessed 11 January 2012.

126 Michael St J. Raggett and Malcolm Clarkson, 'A proposal for an extended role for the Open University', *Teaching at a Distance*, 5 (March 1976), 59.

127 *Review of the Open University*, p. 52.

128 John Cowan, OU Oral History Project. John Cowan attended High School in Glasgow and after he studied at the University of Edinburgh he became an engineering apprentice. He taught at Heriot-Watt College and became the first Professor of Engineering Education in the UK. He worked with the British Council, became specialist adviser for the CNAA on teaching, learning and assessment and was Director of the OU in Scotland 1987–97.

129 www8.open.ac.uk/researchprojects/historyofou/story/students, accessed 23 April 2012.

130 Terry D. Evans, 'Review', *Distance Education*, 30:3 (2009), 447.

131 Charles P. Snow, *Science and government* (Cambridge, MA: Harvard University Press, 1961).

132 Dame Jocelyn Bell Burnell, OU Oral History Project. Professor Jocelyn Bell Burnell became a tutor for OU in 1973 and in 1991 she was appointed Head of the Department of Physics at the OU until she left in 2001. Her appointment as a professor at the OU doubled the number of female professors of physics in the UK. She was the first female president of the Institute of Physics.

133 See 'Editorial', *History Workshop Journal*, 4 (Autumn 1977), 2.

134 *Sesame* (July/August 1984) and *Sesame* (January/February 1985). In order to aid internal communication major decisions were recorded in *The Gazette* and, from 1970, 'a weekly journal of news, views and information for and

by the staff of the Open University', *Open House*, was produced. *Open Forum*, intended to connect staff and students, was produced for television. *Sesame* was launched in 1972 and sent to all students (about 35,000 of them) and staff (about 5,000 people). Michael Drake, who chaired the interim editorial advisory group, announced in the first issue that *Sesame* (8 May 1972) had to be 'more than a vehicle for student outrage or Walton Hall pap. It has got to be seen to be independent.' In 1998 *Open Eye*, which called itself 'the monthly bulletin of The Open University community', was launched in conjunction with the *Independent* (Plate 7).

135 Students at the polytechnic passed a vote of no confidence in Cox, who co-authored an account of Marxist bias within her own workplace. See Keith Jacka, Caroline Cox and John Marks, *Rape of reason: The corruption of the Polytechnic of North London* (London: Churchill, 1975). *The Times* columnist Bernard Levin wrote in praise of the book several times.

136 *Sesame* (May 1976); *Sesame* (June/July 1976).

137 *The Times* (10 December 1976). There was a letter by way of response from the Deputy Chair of Senate in *The Times* (16 December 1976).

138 In 1977 the Institute for the Study of Conflict argued that the OU's *Schooling and society*, E202, and particularly one book – Roger Dale, Geoff Esland and Madeleine MacDonald (eds), *Schooling and capitalism: A sociological reader* (London: Taylor and Francis, 1976) – favoured Marxism. In *Sesame* (August 1977) Julius Gould and Geoff Esland presented their views about E202, and Robert Nicodemus collated student views for the following issue. There were a number of accounts in the *Guardian*, *Observer* and *The Times*. See also *Sesame* (August 1977), *Sesame* (September/October 1977) and *Sesame* (November 1977); *Open House*, 147 (22 February 1977); *Open House*, 153 (5 July 1977).

139 *Observer* (25 September 1977). There was also criticism of *Modern art and modernism: Manet to Pollock*, A315 (1983–92), and of its external assessor, T. J. Clark, in *The New Criterion* in 1982 and 1985. For an account by the Chair of A315 see Francis Frascina, *Pollock and after: The critical debate*, 2nd edn (London and New York: Routledge, 2000) pp. 15–16, n2.

140 David Harris, 'On Marxist bias', *Journal of Further and Higher Education*, 2:2 (1978), 68–71; Julius Gould, *The attack on higher education: Marxist and radical penetration. Report of a study group of the Institute for the Study of Conflict* (London: Institute for the Study of Conflict, 1977).

141 *Sesame* (September 1981); *Sesame* (October/November 1981). The focus was on P. Lee (ed.), *Racism in the workplace and community: Introduction and guide* (Milton Keynes: The Open University, 1983). For the internal inquiry see S/74/7 (September 1982) and S/73/9 (November 1982). OU Archive.

142 *The Times* (6 August 1984).

143 George Walden, 'Painting and politics', *The Spectator* (13 July 1985), 28–9. For Walden's remarks in the Commons, 26 October 1984, see http://

hansard.millbanksystems.com/commons/1984/oct/26/higher-education #S6CV0065P0_19841026_HOC_95, accessed 20 May 2011.

144 Andrew Denham and Mark Garnett, *Keith Joseph: A life* (Chesham: Acumen Press, 2001), p. 387; memo of 10 June 1985 (visits to the University of Sir Keith Joseph 17 and 20 July 1985) IM papers Box 3. OU Archive.

145 Elaine Storkey, 'Laissez-faire government and the Open University', *Third Way* 7:8 (September 1984), 8-9.

146 *The Times* (2 July 1984).

147 Academic Board Meeting 16. OU Archive.

148 *Sesame* (January/February 1983) and *Sesame* (July/August 1984). See S/79/M (September 1985) Appendix 1. OU Archive.

149 Quoted in Tim Dalgleish (ed.), *Lifting it off the page: An oral portrait of OU people* (Milton Keynes: The Open University, 1995), pp. 43–4; Horlock, *An open book*, p. 64.

150 Asa Briggs, OU Oral History Project.

151 *Report of the Vice-Chancellor, 1972*, p. 98. Norman Woods, OU Oral History Project, recalled that 'before I left I had a visitors' book with over 500 signatures in it of people or groups of people who'd come from overseas'.

152 Neil McLean, *A study of the utilization of electronic technology in post-secondary education in Britain and West Germany: Prepared for the Commission on Post-Secondary Education in Ontario* (Toronto: W. Kinmond, Queen's Printer, 1972); Bernard Trotter, *Television and technology in university teaching: A report to the Committee on University Affairs, and the Committee of Presidents of Universities of Ontario* (Toronto: Information Branch of the Department of University Affairs, 1970).

153 Cited in J. Dodd and G. Rumble, 'Planning new distance teaching universities', *Higher Education*, 13 (1984), 249.

154 Personal correspondence with the author.

155 Gordon Lammie, OU Oral History Project.

156 *The Times* (6 March 1975). *The Times*, 25 August 1976, reported that some staff objected to this consultancy agreement.

157 The university admitted its first students, 2,267 of them, in 1976. It expanded to enrol 8,525 in 1981 and 23,791 in 1995. See Sarah Guri-Rosenblit, 'Trends in access to Israeli Higher Education 1981–1996: From a privilege to a right', *European Journal of Education*, 31:3 (1996), 331–2.

158 www8.open.ac.uk/researchprojects/historyofou/story/first-forays-overseas, accessed 23 May 2012.

159 AcB/8/M Appendix 3. OU Archive.

160 Briggs, *Michael Young*, p. 160.

161 Silver, 'Higher technological education', p. 308.

162 Jones, *Education in Britain*, p. 39; Marwick, *British society*, p. 178.

163 Isaac Krannick (ed.), *Is Britain dying?: Perspectives on the current crisis* (Ithaca, NY, and London: Cornell University Press, 1979); Samuel H. Beer,

Britain against itself: The political contradictions of collectivism (New York and London: W. W. Norton, 1982); Robert Bacon and Walter Eltis, *Britain's economic problem: Too few producers* (London: Macmillan, 1976); Tom Nairn, *The break-up of Britain: Crisis and neonationalism* (London: New Left Books, 1977); Stuart Hall, Chas Critcher, Tony Jefferson, John N. Clarke and Brian Roberts, *Policing the crisis: Mugging, the state and law and order* (London: Palgrave Macmillan, 1978).

164 Wagner, 'The economics of the Open University', p. 183. See also Leslie Wagner, 'The economics of the Open University revisited', *Higher Education*, 6 (1977), 359–81.

165 Charles F. Carter, 'The economics of the Open University: A comment', *Higher Education*, 2:1 (February 1973), 69–70. A decade earlier he had noted the possible costs to be placed on public libraries by the opening of the OU. See C. F. Carter, 'The economics of higher education', *Manchester School of Economic and Social Studies*, 33:1 (January 1965).

166 Perry, *Open University: A personal account*, pp. 228–9, 233, 238.

167 Leslie Wagner, 'The Open University and the costs of expanding higher education', *Universities Quarterly*, 27:4 (Summer 1973), 394–406; Richard Layard and Gareth Williams, 'Meeting the cost restraint', in George Brosan, Charles Carter, Richard Layard, Peter Venables and Gareth Williams (eds), *Patterns and policies in higher education* (Harmondsworth: Penguin, 1971), pp. 19–44; Robert S. Love, 'The economic effects of the Open University', *Universities Quarterly*, 25:4 (Autumn 1971), 435–45; Wagner, 'The economics of the Open University'.

168 Margaret Cole, letter in *The Times*, 6 September 1974.

169 Bruce Laidlaw and Richard Layard, 'Traditional versus Open University teaching methods: A cost comparison', *Higher Education*, 3:4 (1974), 455; K. G. Lumsden and C. Ritchie, 'The Open University: A survey and economic analysis', *Instructional Science*, 4 (1975), 237–91; Greville Rumble, 'The economics of the Open University of the United Kingdom', Open University mimeo, 1976. OU Archive.

170 John Mace, 'Mythology in the making: Is the Open University really cost effective?', *Higher Education*, 7:3 (August 1978), 307.

171 Thomas Hülsmann, *The costs of open learning: A handbook* (Oldenburg: Bibliotheks- und Informationssystem der Universität Oldenburg, 2000).

172 Greville Rumble (ed.), *Papers and debates on the economics and costs of distance and online learning* (Oldenburg: Bibliotheks-und Informationssystem der Carl von Ossietzky Universität, 2004).

173 Department of Education and Science, *Open University Review Study of the costs of part-time higher education provision in three comparator institutions* (London: HMSO, 1991), p. 67.

174 Hilary Perraton, *Open and distance learning in the developing world* (London: Routledge, 2000).

175 Much of the research for this box was done by Rachel Gibbons.

176 Committee on Higher Education, *Higher education: Report of the Committee appointed by the Prime Minister under the chairmanship of Lord Robbins 1961–63*, Cmnd 2154 (London: HMSO, 1963), p. 705.

177 Royal Charter (RC 000391) establishing the Open University, 30 May 1969, pp. iv, v. Online at www.open.ac.uk/about/documents/about-univer sity-charter.pdf, accessed 23 May 2013.

178 All three are quoted in Malcolm Cross and R. G. Jobling, 'The English new universities: A preliminary enquiry', *University Quarterly*, 23:2 (Spring 1969), 175.

179 *The Spectator*, 11 September 1970.

180 Steven Rose, OU Oral History Project. Appointed in 1969, Steven Rose was the first Professor of Biology at the OU. He was Head of the Department of Life Sciences until 1999.

181 *Report of the Vice-Chancellor to the Council, 1972*, p. 98.

182 *Report of the Vice-Chancellor, 1990* (Milton Keynes: The Open University, 1989), p. 12.

183 *The Times* (9 July 1984).

184 Horlock, *An open book*, pp. 65, 66.

185 Horlock, *An open book*, p. 66.

186 John Horlock, OU Oral History Project.

187 DES, 'The Open University: Commentary on the campaign about govern-ment funding', Aug 1984 IM papers, Box 3. OU Archives.

188 S/74/7 (September 1982) *Sesame* (September/October 1982); Senate Minutes, S/86/6 Appendix 1. OU Archives.

189 Letter 18 January 1984 filed in S/77/8 (February 1984) Appendix 1 Annex 2(ii).

190 Senate S/82/M (November 1985). OU Archives; Horlock, *An open book*, p. 62.

191 *Report of the Vice-Chancellor, 1990* (Milton Keynes: The Open University, 1989), p. 3.

192 The OU also received sums for the continuing education programme and in 1990, for example, an income of about £1 million per annum from the marketing of course materials and recording rights, the sale of computer time, consultancies and contract research and training.

193 From 1990 the undergraduate and associate programme fees were permitted to vary and a variety of fees were charged.

194 Students also paid additional sums for equipment, notably computers and books, for residential schools and for travel to tutorials. By 1989 summer school income, which stood at £4.6 million, amounted to 5 per cent of the cost of the undergraduate programme. The income from summer schools rose by 62 per cent during the 1980s. *Review of the Open University*, p. 70.

195 *Committee on Continuing Education, Report* (Milton Keynes: The Open University, 1977).

196 Some of the funding came from the Science and Engineering Research Council, some through the Professional, Industrial and Commercial Updating Programme.

197 *Into the 1990s*, p. 45.

198 Birgitta Willén, 'What happened to the Open University: Briefly', *Distance Education*, 9:1 (1988), 78–9.

199 Robin Wilson, OU Oral History Project.

200 R. Edwards, *Changing places: Flexibility, lifelong learning and a learning society* (London: Routledge, 1997).

201 J. Pratt, 'Unification of higher education in the United Kingdom', *European Journal of Education*, 27:1/2 (1992), 38.

202 *Report of the Vice-Chancellor, 1984*, p. 2; *Report of the Vice-Chancellor, 1985*, p. 5.

203 DES, *The development of higher education into the 1990s*, Cmnd 9524 (London: HMSO, 1985), p. 6.

204 Confederation of British Industry, *The skills revolution* (London: CBI, 1991).

205 DES, *Higher education: Meeting the challenge*, Cmnd 114 (London: HMSO, 1987). On the developments of this period see C. Ball, *Learning pays: The role of post compulsory education and training* (London: Royal Society of Arts, 1991) and Edwards, *Changing places*.

206 'Open University Professor of Planetary and Space Science Awarded a CBE', *OU News*, 19 January 2012, www3.open.ac.uk/media/fullstory. aspx?id=23622.

207 1988 Education Act, Section 202, www.legislation.gov.uk/ukpga/1988/40/ section/202, accessed 19 April 2014.

208 *Report of the Vice-Chancellor, 1993* (Milton Keynes: The Open University, 1994), p. 4.

209 T. Besley and M. Peters, 'Neoliberalism, performance and the assessment of research quality', *South African Journal of Higher Education*, 20:6 (2006), 814–32; B. Regan, 'Campaigning against neo-liberal education in Britain', *Journal for Critical Education Policy Studies*, 5:1 (2007), 1–19; *Report of the Vice-Chancellor, 1996* (Milton Keynes: The Open University, 1997), pp. 4, 10.

210 *Report of the Vice-Chancellor, 1996*, pp. 4, 10.

211 *Report of the Vice-Chancellor, 1993*, p. 9; *Report of the Vice-Chancellor, 1992*, p. 4. See also John Daniel, Geoff Peters and Martin Watkinson, 'The funding of the United Kingdom Open University', in Ian Mugridge (ed.), *The funding of open universities* (Vancouver: The Commonwealth of Learning, 1994), pp. 13–20, and G. Peters and J. S. Daniel, 'Comparison of public funding of distance education and other modes of higher education

in England', in G. Dhanarajan *et al.*, *Economics of distance education: Recent experience* (Hong Kong: Open Learning Institute Press, 1994), pp. 31–41.

212 *Times Higher Education Supplement* (7 March 2003).

213 http://pelagios-project.blogspot.co.uk, accessed 1 December 2012; www.open.ac.uk/Arts/reading/UK/index.php, accessed 1 December 2012.

214 Cabinet Office, *Investing in innovation: A strategy for science, engineering and technology* (London: HMSO, 1987); DfES, *The excellence challenge* (London: HMSO, 2003); DfES, *The Future of Higher Education*, Cmd 5735 (London: HMSO, 2003).

215 C. Clarke, 'Foreword' to *The Future of Higher Education*, DfES White Paper (London: HMSO, 2003), p. 2, www.dfes.gov.uk/hegateway/uploads/White%20Pape.pdf, accessed 18 April 2012.

216 http://webarchive.nationalarchives.gov.uk/+/http://www.hm-treasury.gov.uk/media/9/0/lambert_review_final_450.pdf, accessed 1 October 2012.

217 Richard Lambert, *Inaugural universities UK speech*, delivered 11 December 2007, www.cbi.org.uk/ndbs/press.nsf/0363c1f07c6ca12a8025671c00381cc7/99671dd107d3a624802573ae0051697a?OpenDocument, accessed 18 April 2012.

218 http://academy.bcs.org/upload/pdf/wilson-review.pdf, accessed 1 October 2012.

219 Alan Woodley, OU Oral History Project.

220 *Report of the Vice-Chancellor, 1990* (Milton Keynes: The Open University, 1991), pp. 1, 4, 27.

221 *Report of the Vice-Chancellor, 1989* (Milton Keynes: The Open University, 1990), pp. 1–2.

222 *Report of the Vice-Chancellor, 1990*, p. 1; Robin Wilson, OU Oral History Project; Daniel Weinbren, 'Oxford may have snubbed Margaret Thatcher – but higher education owes her a debt', *Daily Telegraph* (9 April 2013), www.telegraph.co.uk/education/universityeducation/9980159/Oxford-may-have-snubbed-Margaret-Thatcher-but-higher-education-owes-her-a-debt.html, accessed 10 April 2013. Mrs Thatcher's Under Secretary at the DES, Norman St John Stevas, said: 'I have always thought that the Open University was making a most important contribution to education. I was glad when it was founded.' Commons, 10 April 1973 http://hansard.millbanksystems.com/commons/1973/apr/10/adult-education#S5CV0854P0_19730410_HOC_81, accessed 20 May 2011.

Chapter 4

1 Inauguration speech of Baron Crowther, www.col.org/SiteCollection Documents/Daniel_CROWTHER_Speech_1969.pdf, accessed 20 September 2012.

2 F. Castles, 'Divide and teach: The new division of labour', in Jeremy Tunstall (ed.), *The Open University opens* (London: Routledge and Kegan Paul, 1974), p. 115.

3 Open University, *An introduction to the Open University* (Milton Keynes: The Open University, 1977).

4 Michael Macdonald-Ross, 'Janus the consultant: Educational technology at the Open University', *British Journal of Educational Technology*, 1:7 (January 1976), 65.

5 Alan Woodley, OU Oral History Project.

6 David Harris, 'Educational technology at the Open University: A short history of achievement and cancellation', *British Journal of Educational Technology*, 1:7 (January 1976), 44.

7 *Saturday Review* (29 April 1972) referred to the classroom and the image of the flash which challenged was said by Peter Mandelson, *Guardian* (24 June 2009) www.guardian.co.uk/education/2009/jun/24/open-university-mandelson-comment, accessed 5 June 2012.

8 Surveys indicated that reception of broadcasts was uneven and that many broadcasts were ignored or had little influence on students' achievements. Robert Rowland, 'Some thoughts on the use of broadcasting in the Open University', *Teaching at a Distance*, 2 (February 1975), 61–5; A. Bates, 'Student use of Open University broadcasting', mimeo. Paper on Broadcasting No. 44 IET, 1975; Richard E. Clark, 'Reconsidering research on learning from media', *Review of Educational Research*, 53:4 (1983), 445, 450.

9 John Field, 'Behaviourism and training: The programmed instruction movement in Britain, 1950–1975', *Journal of Vocational Education and Training*, 59:3 (September 2007), 326.

10 A. W. Bates, 'Success and failure in innovation at the Open University', *Programmed Learning and Educational Technology*, 11:1 (January 1974), 16–23.

11 Department of Education and Science, *The Open University: Report of the Planning Committee (Venables Report)* (London: HMSO, 1969), p. 20.

12 *Report of the Vice-Chancellor, 1971*, p. 107; see also pp. 108–11; J. Riley, 'Course team alternatives', *Teaching at a Distance*, 19 (1981), 69–71.

13 Macdonald-Ross, 'Janus the consultant', p. 68.

14 Bates, 'Success and failure in innovation'; Hoult, 'The Open University', p. 55.

15 Kate Bradshaw, OU Oral History Project. Kate Bradshaw completed a PhD at the OU and was then an academic in earth sciences for five years. She subsequently produced science multi-media courseware and websites, and short films for science modules.

16 Robin Wilson, OU Oral History Project.

17 Charles Curran, report on the relationship between The Open University and the BBC, R103/218 G21/72 21 January 1972 BBC Archives, Caversham.

George Howard, speech at Leeds Polytechnic, 'The BBC, educational broadcasting and the future', 3 March 1981, copy in Broadcasting File 2, OU Archives.

18 G. Foster, 'Lessons from team work: Towards a systematic scheme for course development', *Higher Education*, 24 (1992), 210. See also J. Riley, 'Course teams at the Open University', *Studies in Higher Education*, 1:1 (1976), 57–61; C. R. Wright, 'The independent/distance study course development team', *Educational Technology*, 28:12 (December 1988), 12; J. Mason and S. Goodenough, 'Course creation', in A. Kaye and G. Rumble (eds), *Distance teaching for higher and adult education* (London: Croom Helm in association with the Open University Press, 1981), pp. 109, 113.

19 Raymond Williams, 'Raymond Williams thinks well of the Open University', *The Listener*, 23:14 (October 1971), 5.

20 Brian N. Lewis, 'Course production at the Open University I: Some basic problems', *British Journal of Educational Technology*, 2:1 (January 1971), 4–13; Brian N. Lewis, 'Course production at the Open University II: Activities and activity networks', *British Journal of Educational Technology*, 2:2 (May 1971), 111–23; Brian N. Lewis, 'Course production at the Open University III: Planning and scheduling', *British Journal of Educational Technology*, 2:3 (October 1971), 189–204; Brian N. Lewis, 'Course production at the Open University IV: The problem of assessment', *British Journal of Educational Technology*, 3:2 (May 1972), 108–28.

21 Roger Lewis and John Meed, *How to manage the production process* (London: Council for Educational Technology, 1986).

22 Anthony R. Kaye, 'Design and evaluation of science courses at the Open University', *Instructional Science*, 2 (1973), 119–85; Anthony R. Kaye, *Computer networking for development of distance education courses*, CITE Technical Report No. 146 (Milton Keynes: IET, The Open University, 1991).

23 John S. Daniel and M. A. Stroud, 'Distance education: A reassessment for the 1980s', *Distance Education*, 2:2 (1981), 153.

24 David G. Hawkridge, 'The University's self-improving instructional system', unpublished circular quoted in David Harris, 'Educational technology at the Open University: A short history of achievement and cancellation', *British Journal of Educational Technology*, 1:7 (January 1976), 50. On the evaluation systems see Naomi E. McIntosh, 'Research for a new institution: The Open University', in *Innovation in higher education* (London: SRHE, 1972), and Anthony R. Kaye, 'The design and evaluation of science courses at the Open University', *Instructional Science*, 1:2 (1973).

25 Clive Lawless and Adrian Kirkwood, 'Training the educational technologist', *British Journal of Educational Technology*, 1:7 (January 1976), 59.

26 Alan Woodley, OU Oral History Project.

27 *The Times Educational Supplement* (22 January 1965), 186.

28 Department of Education and Science, *Venables Report.*

29 Perry, *Open University: A personal account*, p. 264. The people were Peter Montagnon and Bob Rowlands.

30 Martin Trow, *Problems in the transition from elite to mass higher education* (Berkeley, CA: Carnegie Commission on Higher Education, 1973), p. 27.

31 Universities Grant Committee, *Report of the Committee on University teaching methods* (chairman Sir Edward Hale) (London: HMSO, 1964).

32 David Butt, 'The future of ETV', *Scottish Educational Journal*, 15 (January 1971), 36–7.

33 John Ferguson, 'Classics in the Open University', *Greece & Rome*, 21:1 (April 1974), 4.

34 Ruth Weinstock, 'British Open University: Media used in context', *Planning for higher education*, 4:2 (3/5 April 1975), n.p.

35 Letter to *Open Eye*, an Open University newsletter, in 2001, www. independent.co.uk/student/news/small-screen-heroes-1679166.html, accessed 5 October 2010.

36 Nicholas Valéry, 'Students of the air', *New Scientist*, 52:775 (23 December 1971), 208–9.

37 Amanda Wrigley, *Drama: A307, Woyzeck, BBC / The Open University, 1977*, online at http://screenplaystv.wordpress.com/2012/11/15/woyzeck-bbc-the-ou-1977, accessed 31 December 2012.

38 Interview with Nick Levinson by Amanda Wrigley, 19 June 2012. Archived at the University of Westminster. Thanks to Amanda Wrigley for access to this material.

39 'A Guide to the Course' and 'Supplementary Material A307', 1977; radio programme A307/03, *Theatre and Television*, produced by Richard Callanan.

40 Obituary of Glynne Wickham, *Guardian* (25 February, 2004), www. guardian.co.uk/news/2004/feb/25/guardianobituaries.highereducation, accessed 12 February 2013.

41 Brian Stone, *Studying drama: An introduction, Unit 1 Study 1* (Milton Keynes: The Open University, 1977), p. 7.

42 This material is derived from Amanda Wrigley's blog postings, http://screen playstv.wordpress.com/2011/09/09/macbeth-bbc-ou-1977; http://screen playstv.wordpress.com/2011/09/02/oedipus-the-king-bbc-ou-1977; http:// screenplaystv.wordpress.com/2012/10/31/the-balcony-bbc-the-ou-1977; http://screenplaystv.wordpress.com/2012/09/21/six-characters-bbc-ou-1977, accessed 31 December 2012.

43 On *Clouds* see Ferguson, 'Classics', pp. 4–5.

44 Interview with Cicely Havely by Amanda Wrigley, 18 June 2012. Archived at the University of Westminster.

45 Television programme A100/23, '*Hamlet*' I: Studies in Interpretation*, produced by Richard Callanan.

46 Naomi E. McIntosh and Val Morrison, *A unit-by-unit analysis of students' study patterns and their reactions to the foundation course materials* (Milton Keynes: The Open University, 1972).

47 *Education + Training*, 14:3 (March 1972), 79.

48 William S. Dorn, 'Technology in education: A case study of the Open University', *International Review of Education*, 20:1 (1974), 65.

49 Margaret Gayfer, 'Can the open university concept de-mystify the instructional process?', *Canadian University & College* (March/April 1972), 22. For an assessment of the OU's early broadcasts and some of the printed materials see Marghanita Laski, 'Hey Jude, or the Open University', *The Listener*, 2197 (6 May 1971), 569. She noted some errors and the 'permeating Marxism' but was generally impressed. There was further analysis in the same issue of *The Listener*, Raymond Williams, 'Open Teaching', *The Listener*, 2197 (6 May 1971), 594 and Philip Elliot, 'Second chance', *The Listener*, 2197 (6 May 1971), 595.

50 Stephen Jessel, *The Times* (26 June 1973).

51 Department of Education and Science, *Venables Report*, p. 6.

52 Williams, 'Raymond Williams thinks', p. 5.

53 R. C. L. Wilson, 'The Open University', *Geotimes*, 28 (August 1971), 18.

54 Naomi E. McIntosh and Alan Woodley, 'The Open University and second-chance education: An analysis of the social and educational background of Open University students', *Paedagogica Europaea: Review of Education in Europe*, 9:2 (1974), 85–6.

55 Ferguson, *The Open University from within*, pp. 17, 78–9.

56 Tom Prebble, *From a Distance: 50th Jubilee of distance learning* (Palmerston North: Massey University, 2010), p. 79. On the emphasis on technology see also Pratt 'Open University!', pp. 6–24.

57 Quoted in P. Kelly and B. Swift, *Tuition at post foundation level in the Open University: Student attitudes towards tuition*, mimeo (Milton Keynes: RAS/ IET, The Open University, 1983).

58 June Purvis, 'Some problems of teaching and learning within the Open University', *Educational Research*, 21:3 (1979), 172.

59 See Steve Murgatroyd, 'What actually happens in tutorials?', *Teaching at a Distance*, 18 (Winter 1980), 44; Moreen Dochety, 'A case study of student progress', *Teaching at a Distance*, 18 (Winter 1980), 69; Anne Jelfs, John T. E. Richardson and Linda Price, 'Student and tutor perceptions of effective tutoring in distance education', *Distance Education*, 30:3 (November 2009), 419–41.

60 Pauline Kirk, 'The loneliness of the long distance tutor', *Teaching at a Distance*, 7 (November 1976), 3–6.

61 For this view of the impact of the two foundation courses in social sciences and arts, D102 and A101, see Geoffrey Wood, 'Does distance lend enchantment? The politics of knowledge at the Open University', *Universities Quarterly Culture Education & Society*, 39:2 (Spring 1985), 127, 134–5.

62 Tony Bennett, 'Out in the open: Reflections on the history and practice of cultural studies', *Cultural Studies*, 10:1 (1996), 141.

63 N. Farnes, 'Student-centred learning', *Teaching at a Distance*, 3 (May 1975), 2–6.

64 Dave Harris and John Holmes, 'Openness and control in higher education: Towards a critique of the Open University', in Roger Dale, Geoff Esland and Madeleine MacDonald (eds), *Schooling and capitalism: A sociological reader* (London: Routledge and Kegan Paul, 1976), pp. 78–87. This book was part of the materials for *Schooling and society*, E202.

65 Bell, '"Education for adults" (E355): An Open University case study', *Open Learning*, 4:1 (1989), 39.

66 Elizabeth Taylor and Tony Kaye, 'Andragogy by design? Control and self-direction in the design of an Open University course', *Programmed Learning and Educational Technology*, 23:1 (1986), 63.

67 Jeremy Millard, 'Local tutor-student contact in the Open University', *Teaching at a Distance*, 26 (Autumn 1985), 12.

68 Ray Woolfe, 'Learning in groups', *Teaching at a Distance*, 26 (Autumn 1985), 65.

69 Judith Fage quoted Elizabeth J. Burge, *Flexible, higher education: Reflections from expert experience* (London: The Society for Research into Higher Education, 2007), p. 31.

70 Hilary Perraton, 'Is there a teacher in the system?', *Teaching at a Distance*, 1 (1974), 55–60.

71 Open University, *Teaching by Correspondence in the Open University* (Milton Keynes: The Open University, 1973), p. 30.

72 Tony Bates, *Guidelines to tutors and counsellors on the use of broadcasts* (Milton Keynes: The Open University, 1973), pp. 1, 14.

73 Open University, *Teaching for the Open University* (Milton Keynes: The Open University, 1982), p. 57.

74 R. Lewis, 'The place of face-to-face tuition in the Open University system', *Teaching at a Distance*, 3 (May 1975), 26–31; G. Gibb and N. Durbridge, 'Characteristics of the Open University tutors (part 1)', *Teaching at a Distance*, 6 (June 1976), 96–102; G. Gibb and N. Durbridge, 'Characteristics of the Open University tutors (part 2)', *Teaching at a Distance*, 7 (November 1976), 7–22.

75 Hollister and Pentz, 'Science and technology', 98.

76 Paulo Freire, *Pedagogy of the Oppressed*, revised twentieth anniversary edn (New York: Continuum, 1998), p. 54. The book was first made available in English in 1972.

77 The literature is surveyed in Frankie Todd and Roy Todd, 'Talking and learning: Towards an effective structuring of student-directed groups in higher education', *Journal of Further and Higher Education*, 3:2 (Summer 1979).

78 See N. MacKenzie, M. Eraut and H. C. Jones, *Teaching and learning: New methods and resources in higher education* (Paris: Unesco/International Association of Universities, 1970).

79 John Stuart and R. J. D. Rutherford, 'Medical student concentration during lectures', *The Lancet*, 8088 (2 September 1978), 514–16; John McLeish, *The lecture method* (Cambridge: Cambridge Institute of Education, 1968); Donald A. Bligh, *What's the use of lectures?*, 2nd edn (Harmondsworth: Penguin, 1972).

80 Ferguson, *The Open University from within*, p. 6.

81 Michael Drake, OU Oral History Project. Having worked at the universities of Belfast, Kent and Trinity College, Dublin, Michael Drake was appointed as the first Dean of Social Sciences in 1969. He later left the post, was subsequently elected as Dean for a further term, contributed to numerous courses and helped establish, with former students, the Family and Community Historical Research Society and retired as Emeritus Professor.

82 Chris Dunkley, 'Uncle Ebenezer's view', in Holloway (ed.), *The first ten years*, p. 28.

83 Quoted in Huw Richards, 'Goodbye to kipper ties and sideburns', *Times Higher Education Supplement* (15 December 2006), www.timeshigheredu-cation.co.uk/features/goodbye-to-kipper-ties-and-sideburns/207205.article, accessed 2 July 2011.

84 David Harris, 'On Marxist bias', *Journal of Further and Higher Education*, 2:2 (1978), 68–71. See also Harris, 'Educational technology', pp. 46, 48.

85 Freire's degree is reported in Ferguson, *The Open University from within*, p. 29.

86 Russell argued that 'I write my plays to be played, not studied ... I hope you will find *Educating Rita* understandable without lengthy analysis.' See Willy Russell, *Education Rita*, ed. and annotated Albert-Reiner Glaap (Frankfurt am Main: Verlag Moritz Diesterweg, 1984), pp. 5–6. Nevertheless, some engagement with the play illuminates the history of the OU.

87 For use of the 'revolving door' image of the OU see Naomi E. McIntosh and Alan Woodley, *Excellence, equality and the Open University* (Milton Keynes: The Open University, Survey Research Department, 1975).

88 On the advice to Russell provided by OU staff see Mike Bullivant, quoted in Dalgleish (ed.), *Lifting it off the page*, p. 35.

89 Gill Kirkup, 'Women's studies "at a distance": The new Open University course', *Women's Studies International Forum*, 6:3 (1983), 273.

90 Russell, *Educating Rita*, pp. 36–7.

91 Email to author, 15 July 2010.

92 www3.open.ac.uk/near-you/south-east/p3.asp, accessed 7 January 2010. There is a review of the performance in a prison at www.prisonerseduca tion.org.uk/index.php?id=362, accessed 2 October 2012.

93 When *Educating Rita* ran at the Derby Playhouse 7 September–8 October 1983, this was the advertisement from The Open University in the programme.

94 Perry, *Open University: A personal account*, pp. 85, 91.

95 Dorn, 'Technology in education', p. 64.

96 John S. Daniel, *Mega-universities and knowledge media: Technology strate-gies for higher education* (London: Kogan Page, 1996), p. 196.

97 John Mason and Michael Moore, 'Editorial', *Teaching at a Distance*, 18 (Winter 1980), 1–2.

98 Michael Macdonald-Ross and Robert Waller, 'The transformer revisited', *Information Design Journal*, 9:2–3 (2000), 178.

99 Charles Newey, 'On being a course team chairman', *Teaching at a Distance*, 4 (November 1975), 48.

100 Hung-Ju Chung, 'The nature of the course team approach at the UK Open University' (PhD, The Open University, 2001), p. 274; David Hawkridge, 'Which team for open and distance learning materials production?', in F. Lockwood (ed.), *Materials production in open and distance learning* (London: Paul Chapman, 1994), p. 98.

101 W. Gordon Lawrence and Irene Young, *The Open University* (London: Tavistock Institute of Human Relations, 1979) p. 3; Michael Drake, 'The curse of the course team', *Teaching at a Distance*, 16 (Winter 1979), 51–2.

102 *Open House*, 74 (31 January 1973); *Open House*, 75 (15 February 1973); *Open House*, 130 (24 February 1976); *Open House*, 133 (29 April 1976).

103 George Low, OU Oral History Project.

104 Lawrence and Young, *The Open University*.

105 Joan Whitehead, OU Oral History Project.

106 Newey, 'On being a course manager', p. 51.

107 Walter Perry, 'The Open University', *New University* (March/April 1970), 19; Drake, 'The curse'.

108 Andy Blowers, 'Carry on course teams', *Teaching at a Distance*, 16 (Winter 1979), 54–7; N. Costello, 'The curse of the course team: A comment', *Teaching at a Distance*, 16 (Winter 1979), 53–4.

109 Malcolm Tight, 'Do we really need course teams?', *Teaching at a Distance*, 26 (Autumn 1985), 48–50.

110 Riley, 'Course teams', p. 61.

111 Ken Jones, *Given half a chance: A study of some factors in cultural disad-vantage affecting the acquisition of learning skills in adults*, Open University internal paper, 1977.

112 Ivor Wymer, 'Back in 10 minutes: Preparing Open University students', *Education & Training*, 12:10 (October 1970), 376.

113 Perry, *Open University: A personal account*, p. 36.

114 Paulo Freire, *Cultural action for freedom* (Harmondsworth: Penguin, 1972).

115 John Cowan and Judith George, *Ten years of action research: A reflective review 1987–1997* (Edinburgh: The Open University in Scotland, 1999).

116 Weinstock, 'British Open University'.

117 George Howard, *The BBC, educational broadcasting and the future: A speech given by George Howard at Leeds polytechnic, Tuesday 3 March 1981* (London: BBC, 1981).

118 Perry, *Open University: A personal account*, pp. 264–5.

119 Perry, 'The Open University', p. 19.

120 Conrad Russell, 'Open University: Preliminary progress reports', *Times Educational Supplement* (15 May 1971). *Einstein's Universe*, a 120-minute TV film produced and directed by Martin Freeth for the BBC and WGBH, was presented by Peter Ustinov, written by Nigel Calder, and first broadcast on the centenary of Einstein's birth, 14 March 1979. The book that accompanied the programme, *Einstein's Universe* by Nigel Calder, was well received by *Nature*, the *Evening Standard* and the *Irish Times*. http://calde-rup.wordpress.com/2010/05/01/about-einsteins-universe-3, accessed 5 May 2010. The categorisation 'slick' was Russell's description of a second-level arts programme on ancient Greece, *The Agora of Athens*, and a third-level one, *The Rise of Modernism in Music*.

121 *Saturday Review* (29 April 1972).

122 P. Macguire, 'Book review', *Journal of Design History*, 8:2 (1995), 155.

123 Russell, 'Open University: Preliminary'.

124 Grahame Thompson, 'Television as text: Open University "case study" programmes', in Michèle Barrett, Philip Corrigan, Annette Kuhn and Janet Wolff (eds), *Ideology and cultural production* (London: Croom Helm, 1979), pp. 160–97.

125 Colin Robinson, OU Oral History Project.

126 Quoted in Richards, 'Goodbye'.

127 Donald Grattan, OU Oral History Project.

128 Perry, *Open University: A personal account*, p. 264. See also *Ariel*, 13 (11 November 1968); Perry, 'The Open University', p. 19.

129 Agreement, 16 December 1971, Broadcasting File 2, OU Archives, Schedule 1, pp. 15–16.

130 Agreement, 16 December 1971, Broadcasting File 2, OU Archives, Clause 3, p. 2.

131 Dorn, 'Technology in education', p. 65.

132 Russell, 'Open University: Preliminary'; Sparkes quoted in Richards, 'Goodbye'.

133 Wilson, 'The Open University', *Geotimes*.

134 *The Times* (23 May 1977); *Observer* (15 May 1977); *Observer* (1 May 1977); Letter to the Editor, *Guardian* (23 May 1977); *Guardian* (24 May 1977).

135 Open House 148 (24 May 1977); *Open House*, 153 (5 July 1977). See also Brian Stone and Pat Scorer, *Sophocles to Fugard* (London: BBC, 1977). The BBC evoked the Agreement, 16 December 1971, with the OU. See Broadcasting File 2, OU Archives, Clause 4, p. 3. Copy in Broadcasting File 2, OU Archives.

136 Agreement, 16 December 1971, Clause 8, p. 5. Broadcasting File 2, OU Archives; OU Archives Mudridge File 10, 17/10/1972; Editor (Arts Programmes) Peter Scroggs in a note to the Senior Presentation Editor OU File Mugeridge 10, 17/10/1972; Perry, 'The Open University', p. 19; Perry, *Open University: A personal account*, p. 265; Agreement, 16 December 1971, Clause 8, p. 5. Broadcasting File 2, OU Archives; OU Archives Mudridge File 10, 17/10/1972.

137 Quoted in Richards, 'Goodbye'; RGJ/JFW, 24 April 1977, notes of a meeting of 24 March 1977; Open House, 138 (31 August 1976); Perry, *Open University: A personal account*, p. 269.

138 Hilary Perraton, 'Why use television?', *Adult Education*, 39 (1966), 266.

139 Agreement, 16 December 1971, Broadcasting File 2, OU Archives, Clause 10, p. 6.

140 Tony Bates and Margaret Gallagher, 'The development of research in broadcasting at the Open University', *British Journal of Educational Technology*, 1:7 (January 1976), 34.

141 A. W. Bates, 'The television transmission problem: The current situation', MPAG/2/4 1981. Copy in Broadcasting File 2, OU Archives.

142 The Open University Media Policy Advisory Group meeting Minutes, 15/4/81. Copy in Broadcasting File 2, OU Archives.

143 *The Times* (13 July 1973).

144 Ohliger, 'Adult education', p. 262.

145 Tony Bates, 'Trends in the use of audio-visual media in distance education systems', in John S. Daniel, M. A. Stroud and J. R. Thompson (eds), *Learning at a distance: A world perspective* (Edmonton: Athabasca University, Alberta, 1982).

146 Bates, 'The television', pp. 4–5; Naomi McIntosh and V. Morrison, 'Students' study habits and their reactions to Foundation Course materials', Open University, mimeo, 1972; A.W. Bates, *Student use of open university broadcasting*, IET Paper No. 79 (Milton Keynes: The Open University, 1975); J. Meed, 'The use of radio in the Open University's multi-media educational system', *Educational Broadcasting International*, 9:2 (1976); A. W. Bates, 'Whatever happened to radio at the Open University?', *Educational Broadcasting Press*, 12 (1979), 4–19; H. Grundin, *Audio-visual and other media in 91 Open University courses: The results of the 1979 undergraduate survey* (Milton Keynes: The Open University, 1980); H. Grundin, *The 1982 Media Survey* (Milton Keynes: The Open University, 1983); A. W. Bates, 'Recent trends in the use of radio and cassettes', in *Radio: The forgotten medium?*, mimeo. Papers on broadcasting No. 185 (Milton Keynes: IET, The Open University, 1981); Open University Broadcast & Audio-Visual Sub-Committee, *Interim report of the Radio Transmissions Working Group* (Milton Keynes: The Open University, 1988); Media Policy Advisory Group report to Planning Board, 8 January 1981. Copy in Broadcasting File 2, OU Archives.

147 Andrew Lane, Dick Morris and Sue Thompson, 'Open learning down on the farm', *Open Learning*, 3:1 (February 1988), 29–34 (p. 32).

148 D. G. Hawkridge, 'Space for the Open University', *Proceedings of the Royal Society of London: Series A, Mathematical and Physical Sciences*, 345:1643 (7 October 1975), 567–73.

149 Quoted in Richards, 'Goodbye'.

150 On BBC2 see Walter Perry, 'Continuing education', *Higher Education*, 2:2 (May 1973), 176–7; Bates, 'Trends', p. 9.

151 David Murray, OU Oral History Project.

152 *Sesame* (June/July 1977), p. 7; the last course-specific programme, *Art: A Question of Style. Neo-Classicism and Romanticism* was screened at 5.30am on 16 December 2006: Richards, 'Goodbye'.

153 Bates, 'Trends'.

154 Paul Du Gay, Stuart Hall, Linda Janes and Hugh Mackay, *Doing cultural studies: The story of the Sony Walkman* (London: Sage, in association with The Open University, 1997).

155 Bates, 'Recent trends in the use of radio and cassettes'; Open University Broadcast & Audio-Visual Sub-Committee, *Interim report of the Radio Transmissions Working Group* (Milton Keynes: The Open University, 1988).

156 Michael Young and Peter Wilmott, *Family and kinship in East London* (London: Routledge, 1957); Peter Wilmott and Michael Young, *Family and class in a London suburb* (London: Routledge and Kegan Paul, 1960).

157 Young and Wilmott, *Family and kinship*, p. 157.

158 Brian Jackson and Dennis Marsden, *Education and the working class* (Harmondsworth: Pelican, 1962).

159 Obituary, *The Herald*, www.heraldscotland.com/comment/obituaries/norman-mackenzie.21440715, accessed 30 July 2013.

160 Asa Briggs, 'The years of plenty', in Roger Blin-Stoyle and Geoff Ivey (eds), *The Sussex opportunity: A new university and the future* (Brighton: Harvester Press, 1986), p. 11.

161 Alan Tuckett, 'Introduction', in Andrew McIntosh, Derek Jones, Alan Tuckett and Alan Woodley, *Lifelong learning: A brave and proper vision. Selected writings of Naomi Sargant* (Leicester: NIACE, 2009), p. 2.

162 M. Savage, *Identities and social change in Britain since 1940: The politics of method* (Oxford: Oxford University Press, 2011), pp. 158–60.

163 On this concept see Mike Savage, Gaynor Bagnall and Brian J. Longhurst, *Globalization and belonging* (London: Sage, 2005).

164 Savage, *Identities and social change*, p. 47.

165 Savage, *Identities and social change*, p. 133.

166 Savage, *Identities and social change*, p. 201.

167 McIntosh, 'Research for a new'.

168 N. E. McIntosh, 'Institutional research: Needs and uses', *Teaching at a Distance*, 2 (1975), 35–48.

169 M. Warner, 'Publics and counterpublics', *Quarterly Journal of Speech*, 88:4 (November 2002), 413–25.

170 On McArthur's design award see *The Times* (22 May 1970). His obituary appeared on *The Times* (8 May 1996).

171 Valéry, 'Students of the air', pp. 208–9.

172 Gayfer, 'Can the open university concept', p. 22; David Sewart, 'Some observations on the formation of study group', *Teaching at a Distance*, 2 (February 1975), 2–6; Olga Camm, 'Looking back at early student days at OU', *OU Student* (September 2010), 2. Camm became the first chair of the OU Graduates Association.

173 www8.open.ac.uk/researchprojects/historyofou/story/students, accessed 23 April 2012.

174 Pauline Swindells cited in Patricia W. Lunneborg, *OU women: Undoing educational obstacles* (London: Cassell, 1994), pp. 25–31.

175 Ernie Barnhurst, OU Oral History Project. Ernie Barnhurst started studying with The Open University in 1971. He subsequently worked for the OU as an associate lecturer, part-time adviser, disability adviser and assessor.

176 Diana Purcell, OU Oral History Project. In 1971 Diana Purcell as a part-time OU counsellor while working full-time as a lecturer at another institution. She became a senior counsellor in the 1980s and was responsible for the OU in prison teaching.

177 Cited in Angie Ballard, 'Community education and the limits of openness', in Vivien E. Hodgson, Sarah J. Mann and Robin S. Snell (eds), *Beyond distance teaching towards open learning* (Milton Keynes: The Society for Research into Higher Education and The Open University, 1987), 127–41 (pp. 134, 135). There were a dozen courses and fifteen packs of non-degree materials.

178 M. Foucault, 'Of other spaces', *Diacritics*, 16 (Spring 1986), 22–7.

179 Foucault 'Of other spaces'.

180 Arthur Marwick, 'History at the Open University', *Oxford Review of Education*, 2:2 (1976), 130–1, 133.

181 Gerald Isaaman, obituary of Arthur Marwick, *Camden New Journal* (2 November 2006), www.thecnj.com/camden/110206/obit110206_01.html, accessed 11 April 2014.

182 *Daily Telegraph* (4 October 2006), www.telegraph.co.uk/news/obituaries/1530467/Professor-Arthur-Marwick.html, accessed 11 April 2014.

183 Bernard Harrison, 'The teaching-learning relationship in correspondence tuition', *Teaching at a Distance*, 1 (November 1974), 2, 3.

184 Moreen Dochety, 'A case study of student progress', *Teaching at a Distance*, 18 (Winter 1980), 69.

185 Ferguson, *The Open University from within*, p. 6.

186 Ferguson, 'Classics', p. 2.

187 Dorn, 'Technology in education', p. 68.

188 *Education + Training*, 14:3 (March 1972), 79.

189 *Education + Training*, 14:2 (February 1972), 48.

190 Marwick, 'History at the Open University', pp. 130–1, 133.

191 Perry, *Open University: A personal account*, p. 269.

192 Perry, *Report*, pp. 85, 103.

193 The title also echoes that of a popular radio series of the 1950s (and briefly a television series) in which a pupil constantly outwits a series of tutors, *Educating Archie*.

194 Russell, *Educating Rita*, p. 23. See pp. 54, 32, 37, 39, 77, 74, 51, 63 for other quotations in this box.

195 In Russell's introduction to the 1983 edition, he denied that Rita was meant to echo Delilah, who denied Samson his powers by cutting his hair. Rather the activity was 'merely … a joke'. See Russell, *Educating Rita*, p. 6.

196 *The Times* (9 September 1963).

197 This image owes something to Mary Thorpe, 'When is a course not a course?', *Teaching at a Distance*, 16 (Winter 1979), 13–18.

198 J. Gregson, 'Ars docendi, artium liberalium', *Cam: Cambridge University Alumni Magazine* (Michaelmas 1993), 8.

199 Robert Millward, 'The rise of the service economy', in Roderick Floud and Paul Johnson (eds), *The Cambridge economic history of modern Britain*, volume III: *Structural change and growth, 1939–2000* (Cambridge: Cambridge University Press, 2004), pp. 240–7.

200 David Harris, 'The micro-politics of openness', *Open Learning*, 3:2 (June 1988), 13–16 (p. 15); Andy Northedge, 'Returning to study', in Mary Thorpe and David Grugeon (eds), *Open learning for adults* (Harlow: Longman, 1987).

201 Macdonald-Ross, 'Janus the consultant', p. 68.

Chapter 5

1 On the new structures see B. Davies, M. Gottsche and P. Bansel, 'The rise and fall of the neo-liberal university', *European Journal of Education*, 41:2 (2006), 305–19; George Ritzer, 'The McDonaldization of society', *Journal of American Culture*, 6:1 (1983), 100–7; Christian Garland, 'The McDonaldization of higher education? Notes on the UK experience', *Fast Capitalism*, 4:1 (2008), www.uta.edu/huma/agger/fastcapitalism/4_1/garland.html, accessed 18 April 2012.

2 www.bbc.co.uk/news/education-11627843, accessed 2 January 2013.

3 Adrianna Kezar, 'Obtaining integrity? Reviewing and examining the charter between higher education and society', *The Review of Higher Education*, 27:4 (Summer 2004), 430, 433.

4 The term 'quasi-markets' was employed in Julian Le Grand, 'Quasi-markets and social policy', *The Economic Journal*, 101:408 (September 1991), 1256–67;

and in Julian Le Grand and Will Bartlett (eds), *Quasi-markets and social policy* (Basingstoke: Palgrave Macmillan, 1993). For the term 'hollowed-out state' see R. A. W. Rhodes, 'The hollowing out of the state: The changing nature of public service in Britain', *Political Quarterly*, 65:2 (April–June 1994), 138–51.

5 F. Rizvi and R. Lingard, *Globalising educational policy* (London: Routledge, 2010).

6 Department for Education and Employment, *Statistical bulletin* (London: HMSO, 1992); The Open University, *Enquirers, market share, gone elsewhere study* (September 2002). The data is derived from HESA data: *All HE students by subject of study, domicile and gender*, 1996/97, 97/98, 98/99, 99/00, 00/01 cited in *Size and shape: The Open University curriculum and awards strategy, 2001–2006*. Academic Board 106/14.

7 Alan Tait and Roger Mills (eds), *The convergence of distance and conventional education: Patterns of flexibility for the individual learner* (London: Routledge, 1999), p. 2.

8 Grants were recommended by Ministry of Education, *Grants to Students, 1959/60*, Cmd 1051 (London: HMSO, 1960). A nationwide university admissions service was opened in 1961.

9 *Size and shape, 2003–2008: The OU curriculum and awards strategy*, Academic Board/110/9 Para. 20 p. 5.

10 Department of Education and Science, *Higher education: Meeting the challenge*, Cmnd 114 (London: DES, 1987).

11 C. M. Savage, *Fifth generation management: Co-creating through virtual enterprising, dynamic teaming and knowledge networking* (Boston, MA: Butterworth-Heinemann, 1990).

12 Burton R. Clark, *Places of inquiry: Research and advanced education in modern universities* (Berkeley, CA: University of California Press, 1995), p. 66.

13 They were the Higher Education Funding Council for England, the Higher Education Funding Council for Wales and the Scottish Higher Education Funding Council (later the Scottish Funding Council for Further and Higher Education) and the Department for Employment and Learning (from 2009 The Northern Ireland Charity Commission for Northern Ireland).

14 *Realising our potential: A strategy for science, engineering and technology*, Cmnd 2250 (London: The Stationery Office, 1993), p. 5.

15 Martin Watkinson, 'Recollections', p. 6. Notes electronically submitted to author 21 August 2011.

16 Department of Education and Science, *Higher education: A new framework*, Cmnd 1541 (London: HMSO, 1991), p. 12, para. 54.

17 *The development of higher education into the 1990s* cited in *Review of the Open University*, p. 76.

18 In 1995 there were at least eight other universities in the Midlands which offered part-time provision. See Pat Rickwood, 'Others like us? A study of part-time degree provision outside the Open University', *Open Learning*, 10:3 (November 1995), 24; T. Borner, A. Reynolds, M. Hamed and R. Barnett, *Part-time students and their experience of higher education* (Buckingham: The Open University, 1991); M. Tight, *Higher education: A part-time perspective* (Buckingham: The Open University, 1991); D. Watson and R. Taylor, *Lifelong learning and the university: A post-Dearing agenda* (London: Falmer, 1998).

19 Sir Ron Dearing (chair), *Higher education in the learning society: Report of the National Committee of Inquiry into Higher Education* (London: HMSO, 1997), https://bei.leeds.ac.uk/Partners/NCIHE, accessed 20 April 2012; P. Davies, 'Half full, not half empty: A positive look at part-time higher education', *Higher Education Quarterly*, 53:2 (1999), 141–55.

20 Higher Education Statistics Agency data, 2006, www.hesa.ac.uk, accessed 24 October 2011.

21 Centre for Higher Education Research and Information and London South Bank, *Survey of higher education students' attitudes to debt and term-time working and their impact on attainment: A report to Universities UK and HEFCE by the Centre for Higher Education Research and Information (CHERI) and London South Bank University* (London Universities UK, 2005), www.universitiesuk.ac.uk/Publications/Documents/termtime_work.pdf, accessed 2 October 2012.

22 The Open University, *Enquirers, market share*.

23 *Size and shape, 2003–2008*, para. 20 p. 5; National Statistics Office website: www.statistics.gov.uk/census2001, accessed 13 April 2014.

24 *Report of the Vice-Chancellor, 1993*, p. 4; *Report of the Vice-Chancellor, 1994* (Milton Keynes: The Open University, 1995), p. 4.

25 *Review of the Open University*, p. 76.

26 Martin Watkinson, 'Funding and strategy', paper for the History of The Open University Project, October 2011.

27 *Review of the Open University*, pp. 64–6.

28 On the impact on the OU see *Report of the Vice-Chancellor, 1992*, p. 4; *Report of the Vice-Chancellor, 1993*, pp. 3, 4, 9; *Report of the Vice-Chancellor, 1994*, pp. 4, 7; *Report of the Vice-Chancellor, 1995* (Milton Keynes: The Open University, 1996), pp. 3, 5; *Report of the Vice-Chancellor, 2000* (Milton Keynes: The Open University, 2001), p. 5.

29 *Report of the Vice-Chancellor, 1994*, p. 4; *Report of the Vice-Chancellor, 1995*, p. 3; *Report of the Vice-Chancellor, 1996*, p. 3.

30 *Report of the Vice-Chancellor, 2000*, p. 5.

31 www.leeds.ac.uk/educol/ncihe, accessed 2 October 2012.

32 *The Times* (4 June 1970).

33 National Committee of Inquiry into Higher Education Report 2, Section 2.44.

34 www.publications.parliament.uk/pa/cm199798/cmstand/f/st980421/ am/80421s01.htm, accessed 28 March 2013.

35 Dearing (chair), *Higher education*, pp. 1–2. For the externalities see the Appendix. The committee also noted that universities had a cultural herit- age, a public-service function and a spiritual dimension. For the relation- ship between human capital theory and education see P. Fitzsimons and M. Peters, 'Human capital theory and the industry training strategy in New Zealand', *Journal of Education Policy*, 9:2 (1994), 245–66. Australia and New Zealand were among other OECD countries which reviewed their ter- tiary education systems during this period. For a comparison see M. Peters and P. Roberts, 'Agendas for change: Universities in the 21st century', *New Zealand Annual Review of Education*, 7 (1998), pp. 5–28. See also Gareth Parry, 'Education research and policy making in higher education: The case of Dearing', *Journal of Educational Policy*, 14:3 (1999), 232.

36 Tony Blair's account of his priorities for government in a speech to the Labour Party conference, October 1996.

37 Tony Blair, *A journey* (London: Hutchinson, 2010), pp. 481–2, 495.

38 Between 1977 and 1984 there were means-tested maintenance grants as well as fees paid by Local Education Authorities, and students could claim hous- ing and unemployment benefits in the vacations. The value of grants was then frozen, eligibility for benefits was removed and gradually loans were introduced. See Jo Blanden and Stephen J. Machin, 'Educational inequality and the expansion of UK Higher Education', *Scottish Journal of Political Economy*, 51:2 (May 2004), 230–49.

39 *Report of the Vice-Chancellor, 1993*, p. 3; *Report of the Vice-Chancellor, 1995*, p. 3.

40 Legislation to create a Single European Market was introduced in 1992. Membership of the EEC (the EU from 1993) determined that nationals from other member states be treated with parity.

41 Blair, *A journey*, p. 480.

42 The Northern Ireland Assembly was elected in 1998 but suspended until 1999. It was further suspended and its impact on HE policy has been minor.

43 *Annual Report 2005* (Milton Keynes: The Open University, 2007), p. 29.

44 www.gov.uk/government/uploads/system/uploads/attachment_data/file/324 00/11-1046-government-response-to-browne-review.pdf, accessed 12 March 2013.

45 *Times Higher Education* (21 March 2013), www.timeshighereducation. co.uk/news/elq-loans-could-turn-part-time-rhetoric-into-reality/2002674. article, accessed 16 April 2013.

46 Other higher educational bodies funded directly by the DES were Goldsmiths College, the College of Guidance Studies, Cranfield Institute of Technology and the Royal College of Art.

47 *Review of the Open University*, p. 57.

48 *Report of the Vice-Chancellor, 1990*, p. 3.

49 *Report of the Vice-Chancellor, 1991*, p. 3.

50 *Report of the Vice-Chancellor, 1991*, p. 3.

51 *Report of the Vice-Chancellor, 1992*, pp. 2, 4; *Report of the Vice-Chancellor, 1993*, p. 4; *Report of the Vice-Chancellor, 1994*, p. 5; Watkinson, 'Funding and strategy'.

52 *Report of the Vice-Chancellor, 1990*, p. 12.

53 *Report of the Vice-Chancellor, 1990*, p. 11.

54 *Report of the Vice-Chancellor, 1991*, p. 28.

55 Alan Tait, 'Leadership development for distance and e-learning', in Terry Evans, Margaret Haughey and David Murphy (eds), *The international handbook of distance education* (Bingley: Emerald, 2008), p. 507.

56 Alex Jarratt, *Report on efficiency studies in universities* (London: CVCP, 1985), p. 33.

57 Janet Newman, 'Rethinking "the public" in troubled times', *Public Policy and Administration*, 22:1 (February 2007), 30.

58 A. Kirkwood, 'Interaction upon interaction: Combining interactive video with group sessions in management training', *Computers in Adult Education and Training*, 2:3 (December 1991); A. Kirkwood, 'Bearing fruit: The longer-term effects of management training using interactive video', *Education and Training Technology International* (December 1993); M. Stratford, 'Evaluation of the flowcharting interface and video in terminal RISK' (internal report, January 1992); M. E. V. Taylor, A. T. Vincent and D. A. Child, 'Alternatives to print for visually impaired students: Feasibility project report', (internal report, February 1992).

59 J. Taylor, T. O'Shea, E. Scanlon, C. O'Malley and R. Smith, 'Discourse and harmony: Preliminary findings in a case-study of multi-media collaborative problem solving', in R. Glanville and G. de Zeeuw (eds), *Interactive interfaces and human networks* (Amsterdam: Thesis, 1993).

60 Diana Laurillard, 'Mediating the message: Programme design and students' understanding', *Instructional Science*, 20:1 (1991), 3–24.

61 *Annual Report 2002* (Milton Keynes: The Open University, 2003), p. 17.

62 John W. Meyer, Francisco O. Ramirez, David John Frank and Evan Schofer, *Higher education as an institution*, Working Paper 57, Center on Democracy, Development and The Rule of Law, Stanford University (May 2006), http://cddrl.stanford.edu, accessed 20 September 2011.

63 www.ond.vlaanderen.be/hogeronderwijs/bologna/about, the official Bologna Process website July 2007–June 2010, accessed 2 October 2012. World Bank, *Constructing knowledge societies: New challenges for tertiary education* (Washington, DC: World Bank, 2002).

64 P. Zgaga, 'Higher education and citizenship: The full range purposes', in *European Educational Research Journal*, 8:2 (2009), 185; R. Edwards,

Changing places: Flexibility, lifelong learning and a learning society (London: Routledge, 1997).

65 *Report of the Vice-Chancellor, 2000*, p. 16; *Report of the Vice-Chancellor, 2001* (Milton Keynes: The Open University, 2002), p. 11; *Report of the Vice-Chancellor, 2003* (Milton Keynes: The Open University, 2004), p. 14.

66 John Brennan, 'Higher education and social change', *Higher Education*, 56 (2008), 384.

67 M. Olssen and M. A. Peter, 'Neoliberalism, higher education and the knowledge economy: From the free market to knowledge capitalism', *Journal of Education Policy*, 20:3 (2005), 345.

68 Inauguration speech of Baron Crowther, www.col.org/SiteCollection Documents/Daniel_CROWTHER_Speech_1969.pdf, accessed 20 September 2012.

69 Ellie Chambers and Kevin Wilson, 'International partnership and collaboration for cost-effective distance education', in Terry Evans, Margaret Haughey and David Murphy (eds), *The international handbook of distance education* (Bingley: Emerald, 2008), pp. 841–4.

70 The OU carried out analysis of aspects of the two bodies. See Chris Kubiak and Keir Thorpe, *Advice for versioning from the USOU experience* (May 2002); Keir Thorpe, *CURVE-L22: Lessons from versioning for the Arab OU* (November 2001); and Keir Thorpe, *CURVE-L37: Lessons from developing conferencing for the Arab OU on TU170 and T171* (April 2002).

71 The NASDAQ stock index rose from 600 to 5,000 points between 1996 and 2000 but then fell to 800 by 2002.

72 Tom Stein, 'VCs go back to the drawing board', *Red Herring Magazine* (25 February 2001), quoted in Thomas M. Duffy and Jamie Kirkley, 'Theory and practice in distance education: An introduction', in Thomas M. Duffy and Jamie Kirkley (eds), *Learner-centred theory and practice in distance education* (Mahwah, NJ: Lawrence Erlbaum and Associates, 2004), p. 2, www.gse.harvard.edu/~uk/otpd/participants/papers/duffy_kirkley_ch1.pdf, accessed 18 August 2011.

73 These included some for-profit bodies. See Dan Carnevale, 'Legislative audit criticizes Western Governors University', *The Chronicle of Higher Education* (14 July 2000), http://chronicle.com/weekly/v47/i06/06a04802. htm, accessed 18 August 2011; Scott Carlson and Dan Carnevale, 'Debating the demise of NYUonline', *The Chronicle of Higher Education* (12 December 2001), http://chronicle.com/article/Debating-the-Demise-of/23290, accessed 18 August 2011.

74 Katrina A. Meyer, 'The closing of the U.S. Open University', *Educause Quarterly*, 29:2 (2006), pp. 5–7; Lynette M. Krenelka 'A review of the short life of the US Open University', *New Directions for Higher Education*, 146 (Summer 2009), 65–72; Michael Arnone, 'United States Open U. to close after spending $20 million', *The Chronicle of Higher Education* (15

February 2002), http://chronicle.com/article/United-States-Open-U-to-Close/24049, accessed 18 August 2011.

75 Table 182, National Center for Educational Statistics, Fall Enrollment and Number of Institutions of Higher Education and Degree-Granting Institutions, by Affiliation 1980 to 1997, http://nces.ed.gov/programs/digest/d99/d99t182.asp, accessed 18 August 2011.

76 www.onlinems.umbc.edu, accessed 1 October 2012.

77 www.open.ac.uk/johndanielspeeches/FIEKansas.htm, accessed 15 August 2011; Sir John Daniel, 'Offering a high-quality engineering degree by distance education', paper to Frontiers of Education conference, Kansas City, 2000. Available at www.open.ac.uk/johndanielspeeches/FIEKansas.htm, accessed 15 August 2011. Jarvis attended this speech; *Independent*, 3 August 1999, www.independent.co.uk/life-style/open-eye-chancellor-for-usou-1110335.html, accessed 18 August 2011. 'Sister institution' was a term also used by Lynette M. Krenelka, 'A review of the short life', p. 65. *The Chronicle of Higher Education* preferred 'Open U.'s American spinoff' (15 September 2000), http://chronicle.com/article/Open-Us-American-Spinoff/8438, accessed 18 August 2011.

78 Goldie Blumenstyk, 'Distance learning at the Open University', *The Chronicle of Higher Education* (23 July 1999), http://chronicle.com/article/Distance-Learning-at-the-Open/23488, accessed 18 August 2011.

79 *Business Wire*, 21 August 2001, www.thefreelibrary.com/At+the+U.S.+Open+University+the+Quest+For+Knowledge+Is+As+Easy+As+...-a077366737, accessed 18 August 2011.

80 There were some British terms which need to be changed to make the language comprehensible to North Americans. See G. Blumenstyk, 'Logging in with … Richard S. Jarvis', *The Chronicle of Higher Education* (22 August 2000), http://chronicle.com/article/Open-Us-American-Spinoff/106475, accessed 18 August 2011; www.open.ac.uk/johndanielspeeches/ScotFund.htm, accessed 24 October 2011.

81 Conference speech in Kansas in October 2000, www.open.ac.uk/johndanielspeeches/FIEKansas.htm, accessed 15 August 2011.

82 Conference speech in Kansas in October 2000. Born in Nottingham, Jarvis was an undergraduate and doctoral student at Cambridge, UK, before becoming the Chancellor of the University and Community College System of Nevada. He was later Provost at the University of Texas at El Paso. See Rick Shearer, 'Speaking personally with Dr. Richard S Jarvis', *American Journal of Distance Education*, 13:3 (1999), 73–8 (p. 73), www.tandfonline.com/doi/abs/10.1080/08923649909527037, accessed 18 August 2011.

83 'Banking on its reputation, the Open University starts an operation in the U.S.' was the headline employed by *The Chronicle of Higher Education* (23 July 1999), http://chronicle.com/article/Banking-on-Its-Reputation-the/12231, accessed 18 August 2011.

84 Mohammed I. Zakari and Fahad Alkhezzi, 'The role of the Arab Open University, as a distance education institution, in social communication and development in the Arab Region', *Education*, 131:2 (2010), 279, 280.

85 Title IV Programs, http://federalstudentaid.ed.gov/about/title4_programs. html, accessed 18 August 2011.

86 www.arabou.edu.kw/index.php?option=com_k2&view=item&id=85: open-learning&Itemid=446&tmpl=component&print=1&lang=en, accessed 9 July 2012.

87 Shearer, 'Speaking personally with Dr. Richard S Jarvis', p. 73.

88 www.ouworldwide.com/pdfs/AOUpartnership.pdf, accessed 1 July 2013.

89 www.open.ac.uk/platform/news-and-features/despite-the-turmoil-its-busi ness-usual-arab-ou, accessed 1 July 2013.

90 Zakari and Alkhezzi, 'The role of the Arab Open University', pp. 281, 283.

91 See Keir Thorpe, *CURVE L-48: Lessons from the Certificate in Management Short Courses* (November 2002). Available via the OU's Knowledge Network.

92 Angela Harrison, '"Shameful waste" on e-university', *BBC News*, 9 June 2004, http://news.bbc.co.uk/1/hi/education/3791001.stm, accessed 18 April 2013. For a fuller account see Richard Garrett, 'The real story behind the failure of U.K. eUniversity', *Educause Quarterly*, 4 (2004), 4–6, http://net. educause.edu/ir/library/pdf/eqm0440.pdf, accessed 18 April 2013.

93 Quoted in the report on the UKeU made to the Commons, House of Commons Education and Skills Committee, *UK e-University Third Report of Session 2004–05*, Q373, Ev 54, www.publications.parliament.uk/pa/ cm200405/cmselect/cmeduski/205/205.pdf, accessed 18 April 2013.

94 www.ouworldwide.com/pdfs/simfactsheet.pdf, accessed 2 October 2012.

95 Between 2004 and 2006 an Australian university delivered a virtual degree programme to Kenya, Ethiopia, Tanzania and Rwanda. See Victor Egan, 'The promise and polemics of virtual higher education in Sub-Saharan Africa: A case study of a transnational business program', *Journal of the World Universities Forum*, 5:1 (2012), 23–6.

96 www.open.ac.uk/deep/Public/web/index.php, accessed 2 October 2012.

97 J.-C. Smeby and J. Trondal, 'Globalisation or Europeanisation? International contact among university staff', *Higher Education*, 49:4 (2005), 450; Peter Scott, 'Massification, internationalisation and globalisation', in P. Scott (ed.), *The globalisation of higher education* (Buckingham: SHRE, The Open University, 1998), pp. 108–29. The relationship is also considered in Annneliese Dodds, 'How does globalisation interact with higher education? The continuing lack of consensus', *Comparative Education*, 44:4 (November 2008), 505–17.

98 Christine T. Ennew and Yang Fujia, 'Foreign universities in China: A case study', *European Journal of Education*, 44:1 (2009), 21–36.

99 www.liv.ac.uk/xjtlu/vision-strategy/index.htm, accessed 24 October 2011.

100 *Financial Statements for the year ended 31 July 2010* (Milton Keynes: The Open University, 2010), p. 10.

101 *The Times* (21 June 1976).

102 Sector-wide performance indicators were introduced in 1992, and from 1999 there were also sector-wide statistical benchmarks.

103 OU Senate S/87/Min 21.6. Available in The Open University Archive.

104 Alan Woodley, Lee Taylor and Bernadette Butcher, 'Critical reflections on developing an equal opportunities action plan for black and ethnic minorities', in Terry Evans and Daryl Nation (eds), *Reforming open and distance education: Critical reflections from practice* (London: Kogan Page, 1993), p. 156.

105 Woodley, Taylor and Butcher, 'Critical reflections', pp. 151, 157.

106 The Polytechnic Central Admissions System and the Universities Central Council on Admissions began monitoring in 1990.

107 John Daniel, *Mega-universities and knowledge media: Technology strategies for higher education* (London: Kogan Page, 1998).

108 Martin Trow, 'Academic standards and mass higher education', *Higher Education Quarterly*, 41:3 (June 1987), 268–92; Martin Trow, 'American higher education: Past, present future', *Educational Researcher*, 17:3 (April 1988), 13–23.

109 On the evidence of effectiveness see Michael L. Shattock, 'Research, administration and university management: What can research contribute to policy?', in R. Begg (ed.), *The dialogue between higher education research and practice* (Dordrecht: Kluwer Academic, 2003).

110 Henkel, *Academic identities*, p. 227.

111 John Daniel, 'The future of distance learning in management development', *Executive Development*, 7:5 (1994), 24, 26.

112 Bruce King, 'Managing the changing nature of distance and open education at institutional level', *Open Learning*, 16:1 (2001), 48.

113 Bruce King, 'Managing change for sustainability', in A. Hope and P. Guiton (eds), *Strategies for sustainable open and distance learning* (London: Routledge, 2005).

114 Maureen Barrett, 'The attitude of industry to the Open University', *Teaching at a Distance*, 18 (Winter 1980), 65–6.

115 N. McIntosh and M. Rigg, *Employers and the Open University*, mimeo, Survey Research Department Paper No. 162 (Milton Keynes: The Open University, 1982); A. Kirkwood, N. Farnes, G. Hales and A. Hughes, *Employers study 1992: Report on the qualitative phase*, Student Research Centre Report No. 72 (Milton Keynes: IET, The Open University, 1992).

116 *Intellect* represented around 800 organisations including BAE Systems, BT, HP, IBM, Intel, Logica, Microsoft, Motorola, Nokia, Philips, SAP and Sony.

117 Organisations participating in Postgraduate Certificate in IT Professional Practice, the first part of the e-Skills Professional Programme, included

British Airways, the Cabinet Office, Metropolitan Police, NHS IT and the Prison Service.

118 Lord Browne *et al.*, *Securing a sustainable future for higher education: An independent review of higher education funding and student finance* (London: Department for Employment and Learning, October 2010), p. 14, www.delni. gov.uk/index/publications/pubs-higher-education/browne-report-student-fees.htm, accessed 4 November 2011.

119 Ernie Lowe, www8.open.ac.uk/researchprojects/historyofou/story/students, accessed 4 November 2011. For accounts of career moves by other students see Rob Catlow, Doris Lawrence, Roger Daniels, Patricia Palmer, Maggie Bailey, Dr Georgina Lang, Professor Anthony Johnson, Lewis Evans, Frank Cripps, Sheila A. Evans, Linda Kirk, Alan Gordon, Martyn Perks and John Whatmore, www8.open.ac.uk/researchprojects/historyofou/story/students, accessed 4 November 2011. There is also the example of Terry Lewins, OU Oral History Project. Terry Lewins was a teacher without a degree who studied through the OU, graduated in 1973 and went on to become a headteacher and an inspector. Jacqueline Cooper and Vanessa Worship made similar points about the impact of their studies. They were interviewed by Ronald Mcintyre. The recordings were made with the support of a grant from the Society for Research into Higher Education.

120 Anne Vickers, 'An open learning system for careers guidance', *Open Learning*, 6:1 (February 1991), 63, 60.

121 B. Swift, *What OU graduates have done* (Milton Keynes: The Open University, 1982); Alan Woodley, 'Graduation and beyond', *Open Learning*, 3:1 (1988), 13–17.

122 Alan Woodley and Claire Simpson, 'Learning and earning: Measuring rates of return among mature graduates from part-time distance courses', *Higher Education Quarterly*, 55:1 (2001), 32.

123 Patricia Lunneborg, *OU men: Work through lifelong learning* (Cambridge: Lutterworth, 1997), pp. 130–1.

124 Jim Gallacher and Fiona Reeve, *Work-based learning: The implications for higher education and for supporting informal learning in the workplace*, Working Papers of the Global Colloquium on Supporting Lifelong Learning (Milton Keynes: The Open University, 2000), www.open.ac.uk/lifelong-learning/papers/3937BC34-0008-6511-0000015700000157_freevejgallacher paper-noabstract.doc, accessed 9 September 2011.

125 Naomi Sargent, 'The Open University', in Roger Fieldhouse, *A history of modern British adult education* (Leicester: NIACE, 1996), pp. 290–307.

126 *Report of the Vice-Chancellor, 1990*, p. 4.

127 Intended to be one of a number of low-cost, low-maintenance postgraduate courses, D833 took over two years to prepare. A number of texts were commissioned and extensive software updates were required. In 2000 the Chair

personally observed negotiations at the UN in New York. Presentation costs were high and the course attracted only seventeen students.

128 See David Humphreys, 'The pedagogy and practice of role-play: Using a negotiation simulation to teach social science theory', *Proceedings of the International Conference on Computers in Education (ICCE) 'Learning Communities on the Internet: Pedagogy in Implementation'* (Auckland, New Zealand, 3–6 December 2002).

129 Linda Price, *D833 Review* (PLUM Report, Institute of Educational Technology, The Open University, 2003). At the conclusion of the first presentation of D833 many of the students gathered to meet one another in real life.

130 *Report of the Vice-Chancellor, 2000*, pp. 11, 16; *Report of the Vice-Chancellor, 2002*, p. 14.

131 *Report of the Vice-Chancellor, 2000*, p. 11.

132 COBE, *Action research: A guide for associate lecturers* (Milton Keynes: The Open University, 2005), pp. 11, 15, www.open.ac.uk/cobe/docs/AR-Guide-final.pdf, accessed 15 April 2013.

133 Daniel, 'The future', p. 24.

134 Dearing (chair), *Higher education*, p. 1.

135 Caroline Bucklow and Paul Clark, 'The role of the Institute for Learning and Teaching in Higher Education in supporting professional development in learning and teaching in higher education', *Teacher Development*, 4:1 (2000), 7–13.

136 On the developments of this period see C. Ball, *Learning pays: The role of post compulsory education and training* (London: Royal Society of Arts, 1991); QAA, *The framework for qualifications of higher education institutions in Scotland* (London: QAA, 2001); QAA, *The framework for higher education qualifications in England, Wales and Northern Ireland*, 2nd edn (London: FHEQ, 2008).

137 Celia Whitchurch, *Reconstructing identities in higher education: The rise of the 'third space' professional* (London: Routledge, 2012); *Times Higher Education* (7 October 2010), www.timeshighereducation.co.uk/news/market-forces-blamed-for-30-increase-in-managers/413740.article, accessed 18 August 2012.

138 S. Court, *Long hours, little thanks: A survey of the use of time by full-time academic and related staff in the traditional UK universities* (London: Association of University Teachers, 1994), p. 14; Association of University Teachers, Update 50, 30 April 1998, p. 1; Mark Baimbridge, 'Academic staff salaries: Equity and exploitation', *Applied Economics Letters*, 2:12 (1995), 469–72.

139 Alan Woodley, 'But does it work? Evaluation theories and approaches in distance education', in Terry Evans, Margaret Haughey and David Murphy (eds), *The international handbook of distance education* (Bingley: Emerald, 2008), p. 587.

140 *Review of the Open University*, p. 49. Further and Higher Education Act 1992, c.13, Part II, Section 68.

141 The term was said to be used by some of his colleagues according to Joe Haines, *Independent* (1 October 1998), www.independent.co.uk/news/education/education-news/open-eye-how-harolds-pet-project-became-his-monument-1175330.html, accessed 2 January 2013.

142 Richard Taylor and Tom Steele, *British labour and higher education, 1945 to 2000: Ideologies, policies and practice* (London: Continuum, 2011), pp. 112, 22.

143 Taylor and Steele, *British labour*, p. 11. See also George Monbiot, *Captive state: The corporate takeover of Britain* (London: Pan, 2001).

144 On this notion of the role of universities see Pierre Bourdieu and Jean-Claude Passeron, *Reproduction in education, society and culture*, trans. Richard Nice (London: Sage, 1990).

145 www.insidegovernment.co.uk/economic_dev/higher-education-system, accessed 24 October 2011.

Chapter 6

1 Stephen Brookfield, *Self-directed learning: From theory to practice* (San Francisco: Jossey-Bass, 1985), p. 9.

2 Greville Rumble, 'Labour market theories and distance education III: Post-Fordism – the way forward?', *Open Learning*, 10:3 (November 1995), 25–42.

3 On a few modules students do not have tutors allocated to them.

4 Alison Ashby, 'Monitoring student retention in the Open University: Definition, measurement, interpretation and action', *Open Learning*, 19:1 (February 2004), 71.

5 Anne Vickers, 'An open learning system for careers guidance', *Open Learning*, 6:1 (1991), 59; Judith Fage, 'Vocational guidance provision: An international survey', *Open Learning*, 3:1 (1991), 53; P. Maher, 'The UK OU "Enterprise in Higher Education" programme', *Open Learning*, 6:1 (1991), 51.

6 Michael Fielding, 'Valuing difference in teachers and learners: Building on Kolb's learning styles to develop a language of teaching and learning', *The Curriculum Journal*, 5:3 (1994), 393–417.

7 David A. Kolb, *Experiential learning: Experience as the source of learning and development* (Englewood Cliffs, NJ: Prentice-Hall, 1984), p. 38.

8 Anne Vickers, 'New open learning programme on personal and career development', *Open Learning*, 8:1 (February 1993), 54.

9 Vickers, 'New open learning programme', p. 55.

10 Mary Thorpe, 'Encouraging students to reflect as part of an assignment process: Student responses and tutor feedback', *Active learning in higher education*, 1:1 (2000), 79–92.

11 'Notes from the Precambrian of the OU', uploaded by Matt Kendall, www8. open.ac.uk/researchprojects/historyofou/memories/notes-the-precambrian-the-ou, accessed 29 July 2011.

12 A. Jones, E. Scanlon, C. Tosunoglu, S. Ross, P. Butcher, P. Murphy and J. Greenberg, 'Evaluating CAL at the OU, 15 years on', *Computers and Education*, 26:1–3 (1996), 5–15.

13 T. Evans and D. Nation (eds), *Critical reflections on distance education* (Lewes: Falmer, 1989); Tony Bates, 'Computer assisted learning or communications: Which way for information technology in distance education?', *Journal of Distance Education / Revue de l'Éducation à distance*, 1:1 (1986).

14 By 1995 the number of courses requiring a computer stood at twenty. Jones *et al.*, 'Evaluating CAL', pp. 5–6.

15 Robin Mason and Paul Bacsich, 'Embedding computer conferencing into university teaching', *Computers & Education*, 30:3–4 (1998), 249.

16 Robin Mason, 'From distance education to online education', *Internet and Higher Education*, 3 (2000), 69.

17 Mason and Bacsich, 'Embedding', p. 249 for the figure of 13,000; Mason, 'From distance education', p. 69, for the 50,000.

18 On the impact and possibilities for online communication, specifically CoSy, for OU students see Mason and Kaye, *Mindweave*.

19 Gary Alexander, *Renewable energy technology: An interactive open learning course with technology-based support. Final report to the Training, Enterprise and Education Directorate, Department of Employment*, Report No. 52, Centre for Electronic Education (Milton Keynes: The Open University, 1994).

20 Mason and Bacsich, 'Embedding', pp. 250, 252.

21 Mason and Bacsich, 'Embedding', pp. 253, 255.

22 Christopher Bissell, 'Revitalising the engineering curriculum: The role of information technology', *Engineering Science and Education Journal*, 5:3 (June 1996), 135, 136.

23 G. Kirkup, A. Jelfs and N. Heap, *THD204 Information technology and society: First survey of tutors*, Report No. 54, Programme on Learner Use of Media (Milton Keynes: IET, The Open University, 1995), p. 17.

24 Gilly Salmon, *E-moderating: The key to teaching and learning online* (London: Kogan Page, 2000).

25 Martin Weller, 'The use of narrative to provide a cohesive structure to a web based course', *Journal of interactive media in education* (1 August 2000), 3, www-jime.open.ac.uk/article/2000-1/49, accessed 1 March 2013.

26 Mary Thorpe, *H802 study guide: Socio-cultural perspectives* (Milton Keynes: The Open University, 2002), http://kn.open.ac.uk/public/index.cfm?wpid=3796, accessed 15 April 2012.

27 Alan Tait, 'Planning student support for open and distance learning', *Open Learning*, 15:3 (2000), 289.

28 Weller, 'The use of narrative', p. 7.

29 R. Dickinson, *An evaluation of the use of video cassette machines in the regions, January 1979 to June 1980*, IET Paper on Broadcasting No. 150, mimeo (Milton Keynes: IET, The Open University, 1980).

30 S. Brown and H. U. Grundin, *The 1982 video-cassette loan service: Interim evaluation report*, IET Paper on Broadcasting No. 35, mimeo (Milton Keynes: IET, The Open University, 1982).

31 Adrian Kirkwood, *Access to video equipment for study purposes: Undergraduate students in 1986*, Student Research Centre Report No. 5 (Milton Keynes: IET, The Open University, 1987).

32 Adrian Kirkwood, 'Into the video age: Open University television in the 1990s', *Journal of Educational Television*, 16:2 (1990), 77–85.

33 Beryl Crooks and Adrian Kirkwood, *VCR access and television viewing rates: Undergraduate students in 1988*, Student Research Centre Report, No. 26, mimeo (Milton Keynes: IET, The Open University, 1989).

34 Josie Taylor, 'Access to new technologies survey 1991: Access to televisual and video-recording equipment for study purposes' (internal document, June 1992).

35 Adrian Kirkwood, 'The video cassette downloading scheme: Report of a survey in 1993' (internal report, n.d.).

36 Quoted in the *Times Higher Education Supplement* (15 December 2006).

37 A. W. Bates and M. Gallagher, *Improving the effectiveness of Open University television case studies and documentaries*, Papers on Broadcasting No. 77, mimeo (Milton Keynes: IET, The Open University, 1977).

38 Kirkwood, 'Into the video age'.

39 Beryl Crooks and Adrian Kirkwood, 'Video-cassettes by design in Open University courses', *Open Learning*, 3:3 (November 1988), 15.

40 The OU was not alone in this perception. See, for example, David R. Arendale, *History of supplemental instruction (SI): Mainstreaming of developmental education* (Kansas City: University of Missouri-Kansas City, 2000), http://a.web.umkc.edu/arendaled/SIhistory02.pdf, accessed 29 February 2012.

41 Pat Atkins and Jo Beard, *Learning with practitioners. Rationale: frameworks: learning* (Milton Keynes: The Open University, 2010), p. 21.

42 www8.open.ac.uk/researchprojects/historyofou/story/students, accessed 2 February 2012.

43 www8.open.ac.uk/researchprojects/historyofou/story/students, accessed 2 February 2012.

44 Jacqueline Cooper, interviewed by Ronald Mcintyre, 12 January 2012. This recording was made with the support of a grant from the Society for Research into Higher Education.

45 Michael Drake, 'The democratisation of historical research: The case for DA301', *Journal of the Society of Archivists*, 17:2 (1996), 201.

46 Students could also use course-specific radio and television broadcasts. The MSc programme in *Industrial applications of computers* involved substantial home kit components, including the HEKTOR III microcomputer system and a fully programmable robot, while students on *Robotics in manufacturing*, PT615 (1984–91), received a robot arm in the post.

47 *The end of the course*, Open University, T100/34, contributors Dr Keith Attenborough, Geoffrey Holister and John Beishon. 25min.00sec, The Open University, 1972. Some broadcast material is available via the OU Archives.

48 Jonathan Silvertown, OU Professor of Ecology, quoted on www8.open. ac.uk/science/main/about-the-faculty/case-studies/geographical, accessed 16 October 2010.

49 Jane Henry, 'The course tutor and project work', *Teaching at a Distance*, 9 (July 1977), 1–12.

50 Jane Henry, *Teaching through projects* (London: Kogan Page in association with IET, 1984), p. 17.

51 L. M. Cook, G. S. Mani and M. E. Varley, 'Postindustrial melanism in the peppered moth', *Science*, 231 (1986), 611–13.

52 The East Anglian Studies Resources pack, PA730 (1984–97). See Jill Turner, 'Open learning resources for local studies', *Open Learning*, 2:1 (February 1987), 43–5.

53 Jane Matthews, 'All they ever wanted to know about energy use', in *Learn & Live* (Milton Keynes: The Open University, 1994), p. 21.

54 Diana Laurillard, 'Multimedia and the learner's experience of narrative', *Computers and Education*, 31:3 (1998), 233.

55 Robin Mason, 'Effective facilitation of online learning: The Open University experience', in John Stephenson (ed.), *Teaching and learning online: Pedagogies for new technologies* (London: Kogan Page 2001), 71.

56 Robin Mason, *IET's Masters in Open and Distance Education: What have we learned?*, CITE Report No. 248 (Milton Keynes: IET, The Open University, 1999), p. 7, http://kn.open.ac.uk/document.cfm?documentid=142, accessed 1 November 2012.

57 Mason, 'Effective facilitation', p. 75.

58 Diana Laurillard, 'The E-University: What have we learned?', *International Journal of Management Education*, 1:2 (2001), 4.

59 Open University, *Becoming a student: Frequently asked questions* (2006), cited in Sarah Cornelius and Janet Macdonald, 'Online informal professional development for distance tutors: Experiences from The Open University in Scotland', *Open Learning*, 23:1 (February 2008), 44.

60 Stephen Peake, James Aczel and Pascale Hardy, *Opportunities and barriers in relation to use of various types of ICTs, a report prepared for the United Nations Institute of Training and Research Climate Change Capacity Development Project* (Milton Keynes: The Open University, 2005), p. 13.

61 On T885 see M. Thorpe and R. Edmunds, 'Practices with technology: Learning at the boundary between study and work', *Journal of Computer Assisted Learning*, 27:5 (2011), 385–98.

62 Jim Moffatt, Mary Thorpe, Robert Edmunds, Mark Endean, Barbara Jones, Bob Reuben and George Weidmann, 'Technology supports distributed team working: The case of T885, *Team Engineering at the Open University*', paper for ICL2009 (23–25 September 2009), Villach, Austria, www.icl-conference.org/dl/proceedings/2009/program/pdf/Contribution_121.pdf, accessed 12 March 2013.

63 See www3.open.ac.uk/study/undergraduate/course/t189.htm, accessed 2 February 2012.

64 http://learn2.open.ac.uk/mod/oucontent/view.php?id=56319, accessed 1 May 2012.

65 http://learn.open.ac.uk/mod/oucontent/view.php?id=576650&section=3, accessed 21 March 2012.

66 Dave Philips, interviewed by Ronald Macintyre, 30 May 2012. This recording was made with the support of a grant from the Society for Research into Higher Education.

67 Phil Carey, Julie Ann Cole, Michael John Deller and others, comments, www3.open.ac.uk/coursereviews/course.aspx?course=t189, accessed 2 February 2012.

68 Two student reviews posted on www3.open.ac.uk/coursereviews/course.aspx?course=t189, accessed 20 October 2012.

69 www.flickr.com/help/general/#1, accessed 20 April 2012.

70 E. Chambers and J. Rae, *Evaluation of the Homer CD-ROM: Final report* (Milton Keynes: The Open University, 1999). http://kn.open.ac.uk/public/getfile.cfm?documentfileid=111, accessed 20 April 2012.

71 Diana Laurillard, 'Multimedia and the learner's experience', p. 239; Jeremy Burke and Marianthi Papadimitriou, 'Narratives and maps for effective pedagogy in hypermedia learning environments', *Goldsmiths Journal of Education* (2001), 1–13, www.mendeley.com/research/narratives-maps-effective-pedagogy-hypermedia-learning-environments, accessed 23 March 2012; Diana Laurillard, M. Stratford, R. Luckin, L. Plowman and J. Taylor, 'Affordances for learning in a non-linear narrative medium', *Journal of Interactive Media in Education*, 2 (2000), 6.

72 Peake *et al.*, *Opportunities and barriers*, p. 13. For the news release see www3.open.ac.uk/media/fullstory.aspx?id=411, accessed 2 July 2013.

73 On the wider technological context see www.schome.ac.uk/wiki/An_history_of_new_technology_at_the_Open_University, accessed 16 April 2012.

74 Denise Whitelock, *Going live to the Galapagos Islands and an oak wood: S103 student responses to some biological multimedia programs (Blocks 4/5)*, PLUM report 138 (Milton Keynes: IET, The Open University, 1998).

75 The S216 Teign Valley Virtual Field Trip won the Society for Screen-Based Learning Interactive Adult Learning Award in 2003.

76 Allan Jones, Christopher Bissell and David Chapman, 'Open resources for case studies and assignments', paper presented to EADTU (European Association of Distance Teaching Universities) 25th Annual Conference 2012, 'The role of open and flexible education in European higher education systems for 2020: New models, new markets, new media' (Paphos, Cyprus, 27–28 September 2012), www.open.ac.uk/blogs/sirg/author/jonesa, accessed 7 November 2013.

77 Jones *et al.*, 'Evaluating CAL', p. 7.

78 http://intranet6.open.ac.uk/inclusion-collaborative-partnerships/main/files/cic-i/file/ecms/web-content/Undergraduate-Levels-Framework.pdf, accessed 1 March 2013.

79 *Annual Report 1992* (Milton Keynes: The Open University, 1993), p. 2.

80 *Annual Report 1992*, p. 6.

81 Daisy Mwanza-Simwami, Patrick McAndrew and Matete Madiba, 'Fostering open educational practices in cross-cultural contexts', *IST-Africa 2008 Conference Proceedings,* pp. 1–8, p. 3, www.ist-africa.org/conference 2013/default.asp?pagestart=501&page=paper-repository&, accessed 1 November 2013.

82 Kim Hammond, *Teaching of environmental studies at the Open University 1971–2009* (Report for the History of the Open University Project, October 2012).

83 See Peter Green, *Design education: Problem solving and visual experience* (London: Batsford, 1984). See also the Design Council reports *Design education at secondary level* (London: Design Council, 1980) and *Design and primary education* (London: Design Council, 1987), and K. Baynes, 'Defining a design dimension of the curriculum', *Journal of Art & Design Education*, 4:3 (1985), 237–43. In 1980 a degree which assessed the relationship between technologies and the environment, Engineering Design and Appropriate Technology, was first offered at the University of Warwick.

84 Margaret E. Varley, 'Ecology projects: An innovation', *Teaching at a Distance*, 2 (February 1975), 27–30.

85 *Panorama: The Challenge of the Sixties* (1960); *Spotlight: Population* (1965); *Tomorrow's World: Population Explosion* (1966). Thanks to Kim Hammond for this information. The text was Donella H. Meadows, Dennis L. Meadows, Jørgen Randers and William W. Behrens III, *The limits to growth* (London: Universe Books, 1972).

86 *Report of the Vice-Chancellor, 1990*, p. 10.

87 Philip Sarre interviewed by Kim Hammond. Quoted in Hammond, *Teaching of environmental studies*, p. 14.

88 Hammond, *Teaching of environmental studies*, pp. 11, 14, 15.

89 Mary Thorpe and Steve Godwin, 'The impact of interaction on U316, *The environmental web*: The tutors' perspective', *ICHE: The Impact of Interaction and Integration in computer-mediated teaching in higher education: Report 3* (2006), pp. 2, 11, http://kn.open.ac.uk/document. cfm?docid=7727, accessed 20 April 2012.

90 http://ispot.org.uk, accessed 19 October 2012.

91 www.open.ac.uk/platform/news-and-features/ou-senior-lecturer-named-most-innovative-teacher-the-year, accessed 29 April 2013.

92 Aletha C. Huston, Edward Donnerstein, Halford Fairchild, Norma D. Feshbach, Phyllis A. Katz, John P. Murray, Eli A. Rubinstein, Brian L. Wilcox and Diana M. Zuckerman, *Big world, small screen: The role of television in American society* (Lincoln, NE, and London: University of Nebraska Press, 1992).

93 Josie Taylor, 'Report on the Open University drop-in viewing audience pilot survey' (internal report, 1991).

94 www.bbc.co.uk/programmes/p00p138b, accessed 25 November 2013.

95 OpenLearn Web site: http://openlearn.open.ac.uk, accessed 13 April 2014.

96 http://creativecommons.org, accessed 1 June 2013.

97 Reported to the author by another Pro-Vice-Chancellor, David Vincent, email 29 November 2013.

98 Mwanza-Simwami, McAndrew and Madiba, 'Fostering open educational practices'.

99 https://moodle.org/mod/forum/discuss.php?d=34002; A. Walton, M. Weller and G. Conole, 'Social:Learn – Widening participation and the sustainability of higher education', paper to *EDEN 2008: Annual Conference of the European Distance and E-Learning Network* (11–14 May 2008), Lisbon, www.citeulike.org/user/marclijour/article/3075323, accessed 1 November 2012; Social:Learn Web site: http://sociallearn.open.ac.uk, accessed 1 November 2012.

100 Accessibility, sustainability, excellence: how to expand access to research publications. Report of the Working Group on Expanding Access to Published Research Findings, June 2012, www.researchinfonet.org/wp-content/uploads/2012/06/Finch-Group-report-FINAL-VERSION.pdf, accessed 14 November 2012.

101 House of Lords debate 24 July 2013, *Hansard*, column GC481, www. publications.parliament.uk/pa/ld201314/ldhansrd/text/130724-gc0001. htm#13072463000085, accessed 31 July 2013.

102 Wenger, *Communities of practice*, p. 96.

103 Interviews with Dick Hunter, Anne Langley, Diane Mehew and Michael Kemp by Ronald Mcintyre with the support of a grant from the Society for Research into Higher Education.

104 Details to be found on the FACHRS website, www.fachrs.com, accessed 2 February 2012.

105 Henry, 'The course tutor', p. 7.

106 In 1986 a tutor for the Cambridge University Board of Extra-Mural Studies organised a residential course based on the pack. Another group of learners met one another through an advertisement in a parish newsletter. See Turner, 'Open learning resources', pp. 43–5.

107 Screenshots of some of A427's CD-ROM materials were reproduced in Rosemary O'Day, 'Charles Booth and social investigation in nineteenth-century Britain', *CRAFT: The newsletter of the CTI Centre for History, Archaeology and Art History, University of Glasgow*, no. 16 (1996–97), www.arts.gla. ac.uk/CTICH/Publications/craft16_1.htm, accessed 19 April 2014.

108 Dave Philips, interview.

109 This paragraph is based on material on the online sites of the groups and on student comments on the module. See www.flickr.com/people/woodycheese; www3.open.ac.uk/coursereviews/course.aspx?course=t189; www.flickr. com/photos/woodycheese/6247405180/in/photosof-markjpearce; www. flickr.com/photos/64883940@N08/5902448713/in/photosof-markjpearce; www.flickr.com/photos/woodycheese/5607823922/in/photosof-julieswright; www.flickr.com/photos/markjpearce/5898339085/in/photosof-markjpearce; www.flickr.com/people/julieswright; www.flickr.com/groups/744249@ N20/discuss/72157625281747413; www.flickr.com/groups/744249@N20/ discuss/72157622261438891; www.flickr.com/groups/744249@N20/dis- cuss/72157621863530934; www.flickr.com/groups/1197338@N24/ and www.flickr.com/people/markjpearce; www.flickr.com/groups/744249@ N20/discuss/72157622261438891; www.flickr.com/people/fromo99, all accessed 29 February 2012. It is also based on interviews recorded by Ronald Mcintyre with Winston Edwards, Mark Pearce, Graham Shaw, Christine Cheung and Mark Simmons. These recordings were made with the support of a grant from the Society for Research into Higher Education. See also www.bursledonbrickworks.org.uk/index.php, accessed 13 April 2014.

110 Tony Whittaker, interviewed by Ronald Mcintyre, 12 January 2012. This recording was made with the support of a grant from the Society for Research into Higher Education.

111 Adrian Kirkwood, Ann Jones and Anne Jelfs, *Changing the role of tutors in distance education with information and communication technologies*, PLUM Paper 66 (January 1996), p. 1.

112 Initially each OU student was given access to both a tutor and a counsellor. Due to low student numbers in rural Wales, the roles were combined in Wales, an idea which was adopted across the rest of the OU in 1976.

113 Perry, *Open University: A personal account*, p. 113.

114 This recollection was written for the OU. See www.open.ac.uk/researchpro- jects/historyofou/memories/pioneer-counsellor, accessed 1 November 2013.

115 A. Woodley, O. Simpson and A. Jelfs, 'Early results from the 1997 costs survey', IET internal report (Milton Keynes: The Open University, 1997).

116 Interviewee recorded by Dr Wendy F. Berndt: see http://intranet.open.ac.uk/cetl/pilsintranet/pics/d63032.doc, accessed 19 April 2014.

117 O. Simpson and V. Stevens, 'Promoting student progress', *Open Learning*, 3:2 (1988), 56; M. Thorpe, *Evaluating open and distance learning* (Harlow: Longman, 1988), p. 118; J. Fage, *A strategy for counselling in academic studies: Expansion, quality and change in the 1990s*, mimeo (Milton Keynes: The Open University Regional Academic Services, 1992). See also Alan Tait, 'Guidance and counselling in the Open University', in Megan Crawford, Richard Edwards and Lesley Kidd (eds), *Taking issue: Debates in guidance and counselling in learning* (London: RoutledgeFalmer, 1998).

118 Perry, *Open University: A personal account*, p. 113. Alan Tait, 'Rethinking learner support in the Open University UK: A case study', in Alan Tait and Roger Mills (eds), *Rethinking learner support in distance education: Change and continuity in an international context* (London: RoutledgeFalmer, 2003), p. 187.

119 www8.open.ac.uk/researchprojects/historyofou/story/students, accessed 23 April 2012.

120 www8.open.ac.uk/researchprojects/historyofou/story/students, accessed 23 April 2012.

121 Lunneborg, *OU women*, pp. 32–8. See also Daniel Knibb, Sarah Watt, Susan O'Donnell and Susan Jones www8.open.ac.uk/researchprojects/historyofou/story/students, accessed 23 April 2012.

122 Ashworth, *The Open University in Wales*, p. 14.

123 See J. W. George, 'Telephone counselling', in M. Crawford, R. Edwards and L. Kydd (eds), *Taking issue: Debates in guidance and counselling in learning* (London: Routledge in association with The Open University, 1998). See also *On the line: Counselling and teaching by telephone*, P519 (1983).

124 B. Robinson, I. Harrison, H. Richards, D. Brown and M. Bunker, *Tutoring by telephone: A handbook* (Milton Keynes: Regional Tutorial Services, The Open University, 1982).

125 P. Atkins, C. Baker, S. Cole, J. George, M. Haywood, M. Thorpe, N. Tomlinson and S. Whitaker, *Supporting open learners reader: A staff development reader for Open University Associate Lecturers* (Milton Keynes: The Open University, 2002), p. 98.

126 Atkins *et al.*, *Supporting open learners reader*, pp. 108, 109.

127 Atkins *et al.*, *Supporting open learners reader*, p. 106.

128 'Tutor E', who taught U316. See Mary Thorpe, 'Effective online interaction: Mapping course design to bridge from research to practice', *Australasian Journal of Educational Technology*, 24:1 (2008), 57–72.

129 Mary Thorpe, 'Rethinking learner support: The challenge of collaborative on-line learning', *Open Learning*, 17:2 (2002), 105–20.

130 Mary Thorpe, 'Collaborative on-line learning: Transforming learner support and course design', in Alan Tait and Roger Mills (eds), *Rethinking learner support in distance education* (London: RoutledgeFalmer, 2003), p. 201.

131 Roger Mills, 'The role of study centres in open and distance education: A glimpse of the future', in Roger Mills and Alan Tait (eds), *Supporting the learner in open distance learning* (London: Pitman, 1996), pp. 75, 78, 73.

132 Mary Thorpe, 'Rethinking learner support', 106.

133 Atkins *et al.*, *Supporting open learners reader*, p. 11.

134 Alan Tait, 'Planning student support for open and distance learning', *Open Learning*, 15:3 (2000), 287–99.

135 Hewitt *et al.*, 'How do I know?', p. 9.

136 A. Northedge and J. McArthur, 'Guiding students into a discipline: The significance of the teacher', in Carolin Kreber (ed.), *The university and its disciplines: teaching and learning within and beyond disciplinary boundaries* (New York and Oxford: Routledge, 2009), pp. 107–18.

137 *Times Higher Education* (23 April 2009), www.timeshighereducation. co.uk/story.asp?storyCode=406249&sectioncode=26, accessed 20 April 2012; HM Treasury, *Securing the recovery: Growth and opportunity*, Pre-Budget Report, CM 7747 (London: HM Treasury, 2009), p. 114.

138 www.open.ac.uk/opencetl/practice-based-professional-learning/activities-projects/funded-projects-and-investigations/co-creating-learning-tutor-reflection, accessed 13 March 2013.

139 Pat Atkins, 'Transformation and integration through research and enquiry: A Centre for Excellence in Teaching and Learning perspective', in Margaret Weaver (ed.), *Transformative learning support models in higher education: Educating the whole student* (London: Facet Press, 2008).

140 M. McLure Wasko and S. Faraj, '"It is what one does": Why people participate and help others in electronic communities of practice', *The Journal of Strategic Information Systems*, 9:2–3 (September 2000), 155–73; PILS (Personalised Integrated Learning Support) CETL, *Supporting student progression: Theory: context: practice* (Milton Keynes: The Open University, 2010), p. 3.

141 *Report of the Vice-Chancellor, 1992*, p. 8.

142 *Report of the Vice-Chancellor, 1990*, p. 22.

143 Atkins *et al.*, *Supporting open learners reader*, p. 15.

144 G. Gibbs and O. Simpson, 'Conditions under which assessment supports students' learning', *Studies in Higher Education*, 32:1 (2004–05), 3–31. See also *Open University toolkit* (Milton Keynes: The Open University, 2004), and *Teaching and learning with the Open University: A guide for associate lecturers* (Milton Keynes: The Open University, 2008).

145 Quoted in Elizabeth J. Burge, *Flexible higher education: Reflections from expert experience* (London: The Society for Research into Higher Education and The Open University, 2007), p. 31.

146 Atkins *et al.*, *Supporting open learners reader*, pp. 123–36.

147 P. Hewitt, H. Lentell, M. Philips and V. Stevens, 'How do I know I am doing a good job?', *Open University toolkit* (Milton Keynes: The Open University, 1997), p. 5.

148 *Supported open learning reader* (Milton Keynes: The Open University, 1996), p. 114.

149 James P. Warren and Anne F. Gaskell, 'Tutors as learners: Overcoming barriers to learning ICT skills', in *The European Conference on Educational Research, ECER, 2002* (Lisbon, 11–14 September 2002), pp. 5, 11.

150 Atkins *et al.*, *Supporting open learners reader*, pp. 33–4.

151 Pat Atkins, Joanne Bard, Patrick Kelly and Charlotte Stevens, *PILS CETL: Final evaluation report 2010* (Milton Keynes: The Open University, 2010), p. 27.

152 Maggie Coats, *Action research: A guide for associate lecturers* (Milton Keynes: The Open University, 2005), p. 11.

153 Coats, *Action research*, p. 12.

154 Coats, *Action research*, pp. 13–14.

155 Leaflet produced by the PILS CETL that sought to better integrate learner support at the university with the development and delivery of curriculum. The Open CETL www8.open.ac.uk/opencetl/files/opencetl/file/ecms/web-content/PILS-Consultants-Leaflet.pdf, accessed 1 December 2012.

156 Natasha Sigala, 'Investigating the use of tutorial group conferences as a teaching tool', www8.open.ac.uk/opencetl/personalised-integrated-learning-support/activities-projects/investigating-the-use-tutorial-group-conferences-teaching-tool, accessed 1 December 2012.

157 Isobel Shelton, 'Geographical skill development and the identity of students as geographers', www8.open.ac.uk/opencetl/personalised-integrated-learning-support/activities-projects/geographical-skill-development-and-the-identity-students-geographer, accessed 1 December 2012.

158 *PILS collection* (Milton Keynes: The Open University, 2010), pp. 63–6.

159 eBooks and Mobiles Project Blog, www.open.ac.uk/blogs/ebooksmobiles, accessed 1 December 2012.

160 Christensen *et al.*, 'Disruption in education', pp. 19–44, 26–32.

Chapter 7

1 Part of the mission of the OU was, noted its inaugural Chancellor, to be open as to people, places, methods and ideas.

2 Address by Lord Geoffrey Crowther at the formal inauguration of The Open University, July 1969.

3 For the wider picture see H. Willmott, 'Managing the academics: Commodification and control in the development of university education in the UK', *Human Relations*, 48 (1995), 993–1025.

4 Ormond Simpson, 'Does the OU do more harm than good?' Paper presented to *Widening participation in the 21st century: A decade of learning*, conference, 24 and 25 June 2010, www8.open.ac.uk/about/wideningparticipation/files/wideningparticipation/Ormond%20Simpson%20-%20DOES%20

THE%20OU%20DO%20MORE%20HARM%20THAN%20GOOD. pdf, accessed 10 November 2010.

5 Students' learning journals quoted in Pat Atkins and Jo Beard, *Learning with practitioners. Rationale: frameworks: learning* (Milton Keynes: The Open University, 2010), p. 26.

6 www8.open.ac.uk/platform/services/study-support/residential-school-students-tell-it-it, accessed 5 September 2012.

7 'There was a lorry driver, there was a retired dentist, there were women who worked in shops, there was a librarian, there were a couple of teachers, there was people that worked in factories. I mean it was a huge big spread.' Description of a first tutorial by Ailsa Swarbrick, OU Oral History Project. Ailsa Swarbrick worked in Adult Education in Tanzania for five years before she joined The Open University in 1974 as a part-time counsellor. She became a tutor-counsellor, a part-time tutor 1978, an assistant staff tutor and then a full-time senior counsellor for Yorkshire, 1982–98.

8 The University of Sussex opened in 1961 with 52 students and plans for 3,000 by 1970: Norman MacKenzie, 'Starting a new university', *Universities Quarterly*, 15 (1960–61), 139–51. In 1965 the University of Warwick opened with 450 undergraduates.

9 *The Times* (1 August 1970); *The Times* (24 June 1970); editorial 'Over the air', *The Times* (14 August 1970).

10 *The Times* (13 August 1970).

11 Martin Trow, *Problems in the transition from elite to mass higher education*, (Berkeley, CA: Carnegie Commission on Higher Education, 1974); G. Neave, 'The future of the city of intellect', *European Education: Issues and Studies*, 34:3 (2002), 20–41.

12 Ferguson, *The Open University from within*, p. 117.

13 www.independent.co.uk/student/news/the-televised-revolution-1679156. html, accessed 20 May 2011.

14 Michael Drake quoted in Ferguson, *The Open University from within*, p. 117.

15 Quoted in Simpson, 'This door is alarmed', 15.

16 W. E. Styler, 'Part-time degrees: The missing element in British universities', *Adult Education*, 41:2 (July 1968), 75. These first OU graduates were not full-time but were ones who had prior credits from other institutions.

17 Wilson, *Memoirs*, p. 196.

18 Quoted in Gayfer, 'Can the open university concept', p. 21.

19 www8.open.ac.uk/about/main, accessed 17 August 2012.

20 Accurate data about students' destinations is difficult to obtain as once students have completed the modules they require at the OU they simply cease to sign on for further modules.

21 www8.open.ac.uk/researchprojects/historyofou/story/students, accessed 2 February 2012.

22 There is a building named after him on East Campus, Milton Keynes.

23 A study of full-time young students who dropped out of universities who were not OU students indicated that they had a higher chance of depression and other illness than graduates. See J. Bynner, P. Dolton, L. Feinstein, G. Makepeace, L. Malmberg and L. Woods, *Revisiting the benefits of higher education* (London: HEFCE, 2003).

24 Naomi E. McIntosh and Alan Woodley, 'The Open University and second-chance education: An analysis of the social and educational background of Open University students', *Paedagogica Europaea: Review of Education in Europe*, 9:2 (1974), 85–6. It has also been suggested that by 1981 almost 60 per cent of those who enrolled since 1971 had graduated: see Peter Gosden, *The education system since 1945* (Oxford: Martin Robinson, 1983), p. 162.

25 Data compiled by IET Student Statistics Team, 13 March 2012.

26 There are a number of definitions as to who can be considered a student and what constitutes equivalence to a full-time student. Many of those who learn through the OU have studied packs or individual modules, not for degrees.

27 *The Times* (28 January 1977).

28 *The Economist* (29 November 1976).

29 Quoted in Lunneborg, *OU men*, p. 117. Flintoff, a professional actor and director, has appeared on an OU iTunesU compilation, *Science communication and public engagement*, www.open.edu/openlearn/science-maths-technology/science/across-the-sciences/science-communication-and-public-engagement, accessed 19 April 2014.

30 Roger Thompson, quoted in Ferguson, *The Open University from within*, p. 95.

31 Gary Slapper, OU Oral History Project. Born in 1958, Gary Slapper was Director of the Law Degree at the University of Staffordshire before becoming Director of The Open University Law Programme in 1997. He left The Open University in October 2011.

32 Alan Woodley, '"Open as to people": The people's response to the Open University of the United Kingdom 1971–2009', *Éducation et sociétés*, 2:26 (2010), 13–27.

33 Data compiled by IET Student Statistics Team, 13 March 2012; www.open.ac.uk/about, accessed 2 February 2010. In regard to the 50 per cent of students who 'hold qualifications above A level on entry' see Alan Woodley, Leslie Wagner, Maria Slowey, Mary Hamilton and Oliver Fulton, *Choosing to learn: Adults in education* (Milton Keynes: SRHE and The Open University, 1987), p. 45.

34 Richard Baldwyn, *Only yesterday: Times of my life* (Wokingham: Kendal and Dean, 2008).

35 www8.open.ac.uk/researchprojects/historyofou/story/students, accessed 2 February 2012.

36 www8.open.ac.uk/researchprojects/historyofou/story/students, accessed 2 February 2012.

37 These accounts were contributed to the HOTOUP website: see www8. open.ac.uk/researchprojects/historyofou/story/students, accessed 2 February 2012. When nearing her retirement age, Dr Platt was awarded a PhD from Lancaster University: www.research.lancs.ac.uk/portal/en/clippings/postgraduate-history-student-vida-jane-platt-successfully-defends-phd (4caef491-5480-4710-aa1a-9cc2e5ff8545).html, accessed 2 February 2012.

38 www8.open.ac.uk/researchprojects/historyofou/story/students, accessed 2 February 2012.

39 www8.open.ac.uk/researchprojects/historyofou/story/students, accessed 2 February 2012.

40 House of Commons debates, 2 April 1965, www.theyworkforyou.com/debates/?d=1963-04-02, accessed 24 July 2011.

41 Hollis, *Jennie Lee*, p. 311.

42 Jennie Lee speaking at Llandaff College of Education, quoted in *South Wales Echo* (29 June 1971).

43 Holloway, 'in the beginning', p. 3.

44 Terry Lewins, OU Oral History Project.

45 *The Times* (10 April 1976).

46 Ray Woolfe, 'Social equality as an Open University objective', *Teaching at a Distance*, 1 (November 1974), 41; Tyrell Burgess, 'The Open University', *New Society* (27 April 1972). Scupham was familiar with theories relating to adult education, as his review of books on mass communication and television for higher technical education in *Adult Education,* 42:2 (July 1969), 126–7, demonstrates.

47 Naomi E. McIntosh, 'The response to the Open University: Continuity and discontinuity', *Higher Education*, 2:2 (May 1973), 186–95.

48 *The Economist* (2 June 1979).

49 *Independent* (25 October 2009), www.independent.co.uk/news/education/education-news/colleges-told-raise-standards-if-you-want-more-cash-18091 40.html, accessed 2 February 2012; Naomi E. McIntosh *et al.*, *A degree of difference* (London: Society for Research into Higher Education, 1976). See also Woodley, 'Open as to people'.

50 *Guardian* (19 April 1997).

51 Tony Blair, 'Education and regeneration', speech in Sedgefield, 18 November 2005, ftp://trf.education.gouv.fr/pub/edutel/siac/siac2/jury/2006/caplp_ext/lv5.pdf, accessed 26 March 2012; Office for National Statistics, *Focus on social inequalities: 2005 edition* (London: The Stationery Office, 2005).

52 Roy Lowe, 'The development and significance of external degrees in the UK: A historian's view', *Research in Academic Degrees*, 6 (August 1997).

53 www.russellgroup.ac.uk/about-russell-group, accessed 2 February 2013.

54 *Times Higher Education* (5 September 2012), www.timeshighereducation.co.uk/story.asp?sectioncode=26&storycode=421077&c=1, accessed 5 September 2012.

55 Judith Potter, 'Beyond access: Student perspectives on support service needs in distance learning', *Canadian Journal of University Continuing Education*, 24:1 (Spring 1998), 63.

56 Stephen J. Ball, Jackie Davies, Miriam David and Diane Reay, '"Classification" and "Judgement": social class and the "cognitive structures" of choice of Higher Education', *British Journal of Sociology of Education*, 23:1 (2002), 70, 69.

57 Bernard Harrison, 'The teaching-learning relationship in correspondence tuition', *Teaching at a Distance*, 1 (November 1974), 3.

58 Stuart Hall, 'The new student', *Universities Quarterly*, 15 (1960–61), 155–6.

59 www8.open.ac.uk/researchprojects/historyofou/story/students, accessed 2 February 2012.

60 www.nytimes.com/1982/07/27/science/about-education.html?pagewanted=2, accessed 18 May 2011.

61 John Kirkaldy, 'Bags of Plato but no nookie', *Times Higher Education Supplement* (27 August 2004).

62 www8.open.ac.uk/researchprojects/historyofou/story/students, accessed 2 February 2012.

63 M. Castells, 'The university system: Engine of development in the new world economy', in J. Salmi and A. Verspoor (eds), *Revitalizing higher education* (Oxford: Pergamon, 1994), pp. 14–40. See also www.thedailybeast.com/newsweek/2005/03/06/not-the-queen-s-english.html, accessed 2 February 2013.

64 William Kenneth Richmond, *The literature of education: A critical bibliography 1945–1970* (London: Taylor and Francis, 1972), p. 2.

65 D. Greenaway and M. Haynes, 'Funding higher education in the UK: The role of fees and loans', *Economic Journal*, 113 (2003), 150–67.

66 'University places for older students', *Where?*, 38 (July 1968), 22.

67 Edward Lee Thorndike, *The measurement of intelligence* (New York: Columbia University, 1927).

68 Donald O. Hebb, *A textbook of psychology* (Philadelphia: W.B. Saunders, 1972), available at http://homepage.smc.edu/russell_richard/Psych2/Lecture%20Outlines/Hebb%20Reprint/Hebb%20Reprint.htm, accessed 13 June 2013.

69 Jagannath Mohanty, 'The British Open University: A model of distance education', in J. Mohanty (ed.), *Studies in distance education. Concepts and development, need and role: A critical assessment* (New Dehli: Deep and Deep, 2001), p. 68.

70 For example the 1970 Chronically Sick & Disabled Persons Act gave people with disabilities the right to equal access to recreational and educational facilities. Further legislation followed, including the 1995 Disability Discrimination Act, which made it illegal to discriminate against people with disabilities in employment or the provision of goods and services.

71 Geoffrey Tudor, 'The study problems of disabled students in the Open University', *Teaching at a Distance*, 9 (July 1977), 43–9; Perry, *Open University: A personal account*, pp. 169–73.

72 Maggy Jones, 'OUSA study tour to Rome', in Disabled students on a study tour of Rome, *Have wheels: Will travel* (Reading: Educational Explorers, 1976), p. 12. Her article about a study tour to Rome first appeared in *The Times Educational Supplement*.

73 *The Times* (31 January 1975).

74 blackrose, www.dooyoo.co.uk/universities/open-university-in-general/329 952, accessed 17 August 2012.

75 Woodley, 'Open as to people', p. 18. There are other ways of calculating the number of students with disabilities and as disability is a complex term and some students do not report their disability to the OU the figures are not completely reliable.

76 John Cowan, OU Oral History Project.

77 C. Newell and M. Debenham, 'Disability, chronic illness and distance education', in Patricia L. Rogers, Gary A. Berg, Judith V. Boettcher, C. Howard, Lorraine Justice and Karen D. Shenk (eds), *Encyclopedia of distance learning*, volume 2 (Hershey and London: Information Science Reference, 2009), pp. 646–54.

78 *Aberdeen Evening Express* (15 January 1971).

79 Holloway (ed.), *The first ten years*, p. 27.

80 Michael Drake, OU Oral History Project.

81 P. Rickwood and V. Goodwin, 'Travellers' tales: Reflections on the way to learner autonomy', *Open Learning*, 15:1 (2000), 47–55.

82 E. Burge, J. Howard and D. Ironside, *Mediation in distance learning: An investigation of the role of tutoring* (Toronto: Ontario Institute for Studies in Education, 1991); Andy Lane, 'Am I good enough? The mediated use of open educational resources to empower learners in excluded communities', Fifth Pan-Commonwealth Forum on Open Learning, 13–17 July 2008, London, http://oro.open.ac.uk/17829, accessed 5 March 2012.

83 Ray Mason, 'Mature students and higher education: The Further Education and Training Scheme', *Journal of Educational Administration and History*, 21:2 (July 1989), 35–45 (p. 43). See also David Ben Rees, *Preparation for crisis: Adult education 1945–80* (Ormskirk and Northridge: G. W. & A. Hesketh, 1982), p. 2.

84 Caroline Moorehead, 'The "little women" who graduated to a new freedom', *The Times* (26 October 1984). Other quoted accounts in this section are derived from the material uploaded to www8.open.ac.uk/research projects/historyofou/story/students, accessed 2 February 2012. For other examples of an emphasis on a notion of confidence see the testimony of Christine Smith, Ann Pollard, Gwen Rowan, Lorelei Henley, Judy Sims, Priscilla Hogan, Pat Elliott, Susan O'Donnell and Russel Mohan.

85   Moorehead, 'The "little women"'.

86   *The Times* (4 July 1973).

87   Ferguson, *The Open University from within*, p. 116.

88   www8.open.ac.uk/researchprojects/historyofou/story/students, accessed 2 February 2012.

89   Adapted from O. Simpson, *Supporting students in online, open and distance education* (London: Routledge, 2002), p. 120.

90   Mark Pearce, interview with Ronald Mcintyre, 29 December 2011. This recording was made with the support of a grant from the Society for Research into Higher Education (henceforth SRHE collection). For similar conclusions about the significance attributed to kin, see the online accounts by Charlene Buckley, Vida Jane Platt, Joanne Greenwood, Jim Bailey, Maureen Bowman, Iain Boyle and Mark Pearce. Kayleigh Carey mentioned her husband; Gwen Rowan her boyfriend, later husband; Claire Smith an OU student who was her boyfriend, later fiancé; Ian Ellson was encouraged by his wife and her family, and Patricia Palmer by her husband and children: www8.open.ac.uk/researchprojects/historyofou/story/students, accessed 2 February 2012.

91   Lunneborg, *OU men*, pp. 4, 39. Rosemary Jamieson, Joan Knox and Pam Gilham all called their spouses 'supportive'. www8.open.ac.uk/researchprojects/historyofou/story/students, accessed 2 February 2012.

92   www8.open.ac.uk/researchprojects/historyofou/story/students, accessed 2 February 2012.

93   Naomi McIntosh, 'Women and the OU', in *Staff development in universities programme: Women in higher education*, papers from a conference held in London on 29 June 1973 (London: University of London Teaching Methods Unit, 1975), p. 12.

94   The image of the basket illustrates Patrick Kelly, 'How open is the Associate Student programme?', *Teaching at a Distance*, 18 (Winter 1980), 24.

95   Noel J. Entwhistle, 'The student in mass higher education', *Higher Education*, 2:2 (May 1973), 240.

96   *The Times* (4 July 1973).

97   *Times Higher Education Supplement* (20 January 1978); Open University, *An introduction to the Open University* (Milton Keynes: The Open University, 1977).

98   John T. E. Richardson, Alistair Morgan and Alan Woodley, 'Approaches to studying in distance education', *Higher Education*, 37 (1999), 50.

99   Peter Scott, *The meanings of mass higher education* (London: SRHE and The Open University, 1995).

100   *Radio Times* (7 January 1971).

101   McIntosh, 'Women and the OU'.

102   Pauline Kirk, 'Female students and the Open University', *Times Higher Education Supplement* (24 February 1978).

103 *The Spectator* (9 January 1971).

104 A. H. Halsey, A. Heath and J. M. Ridge, *Origins and destinations: Family, class and education in modern Britain* (Oxford: Clarendon, 1980).

105 Gill Kirkup and Elizabeth Whitelegg, 'The legacy and impact of Open University women's/gender studies: 30 years on', *Gender and Education*, 25:1 (2013), 6–22.

106 *The Times* (26 October 1984).

107 Jill MacKean, 'Housewife with five children', in Jeremy Tunstall (ed.), *The Open University opens* (London: Routledge and Kegan Paul, 1974), pp.65–6.

108 Alex Richards, 6 January 2012. SRHE collection. Alex subsequently completed OU courses in 1986, 1987, 2007 and 2008.

109 www8.open.ac.uk/researchprojects/historyofou/story/students, accessed 2 February 2012.

110 Moorehead, 'The "little women"'.

111 Tony Whitaker, 4 January 2012. SRHE collection. *Mr Sheen* is a brand of cleaning materials.

112 Anonymous secretary quoted in Ferguson, *The Open University from within*, p. 116. Clare Burdett, 'Professionally speaking', in Disabled students on a study tour of Rome, *Have wheels*, p. 8 and www8.open.ac.uk/researchprojects/historyofou/story/students, accessed 2 February 2012.

113 *The Times* (4 July 1973).

114 Alan Gordon was an 'E' year student, Sylvia an 'A' year student. She was a founder member of the Southend OU Students Association, a member of the Regional Consultative Committee and a member of the General Assembly.

115 Christine von Prümmer, 'Women-friendly perspectives in distance education', *Open Learning*, 9:1 (1994), 3–12.

116 *The Times* (4 July 1973).

117 Central Statistical Office, *Social Trends* 22 (London: HMSO, 1992).

118 Peter Cook's monologue *The Tadpole Expert*, first broadcast in 1964 and reproduced in William Cook, *Tragically I was an only twin: The complete Peter Cook* (London: Arrow, 2003), pp. 64–5 does not relate to this course, TAD292. However, 'I've always fancied being a tadpole expert. It's a wonderful life if you become an experty tadpoleous' pre-empts the type of perspective that the course sought to promote.

119 J. Roby Kidd, 'How adults learn: What's new', *Canadian Journal of University Continuing Education*, 4:1 (Summer 1977), 27.

120 Tait, 'Planning student support', pp. 287–99.

121 Philippe C. Duchastel, 'TAD292 – and its challenge to educational technology', *Programmed Learning & Educational Technology*, 13:4 (October 1976), p. 62.

122 Duchastel, 'TAD292', p. 63.

123 Quoted in Lunneborg, *OU women*, pp. 4–10.

124 The idea of students running their own camp had been proposed before. In 1972 an OU counsellor suggested to students on a second-level course which did not have an associated residential school that they establish their own *Education + Training*, 14:3 (March 1972), 79.

125 www.open.ac.uk/ousa/societies.php, accessed 8 March 2012.

126 Alex Richards, 6 January 2012. SRHE collection.

127 Tony Whitaker, 4 January 2012. SRHE collection; Alex Richards, SRHE collection.

128 Alex Richards, SRHE collection; John Leach, 6 March 2012, SRHE collection; Edwina Nixon, 8 March 2012, SRHE collection.

129 Tony Whitaker and four others from the course trained with the choreographer of the Beijing Olympics Opening Ceremony. See www8.open.ac.uk/researchprojects/historyofou/story/students, accessed 2 February 2012.

130 Alex Richards, SRHE collection.

131 Eric Summers, 6 June 2012, SRHE collection.

132 Gill Kirkup and Christine von Prümmer, 'Support and connectedness: The needs of women distance education students', *Journal of Distance Education*, 5:2 (1990), 9–31.

133 L. Feinstein, T. Anderson, C. Hammond, A. Jamieson and A. Woodley, *The social and economic benefits of part-time, mature study at Birkbeck College and The Open University* (Milton Keynes and London: The Open University, Centre for the Wider Benefits of Learning, Institute of Education and Birkbeck College, 2007). See also E. Fenster, *College attendance by working adults and its effects on the educational motivation of their children* (Detroit: To Educate the People Consortium, 1982).

134 www8.open.ac.uk/researchprojects/historyofou/story/students, accessed 2 February 2012.

135 www8.open.ac.uk/researchprojects/historyofou/story/students, accessed 2 February 2012.

136 www8.open.ac.uk/researchprojects/historyofou/story/students, accessed 2 February 2012.

137 David R. Arendale, *History of supplemental instruction (SI): Mainstreaming of developmental education* (Kansas City: University of Missouri-Kansas City, 2000), http://a.web.umkc.edu/arendaled/SIhistory02.pdf, accessed 29 February 2012. In 2001 the Higher Education Funding Council for England offered support for peer-assisted learning and peer-assisted study sessions.

138 Feinstein *et al.*, *The social and economic benefits*. Enjoyment was more important among Birkbeck students, who wanted to meet people and who studied through attendance at evening classes, unlike the OU students who were likely to be more geographically isolated from one another.

139 For narratives which refer to fulfilment and stimulus see Rosemary Jamieson, John Driscoll, Ann Eastaway and Joan Knox, www8.open.ac.uk/

researchprojects/historyofou/story/students, accessed 2 February 2012. See also Jacqueline Cooper, 12 January 2012, SRHE collection.

140   www8.open.ac.uk/researchprojects/historyofou/memories/contribution-the-history-the-ou, accessed 2 February 2012.

141   www8.open.ac.uk/researchprojects/historyofou/story/students, accessed 2 February 2012.

142   www8.open.ac.uk/researchprojects/historyofou/story/students, accessed 2 February 2012.

143   www8.open.ac.uk/researchprojects/historyofou/story/students, accessed 2 February 2012.

144   www8.open.ac.uk/researchprojects/historyofou/story/students, accessed 2 February 2012.

145   'It is the unanimous testimony of tutors that they never met such dedicated students. The Norwich paper which bore the headline "Short-haired students keen to work" spoke nothing but the truth.' Ferguson, *The Open University from within*, p. 94.

146   Young, 'Whose story counts?', p. 105, noted both that OU summer schools had 'a reputation for romantic liaisons' and also that many of her OU interviewees 'were reluctant to talk about this particular myth'.

147   There was also a death to report. Dr Elizabeth Howe was murdered while working as an OU summer school tutor, *The Times* (27 July 1992).

148   *The Times* (30 November 2004).

149   Stuart Hall, OU Oral History Project.

150   Nina Halttunen, 'Changing missions: The role of open university education in the field of higher education in Finland', *Scandinavian Journal of Educational Research*, 50:5 (November 2006), 503–17. See also Marion Royce, 'Study circles in Finland', *Convergence*, 3:1 (1970), 69–73; Donald Garside, 'Short-term residential colleges: Their origins and values', *Studies in Adult Education*, 1 (April 1969), 2; MacKenzie, 'Genesis', p. 714; Geoffrey Crowther, *Schools and universities*, a lecture at LSE 1961, cited in Briggs, *Michael Young*, p. 196; Young, 'Announcing', pp. 16–17.

151   www8.open.ac.uk/platform/services/study-support/residential-school-students-tell-it-it, accessed 5 September 2012.

152   *Education + Training*, 14:3 (March 1972), 79; *Independent* (31 July 1997).

153   Sue Danks, 'Day in the life … of a biochemist at Open University summer school', www.biochemistry.org/Portals/0/Education/OU%20summer%20school%20biochemist.pdf, accessed 17 August 2012.

154   Although not all residential schools were held during the summer months it is by the alliterative title that they came to be known. In 1972, the second year of accepting students for study at the OU, a fifth foundation course in technology was added alongside eleven second-level courses, and the number of different summer schools was increased from four to twelve. A residential element was not arranged for all courses.

155 Ferguson, *The Open University from within*, p. 94.

156 Kirkaldy, 'Bags of Plato'.

157 *The Times* (6 September 1973). The headline referred to how, as a teaching aid, Arthur Marwick opened a can of beer at an evening lecture. The latter story, about TAD292 at Sussex, was broadcast on a BBC radio news programme. It was also used as part of a report on the TAD292 summer school at Sussex on *Open Forum*, 31, 1976. Recording made available through The Open University Archive. Others took up this matter. The *Times Higher Education Supplement* headline on this matter was 'OU students get behind on project'. A film made as part of the TAD292 summer school at Brighton in 1976 is available at www.open.edu/openlearn/education/educational-technology-and-practice/educational-technology/1976-summer-school, accessed 17 August 2012.

158 www.open.ac.uk/Arts/arthur-marwick.htm, accessed 15 April 2014. On the other hand, Sebastian Barnes met the person whom he later married at summer school, and Mary Connor and her spouse James Connor studied the same courses. See www8.open.ac.uk/researchprojects/historyofou/story/students, accessed 2 February 2012.

159 *Sesame* (September 1974).

160 Stuart Hall, OU Oral History Project.

161 Ferguson, *The Open University from within*, p. 66.

162 Chris Haines, 'Let's talk mathematics', *Teaching at a Distance*, 18 (Winter 1980), 37.

163 J. M. Ekins, 'Pedagogic issues in opening up mathematics to a wider audience', *The new learning environment: A global perspective. The 18th ICDE-World Conference, June 2–6 1997* (Pennsylvania State University: International Council for Distance Education, 1997), p. 194.

164 John Daniel, 'The summer school experience', *Open Eye* (September 2000), www.open.ac.uk/johndanielspeeches/Open-Eye-September-2000.htm, accessed 14 August 2012.

165 Alistair Morgan and Mary Thorpe, 'Residential schools in open and distance education: Quality time for quality learning?', in Terry Evans and Daryl Nation (eds), *Reforming open and distance education: Critical reflections from practice* (London: Kogan Page, 1993), pp. 72–87.

166 Arthur Marwick, 'History at the Open University', *Oxford Review of Education*, 2:2 (1976), 135.

167 www.open.ac.uk/Arts/charles-harrison/index.shtml, accessed 17 August 2012.

168 Naomi E. McIntosh, 'The place of the summer school in the Open University', *Teaching at a Distance*, 3 (May 1975), 59.

169 G. Burt, *Face to face with distance education* (Milton Keynes: Open and Distance Education Statistics, 1997), pp. 10, 18, 11.

170 This student went on to gain a distinction: see *Education + Training*, 14:9 (March 1972), 79.

171 *The Times* (1 August 1973).

172 *The Times* (6 September 1973). There may have been some bitterness towards the OU from this newspaper because, in the early 1960s, Geoffrey Crowther, the founding Chancellor of the OU, played a major part in resisting the take-over by the *News of the World* of a printing company which he chaired.

173 *Sesame* (September 1975).

174 *Independent* (31 July 1997).

175 Tilly Bud and the Laughing Housewife, 2011, http://thelaughinghousewife. wordpress.com/2012/07/19/olive-what-shes-having, accessed 17 August 2012.

176 www.helium.com/items/567216-testimonies-open-university-summer-schools, accessed 17 August 2012.

177 Joan Christodoulou, OU Oral History Project.

178 Michael Drake, OU Oral History Project.

179 Sean Cubitt, 'Cancelling popular culture', *Screen*, 32:6 (1986), 91–3.

180 Mike Hey, 'How wide is your bed? Twenty years of Stirling summer schools' (1998), web.me.com/penicuik/mjh/ssbook.pdf, accessed 24 July 2011, p. 9. For other accounts of residential schools see *Sesame*, 1:2 (June 1972); *Sesame*, 1:3 (July 1972); *Sesame*, 1:5 (September 1972); *Sesame*, 2:1 (January 1973); *Sesame*, 6:5 (September/October 1977); and the double spread in *Open House*, 273 (August 1989).

181 Mason said that he was influenced by Kurt Simo's 1966 film *Let us keep guessing*, in which a teacher sets a problem and encourages undergraduates to solve it. See www.mcs.open.ac.uk/people/j.h.mason, accessed 24 July 2011.

182 Sir John Daniel, speech given in 2010, www.col.org/resources/speeches/2010presentation/Pages/2010-05-13.aspx, accessed 27 September 2010. John Daniel's full-time university education was in metallurgy at the universities of Oxford and Paris. He then started on a part-time Master's degree in educational technology at Concordia University. The internship for this took him to the OU in 1972, which changed the course of his life. He subsequently held appointments at the Télé-université, Québec (Directeur des Études, 1973–77); Athabasca University, Alberta (Vice-President for Learning Services, 1978–80); Concordia University, Montreal (Vice-Rector, Academic, 1980–84); and Laurentian University, Ontario (President, 1984–90) before he returned the OU as the Vice-Chancellor, 1990–2001. While at the OU he completed his thesis, after twenty-five years, and his book based on it, *Mega-universities and knowledge media: Technology strategies for higher education* (London: Kogan Page, 1996), was published. He was knighted for services to higher education.

183 Transcript of a seminar in 1973: Peter Montagnon, *The media and edu-cational development: A seminar held in Dublin, 21–22 February, 1973* (Dublin: RTE Education, 1974), p. 50. Peter Montagnon was a member of the BBC Schools Television Department, who produced the first television language-learning series, *Parliamo Italiano*. He became Head of Open University Productions nine months before its first year of operation.

184 *Education + Training*, 14:7 (June 1972), 216–17.

185 *The Times* (6 September 1973).

186 Christopher Harvie MSP, Scottish Parliament debate on motion S3M-5328.

187 Hilary Perraton, 'Is there a teacher in the system?', *Teaching at a Distance*, 1 (November 1974), 58.

188 McIntosh, 'The place of the summer school', p. 59.

189 J. Eiseman, 'Redefining the role of residential schools in distance educa-tion', *Distance Education Association of New Zealand Bulletin*, 15 (1992), 45–52.

190 Alan Gillie and Alan Woodley, 'Residential summer schools attendance and students' assessed performances on Open University Foundation Courses', *Open Discussion Papers in Economics* (June 1995); Alan Gillie, 'Efficiency in universities and resource-based learning: A case study of assumptions versus analysis', *Public Money & Management*, 19:3 (July 1999), 43–9.

191 *Guardian* (18 June 2010).

192 www.dooyoo.co.uk/universities/open-university-in-general/329952, accessed 17 August 2012.

193 One of these modules was *Exploring psychology online*, DZX222. Formerly the embedded residential school of *Exploring psychology*, DSE212, it retained close links to its parent. Students worked in groups, designing, conducting and analysing a psychological study. DZX222 was a virtual resi-dential school conducted using online forums for tutor support, group dis-cussions and activities. There was also DZX222's counterpart, a week-long residential school, *Exploring psychology project*, DXR222, which offered opportunities to develop the same skills.

194 This appeared under the headline, 'Crime does pay if you want to take OU course:Taxpayersfunding1,600prisonersthisyear',*DailyMail*(9March2011), www.dailymail.co.uk/news/article-1364279/Crime-does-pay-want-OU-course-Taxpayers-funding-1-600-prisoners-year.html#ixzz24TWiPayD, accessed 20 August 2012.

195 Written evidence to the Select Committee on Education and Skills, December 2006, www.publications.parliament.uk/pa/cm200607/cmselect/cmeduski/170/170we15.htm, accessed 1 March 2012.

196 There were precedents for teaching within prisons. In 1961 there were 3,000 weekly classes being run by local authorities. Rees, *Preparation for crisis*, p. 8.

197 By 2011 other universities offered some provision. A distance-learning degree in law was available through both Nottingham Trent University and Birkbeck College, University of London. See www.guardian.co.uk/education/2011/apr/25/prisoners-law-degrees, accessed 17 August 2012. In addition, an undergraduate workplace foundation degree in offender management was run by Staffordshire University and Stafford College at Dovegate prison. It was for prison officers and was not available to prisoners: www.guardian.co.uk/education/2011/mar/29/first-workplace-degree-dovegate-prison, accessed 17 August 2012.

198 Barry and Johnny of HMP Maghaberry were interviewed by Kirsten Dwight for a conference on offender learning hosted by The Open University in 2010. See www8.open.ac.uk/about/offender-learning/information-and-developments, accessed 12 March 2012.

199 Katla Helgason, OU Oral History Project. Katla Helgason started to study at the OU in 1971. She became a tutor, established the Scottish Prison Scheme which replaced *ad hoc* arrangements with prisons, and later became the Assistant Director OU in Scotland.

200 Ferguson, 'Classics in the Open University', p. 5.

201 Moira MacLean, 'Open learning in closed conditions', *Open Learning*, 2:3 (November 1987), 46.

202 Quoted in The Open University, *Studying with the Open University: A guide for learners in prison* (Milton Keynes: The Open University, 2011), http://labspace.open.ac.uk/file.php/3427/Studying_with_the_OU_-_a_guide_for_learners_in_prison.pdf, accessed 15 April 2014.

203 For the source of this material see following note.

204 John and Trevor of HMP Maghaberry and James of HMP Shotts were interviewed by Kirsten Dwight for a conference on offender learning hosted by The Open University in 2010. See www8.open.ac.uk/about/offender-learning/information-and-developments, accessed 12 March 2012.

205 www8.open.ac.uk/about/offender-learning/information-and-developments, accessed 12 March 2012. This student completed *Introducing astronomy*, S194; *How the universe works*, S197; *Understanding human nutrition*, SK183; and *Inside nuclear energy*, ST174.

206 Quoted in Open University, *A guide for learners in prison*, p. 1.

207 www8.open.ac.uk/about/offender-learning/information-and-developments, accessed 12 March 2012. Trevor was interviewed by Kirsten Dwight for a conference on offender learning hosted by The Open University in 2010.

208 Open University, *A guide for learners in prison*, p. 2.

209 W. Forster, *The higher education of prisoners* (Leicester: Department of Adult Education, University of Leicester, 1976), cited in Rees, *Preparation for crisis*, p. 8.

210 Perry, *Open University: A personal account*, p. 173.

211 Office of National Statistics, *Focus on the digital age* (London: Palgrave Macmillan, 2007) Table 2.4, p. 10, www.statistics.gov.uk/StatBase/Product. asp?vlnk=14797, accessed 1 November 2013.

212 Anne Pike, COLMSCT CETL *Final report: Building bridges across the digital divide for HE students in prison*, April 2010, p. 11.

213 Katla Helgason, OU Oral History Project.

214 *Inside News: The Open University Newsletter for Prisons* (2 March 2008), 2, http://labspace.open.ac.uk/file.php/3427/Inside_News_2.pdf, accessed 1 November 2013.

215 This is supported by quotations from Student 34, Student 6 and Student 4 in Pike, COLMSCT CETL *Final report*, p. 11. Sally Jordan, 'An unusual degree ceremony', www8.open.ac.uk/science/main/about-the-faculty/case-studies/unusual-degree-ceremony?samsredir=1328029200, accessed 1 November 2010.

216 www.insidetime.org/info-regimes2.asp?nameofprison=HMP_MAGHA BERRY, accessed 14 May 2011.

217 Pike, COLMSCT CETL *Final report*, p. 17.

218 Perry, *Open University: A personal account*, p. 173.

219 Pike, COLMSCT CETL *Final report*, p. 9.

220 Norman Woods, OU Oral History Project.

221 Hindley was a prisoner between 1966 and her death in 2002. The claim regarding her fame was made by Rupa Huq, http://rupahuq.wordpress.com/2008/08/26/as-myra-hindley-courts-olympic-controversy-from-the-grave-ian-brady-slams-new-labour-for-not-paying-him-enough, accessed 20 August 2012.

222 When some of Hindley's documents were made publicly available the *Daily Mail* (13 June 2008) mentioned the extra reading lamp she received to assist her OU studies: www.dailymail.co.uk/news/article-1025973/Revealed-Myra-Hindleys-FAN-mail--13-year-old-told-You-deserve-released.html#ixzz24S3 sdXzx, accessed 20 August 2012.

223 *Observer* (22 January 2012).

224 http://prisonersvoice.blogspot.com/search?q=Open+, accessed 1 November 2011.

225 http://erwinjames.co.uk/biog.html, accessed 24 August 2012.

226 *Guardian* (30 January 2012), www.guardian.co.uk/education/2012/jan/30/prison-education-failures?newsfeed=true, accessed 29 February 2012. He also worked for a rehabilitation charity.

227 *The Open University: The first 40 years. A celebration of four decades of growth and innovation* (Milton Keynes: The Open University, 2009), p. 17, http://intranet.open.ac.uk/anniversary/pics/d117397.pdf, accessed 17 May 2012.

228 'MoD took softer line on loyalist paramilitaries, secret files reveal', *Guardian* (11 October 2010).

229 'Prison sentences proved no bar to degrees for loyalists', *Belfast Telegraph* (18 January 2011).

230 Jane Nelson, 'One day in the life of Jane Nelson', *Sesame,* 1:5 (May 1972), 12. Jane Nelson was a senior counsellor at the OU. She taught some of those imprisoned in Long Kesh.

231 Diana Purcell, OU Oral History Project.

232 Diana Purcell, OU Oral History Project.

233 Jacqueline Dana and Seán McMonagle, 'Deconstructing "criminalisation": The politics of collective education in the H-blocks', *Journal of Prisoners on Prisons,* 8:1–2 (1997), www.jpp.org/documents/forms/JPP8/Danandsean. pdf, accessed 22 June 2013.

234 *Times Higher Education Supplement* (7 January 2000), www.timeshigher-education.co.uk/story.asp?storyCode=149558&sectioncode=26, accessed 1 November 2010.

235 'South's jail swots get Open University', *Irish News* (13 February 1985).

236 Much of this information is derived from an internal report compiled in January 1979 by Diana Purcell.

237 Louise Purbrick, 'The architecture of containment', in Donovan Wylie, *The Maze* (London: Granta Books, 2004), p. 108.

238 Diana Purcell, OU Oral History Project.

239 L. McKeown, *Out of time: Irish Republican prisoners Long Kesh, 1972–2000* (Belfast: Beyond the Pale Publications, 2001).

240 Richard English, *Armed struggle: The history of the IRA* (Oxford: Oxford University Press, 2003), p. 230.

241 English, *Armed struggle,* p. 231.

242 Kirkup, 'Women's studies "at a distance"', p. 279.

243 Diana Purcell, OU Oral History Project; Simona Sharoni, 'Gendering resistance within an Irish Republican prisoner community: A conversation with Laurence McKeown', *International Feminist Journal of Politics,* 1:2 (Spring 2000), 104–23.

244 Gordon Macintyre, 'My 20 years as Regional Director'. These notes are in the OU Archives.

245 English, *Armed struggle,* p. 231.

246 Gordon Macintyre, 'Don's Diary', *Times Higher Education Supplement* (29 May 1987). The events described probably occurred during the week 4–10 April 1987.

247 Macintyre, 'My 20 years'.

248 Report of the committee of Privy Counsellors appointed to consider authorised procedures for the interrogation of persons suspected of terrorism, http://cain.ulst.ac.uk/hmso/parker.htm#3, accessed 22 June 2013.

249 'Bomb meant for Gardiner, IRA claims', *The Times* (15 June 1981).

250 A full-time tutor in the Republic, Pat McManus, gave much of the credit for the initiative to Dr Kevin Warner, the national co-ordinator of prison education 1979–2009, and founding chair of the European Prison Education

Association: *Irish Independent* (11 February 1985). The Irish National Adult Learning Organisation noted that the University of London was also involved in bringing university education to prisons in the Republic. *Aontas Newsletter*, 14:1 (August 1985).

251 Diana Purcell, OU Oral History Project.

252 Rosemary Hamilton, OU Oral History Project.

253 *The Times* (18 May 1985).

254 Naomi Stinson, OU Oral History Project.

255 Gordon Macintyre taught Raymond McCartney, later a Sinn Féin Member of the Legislative Assembly. See also www.irlnet.com/saoirse/maghella. html, accessed 14 March 2012.

256 Peter Smith, 'From prison to political power', *Society Matters* ('The newspaper for all Social Sciences students and staff at The Open University'), 13 (2010–11), 12.

257 Diana Purcell, OU Oral History Project.

258 *Times Higher Education Supplement* (7 January 2000).

259 *Belfast Telegraph* (8 January 2007), www.belfasttelegraph.co.uk/break ingnews/breakingnews_ukandireland/breakingnews_ukandireland_politics/ progressive-unionist-leader-ervine-dies-28414284.html, accessed 22 June 2013.

260 www.open.ac.uk/platform/node/1255, accessed 1 December 2011.

261 Learning Teaching and Student Support Committee, *Offender Learning Steering Group: Final report*, www.open.ac.uk/opencetl/files/opencetl/file/ ecms/web-content/Pike-A-(2008)-Offender-Learning-Steering-Group-Final-Report.pdf, accessed 15 April 2014.

262 *The Times* (9 September 1963).

263 *The Times* (1 August 1973).

264 *Review of the Open University*.

265 Pierre Bourdieu, *The inheritors: French students and their relation to culture* (Chicago: University of Chicago Press, 1979); Pierre Bourdieu, 'The forms of capital', in A. H. Halsey, Hugh Lauder, Philip Brown and Amy Stuart Wells (eds), *Education, culture, economy and society* (Oxford: Oxford University Press, 1997), pp. 27–39.

266 www8.open.ac.uk/platform/news-and-features/2011-national-student-sur vey-launched, accessed 13 March 2012. In 2005 and 2006 the OU was first with regard to student satisfaction, being more popular with its students than any other publicly funded university in the UK.

267 Mpine Makoe, John T. E. Richardson and Linda Price, 'Conceptions of learning in adult students embarking on distance education', *Higher Education*, 55 (2008), 317.

268 Laura McInerney, *Guardian*, 14 October 2013.

269 Perry, *Open University: A personal account*, p. 288.

270 *The Times* (24 December 1968); Pimlott, *Harold Wilson*, pp. 510, 514.

271 Joe Haines, 'Open eye: How Harold's pet project became his monument', *Independent* (1 October 1998), www.independent.co.uk/news/education/ education-news/open-eye-how-harolds-pet-project-became-his-monument-1175330.html, accessed 2 January 2013.

Index

Note: The main text and notes have been indexed. Page numbers for illustrations are shown in italics, and notes are shown as page number, note number (e.g. 123n.100 is page 123, note number 100). Bold type indicates main discussion of a topic. Due to space restrictions and for ease of reading, The Open University is referred to as 'the OU' or 'OU' in the index.